JOHN W. O'MALLEY has been Professor of History
and Chairman of the Department of Religious
Studies at the University of Detroit and is now
Professor of History, Weston School of Theology.
An earlier book was *Giles of Viterbo on Church
and Reform: A Study in Renaissance Thought,*
and he has published articles in many scholarly
journals, among them *Renaissance Quarterly,
Thought, Viator, Traditio, The Catholic Historical Review, Theological Studies,* and *Journal of
Medieval and Renaissance Studies.* He was the
recipient of a John Simon Guggenheim Fellowship, 1975–76, which gave him the opportunity
to write this book.

D0857078

PRAISE AND BLAME IN RENAISSANCE ROME

PRAISE AND BLAME IN RENAISSANCE ROME

Rhetoric, Doctrine, and Reform in the Sacred Orators
of the Papal Court, c. 1450–1521
by JOHN W. O'MALLEY

Duke Monographs in Medieval and Renaissance Studies number 3
DUKE UNIVERSITY PRESS Durham, North Carolina 1979

For ANNA MARIE

© 1979 by Duke University Press, Library of Congress Catalogue card number
79–51220. I.S.B.N. 0–8223–0428–7. Printed in the United States of America by Heritage
Printers, Inc.

TABLE OF CONTENTS

PREFACE

In Rome, in the summer of 1971, the sacred oratory of the papal court first attracted my attention as a distinctive body of literature, distracting me from another project on which I was working. The following spring, at the invitation of Professor Charles Trinkaus, I presented the results of my distraction at the University of Michigan Conference on Late Medieval and Renaissance Religion. At that conference Professor Paul Oskar Kristeller offered comments on my paper. I realized for the first time that he had published an edition of the sermon at the papal court by Guillaume Fichet, 1476, referred to below in Chapter Two, and had elsewhere called attention to the humanist influence on the sacred oratory of the court. He suggested to me that I might undertake further research, this time investigating the impact on the sermons of the revival of classical rhetoric, an aspect of the subject that I had not touched upon.

Grateful though I was to Professor Kristeller for his suggestion, I had no intention of acting upon it. My interests, I thought, lay elsewhere. John McManamon, one of my students, was more perceptive than I, and he began to pursue Professor Kristeller's suggestion as part of his Master's thesis. I was able to put Mr. McManamon in contact with Professor Helen North of Swarthmore College, who expertly introduced him to rhetoric and the rhetorical tradition. These two friends gradually made me perceive how important a study of rhetoric might be for materials I continued to research, but my interest was still tepid and my comprehension dim.

Later, again while working on a project having little to do with oratory, I read Aurelio Brandolini's *De ratione scribendi libri tres*. At some moment during the reading of that treatise—a work described at length in Chapter Two—I finally saw what rhetoric might mean for many of the questions in the Renaissance I had been intrigued with, and I decided to write this book.

Once the decision was taken, I continued to be encouraged and enlightened by friends and colleagues. I am especially grateful to my fellow Jesuit, Mark Henninger, who evening after evening at the Collegio Internazionale del Gesù, Rome, discussed the book with me during the year I did most of the research on it. As the chapters were produced, he read them and offered good criticism. I am also grateful to others who, at some stage, read the manuscript in whole or in part and who made helpful suggestions: Helen North, Paul Oskar Kristeller, Charles Trinkaus, John McManamon, Francis X. Martin, Charles Stinger, Myron Gilmore, Sarah Stever Gravelle, Frederick McGinness, Vernon Ruland, Thomas Porter, Philip Rule, Edmund Miller, and Dayton Haskin.

Without a fellowship from the John Simon Guggenheim Foundation and a leave of absence from the University of Detroit, I would not have been able to spend fifteen months of research in Rome, 1975–76, which made possible the writing of the book. A grant-in-aid from the American Council of Learned Societies allowed me to return to Rome for another period of research in the summer of 1977. The hospitality of the Collegio del Gesù in the persons of Rev. Manuel Acévez, S.J., Rev. Robert Finlay, S.J., and Rev. Carmelo Gatt, S.J., as well as the students at the Collegio, provided me with a congenial atmosphere in which to work. Sarah Stever Gravelle assisted me in compiling the Appendix. Constance Young read the entire manuscript and made many stylistic suggestions. Barbara Butler helped with the indices. Professor Edward P. Mahoney of Duke University, general editor of the series in which the book appears, has been readily available for consultation and made my work easier at every stage of the book's publication. Whatever praise the book merits must be shared with the persons and institutions I have mentioned. Insofar as it deserves blame, the blame is mine alone.

In quoting Latin sources, printed or manuscript, I have standardized the orthography, even for titles. The only exception to this rule is occasionally leaving proper names in the form in which they are found in the sources. Punctuation has been changed, when necessary, to conform it to modern usage. Long titles of old works in Latin have generally been shortened, since full titles can be found in the appropriate catalogues, to which reference is always made for incunabula. Foliation and those portions of imprints given within square brackets do not actually appear as such in the work, and are supplied on a different basis. When a title appears in brackets, I have formulated it myself, usually from the opening words of the work in question. The word "sermon" is used in the book to designate only those orations delivered in church or chapel during the celebration of Mass. The word "oration" includes this category as well as all other forms of sacred and secular oratory.

Finding the materials upon which the book is based has been an arduous and often frustrating task. The search entailed, first of all, an entry-by-entry examination of the standard catalogues of incunabula. For books printed after 1500, the two most useful publications were Fernanda Ascarelli's *Le cinquecentine romane: "Censimento delle edizioni romane del XVI secolo possedute dalle biblioteche di Roma"* (Milan: Etimar, 1972) and Francis S. Isaac's *An Index to the Early Printed Books in the British Museum*, pt. II: MDI–MDXX, sec. 2: Italy (London: B. Quaritch, 1938).

The problem of finding the pertinent materials was considerably compounded for manuscripts, and often only chance or the suggestion of a colleague led me to my sources. John McManamon and Paul Oskar Kristeller deserve my special gratitude for the information and clues they supplied over the course of several years. However, the most important source of information for manuscripts was, not surprisingly, Professor Kristeller's *Iter Italicum*, whose usefulness to me is only faintly indicated by the number of times I refer to it. I searched its pages, especially those dealing with the Roman, Venetian, and Florentine libraries. Thousands of entries described simply as "oratio" or "orationes variae" had to be bypassed, of course, but I tried to pursue entries where the description offered details suggesting materials that might be useful to my investigation. Meanwhile I gradually composed a list of orators and preachers, principally from the diaries of the papal Masters of Ceremonies. I then returned to the *Iter* and other catalogues, looking for further information on the names I had retrieved from these sources. The process of search and verification was dialectical, therefore, as seems to be the case in most historical scholarship.

It was thus that the book was conceived, the search conducted, and the materials gathered. I now dedicate the book, with much affection, to my cousin, Anna Marie Fouts.

ABBREVIATIONS

General

The abbreviations for classical authors and works are taken from *A Latin Dictionary*, ed. Charlton T. Lewis and Charles Short (New York: Oxford University Press, 1962), pp. vii–xi. Abbreviations for books of the Bible are taken from *A Manual of Style*, 12th ed. rev. (Chicago: University of Chicago Press, 1969), pp. 328–31.

ASD	Erasmus, *Opera Omnia* (Amsterdam: North-Holland, 1969—).
Burchard, *Liber Notarum*	Iohannes Burchardus, *Liber Notarum*, ed. Enrico Celani, RIS, 32.1–2 (Città di Castello: S. Lapi, 1906).
Cop. (Hain-Cop.)	W. A. Copinger, *Supplement to Hain's Repertorium Bibliographicum*, 2 vols. (Berlin: J. Altmann, 1926).
DBI	*Dizionario biografico degli Italiani* (Roma: Istituto della Enciclopedia Italiana, 1960—).
GKW	*Gesamtkatalog der Wiegendrucke* (Leipzig: K. Hiersemann, 1925—).
Hain	Ludovicus Hain, *Repertorium Bibliographicum*, 2 vols. (Berlin: J. Altmann, 1925).
Hain-Cop.	*See* Cop.
Hain-Reichling	*See* Reichling.
Kristeller, *Iter*	Paul Oskar Kristeller, *Iter Italicum*, 2 vols. (Leiden: Brill, 1965–67).
LB	Erasmus, *Opera omnia*, ed. J. Clericus, 10 vols. (Lugdini Batavorum: P. Vander, 1703–6).
Mansi	Giovanni Domenico Mansi, *Sacrorum conciliorum nova et amplissima collectio*.
Pastor	Ludwig Pastor, *The History of the Popes*, ed. F. I. Antrobus et al., vols. I–VII (St. Louis: B. Herder, 1923).
PG	Jacques Paul Migne, *Patrologia graeca*.
PL	Jacques Paul Migne, *Patrologia latina*.
Reichling	Dietericus Reichling, *Appendices ad Hainii-*

Copingeri Repertorium Bibliographicum (Munich: J. Rosenthal, 1905–11).

RIS   Lodovico Antonio Muratori, *Rerum italicarum scriptores* (edition as specified).

Libraries and Archives

Arch. Seg. Vat.	Archivio Segreto Vaticano
Aug. Gen. Arch.	Augustinian General Archives, Rome
BAV	Biblioteca Apostolica Vaticana
Bibl. Ambr.	Biblioteca Ambrosiana, Milan
Bibl. Ang.	Biblioteca Angelica, Rome
Bibl. Casan.	Biblioteca Casanatense, Rome
Bibl. Com.	Biblioteca Comunale (city as specified)
Bibl. Estense	Biblioteca Estense, Modena
Bibl. Guarn.	Biblioteca Comunale Guarnacci, Volterra
Bibl. Marc.	Biblioteca Marciana, Venice
Bibl. Ricc.	Biblioteca Riccardiana, Florence
Bibl. Vall.	Biblioteca Vallicelliana, Rome
BL	British Library, London
BN	Bibliothèque Nationale or Biblioteca Nazionale (city as specified)

PRAISE AND BLAME IN RENAISSANCE ROME

INTRODUCTION

This book attempts to do two things that are new in Renaissance studies. First of all, it investigates a new body of evidence. That is to say, it investigates a body of evidence that until now has been almost completely ignored by scholars. This evidence consists principally in orations, sacred and secular, composed in Italy in the Quattrocento and early Cinquecento. The orations that receive the most detailed analysis are over 160 sermons I have located that were delivered before the popes during the sacred liturgies in the Sistine Chapel and Saint Peter's basilica between about 1450 and 1521. These are the orations *coram papa inter missarum solemnia*. Why these orations seemed particularly deserving of study will emerge, it is hoped, in the course of the book. They lead, in any event, to other orations their authors delivered—funeral eulogies, panegyrics of cities and saints, addresses to the Fifth Lateran Council, and addresses to cardinals about to enter conclave. Thus the works of the sacred orators at the papal court, including some of their tracts and treatises, constitute the central material of the book.

Secondly, the book investigates this new body of evidence by making use of a category hitherto practically neglected in the study of sacred oratory in the Renaissance, the so-called *genus demonstrativum*, or epideictic genre, of classical rhetoric. The *genus demonstrativum* was the oratorical genre in which, according to classical theory, "praise and blame" were appropriately distributed. As the title of the book indicates, much of its burden will be to show how important the revival of this genre was in Renaissance Rome. The application of the principles of the *genus demonstrativum* to the works of the sacred orators of the papal court is, in effect, a new hermeneutical device for rendering these works intelligible in ways which until now have escaped scholars. It enables us to arrive at considerable precision in charting the changes in form, mood, and content which the revival of classical rhetoric promoted or effected.

The book places this new material and this new hermeneutical device at the service of three old problems, hoping to contribute to their clarification. The first of these problems concerns the history of Christian preaching. At present we know a great deal about the principles and practice of sacred oratory in the patristic and medieval periods. We know a fair amount about what happened in the Reformation, much less about what happened in the Counter Reformation. We know practically nothing about what happened in the Renaissance, at least insofar as sermons were influenced by the principles of classical oratory. By studying the sermons and other oratory of the court, we fill a gap. Moreover, we provide a foil against which other styles of preaching can be examined so that new light can be thrown on them, and the book in fact does this in a limited way for medieval preaching. A comparison with the preaching of other eras must be left to some other time and, probably, to other scholars. The important role preaching played in the life of these eras, however, needs no proving to anybody who has studied them even superficially. Hence, the justification for an essay towards a history of Renaissance preaching, a history which is still to be written.

By such an essay the book hopes to address a second old problem: the theology and religious world view operative at the papal court during the Renaissance. Despite the scholarly efforts that have been expended on the Italian Renaissance, relatively little has been expended on the religious question. We still nourish ourselves on the broad and often dubious generalizations of scholars from bygone days. In recent years, true, the situation has improved. But Rome remains curiously neglected. In part the reason for this neglect is the absence of a neatly contained *corpus* of theological or religious writings, properly edited and easily accessible. Some of the difficulty is due to the fact that the popes themselves, with the exception of Pius II, left us practically nothing in writing that is of any significant help. We know a great deal about what the Renaissance popes did. We know practically nothing about what they thought; and materials seem lacking which can be of direct help in improving the situation.

On the other hand, even if it seems highly improbable that we shall ever have direct access to the popes' thoughts, we can at least discover what they and their court heard and what they were told they should think—and feel. In order to discover such materials, we must cast a wide net in a vast sea. That is exactly what this book attempts to do, all the while being painfully conscious that its net can capture only a small portion of widely scattered pieces of evidence. Nonetheless, one of the convictions underlying the book is that the style and content of sacred oratory is an effective instrument for discovering the religious sensibilities of an age, especially when the results are confirmed and further specified by other writings of the orators. The members of the papal court, as we know from many sources, discussed what they heard, and they formed through conversation favorable or unfavorable opinions about it. The message of the orators, in other words, did not lie gathering dust on bookshelves but was thrust upon listeners in a social situation where it almost perforce had impact. Orators, in their turn, had in some way to respond to what they thought was expected of them. Therefore, though the book professes to take only a first step in helping us to understand the religion of the papal court in the Renaissance, it takes that step with some confidence that what it discovers will not be misleading.

Finally, the book tries to deal with the nature of Renaissance Humanism. Recent scholarship has provided some extremely helpful clarifications of this old problem, but at the same time it has made us ever more cognizant of the complexity of the problem. The humanists' devotion to the *studia humanitatis* took many forms and found expression in poetry, history, philology, and textual criticism. It was concerned with some branches of philosophy. "Humanists" were schoolmasters, secretaries, diplomats, and chancellors of kings. If scholarship has proved a single point, however, it has proved that in one way or another Renaissance Humanism was intimately, even essentially, related to the revival of classical rhetoric. A "humanist" who made no profession of rhetoric was no humanist at all. And rhetoric, in its classical formulation, meant oratory. We are not, therefore, absurd in postulating that, if we wish to understand Humanism, we must study oratory and orations. Thus we meet the humanists on what was peculiarly their own home territory. It is precisely on that territory that the book attempts to meet them.

The book begins with the pontificate of Nicholas V because that is when the materials I have been describing begin to be available for Rome. This empirical fact coincides with the convention that Nicholas was the first Renaissance pope. The book ends with the death of Leo X because that event, practically coinciding with the excommunication of Luther, seemed to me the earliest date at which a logical break could be made, especially insofar as the book deals with the problem of reform. Good reasons could be adduced for extending the book to the Sack of Rome in 1527, to the establishment of the Roman Inquisition in 1542, or to the end of the Council of Trent in 1563. But I already had more than enough material to interpret, and the early date thus seemed preferable. Indeed, one of the purposes I had in writing the book and in trying to provide as ample documentation as possible was to make this material available to other scholars, who can now give it a more specialized scrutiny and approach it with new and different questions.

CHAPTER ONE. A RENAISSANCE SETTING: CORAM PAPA INTER MISSARUM SOLEMNIA

When the Florentine humanist Giannozzo Manetti praised Pope Nicholas V for the attention he gave to liturgical ceremonies and for his desire to render them ever more dignified and beautiful, he touched an aspect of the Renaissance papacy which was as important in its own day as it has generally been neglected by historians of the era ever since.[1] The observance of the liturgical solemnities by the pope and his court were at the heart of the meaning of papal Rome. This was at least the ideal and the theory, no matter what eclipse these solemnities may from time to time have suffered in the consciousness of those participating in them. The fact that the reform bulls prepared for Sixtus IV and for Alexander VI both treat in the first place of matters concerning the papal liturgies indicates the central and symbolic importance these liturgies continued to enjoy throughout the period.[2] The nature of that centrality and symbolism will be discussed in a later chapter. For the moment it is sufficient simply to point out that for a full understanding of Renaissance Rome the liturgical solemnities cannot be ignored. They are considerably less dramatic than the political and cultural engagements of the popes, but they must nevertheless form an integral part of any authentic portrait of the

1. "Vita Nicolai V, summi pontificis," RIS, 3.2 (Milan: Soc. Palatina, 1734), 923. See also Jean Jouffroy's funeral eulogy for Nicholas, "Oratio in funeralibus Nicolai papae quinti," BAV cod. Vat. lat. 3675, fol. 34ᵛ, and the "De laudibus et divina electione [Nicolai papae]" by Michele Canensi, now edited by Massimo Miglio in his *Storiografia pontificia del Quattrocento* (Bologna: Patròn, 1975), pp. 205–43, esp. 233. Elegance and liturgy are conjoined some decades later by Aurelio Brandolini in his "Epitoma in sacram Iudaeorum historiam," BAV cod. Ottob. lat. 438, fol. 8ʳ.
2. Sixtus IV, "Quoniam regnantium cura non minor," BAV cod. Vat. lat. 3884, fols. 118ᵛ–119ʳ; Alexander VI, "In apostolicae sedis specula," Arch. Seg. Vat., Misc. Arm. XI.88, fols. 1ᵛ–2ᵛ. There is another copy of "Quoniam regnantium" in BAV cod. Vat. lat. 3883, fols. 14ʳ–25ᵛ. There is a second copy of Alexander's bull in the same codex in the Archives, fols. 41ʳ–82ᵛ, and another, in a more difficult hand, in BAV cod. Vat. lat. 3884, fols. 73ʳ–109ᵛ. On these documents, see Léonce Celier, "Alexandre VI et la réforme de l'Église," *Mélanges d'archéologie et d'histoire*, 27 (1907), 65–124, as well as his "L'idée de réforme à la cour pontificale du Concile de Bâle au Concile de Latran," *Revue des questions historiques*, 86 (1909), 418–35. See also the constitution of Calixtus III, Nov. 13, 1456, "Licet ubilibet," in *Bullarium Ordinis Praedicatorum* (Rome: H. Mainardus, 1731), III, 356: ". . . in alma palatii apostolici cappella . . . ea quae apud sedem ipsam aguntur, tamquam praeclarissimum quoddam salubris eruditionis intuetur exemplar."

era. Thus the diaries of the papal Masters of Ceremonies cease being merely mines of discontinuous bits of information, and they assume the function of testifying in their totality to the significance of the liturgical phenomenon at the papal court in the Renaissance.

A modern history of the papal liturgies has yet to be written; my intention is not to attempt one here even for the Renaissance.[3] All that I hope to accomplish in this chapter is to call attention to the importance of the liturgy for Renaissance Rome and then try to reconstruct certain aspects of it that relate to that part of the liturgy that is preaching. To be appreciated as it was appreciated by contemporaries, preaching must be seen in its liturgical context, *inter missarum solemnia*. The liturgical form in which the sermons were encased helped characterize them almost as much as did the literary forms in which they were expressed. We shall eventually see how aesthetically suited to each other these two forms were.

From the early centuries of the Christian era, the solemnity of the liturgies of the *ecclesia Romana* is attested to by many witnesses, and the origin of the cardinalitial dignity itself was related to the liturgy.[4] One of the distinctive characteristics of liturgies in Rome was the consistently important role assigned to churches other than the cathedral of the Lateran. The major basilicas, especially Saint Peter's, as well as the stational churches, all played a part in a liturgical program that over the course of any given year was distributed throughout the city. The Roman liturgy was thus public and urban as in no other city.

By the beginning of the eleventh century, however, the pope and the clerics of his household at times said Office in a private sanctuary in the papal quarters. This was the starting point of a history in which a palace liturgy, separate from the liturgies of the churches, developed. It seems clear, moreover, that the residency of the popes at Avignon in the fourteenth century modified the liturgical traditions of the papacy in ways

3. Despite many inadequacies, Gaetano Moroni's work still contains a considerable amount of helpful information, *Le cappelle pontificie, cardinalizie e prelatizie: Opera storico-liturgica* (Venice: Emiliana, 1841). See, however, esp. S. J. P. van Dijk and J. Hazelden Walker, *The Origins of the Modern Roman Liturgy: The Liturgy of the Papal Court and the Franciscan Order in the Thirteenth Century* (Westminster, Md.: The Newman Press, 1960).

4. See, e.g., Stephan Kuttner, "Cardinalis: The History of a Canonical Concept," *Traditio*, 3 (1945), 129–214; Michel Andrieu, "L'origine du titre de Cardinal dans l'Église romaine," in *Miscellanea Giovanni Mercati*, V, Studi e Testi, No. 125 (Città del Vaticano: BAV, 1946), 113–44.

that would have special significance for the Renaissance and even for centuries thereafter.[5] The liturgies, deprived of their great basilicas and the other churches of Rome, became ever more confined to the chapel of the papal palace. This shift from church to palace meant a shift from a public and urban liturgy to a more private and courtly one. The significance of this change is indicated by the very title, *cappelle pontificie* or *cappelle palatine*, which in time became attached to these liturgies.

After the turmoil of the Schism, when the popes once again took up their residency in Rome, the effects of these developments continued to be felt, with the added distinction that the Vatican palace and the basilica of Saint Peter became the liturgical focus of the city to a greater degree than ever before. Nicholas V's architectural plans and achievements for that quarter of the city meant that henceforth during the period we are considering the papal liturgies would for the most part be celebrated there. When, a few decades after Nicholas V, Sixtus IV demolished the old "cappella magna" of Nicholas III in order to construct the Sistine Chapel, we can say that a definite localization of the *cappelle pontificie* had been accomplished.[6] The great feasts, such as Pentecost and All Saints, would

5. See Moroni, *Cappelle pontificie*, pp. 2–12, and esp. Bernhard Schimmelpfennig, *Die Zeremonienbücher der römischen Kurie im Mittelalter*, Bibliothek des deutschen historischen Instituts in Rom, No. 40 (Tübingen: M. Niemeyer, 1973), pp. 36–39, as well as Schimmelpfennig's "Die Organization der päpstlichen Kapelle in Avignon," *Quellen und Forschungen aus italienischen Archiven und Bibliotheken*, 50 (1971), 80–111; Franz Xaver Haberl, *Die römische "Schola cantorum" und die päpstlichen Kapellsänger bis zur Mitte des 16. Jahrhunderts*, vol. III of *Bausteine für Musikgeschichte*, 3 vols. (Leipzig: Breitkopf und Härtel, 1885–88), 46; Bernard Guillemain, *La cour pontificale d'Avignon, 1309–1376* (Paris: de Boccard, 1966), p. 702; van Dijk and Walker, *Origins of the Modern Roman Liturgy*, pp. 80–87.

6. See Moroni, *Cappelle pontificie*, pp. 8–12; Schimmelpfennig, *Zeremonienbücher*, pp. 132–38; Joaquim Nabuco's introduction to *Le Cérémonial Apostolique avant Innocent VIII: Texte du manuscrit Urbinate Latin 469 de la Bibliothèque Vaticane* établi par Dom Filippo Tamburini, Bibliotheca "Ephemerides Liturgicae," Sectio Historica, No. 30 (Rome: Edizioni Liturgiche, 1966), esp. pp. 9*–38*; Carroll William Westfall, *In This Most Perfect Paradise: Alberti, Nicholas V, and the Invention of Conscious Urban Planning in Rome, 1447–55* (University Park, Pa.: Pennsylvania State University Press 1974); Deoclecio Redig de Campos, *I palazzi Vaticani*, Roma Cristiana, No. 18 (Bologna: Cappelli, 1967); L. D. Ettlinger, *The Sistine Chapel before Michelangelo: Religious Imagery and Papal Primacy* (Oxford: Clarendon, 1965). See also my *Giles of Viterbo on Church and Reform: A Study in Renaissance Thought*, Studies in Medieval and Reformation Thought, No. 5 (Leiden: Brill, 1968), esp. pp. 123–26. The title page of Nicolaus Schomberg's *Orationes vel potius divinorum eloquiorum enodationes* (Leipzig: W. Stöckel, 1512) is incorrect when it indicates these Advent and Lenten sermons for Julius II by this procurator general of the Dominicans were delivered at Rome "in certis stationibus ecclesiarum," fol. [1ʳ]. On the other hand, as late as 1481 the feast of John the Evangelist was celebrated at the Lateran, "ut moris est," as

habitually be celebrated in the basilica of Saint Peter or in one of its chapels, whereas other solemnities, such as the Sundays of Advent and Lent, would be observed in the Sistine Chapel of the palace.

According to Manetti's account, Nicholas V spared no expense in trying to provide rich vestments and other adornments to dignify the papal liturgies.[7] His successors, especially Paul II and Leo X, shared some of the same zeal for making these court ceremonies as visually impressive as possible.[8] A similar zeal for the music of the liturgies was operative, and the papal choir underwent considerable enlargement, particularly during the pontificate of Sixtus IV.[9] The motivation behind these important decisions was doubtless complex. As is clear from so many documents of the era, the popes wanted their court, in all its aspects, to evoke sentiments of respect which were proper to their office and to the Church which they represented. The "authority," the "dignity," and the "honor" of the Apostolic See were what was at stake.[10] Moreover, we know too much about the popes of the Renaissance to exclude a desire for personal recognition, as Manetti admits frankly for Nicholas.[11]

Another motive animating this progressive liturgical solemnization, however, must be accepted in all seriousness. The papal court was a reflection and image of the heavenly court, and the papal liturgies were a reflection and image of the heavenly liturgies. The idea of a correspondence between earthly and heavenly hierarchies and between earthly and heavenly liturgies was of course not new. Nonetheless, the clarity

---

Stephanus Thegliatius states in his *Sermo in materia fidei* [Rome: n. publ., after Dec. 27, 1480], Hain #*15461, fol. [6ʳ]. Jacopo Gherardi confirms that the oration was given in the Lateran, *Il diario romano*, ed. Enrico Carusi, RIS, 23.3 (Città di Castello: S. Lapi, 1904), 32. Professor Egmont Lee of the University of Calgary is preparing an article on Gherardi which he kindly let me read in a preliminary version: "Towards a History of the Papal Court: *The Roman Diary* of Jacopo Gherardi."

7. "Vita Nicolai V," col. 923.

8. See Moroni, *Cappelle pontificie*, p. 12; O'Malley, *Giles of Viterbo*, p. 113; John Shearman, *Raphael's Cartoons in the Collection of Her Majesty the Queen and the Tapestries for the Sistine Chapel* (London: Phaidon, 1972), esp. pp. 1–30.

9. See Haberl, "Schola Cantorum," esp. pp. 45–55. Contemporary scholarship has discovered little to add to the information which Haberl provided. See, however, the dissertation by Richard J. Sherr, "The Papal Chapel ca. 1492–1513 and Its Polyphonic Sources," Diss. Princeton University, 1975, pp. 85–104. I am indebted to Professor Jeremy Noble for the information about Sherr's dissertation.

10. See Manetti, "Vita Nicolai V," cols. 921–23, 925, 950–51. See also, e.g., Domenico de' Domenichi, *Tractatus de reformationibus Romanae curiae* (Brescia: Baptista Farfengus, 1495), GKW #8638, fol. [5ʳ–ᵛ].

11. "Vita Nicolai V," col. 925.

with which this comparison occurs in such acute observers at the papal court as Manetti and Pope Pius II himself, as well as others, makes us stop to take notice.[12] Eventually the correlation between the earthly and heavenly liturgies must be set in the context of a broader correlation of the earthly with the heavenly Church, which, as we shall see, recurs as an insistent theme in the preaching at the court and which is of great importance for understanding Roman reform ideals.

Besides the splendor and magnificence of the papal liturgies, what specifically suggested Pius II's comparison of them with the heavenly liturgies was their ordered ranks. He describes how each grade in the chapel had its assigned place in a gradually descending hierarchy. From Pius's description of these grades, we see how the congregation had become almost restricted to members of the court. Except for the orators of the Christian states and princes, all the grades he mentions are clerical. From other sources we know, however, that members of the laity, like the *Barones* and *Conservatores* of the city of Rome, were present for the liturgies.[13]

As the period moves forward, an ever more stabilized ordering of protocol, ritual, and procedure is introduced. This process is part of the general regularizing of life in Rome as the popes at the end of the Schism began to try to set their city in order. But the liturgical ordering was more particularly due to the emergence of the three great Masters of Ceremonies—Agostino Patrizi (1468–83), Joannes Burchard (1483–1504), and Paris de Grassis (1504–28).[14]

By the time Patrizi was functioning in his office, the Master of Ceremonies clearly enjoyed considerable authority. Indeed, Ambrogio Massari, one of the preachers at the court and later prior general of the Hermits of Saint Augustine, relates with some show of indignation how Patrizi gave precedence in seating in the papal chapel to the procurators general of some newer religious orders, displacing the procurators of the Domini-

---

12. Manetti, "Vita Nicolai V," col. 923; Pius II, "Apologia ad Martinum Mayer," in *Commentarii rerum memorabilium* (Rome: D. Basae, 1584), p. 739: "... quod si videres aut celebrantem Romanum Pontificem aut divina audientem, fateris profecto non esse ordinem, non esse splendorem ac magnificentiam, nisi apud Romanum praesulem. ... profecto instar caelestis hierarchiae diceres Romanam curiam, ubi omnia ordinata, omnia ex praescripto statutoque modo disposita, quae profecto cum boni viri intuentur, non possunt nisi laudare."

13. See Shearman, *Raphael's Cartoons*, pp. 21–22.

14. See Nabuco, *Cérémonial Apostolique*, esp. pp. 22*–38*, with the bibliography indicated there.

cans, Franciscans, and Augustinians.[15] The symbolic importance attached to such matters of protocol reveals how great was the authority Patrizi wielded. More significant, however, are the liturgical books he and Burchard edited at the command of Pope Innocent VIII. These books confirmed and promoted the more courtly turn the papal liturgies had already taken.[16]

In addition to these books, the diary describing the papal ceremonies Burchard composed, and its continuation by his successor, guaranteed that ritual order that is the faithful repetition in successive years of the same ceremony for the same occasion. The diaries, consulted year by year to discover how to proceed, began to have prescriptive force.

The changes in the papal liturgies pertinent to our purposes, of course, are those concerning preaching. The most dramatic of these changes certainly consists in the fact that the popes themselves no longer preached. Even at Avignon there were many liturgical occasions when the sermon was not given by the pope himself. Nonetheless, the popes did continue to preach there, as we know from the famous example of Pope John XXII's sermons on the beatific vision, as well as from other examples.[17]

From at least the time of Nicholas V onward, however, not a single

15. (Ambrosius de Cora), *Defensorium ordinis heremitarum s. Augustini* [Rome: G. Herolt, not before 1482, despite Hain #*5684], fol. [34ʳ]. Domenico de' Domenichi's "Oratio pro parte episcoporum" of 1459 before Pius II dramatizes the symbolic importance of precedence in seating in the papal chapel, as Domenichi here thanks the pope for restoring to the bishops their place usurped by the prothonotaries. BAV cod. Ottob. lat. 1035, fols. 28ᵛ–33ᵛ. See Shearman, *Raphael's Cartoons*, pp. 21–30, for a description of the seating arrangements and general layout of the Sistine Chapel during the liturgies.

16. See Nabuco, *Cérémonial Apostolique*, pp. 22*–38*. The two books in question are the *Pontificale Romanum* (Rome: S. Plannck, 1485), Hain #13285, and the "De caeremoniis curiae Romanae libri tres," of 1488, BAV cod. Chigi C.VI.180. The BAV contains two other copies of this work, cod. Vat. lat. 4971 and Vat. lat. 6094. On the variations between these manuscripts and the *Sacrarum caeremoniarum sanctae Romanae ecclesiae libri tres* (Venice: Gregorio de Gregori, 1516), published under the editorship of Cristoforo Marcello, see Nabuco, *loc. cit.* On Innocent VIII's concern to have certain reforms of the *cappelle* codified, see Burchard's *Liber Notarum*, I, 201. It might be useful at this point to note that Paris de Grassis's "Tractatus de oratoribus Romanae curiae," BAV cod. Vat. lat. 12270, does not deal with preachers but with the "orators" of states and princes who enjoyed, in effect, ambassadorial rank at the papal court.

17. See Nabuco, *Cérémonial Apostolique*, pp. 9*–38*; Guillemain, *Cour pontificale*, pp. 48–53; Marc Dykmans, *Les sermons de Jean XXII sur la vision béatifique*, Miscellanea Historiae Pontificiae, No. 34 (Rome: Pontificia Universitas Gregoriana, 1973); Thomas Kaeppeli, "Predigten am päpstlichen Hof von Avignon," *Archivum Fratrum Praedicatorum*, 19 (1949), 388–93; Philibert Schmitz, "Les sermons et discours de Clément VI, O.S.B.," *Revue Bénédictine*, 41 (1929), 15–34.

example of a pope preaching during a *cappella pontificia* seems to have survived, nor is there a single example of a pope delivering a panegyric in honor of a saint on a regular feast day.[18] During the Renaissance protocol forbade the popes from even attending the funeral of a cardinal, and it was by way of a great exception that Sixtus IV appeared and presided at the funeral of Cardinal Bessarion on December 3, 1472, in the cardinal's titular church of Ss. Apostoli.[19]

The popes might, indeed, respond to the "pro obedientia" speeches of the orators of princes and states at their court. In this function Pius II was much esteemed, and some of these responses still survive. The popes might also address the faithful at a canonization or on some other special occasion, as again was true of Pius II at the canonization of Catherine of Siena.[20] But the sermons during the *cappelle* were now invariably delivered by others—in the pope's presence and for his hearing, *coram papa.*

An ever more stable calendar of days when sermons were to be delivered and when they were not was also gradually established. Although the Avignonese calendar for preaching corresponds for certain solemnities with the one that obtained in Rome in Burchard's day, it prescribed or allowed sermons for more occasions. The number per annum certainly exceeded the nineteen that were regular during most of the period we are considering.[21]

At Avignon, for instance, Bernardus Oliver, bishop of Barcelona, preached on the feast of Saint Benedict, 1345 or 1346, for Pope Clement

18. On the other hand, the "De caeremoniis" of Patrizi and Burchard, 1488, still made provision for sermons by the pope, BAV cod. Chigi C.VI.180, fol. 197ᵛ: "Summus Pontifex non convenit facere sermonem alio quopiam celebrante, et tantum dum ipse celebrat."

19. See Niccolò Capranica, "Nicolai episcopi Firmani oratio in funere Bessarionis," in *Kardinal Bessarion als Theologe, Humanist und Staatsmann*, ed. Ludwig Mohler, III (Paderborn: F. Schöningh, 1967), 404. Antonio Casamassa has shown that the "sermo" supposedly by Pope Martin V, "De translatione corporis s. Monicae," was actually written by the humanist Andrea Biglia, "L'autore di un preteso discorso di Martino V," in *Miscellanea Pio Paschini*, Lateranum NS Nos. 14–15, 2 vols. (Rome: Lateranum, 1948–49), II, 109–25. The latest study on Biglia is by Diana M. Webb, "Andrea Biglia at Bologna, 1424–27: A Humanist Friar and the Troubles of the Church," *Bulletin of the Institute of Historical Research*, 49 (1976), 41–59.

20. See *Pii II P. M., olim Aeneae Sylvii Piccolominei Senensis, orationes politicae et ecclesiasticae*, ed. Giovanni Domenico Mansi, 2 vols. (Lucca: P. M. Benedinus, 1755–57), II, 136–44, and Burchard's description of Innocent VIII's "parvam orationem seu sermonem" at the canonization of St. Leopold on Jan. 6, 1485, *Liber Notarum*, I, 100.

21. See Guillemain, *Cour pontificale*, p. 50; Kaeppeli, "Predigten von Avignon," pp. 388–93; Schimmelpfennig, *Zeremonienbücher*, passim. See also *Festa et ordo terminorum sacri palatii apostolici* [Rome: n. publ., n.d.], Hain #*7026.

VI.[22] Franciscus Florentinus (seu Paduanus), a Franciscan, preached a sermon on Holy Thursday, year unknown, for Eugene IV in S. Maria Novella, Florence.[23] We have a sermon on the feast of Saints Peter and Paul (June 29) preached by Rodrigo Sánchez de Arévalo for Nicholas V, and we have another by him for Calixtus III on the feast of the Annunciation (March 25).[24] Guillemus Bodivit preached on the Annunciation in 1484, which seems to be the last time that feast was thus honored in Rome.[25] We have, moreover, two panegyrics of Saint Augustine by Massari delivered respectively before Pius II and Paul II.[26] But these occasions and others had been definitively eliminated by the time Innocent VIII became pope in August, 1484, shortly after Burchard began his diary.[27]

The diaries of Burchard and de Grassis show beyond a doubt how set by their time had become the calendar for preaching *coram papa inter missarum solemnia*. The regular and recurring occasions for these sermons were now the Sundays of Advent and Lent (with the exception of Palm Sunday), and the solemnities of the Circumcision of Christ (January 1), Epiphany (January 6), Ash Wednesday, Good Friday, Ascension Thursday, Pentecost, Trinity Sunday, All Saints (November 1), Saint Stephen (December 26) and Saint John the Evangelist (December 27).

Ancient custom combined with a certain measure of practicality seems to have caused these particular days finally to prevail. One practical norm that Burchard and de Grassis specifically adduce is that there is not to

22. See Kaeppeli, "Predigten von Avignon," p. 391 (#16).

23. "Pro divinissima eucaristia oratio," BN Florence cod. Landau 152, fols. 56ʳ–59ᵛ.

24. "In die apostolorum Petri et Pauli," BAV cod. Vat. lat. 4881, fols. 247ᵛ–250ᵛ; "In die annuntiationis," *ibid.*, fols. 239ᵛ–242ʳ. Marco Maroldi, while Master of the Sacred Palace, preached on the feast of the Annunciation in 1481 for Sixtus IV, *Sententia veritatis humanae redemptionis* [Rome: S. Plannck, after March 25, 1481], Hain #*10778. Gherardi comments on this oration, *Diario*, p. 41: "Orationem habuit Marcus Neapolitanus, sacri apostolici palatii magister, theologo quam oratori convenientiorem. Commendatus ab omnibus fuit." Gherardi notes there was a sermon the next year, 1482, in S. Maria del Popolo, p. 93, and he mistakenly mentions that Sixtus IV forbade the sermon to be given in 1484, p. 130; see the next note. For Avignon, see Schimmelpfennig, *Zeremonienbücher*, p. 303.

25. *In die annuntiationis Virginis sermo* [Rome: B. Guldinbeck, after Aug. 12, 1484], GKW #4503.

26. These are printed in his *Vita praecellentissimi ecclesiae doctoris divi Aurelii Augustini. Commentarii super regula sancti Augustini* (Rome: G. Herolt, 1481), Hain #*5683, fols. [233ʳ–237ᵛ, 241ᵛ–247ᵛ].

27. Practice differed in some particulars from the prescriptions of the "De caeremoniis" of 1488, BAV cod. Chigi C.VI.180, where a sermon is prescribed, for example, for the feast of the Annunciation, fol. 170ʳ. On Dec. 27 there was to be a sermon only if the pope celebrated the Mass, and it was to be given by the pope himself or by a cardinal, fol. 142ᵛ, a provision that was in no way observed.

be a sermon on a day when a procession takes place.[28] According to that norm, sermons would not be given, therefore, on Palm Sunday, Corpus Christi, or the feast of Saints Peter and Paul. From various comments in the diaries of the Masters of Ceremonies, one can easily infer that a general tendency to eliminate sermons when the liturgy was otherwise already very long might explain why there was no sermon on Christmas, with its three Masses. Roman fear of the summer heat seemingly eliminated the possibility for a sermon on the feast of the Assumption, and on August 15, 1505, old hands at the court smiled at the thought that somebody might propose a sermon in such a season.[29] But why in particular certain feasts were observed with a sermon and why others were not is a matter for a specialized study in its own right.

Perhaps of some interest, however, is the fact that at least by 1484 the only two saints who were honored by a *cappella* with sermon were two saints of the New Testament, Stephen and John the Evangelist. Leo X expressed some wonder that John the Baptist was not so honored, and he accordingly instituted a *cappella* for that saint in 1518, though without a sermon.[30] Papal participation ceased in other celebrations in honor of the saints where there might be a sermon. Though the panegyrics in honor of Saint Augustine continued, the popes no longer attended. The feast of Saint Thomas Aquinas was celebrated in Renaissance Rome at the church of S. Maria sopra Minerva with an important panegyric and with the participation of the sacred college,[31] but there is no record that the popes took part in that celebration.

28. See, e.g., Burchard, *Liber Notarum*, Pentecost, 1501, II, 285; Nov. 1, 1505, *ibid.*, II, 495; de Grassis, "Diarium," Nov. 1, 1505, BAV cod. Vat. lat. 12272, fol. 133ᵛ.

29. De Grassis, "Diarium," BAV cod. Vat. lat. 12272, fol. 107ʳ. See also Schimmelpfennig, *Zeremonienbücher*, p. 313.

30. De Grassis, "Diarium," June 24, 1518, BAV cod. Vat. lat. 12275, fol. 299ʳ⁻ᵛ. See also Schimmelpfennig, *Zeremonienbücher*, p. 313.

31. See my "Some Renaissance Panegyrics of Aquinas," *Renaissance Quarterly*, 27 (1974), 174–92, esp. 175–78. Since publishing this article, I have discovered two more panegyrics intended for the sacred college: Rodrigo Sánchez de Arévalo, c.1450, BAV cod. Vat. lat. 4881, fols. 234ʳ–237ʳ, and Francesco Maturanzio, c.1485, BAV cod. Vat. lat. 5358, fols. 35ᵛ–45ʳ. Richard H. Trame mistakenly says that the former oration was delivered in the presence of the pope. *Rodrigo Sánchez de Arévalo, 1404–1470: Spanish Diplomat and Champion of the Papacy* (Washington: Catholic University Press, 1958), p. 72.

During the long Florentine sojourn of Eugene IV, the "Roman clergy" (but not the pope) listened to a panegyric on St. Dominic and one on St. Francis of Assisi by the Franciscan, Franciscus Florentinus (seu Paduanus), BN Florence cod. Landau 152, fols. 62ᵛ–71ʳ. I have found no panegyrics of these two saints for members of the papal court in Rome, 1450–1521.

A further regularization that occurred between the time of the Avignonese residency and the High Renaissance concerned the persons who preached. The cardinals, like the popes, ceased preaching at the *cappelle*. This, too, was contrary to the practice at Avignon. From the accession of Nicholas V in 1447 until the death of Leo X in 1521, I have found no evidence of a cardinal preaching at a *cappella*.[32] This change would explain, for instance, why Nicholas of Cusa—so active in Rome in his later years, so close to Pius II, and otherwise such a prolific preacher—never gave a sermon *coram*.

Until Sixtus IV the assignment of preachers to particular occasions does not follow any clearly discernible pattern. It seems that during that pontificate the Sundays of Advent and Lent were assigned to the procurators general of the mendicant orders in the following sequence: to the Dominicans, the first Sundays; to the Franciscans, the second; to the Augustinians, the third; to the Carmelites, the fourth.[33] A comment of Massari in his *Defensorium*, published probably in 1482, suggests that, at least for the first three of those orders, the sequence was already in force, and other evidence corroborates such an inference.[34] The Servites' right to preach on the feast of the Epiphany and on the fifth Sunday of Lent was much less secure than that of the other mendicants to their days, and even as late as 1508 the Servites were being challenged about the Epiphany. This dispute, with which Burchard also had had to contend, was settled in their favor.[35] Eventually, therefore, about half of the occasions on which there was a sermon *coram papa* was assigned *ex officio* to the procurators of the five great mendicant orders or to their substitutes.

The mendicants had early found it useful to have one of their members present at the papal court to handle their official business with the Holy See. This was the origin of the office of procurator general, and the official business of the order continued to be the principal function of that office

32. The "De caeremoniis" of 1488 still makes provisions for sermons by cardinal bishops and cardinal priests, BAV cod. Chigi C.VI.180, fol. 197ᵛ: "Cardinales non faciunt sermonem in cappella papae nisi celebrante pontifice vel cum ipsemet cardinalis celebrat." Sermons by cardinal deacons are expressly excluded, *ibid.*, fol. 198ʳ: "Et nota quod diaconus cardinalis non praedicat in cappella pontificis, neque alius quispiam non praelatus nisi sit doctor in theologia secundum antiquas et probatas caeremonias. . . ." See also Guillemain, *Cour pontificale*, p. 50.

33. See Moroni, *Cappelle pontificie*, p. 159.

34. *Defensorium*, fol. [34ʳ]. See Gherardi, passim, for the years his *Diario* covers, 1479–84.

35. De Grassis, "Diarium," Jan. 6, 1508, BAV cod. Vat. lat. 12273, fol. 135ʳ; Burchard, *Liber Notarum*, Jan. 6, 1488, I, 217.

even after preaching also became attached to it. Consequently, long before the pontificate of Sixtus IV, the procurators were established figures
at court. This office, obviously, was an important one, and the procurators were chosen by their respective orders with considerable care. Though
sometimes appointed by the superior general of the order, they were in
other instances elected or confirmed by general chapters.[36] The cardinal
protectors of the orders also took an interest in the appointment, as is
clearly seen in Cardinal Oliviero Carafa's successful recommendation of
the young professor of theology, Thomas de Vio (Cajetan), to the Master
General of the Dominicans in 1501.[37] Pope Paul III's refusal in 1538 to
accept the newly elected Augustinian procurator provides us with at least
one instance of direct papal intervention, though it falls slightly outside
the period with which we are dealing.[38] It is difficult to imagine, however,
that the popes at any time remained altogether passive in the face of
such an important appointment. In any case, for the procurators themselves their office, for obvious reasons, often led to further advancement
either in their own order or in the hierarchy of the Church at large.

How were the preachers chosen for those occasions not already pre-
empted by the mendicants? At least by the time Patrizi and Burchard
presented their "De caeremoniis curiae Romanae libri tres" to Innocent
VIII in 1488, the prerogative was firmly in the hands of the Masters of
the Sacred Palace, the popes' official theologians or "masters" in theology.[39]
That office, central to the proper functioning of the *Studium* of the papal
Curia, underwent a significant development during the Avignonese residency, but its authority regarding preaching began to be clearly defined

36. See, e.g., Innocentius Taurisano, *Hierarchia Ordinis Praedicatorum*, 2nd ed.
(Rome: Manuzio, 1916), pp. 81–98; Alessio Rossi, *Manuale di storia dell'ordine dei
Servi di Maria (MCCXXXIII–MCMLIV)* (Rome: S. Marcello, 1956), pp. 797–99; N.
Racanelli, "La Gerarchia Agostiniana: I Procuratori Generali dell'Ordine (1256–1931),"
Bollettino Storico Agostiniano, 10 (1934), 109–14, 141–43, continued through 13
(1937), 150–53.
37. See Daniel-Antonin Mortier, *Histoire des Maîtres Généraux de l'ordre des
Frères Prêcheurs*, V (Paris: A. Picard, 1911), 144. Burchard mentions Carafa's intervention even in the election of the new Master General in 1501. *Liber Notarum*, II, 284.
38. See Racanelli, "Gerarchia Agostiniana," 10 (1934), 143.
39. See BAV cod. Chigi C.VI.180, fol. 195ʳ: "Magister sacri palatii esse convenit
ex ordine praedicatorum et ordinarie quando fit consistorium legit in palatio publice
aliquid in theologia. Ad hunc spectat ordinare qui debeant facere sermones in cappella
apostolica, et eorum sermones praevidere curareque ut nihil dicatur puritati fidei et
gravitati illius loci contrarium. Et sedet vel stat semper post primum auditorem qui
adest, ut ita vidi semper servari meo tempore." The authority of the Master of the
Sacred Palace to assign sermons was, however, sometimes challenged or even defied.
See Burchard, *Liber Notarum*, Jan. 6, 1488, I, 217, and Ash Wednesday, 1489, I, 251.

only with the return of the popes to Rome after the Schism.[40] What we
see here is once again the climax of a gradual evolution. A brief of Eugene
IV of October 30, 1437, conferred a general right of supervision of the
content of the sermons on the then Master, the famous canonist Juan de
Torquemada.[41] Calixtus III renewed, amplified, and strengthened the provisions in his constitution of November 13, 1456, with a special admonition that the Master of the Palace take care that the sermons be not tire-
some by being too long.[42]

The Master of the Sacred Palace's alternate title, *haereticae pravitatis
inquisitor*, has a considerably less pleasant ring. With the safeguarding of
orthodoxy being a major function of the inquisitor's office, we can see
how it might naturally have devolved upon him to appoint the preachers
for the occasions not already assigned. However, contrary to what we
might expect, during the Renaissance the orthodoxy of the sermons does
not seem to have been what gave the Masters of the Palace their real
troubles. Rather, the length and the general propriety of the sermons, as
well as the age, deportment, and dress of the preachers, most often brought
the Masters of the Sacred Palace into conflict with the Masters of Ceremonies and at times even earned for them a rebuke from the popes themselves. From the diaries of Burchard and de Grassis we have detailed, and
often amusing, accounts of how the Masters of the Sacred Palace functioned and of how they and the Masters of Ceremonies handled the
sometimes delicate and difficult situations which arose during the *cappelle pontificie*.

In theory the Master of the Sacred Palace was to see a copy of every
sermon before it was delivered. This provision occurs in the brief of
Eugene IV, in the constitution of Calixtus III, in the unpublished reform
bull of Pius II, in the ceremonial of Patrizi and Burchard, and it was
repeated orally by Leo X in specific terms.[43] The frequency with which
the provision had to be reiterated arouses the suspicion that it was often

---

40. See Raymond Creytens, "Le 'Studium Romanae Curiae' et le Maître du Sacré
Palais," *Archivum Fratrum Praedicatorum*, 12 (1942), 5–83. The list for the Masters of
the Sacred Palace for our period is contained in Taurisano, *Hierarchia Ordinis Praedicatorum*, pp. 46–51. See also Giuseppe Catalani, *De magistro sacri palatii apostolici
libri duo* (Rome: Fulgonus, 1751).

41. "Dudum ex pluribus," in *Bullarium Ordinis Praedicatorum*, III, 81.

42. "Licet ubilibet," *ibid.*, 356.

43. *Ibid.*, 356–57. See also Rudolf Haubst, "Der Reformentwurf Pius' des Zweiten,"
Römische Quartalschrift, 49 (1954), p. 228; Patrizi and Burchard, "De caeremoniis,"
BAV cod. Chigi C.VI.180, fol. 195ʳ; for Leo X, de Grassis, "Diarium," Jan. 1, 1514,
BAV cod. Vat. lat. 12275, fol. 96ᵛ.

honored in the breach. The suspicion is confirmed by the diaries. For
the most part the diaries leave one with the impression that the Masters
of the Sacred Palace, though attentive to this aspect of their duties, were
by no means overly meticulous about it.

There is, however, clear record of several instances when the Master
of the Palace actually refused to allow a particular sermon to be delivered.
For example, there was no sermon on January 1, 1505, because the Master,
Giovanni Rafanelli, said the sermon submitted to him contained "absurd
and improper" ideas, including the prediction that the new year would
be fatal for Pope Julius II and for some of the cardinals.[44] On the same
feast in 1518, Silvester Prierias, Rafanelli's successor, once again wished
to forbid a sermon because the preacher, an unnamed Spaniard, had refused to shorten it. De Grassis informed the pope of Prierias's decision,
and Leo X, after consulting the cardinals, upheld his theologian.[45] Prierias
was embarrassed two years later on Ash Wednesday, when he felt compelled to make his excuses to de Grassis and Leo because he had allowed
another overlong sermon, again by a Spaniard, to slip by him.[46]

Blame for offensive length and content could not always be immediately
assigned to the Master of the Palace. After a particularly trying sermon
by a Servite on the feast of Saint John in 1511, de Grassis reproved Rafanelli for permitting it to be delivered. The Master responded that the
friar had delivered a different sermon from the one he had originally
shown him.[47] Prierias made the same excuse for a sermon on Ascension
Thursday, 1518, stating quite baldly that the preacher had deliberately de-
ceived him.[48] It was, however, after an especially long sermon on the feast
of Saint Stephen in 1508, that Paris de Grassis, still seething the next day,
addressed to Rafanelli a dramatic instruction as to how he was to handle
his office in the future in the case of those who dared to add to what they
had written or to substitute a different sermon: if the preacher digressed
from what had previously been approved, the Master should interrupt
the preacher in the pulpit and insist, then and there, that he adhere to

44. De Grassis, "Diarium," BAV cod. Vat. lat. 12272, fol. 54ᵛ. Burchard has a
much less sensational account of this incident. *Liber Notarum*, II, 467: "Non fuit
sermo, quia frater illum facturus non bene studuit eum, ut dixerunt." For an unsuc-
cessful attempt of the Master of the Sacred Palace to prevent a sermon from being
delivered, see *ibid.*, second Sunday of Advent, 1486, I, 172–73.
45. De Grassis, "Diarium," BAV cod. Vat. lat. 12275, fol. 255ʳ.
46. *Ibid.*, fol. 373ᵛ.
47. De Grassis, "Diarium," BAV cod. Vat. lat. 12269, fol. 484ᵛ.
48. De Grassis, "Diarium," BAV cod. Vat. lat. 12275, fol. 294ʳ.

his text. Rafanelli meekly agreed, but the same Rafanelli suffered the substitute sermon on Saint John to be delivered in 1511.[49] Rafanelli's failure to give satisfaction on this issue was in fact not inconsistent with his own preaching. Burchard describes Rafanelli's sermon for Good Friday, 1505, for instance, as "long and tedious."[50]

Rafanelli, de Grassis, and an unnamed Franciscan were the principal figures in one of the most chaotic incidents to occur during a *cappella*. It was the second Sunday of Advent, 1512. The pope was not present for the Mass. The sermon, as de Grassis perhaps with some exaggeration describes it, began with a commentary on Christ's passion, and then it shifted to an account of all of the wonders wrought by the Father, Son, and Holy Spirit, as well as by the saints, from the creation of the world until the present. By this time the sermon was well on the way towards the hour and a half it was destined to last, a length three or four or five times beyond what was normal. The cardinals, many of whom were now laughing, kept signaling de Grassis to make the friar cease and desist. Needless to say, de Grassis readily received these signals, but his efforts to comply only incited the friar to raise his voice and to shout more loudly. De Grassis at this point turned his wrath on Rafanelli for allowing such nonsense in the first place. With that, the Master of the Sacred Palace finally bestirred himself, rose from his place, and took his turn in trying to silence the preacher. This, too, had no effect. Only the ringing of a bell and the laughter of practically the whole chapel were able to bring the sermon to a close, but not before the friar launched into a eulogy of the absent Julius II. Rafanelli and de Grassis, of course, were not amused. When it was all over, Rafanelli severely reproached the friar for not staying with his original text. De Grassis was more direct. He told the Franciscan that if he ever again dared appear in the papal chapel, he would have him thrown out.[51]

As this incident makes abundantly clear, the decorum and dignity so much desired for the *cappelle pontificie* were not always achieved. Although the particular incident can be dismissed as a unique occurrence, there certainly was a persistent problem in maintaining the silence considered appropriate in the chapel. Indeed, a proclivity for talking during the sermons seems to have been almost ineradicable. In this matter the cardinals

49. De Grassis, "Diarium," BAV cod. Vat. lat. 12273, fol. 183ʳ.
50. *Liber Notarum*, II, 475.
51. De Grassis, "Diarium," BAV cod. Vat. lat. 12269, fol. 601ʳ⁻ᵛ.

themselves were not above reproach, as Domenico de' Domenichi informs us as early as 1458.[52] The reform bull prepared for Alexander VI mentions the problem and indicates penalties for offenders.[53] When Leo X found it difficult to hear the "elegant and learned" sermon for the first Sunday of Advent, 1518, because of the noise in the chapel, he decided to take drastic measures, and ordered that guards be stationed in the chapel to maintain silence. De Grassis found this measure to his liking;[54] but on Ash Wednesday of the very next year the problem recurred, and Leo had in effect to renew his order.[55] Leo ended his days without solving the problem, however, for on Trinity Sunday of 1521 de Grassis noted that the sermon was not heard because of the noise.[56]

This phenomenon of noise and other misbehavior in the chapel reveals at least two things. First of all, despite an ideal of order and elegance and despite considerable achievement of both, these were in many ways still turbulent days, even ceremonially. A rigid code of protocol and convention often combined in public functions with an astonishing degree of spontaneity, even of coarseness. No matter how one explains it, that seems to be the fact. Secondly, as has already been illustrated in several different ways, regulations issued to prevent various abuses were seemingly rather easily forgotten. When Leo in 1519 renewed his order for guards in the chapel, de Grassis's text implies that in the few months which had elapsed since the first such order the guards had already stopped coming—a fact Leo must have been as much aware of as anybody else. We should not, however, too hastily ascribe this negligence to contempt or crass unconcern. It seems, rather, that once the problem which first prompted a regulation was, for the moment at least, under control, there ceased to be any obligation to observe it. We might find such a procedure—or, better, lack of procedure—easier to understand if we recall that in many places in the western world such a day-by-day handling of disciplinary crises has even now not disappeared.

52. *Tractatus*, fol. [7ʳ].
53. "In apostolicae sedis specula," Arch. Seg. Vat., Misc. Arm. XI.88, fol. 2ʳ. Francesco Piccolomini, the future Pius III, was seemingly concerned with the problem, as indicated in his "memorial" done in preparation for Alexander's bull, published by Celier, "Alexandre VI," p. 100. For the effect the chattering had on the preacher for All Saints, 1504, see Burchard, *Liber Notarum*, II, 462. See also the letter of Baptista Mantuanus to Bernardo Bembo, 1488, Bibl. Com. Ariostea, Ferrara, cod. II.162, fol. 129ᵛ.
54. De Grassis, "Diarium," BAV cod. Vat. lat. 12275, fol. 307ʳ.
55. *Ibid.*, fol. 320ʳ.
56. *Ibid.*, fol. 400ʳ.

Irregularities during the *cappelle* like those I have described catch our attention as we read the diaries of the Masters of Ceremonies. We should be careful to balance the evidence, however, by noting how often colorless words like *bonus, doctus,* and *ab omnibus laudatus* occur, or how often there is no comment whatsoever. By and large the ceremonies went off well, and the sermons were deemed satisfactory or more than satisfactory. If we keep this consideration in mind, we shall not be unprepared for the seriousness and high quality of the sermons that survive.

Why some sermons survived and why others did not depended, surely, on a number of factors. From the prefatory letters, it is clear in certain instances that the preachers hoped to win the favor of a patron by publishing the sermon and dedicating it to him. If a sermon were particularly well received, the author might be encouraged to capitalize on its success by circulating it, and occasionally he was encouraged or requested by an important figure at the court to do so. Oliviero Carafa's name, for example, occurs in a number of dedications. The mendicant orders were generally eager to support the publication, in print or manuscript, of the works of their members who distinguished themselves in oratory or who later assumed high office in the order or in the hierarchy of the Church.

We must assume, therefore, that most of the surviving sermons were well regarded, especially if they are now found in print or in a presentation copy. However, the sheer number of sermons still extant, the number of preachers involved, and the relatively even distribution of the sermons across the years under consideration assure that we have a good cross section of the orations *coram papa inter missarum solemnia* in Renaissance Rome. These sermons are listed in the Appendix and represent, at a conservative estimate, about 10 percent of the total number actually delivered, 1450–1521.

Before we turn to a study of the form and content of the sermons, we must take notice of another abiding concern of the Masters of Ceremonies and the Masters of the Sacred Palace—the length of the sermons. From practically every source of information we have about the papal liturgies of the period, the message is the same: brevity was as highly prized and as often enjoined as it was difficult to obtain. In the diaries of Burchard and de Grassis, brevity at times seems almost the measure of excellence. The Masters of Ceremonies here seem to be reflecting faithfully the pervading sentiment of the popes, the cardinals, and the rest of the court, as well as their own. Though we enjoy the benefit of such diaries only for the latter part of the period we are treating, we have no reason to assume that a different sentiment prevailed earlier. The constitution of Calixtus is a basis in fact for such an assumption. There is, nonetheless, unimpeachable evidence that during the pontificate of Sixtus IV the court was more than willing to listen to a long sermon during a *cappella*, provided that the preacher had something truly original to say. The sermon which Flavius Mithridates preached before Sixtus on Good Friday, 1481, lasted two hours. This extraordinary display of knowledge of Hebrew, Arabic, Greek, and "Chaldaic" by the future teacher of Pico della Mirandola won apparently unanimous approval from his distinguished listeners, as he proved that what happened to Jesus in his passion and death had been foretold by the prophets and rabbis.[57] But Mithridates was indeed an exception.

The sermons, after all, were only one part of a religious liturgy which was often long and elaborate. This liturgy, moreover, tried to express at least part of its meaning through the symbolism of song, gesture, movement, flowers, incense, and vestments. Not everything had to be expressed in words, especially as the same cycle of mysteries repeated itself year after year. In any case, the taste of the court ran consistently in favor of short sermons. Leo X doubtless had wide support for his decision in 1514 to limit the length of the sermons to a half hour.[58] Sometime within the next three years, he took a more drastic position, seemingly in consultation with the cardinals, that the sermons should not exceed fifteen minutes. The idea may have been to aim for fifteen minutes in the hope of actually containing the sermon within a half hour. Be that as it may, on the second Sunday of Advent, 1517, after a particularly long sermon, Leo had to tell de Grassis to remind the Master of the Sacred Palace about the fifteen-minute limit.[59]

Despite the insistence on brevity, there was a decided reluctance to omit a sermon on a day for which one was scheduled. Burchard relates the hesitation of Innocent VIII to omit the sermon on Pentecost Sunday, 1490, when the celebrant informed him beforehand that he felt sick.[60] Julius II was clearly more inclined to dispense with the sermon than any

57. Flavius Mithridates, *Sermo de Passione Domini*, ed. Chaim Wirszubski (Jerusalem: Israel Acad. of Science and Humanities, 1963). The favorable reaction to the sermon is described by Gherardi, *Diario*, p. 49.

58. De Grassis, "Diarium," Jan. 1, 1514, BAV cod. Vat. lat. 12275, fol. 96ᵛ.

59. *Ibid.*, fol. 245ᵛ. See also *ibid.*, fourth Sunday of Lent, 1517, fol. 203ʳ.

60. *Liber Notarum*, I, 310. See also *ibid.*, fourth Sunday of Advent, 1502, II, 340–41.

of the other pontiffs of the period, just as he was also the most remiss even in being present for the *cappelle*.[61] Leo X, on the other hand, scrupulously participated, and he also took care to consult the cardinals when a question arose as to whether, in particular circumstances, a sermon should actually be delivered.[62]

Circumstances did arise, of course, that indicated that omission might be the better course. While the basilica was under construction, its exposure to the elements could be adduced as a persuasive argument to omit the sermon when the liturgy was being celebrated there.[63] If the Curia were on the road and the *cappella* being held in some town other than Rome, complications of place and travel might lead to elimination of the sermon.[64] In at least one instance, the celebrant found himself under a compelling need of nature, and without further ado, he in unmistakable terms told de Grassis the sermon was to be foregone.[65] With more frequency than we might expect, preachers at the last minute failed to appear—for reasons of health, bad weather, or for other reasons often never explained. Though in such situations the Master of the Palace might ask somebody to preach ex tempore, the general tendency under these circumstances was to omit the sermon altogether.[66]

The Master of the Sacred Palace in actual practice seems to have exercised considerable latitude in selecting preachers for those occasions when the task fell to him. The choice of Niccolò da Milano to deliver the panegyric on Saint John in 1498, for instance, would seem incautious, even daring. Niccolò was a Dominican friar from the convent of San

61. See de Grassis, "Diarium," e.g., Jan. 1, 1505, BAV cod. Vat. lat. 12272, fol. 54ᵛ; second Sunday of Lent, 1509, BAV cod. Vat. lat. 12273, fol. 198ʳ. De Grassis speaks frankly about Julius II in his entry for the fourth Sunday of Advent, 1509, *ibid.*, fol. 130ᵛ: "Papa quasi omnibus his diebus dominicis de adventu obdormivit quando sermo fiebat."

62. See de Grassis, "Diarium," e.g., fourth Sunday of Lent, 1517, BAV cod. Vat. lat. 12275, fol. 203ʳ.

63. See *ibid.*, e.g., Jan. 6, 1517, fol. 193ʳ.

64. For example, on the first Sunday of Advent, 1515, the sermon was omitted in Florence because some of the cardinals wanted to get an early start for Bologna, where the historic meeting between Leo X and King Francis I would take place. *Ibid.*, fol. 152ᵛ.

65. *Ibid.*, Pentecost, 1515, fol. 138ᵛ: "Sermonem nemo habuit, quia celebrans excusavit se propter urinam, quod non diu posset expectare." A somewhat similar incident occurred on the same feast a year earlier when the pope himself suffered "propter dolorem stomachi." *Ibid.*, fol. 118ᵛ.

66. See, e.g., Gherardi, *Diario*, Trinity Sunday, 1481, p. 57; Burchard, *Liber Notarum*, Nov. 1, 1485, I, 122; *ibid.*, fourth Sunday of Lent, 1487, I, 186; de Grassis, "Diarium," second Sunday of Lent, 1508, BAV cod. Vat. lat. 12273, fol. 141ʳ.

Marco in Florence, and he was Savonarola's secretary for the last three years of his life. He preached the panegyric the same year Savonarola died—before Alexander VI, the pope whom Savonarola so often excoriated and who connived in his execution. Unfortunately, the sermon does not survive.[67]

The reform bulls mentioned earlier enjoined upon the Master of the Palace that the preachers be masters of theology or canon law, or that they had received at least the order of subdiaconate.[68] Though these bulls were never published, their provisions certainly reveal standards supported by some of the more distinguished members of the court, including the important figures of Cardinals Oliviero Carafa and Francesco Piccolomini. Domenichi, basing himself on even earlier legislation, had some decades earlier advocated similar provisions. [69]

For the most part the Masters of the Palace seem to have acted in accord with these standards. Very often they chose friars even for solemnities outside the Sundays of Advent and Lent. Somewhat less often they invited bishops to preach to the court, as well as professors from the *Studium Urbis*. There was also a clear tendency to select preachers from among officials in the Curia as well as from the households or *familiae* of the cardinals. There were, besides, some random choices which fall outside these patterns, and the preachers sometimes recited sermons composed by others.[70] Even in these cases, the individuals generally seem to have been at least in minor orders or tonsured, but this was not invariably true. The "De caeremoniis" of 1488 complains that "today" sermons are sometimes given *coram* by men "without sacred orders."[71] There is no reason

67. See Burchard, *Liber Notarum*, II, 122: "Sermonem fecit frater Nicolaus de Mediolano, ordinis praedicatorum, socius procuratoris eiusdem ordinis, olim cancellarius fratris Hieronymi de Ferraria, dicti ordinis professoris, Florentiae combusti anno superiore."

68. Sixtus IV, "Quoniam regnantium," BAV cod. Vat. lat. 3884, fol. 118^v; Alexander VI, "In apostolicae sedis specula," Arch. Seg. Vat., Misc. Arm. XI.88, fols. 1^v–2^r. See also the "De caeremoniis," BAV cod. Chigi C.VI.180, fol. 198^r.

69. *Tractatus*, fol. [16^r].

70. See de Grassis, "Diarium," e.g., Dec. 26, 1512, BAV cod. Vat. lat. 12269, fol. 608^r; third Sunday of Lent, 1518, BAV cod. Vat. lat. 12275, fol. 270^v; *ibid.*, Dec. 26, 1520, fols. 392^v–393^r.

71. BAV cod. Chigi C.VI.180, fol. 198^r: ". . . hodie non modo inferioris gradus viri sed sine dignitate aut sacro ordine. . . ." In 1482 Gherardi reports, *Diario*, p. 98, that some Romans were shocked that, even after the religious ceremony was over, a poet who was a layman recited verses from the pulpit of S. Maria Maggiore as part of a memorial service for Platina. On the tradition of lay preaching in Renaissance Italy, see Paul Oskar Kristeller, "Lay Religious Traditions and Florentine Platonism," in *Studies in Renaissance Thought and Letters* (Rome: Storia e Letteratura, 1956), pp.

not to accept this complaint at its face value. Moreover, there is at least one specific and unambiguous instance of a preacher who had not received "any ecclesiastical order."

The case in point deserves some elaboration. On the feast of Saint Stephen in 1520, Prierias allowed a boy thirteen years old, the son of a fiscal officer at the court, to deliver the sermon. Sermons by children and youths were, as is well known, a common occurrence in the Renaissance.[72] In 1499 Alexander VI and such an irreproachable member of his court as Oliviero Carafa gave willing ear to the sermons of a boy only ten years old, clad in the habit of the Dominican order. But this "fraterculus" never preached, it would seem, during a papal *cappella*.[73] In 1520 the impropriety of such a sermon *coram papa inter missarum solemnia* by a child not yet constituted in any orders evoked de Grassis's unequivocal indignation. He apparently allowed the young preacher to proceed because he was under some impression that the pope had approved the idea, for he afterwards with some boldness asked Leo why he would permit such a person to preach in his chapel. Leo had in fact had nothing to do with it and, furthermore, seems to have been even more incensed than was de Grassis. In one of the pope's rare displays of high feeling, he told de Grassis to reprimand the Master of the Palace and to inform him that if it ever happened again he would punish him.[74]

There is both direct and indirect evidence that the popes had preferences for certain preachers and that these preferences were honored. Paul II certainly seems to have appreciated Ambrogio Massari, as we infer

---

99–122, esp. 103–6. For a study of early controversy over lay preaching, see Rolf Zerfass, *Der Streit um die Laienpredigt: Eine pastoralgeschichtliche Untersuchung zum Verständnis des Predigtamtes und seiner Entwicklung im 12. und 13. Jahrhundert*, Untersuchungen zur praktischen Theologie, No. 2 (Freiburg: Herder, 1974).

72. See Kristeller, "Lay Traditions," pp. 103–6, and Richard C. Trexler, "Ritual in Florence: Adolescence and Salvation in the Renaissance," in *The Pursuit of Holiness in Late Medieval and Renaissance Religion: Papers from the University of Michigan Conference*, ed. Charles Trinkaus with Heiko Oberman, Studies in Medieval and Reformation Thought, No. 10 (Leiden: Brill, 1974), pp. 200–264.

73. Burchard's account of this phenomenon, May 3, 1499, goes into considerable and interesting detail, *Liber Notarum*, II, 140. For an account of a boy eight or ten years old in the Franciscan habit who preached in Rome in 1485, see Antonio de Vascho, *Il diario della città di Roma*, ed. Giuseppe Chiesa, RIS, 23.3 (Città di Castello: S. Lapi, 1904), 523.

74. De Grassis, "Diarium," BAV cod. Vat. lat. 12275, fols. 392ᵛ–393ʳ. See *ibid.*, Jan. 1, 1514, fol. 96ᵛ, where the question of tonsure is raised in passing. See Burchard, *Liber Notarum*, Ascension, 1496, I, 604, where the youth of the preacher is at issue: "Non fuit sermo quia facturus erat nimis iuvenis scutifer cardinalis Valentini [Cesare Borgia]."

simply from the number of surviving sermons of Massari preached before him. Innocent VIII, for example, personally invited Mariano da Genazzano to be the Augustinian who would preach for him on the third Sunday of Advent, 1487, and in November he refused to allow this already famous preacher and future prior general of the order to leave Rome for a series of Advent sermons in Lucca until after the sermon in the papal chapel.[75] As we might expect from the traditions of his family, Leo X showed a certain preference for Dominicans.[76]

But the popes' interest in their preachers sometimes contains surprises. Julius II compelled the Franciscans of Aracoeli to release from their jail a friar, whom they maintained was an excommunicate, so that he might preach *coram papa* on the second Sunday of Advent, 1504.[77] The same pope, not extraordinarily tolerant of sermons in general and even less tolerant of long sermons in particular, on several occasions invited Giles of Viterbo, then prior general of the Augustinians, to preach in celebration of special events or occasions which fell outside the regular *cappelle*.[78] Giles was notoriously prolix. Paris de Grassis seems to utter an almost audible groan when he several times notes how Giles's orations lasted two or more hours.[79] Giles also had a penchant for repeating in the vernacular what he had just declaimed in Latin. De Grassis stigmatizes this practice as being "contra bonas caeremonias," although it was not dissimilar to the way the popes themselves preached in the Middle Ages.[80] Now,

---

75. See Mariano's *Oratio habita dominica tertia adventus* [Rome: E. Silber, after Dec. 16, 1487], Hain-Cop. #7554, fol. [1ʳ], and esp. David Gutiérrez, "Testi e note su Mariano da Genazzano (†1498)," *Analecta Augustiniana*, 32 (1969), 117–204, esp. 130–32.

76. See de Grassis, "Diarium," e.g., Dec. 26, 1516, BAV cod. Vat. lat. 12275, fol. 191ᵛ; *ibid.*, Jan. 1, 1520, fol. 371ʳ; *ibid.*, Palm Sunday, 1521, fol. 396ʳ⁻ᵛ.

77. See Burchard, *Liber Notarum*, II, 465.

78. See de Grassis, "Diarium," e.g., Trinity Sunday, 1509, BAV cod. Vat. lat. 12273, fol. 218ʳ; June 29, 1512, BAV cod. Vat. lat. 12269, fol. 559ᵛ. See also my "Fulfillment of the Christian Golden Age under Pope Julius II: Text of a Discourse of Giles of Viterbo, 1507," *Traditio*, 25 (1969), 265–338, and Clare O'Reilly, " 'Maximus Caesar et Pontifex Maximus': Giles of Viterbo Proclaims the Alliance between Emperor Maximilian I and Pope Julius II," *Augustiniana*, 22 (1972), 80–117.

79. De Grassis, "Diarium," e.g., March 10, 1506, BAV cod. Vat. lat. 12272, fol. 149ʳ; Trinity Sunday, 1509, BAV cod. Vat. lat. 12273, fol. 218ʳ.

80. De Grassis, "Diarium," Aug. 10, 1510, BAV cod. Vat. lat. 12269, fol. 363ʳ; see also my "Golden Age," p. 269, n. 13. For the practice of the medieval popes, see Marc Dykmans, ed., *Le cérémonial papal de la fin du Moyen Âge à la Renaissance: I. Le cérémonial papal du XIIIᵉ siècle*, Bibliothèque de l'Institut Historique Belge de Rome, No. 24 (Rome: Institut Historique Belge de Rome, 1977), p. 214: "Et [papa] postea incipit thema suum, de quo partem prosequitur in lingua litterali partem in vulgali [sic]." See also Pope Innocent III's "Prologus" to his sermons, PL 217, 311, ". . . quos-

in the Renaissance, Latin was the only language really proper for the papal liturgies.[81]

The language of the sermons, therefore, was important. It was important not only in the sense that the sermons were without exception to be in Latin, but also in the sense that a certain elegance of expression was expected. A graceful Latin, pleasing to the ear, was what was considered appropriate.[82] Thus an aesthetic quality entered also into this part of the liturgy. Sermons were to blend with the beauty and dignity striven for in other parts. Most of the sermons that survive show in their style, as we shall see later, the influence of the classical revival.

Another element of the dignity and aesthetic quality expected in preaching at the court was the dress, appearance, and general deportment of the preachers. When bishops preached, they were to wear their miters, and others were, accordingly, to wear the dress becoming their status.[83] Long hair was considered inappropriate by Burchard and de Grassis, and it had been an issue decades earlier for Domenichi.[84] The reform bull of Alexander VI actually specified for cantors that their hair was not to be so long as to touch their shoulders.[85] In the pulpit theatrical gesticulating consistently evoked smiles and laughter, and Paris de Grassis had harsh words for those preachers who did not know the difference between gestures proper to an orator and those proper to an actor.[86]

---

dam sermones ad clerum et populum, nunc litterali, nunc vulgari lingua proposui et dictavi. . . ."

81. See de Grassis, "Diarium," e.g., May 1, 1509, BAV cod. Vat. lat. 12273, fol. 209^v. The vernacular was excluded. Hebrew, Greek, and even other ancient languages might be employed at least for quotations, as is clear from the case of Mithridates as well as others. See de Grassis, e.g., Jan. 1, 1515, BAV cod. Vat. lat. 12275, fol. 133^r; Burchard, *Liber Notarum*, Pentecost, 1497, II, 24, for a sermon given "graece, hebraice et latine," and also Trinity Sunday, 1498 ("in vesperis"), for one given "in latino, hebraico, caldaico," II, 101.

82. See de Grassis, "Diarium," e.g., Jan. 1, 1507, BAV cod. Vat. lat. 12273, fol. 77^v; *ibid.*, Ascension Thursday, 1509, fol. 213^r; Pentecost, 1516, BAV cod. Vat. lat. 12275, fol. 172^v; *ibid.*, Dec. 26, 1516, fol. 191^v.

83. See de Grassis, "Diarium," e.g., Pentecost, 1506, BAV cod. Vat. lat. 12272, fol. 167^r; Ash Wednesday, 1519, BAV cod. Vat. lat. 12275, fol. 320^v.

84. See, e.g., Burchard, *Liber Notarum*, Ash Wednesday, 1502, II, 318; de Grassis, "Diarium," Jan. 1, 1514, BAV cod. Vat. lat. 12275, fol. 96^v; Dec. 27, 1512, BAV cod. Vat. lat. 12269, fol. 609^r; Domenichi, *Tractatus*, fol. [11^r]. See also Raphael Brandolini's "Oratio ad Lateranense concilium," BAV cod. Ottob. lat. 813, fol. 20^r.

85. Alexander VI, "In apostolicae sedis specula," Arch. Seg. Vat., Misc. Arm. XI.88, fol. 2^v.

86. See de Grassis, "Diarium," e.g., Dec. 26, 1512, BAV cod. Vat. lat. 12269, fol. 608^r; fourth Sunday of Lent, 1516, BAV cod. Vat. lat. 12275, fol. 168^v. Erasmus makes the same distinction between a "histrio" and an "orator" in his *Ciceronianus*, ASD, I.2, 626.

We finally arrive at the most important quality the sermons were expected to have. They were, above all, to be learned. This was clearly the intent of the reform bulls, asking as they did for preachers who were masters in theology or canon law. This is the quality which, with brevity, the Masters of Ceremonies consistently commend, just as they deplore its absence.

The criticism to which preaching at the papal court in the Renaissance has been subjected forces us to inquire closely into the kind of learning the Masters of Ceremonies commended. If we were to believe the most distinguished commentators on these sermons through the ages, we would be convinced that the learning desired was a facile knowledge of the history and literature of ancient Greece and Rome. Erasmus's *Ciceronianus* is the principal source for this assessment. In that dialogue, Bulephorus describes a sermon he supposedly heard preached before Julius II on a Good Friday.[87] Historians like Ludwig Pastor have inferred that Erasmus was recounting for his readers the substance of a sermon he had heard when he visited Rome in 1509.[88] As described by Bulephorus, the sermon exemplifies the substitution of pagan learning, viz., irrelevant stories from Greek and Roman history, for a central Christian mystery. The exordium and peroration, together almost longer than the body of the sermon itself, were filled with elaborate praise of the pope as *Juppiter optimus maximus*, whose power was unlimited and whose right hand brandished a thunderbolt. Bulephorus finally betrays his disgust by exclaiming, "In such fine Roman fashion did that Roman speak that I heard not a word about the death of Christ!"

Jacob Burckhardt does not specifically discuss sermons at the papal court, but his general evaluation of Renaissance preaching is guarded and ultimately negative.[89] Gregorovius assures us that if a Roman from Cicero's day could have assisted at celebrations in honor of Christian saints during the pontificate of Leo X, he would not have been able to discern any difference between the religion of his own age and that of sixteenth-century Rome.[90] Pastor has little to say about the sermons at

87. ASD, I.2, 637–39.
88. *Geschichte der Päpste*, 4th ed. (Freiburg: Herder, 1899), III, 754, omitted in the English edition.
89. *The Civilization of the Renaissance in Italy*, trans. S. G. C. Middlemore, 2 vols. (New York: Harper and Row, 1958), I, 243–44; II, 450–63.
90. *History of the City of Rome in the Middle Ages*, trans. from 4th ed. by Annie Hamilton (1912; rpt. New York: AMS Press, 1967), VIII.1, 295–96.

the court, but he was clearly influenced by Erasmus and Burckhardt in the few observations he makes. Pastor, furthermore, at least implies that sermons at the court dealt as often with "political matters" as they did with the "newly revived pagan philosophy" and the works of "heathen poets and teachers."[91]

In the light of recent research on Renaissance religion in general, few competent historians would today be predisposed to accept these judgments uncritically. But the irreligion of the Renaissance is a deeply imbedded prejudice. As late as 1969, for instance, Johannes Baptist Schneyer in his *Geschichte der katholischen Predigt* summarily dismissed all "humanist" preaching during the Renaissance as doctrinally vacuous or even erroneous.[92] Significantly, he does not cite a single sermon to support his negative assessment.

A few years ago I ventured the opinion, on the basis of some fifty sermons at the court extending from the pontificate of Sixtus IV to that of Clement VII, that the judgments of Erasmus, Burckhardt, Gregorovius, Pastor, and Schneyer were simply wrong.[93] As I trust the following chapters will substantiate, I would now confirm and even more categorically reassert that opinion, this time on the basis of much more extensive documentation. Indeed I will go so far as to state that not a single sermon of those I have examined from the papal court during the Renaissance corresponds with Erasmus's description.[94]

On the other hand, we should not assume that in the Renaissance, with its exuberant enthusiasm for classical learning, no foundation for Erasmus's description existed. In fact, I have discovered an oration for Ash Wednesday, 1520, which in its totality very well fits the central point

91. Pastor, V, 180–81.
92. Freiburg: Seelsorge, 1969, p. 249.
93. "Preaching for the Popes," in *Pursuit of Holiness*, pp. 408–40.
94. Silvana Seidel Menchi has proposed that the "tone and content" of some orations of Battista Casali verify Erasmus's description. "Alcuni atteggiamenti della cultura italiana di fronte a Erasmo (1520–1536)," in *Eresia e riforma nell'Italia del Cinquecento*, Biblioteca del "Corpus Reformatorum Italicorum," Miscellanea I, ed. Luigi Firpo and Giorgio Spini (Florence: Sansoni, 1974), pp. 106–7, n. 169. With precise scholarship, she cites a passage from Casali's Good Friday oration of 1510 before Julius II, and she suggests that Tommaso Inghirami's sacred orations also correspond to what Erasmus deplored. My own assessment, on the other hand, is as follows: the sacred orations of Casali and Inghirami do not as totalities correspond to what Erasmus so globally condemns in the passage I summarized above, no matter how closely an isolated passage might seem to exemplify some of his specific criticisms. But, as I hope I am making clear in this chapter, it is of the utmost importance to distinguish oratory within the sacred liturgy from oratory outside it.

Erasmus was making, except for the part about the pope.[95] The oration does not deal with the pope at all because it is not an oration from the papal court. The oration, in classical form, is filled with quotations and allusions from classical authors. The message is the unrelieved misery of the human condition, without there being explicit correlation of this message with any doctrine specifically Christian. Quite literally, the name of Christ is not mentioned, and the only scriptural reference is a quotation from the Book of Job.

This oration, delivered at Lisieux and printed in Paris, was probably not meant for liturgical purposes. In any case, its importance for us consists in the contrast it affords with the sermons from the papal court. No extant sermon from the court even remotely resembles it. Without doubt, sermons for the popes utilized classical history and classical authors. That is not what is at issue. What we are concerned with, rather, is whether this utilization ultimately swamps the Christian message, as is certainly the case with the oration from Lisieux. My response is that in the papal sermons it does not. The consistent intent of these sermons is to make classical learning serve some other appropriate point, and often that learning is proffered as a *quanto-magis* argument in favor of Christianity.

But we do have to reckon with the fact that not all of the sermons survived. Among those that have not, there does seem to have been one for the feast of Saint John the Evangelist, 1517, that, as we have it described by de Grassis, would give some support to Gregorovius.[96] The unnamed preacher, "a certain student from Narni," invoked gods and goddesses and, in general, proceeded more "in the manner of a pagan than a Christian." De Grassis relates that some in the audience merely laughed at the sermon, whereas others were hotly indignant. Once again the Master of Ceremonies reproved Prierias for letting such a sermon slip by him. Leo X on this occasion "patiently tolerated the matter according to his tolerant and amiable disposition." Nonetheless, in spite of Leo's "tolerance," such a sermon obviously violated the canons of religion and propriety that obtained at the court.[97]

95. Ioannes Vacceus, *Oratio habita in gymnasio Lexoviensi, anno Domini MDXX. idibus februariis, sumpto hinc argumento, Memento homo quia cinis es, et in cinerem reverteris* (Paris: R. Chauldiere, [1520]).

96. De Grassis, "Diarium," BAV cod. Vat. lat. 12275, fol. 254ʳ.

97. See de Grassis also, "Diarium," e.g., Jan. 1, 1512, BAV cod. Vat. lat. 12269, fol. 486ʳ; *ibid.*, Dec. 26, 1512, fol. 608ʳ; fourth Sunday of Lent, 1516, BAV cod. Vat. lat.

As early as 1488, the "De caeremoniis" deplored the fact that sermons were sometimes given by men who were without orders and who had had only a humanist education, "in studiis humanitatis tantum docti."[98] Patrizi and Burchard saw in this practice a violation of "the ancient and approved ceremonies" that provided that the preacher must be either a prelate or a doctor of theology. From this complaint of the "De caeremoniis" we can infer nothing securely about the contentual quality of the sermons delivered by those who were "in studiis humanitatis tantum docti." We can, though, assert quite categorically that in some quarters there was a decided prejudice against anyone who did not hold a degree in scholastic theology. Jacopo Gherardi, in fact, reports in his diary for 1481 that this prejudice existed at the court among those who held such degrees.[99]

There was, therefore, a clear awareness at the court of the difference between preachers who had had a formal training in the traditional theology of the schools and those who had not. In such an atmosphere, sermons empty of doctrinal or theological content could not expect to escape criticism from at least a certain segment of the court. Preachers who wished to adapt their sermons to a classical form would be ill advised to lose sight of this fact, and the fear of such criticism might weigh even more

---

12275, fol. 168ᵛ; *ibid.*, Ascension Thursday, 1521, fol. 398ᵛ. Gherardi's observations about the sermon of the procurator general of the Franciscans for the second Sunday of Advent, 1481, are apposite here. *Diario*, p. 83: "Eius oratio habita est elegans et erudita et caeremoniae diei multum accommodata. Fuit ab omnibus commendatus, id reprehensum dumtaxat: Iuvenalis versiculum recitavit, eum videlicet 'et de virtute locuti, clunem agitant' [Saturae 2.20–21], qui quamvis cursui orationis quadraverit, tamen ob religionem loci parum pudice reputatum dictum est."

98. BAV cod. Chigi C.VI.180, fol. 198ʳ: "Et nota quod diaconus cardinalis non praedicat in cappella pontificis, neque alius quispiam non praelatus nisi sit doctor in theologia secundum antiquas et probatas caeremonias, quamvis hodie non modo inferioris gradus viri sed sine dignitate aut sacro ordine in studiis humanitatis tantum docti, non sine loci et ordinis pontificalis dedecore, onus orandi in totius orbis gravissimo ac celeberrimo consessu [MS=concessu] sibi assumant."

99. Dec. 27, 1481, *Diario*, p. 85: "Orationem habuit de laudibus evangelistae unus ex ordine cubiculariorum pontificis, Albertus nomine, ex nobili et locupleti Zobolorum familia, a Regio Cisalpinae Galliae civitate oriundus; adolescens profecto ingenuus et qui ad gratiam corporis et splendorem familiae litterarum quoque ornamentum addidit. Is attente admodum est auditus et propter florentem aetatem, ut dixi, et propter orationis ornamentum ab omnibus commendatus rostris descendit. Theologiae tantum professores nonnulli, qui soli eo digni munere videri volunt et plerumque saeculari ordini infensi esse dicuntur, enervem orationem fuisse submurmurabant. Ego a ceteris laudatum intelligo, quorum iudicium rectum et absque livore existimatur. Id dumtaxat orationi vitium attribuunt (si vitium dici potest) quod absque argumento, quod ipsi thema appellant, exorsus est et quod versiculis quibusdam orationem absolvit." See also *ibid.*, p. 41, quoted in note 24 above.

heavily on the consciousness of those who came out of a strictly humanist training than of those who were schoolmen.

There is no doubt, however, that the influence of classical form in many of the sermons of scholastic and humanist alike was strong or that that form is of critical importance for understanding them fully. Furthermore, the form did influence the content, but without displacing the Christian message. At least, the preachers certainly wanted to convey a Christian message and thought they were actually doing so.

At the papal court there were indeed occasions when the preachers could not resist the temptation to praise the pope, and we do have instances of generally short sections of sermons which do precisely that. But eulogy of the pope as a subject for discourse *inter missarum solemnia* was considered highly improper, as de Grassis's diary leaves no doubt.[100] In fact, Leo X, as part of his regulation in 1514 which attempted to limit the length of sermons to a half hour, expressly forbade that any part of them be "in laudatione papae." He was in this instance articulating what was already an operative norm. On this occasion, moreover, Leo threatened the Master of the Palace that, unless his directives were honored, he would order that all the sermons for the *cappelle* be delivered by friars.[101] Leo's presumption that the friars were less wordy and less likely to indulge in praise of the pope than the other preachers is from the evidence we possess by no means verified in every instance. However, some credit must be given to Leo's experience in these matters.

In an age when politics and religion were so inextricably intertwined, we might expect to find a blunted sensitivity about excluding strictly political questions from liturgical sermons. If we bypass for the time being the complicated question of the Turkish threat, such was not the case. The preachers avoided taking campaigns, alliances, and the popes' political strategies as subjects for their liturgical discourses, though they certainly did not avoid war and peace insofar as these were viewed as general religious issues. The sermons that professedly treated political events seem to have been very few in number, and they earned disapproval.[102]

What, then, were the sermons to deal with? The answer is clear and consistent. They were to deal with "the Gospel." They were to deal with

100. De Grassis, "Diarium," Nov. 1, 1510, BAV cod. Vat. lat. 12269, fol. 375ᵛ; *ibid.*, second Sunday of Advent, 1512, fol. 601ᵛ.

101. De Grassis, "Diarium," Jan. 1, 1514, BAV cod. Vat. lat. 12275, fol. 96ᵛ.

102. See de Grassis, "Diarium," e.g., Nov. 1, 1510, BAV cod. Vat. lat. 12269, fol. 375ᵛ; *ibid.*, Pentecost, 1512, fol. 543ʳ.

"divine things." They were to deal with the religious solemnity that was being observed.[103] As long as a sermon or oration was delivered *inter missarum solemnia*, i.e., during the religious liturgy and as part of it, the preacher had no other choice, nor was there in this context any other learning which could serve as a viable substitute for an appreciation of Christian mystery. The surviving sermons attempt to fulfill this ideal, though of course they attain it in differing degrees.

Insofar as the popes and Masters of Ceremonies had control of the situation, the practice of the court corresponded to the theory. Orations to celebrate diplomatic or military achievements were supposed to be delivered after the religious liturgy had ended, as we see exemplified in Giles of Viterbo's oration in 1507 on the "golden age" celebrating the successes of King Manuel I of Portugal and in his oration proclaiming the alliance between Emperor Maximilian I and Julius II in 1512.[104] Instances of this procedure could easily be multiplied.[105]

We have, however, one example which strikingly illustrates the scrupulosity with which this distinction was observed and which elucidates the precise religious significance which the phrase *inter missarum solemnia* was meant to convey and safeguard.[106] A preacher by the name of Marcus Antonius Magnus, chancellor for Cardinal Oliviero Carafa, had prepared a sermon "in expositione evangelii" for the feast of Pentecost, May 27, 1509. On the vigil of the feast, Julius II decided that, instead, there should be an oration to celebrate the defeat of the Venetians at Agnadello on May 14 by the League of Cambrai, of which Julius was a member. The preacher rewrote his oration. With the change in subject matter came

---

103. See, e.g., Burchard, *Liber Notarum*, March 25, 1490, I, 301; de Grassis, "Diarium," Jan. 1, 1512, BAV cod. Vat. lat. 12269, fol. 486ʳ; *ibid.*, Pentecost, 1512, fol. 543ʳ; Jan. 6, 1519, BAV cod. Vat. lat. 12275, fol. 310ʳ; *ibid.*, second Sunday of Lent, 1520, fol. 374ᵛ; *ibid.*, Dec. 26, 1520, fol. 392ᵛ; Gherardi, *Diario*, first Sunday of Advent, 1480, p. 28; *ibid.*, Pentecost, 1481, p. 55.

104. See my "Golden Age," and O'Reilly, " 'Maximus Caesar et Pontifex Maximus.' "

105. See, e.g., Burchard, *Liber Notarum*, March 25, 1490, I, 301; Feb. 5, 1492, I, 336–37; de Grassis, "Diarium," June 17, 1509, BAV cod. Vat. lat. 12269, fol. 309ʳ⁻ᵛ; *ibid.*, Aug. 10, 1510, fols. 362ᵛ–363ʳ; *ibid.*, June 29, 1512, fol. 559ᵛ.

106. See de Grassis, "Diarium," BAV cod. Vat. lat. 12273, fol. 214ᵛ. The circumstances are alluded to by Magnus himself in his prefatory letter to Oliviero Carafa, "Oratio de Spiritu sancto," Bibl. Marc. cod. lat. XI.85 (4194), fol. 1ʳ. See also *ibid.*, fols. 3ʳ–4ᵛ. See Domenichi's "Oratio pro victoriis Christianorum" before Paul II on Aug. 30, 1469, found in BAV cod. Ottob. lat. 1035, fols. 77ᵛ–83ʳ, for an exception to this rule about when political orations were to be delivered. But note the early date and the fact that the victories were over the Turks.

the inevitable change of time when the oration was to be given. It was no longer to be delivered during the Mass, between the singing of the Gospel and the singing of the Creed. It was to be delivered only when the Mass was over. An oration like the one Julius requested would be inappropriate *inter missarum solemnia*.

CHAPTER TWO. THE NEW RHETORIC: ARS LAUDANDI ET VITUPERANDI

At some unspecified date in the early sixteenth century when Pietro Bembo was in Padua, he was asked why he did not go to hear the Lenten sermons being preached there. The famous humanist replied that he saw no reason to go. What else would he hear except the "Subtle Doctor" twittering against the "Angelic Doctor," and then he would witness the arrival of Aristotle as a third party to resolve the question which had been proposed.[1] Bembo's reaction to what must have been sermons by a friar is typical of much reaction to scholastic preaching in the late Middle Ages and Renaissance, as we know so well from Erasmus and many other sources. It would be no exaggeration to affirm that one aspect of the general religious crisis of that period was a crisis in preaching.

Bembo's reaction to the friars, however, has some special significance for our purposes. It must be assumed that, since he was a member of the papal court, he heard the sermons preached during the *cappelle*. If that is true, his reaction represents something more than the usual complaints against the friars' style of learning and preaching which were commonplace during the period but which seem too often to have had no specific remedy to propose. Bembo, on the other hand, would have in mind an actual alternative, the new style of preaching which had gradually developed at the papal court from about the time of Nicholas V until his own day. To what we must infer from Bembo's description were the "thematic" sermons of the friar in Padua, he could oppose the "demonstrative" or "epideictic" sermons of the preachers at the papal court. The contrast would be dramatic.

Considerable research has been done on the theory and practice of epideictic oratory in antiquity,[2] and recently there have been some ex-

---

1. The incident is recounted by Ortensio Landi, *Paradossi cioe sententie fuori del comun parere* (Venice: n. publ., 1545), fol. 79[r-v].
2. The basic study is still Theodore C. Burgess, "Epideictic Literature," *Studies in Classical Philology*, 3 (1902), 89–261. See also Vincenz Buchheit, *Untersuchungen zur Theorie des Genos Epideiktikon von Gorgias bis Aristoteles* (Munich: M. Hueber, 1960) and George L. Kustas, *Studies in Byzantine Rhetoric*, Analecta Vlatadon, No. 17 (Thessalonica: Patriarchal Institute, 1973), as well as more general studies such as: D. A. G. Hinks, "Tria Genera Causarum," *Classical Quarterly*, 30 (1936), 170–76; Wilbur Samuel Howell, *Poetics, Rhetoric, and Logic: Studies in the Basic Disciplines*

cellent studies on the impact of epideictic on certain aspects of Renaissance literature, especially poetry.[3] With one notable exception, no attention has been paid to its impact on the sacred rhetoric of the Italian Renaissance.[4] The standard literary histories, in fact, seem unaware that the revival of this particular classical *genus*, or *causa*, or form was of any special importance.[5] My purpose in this chapter and the next is to take

---

of Criticism (Ithaca: Cornell University Press, 1975); Heinrich Lausberg, *Handbuch der literarischen Rhetorik: Eine Grundlegung der Literaturwissenschaft*, 2 vols. (Munich: M. Hueber, 1960); Harry Caplan, *Of Eloquence: Studies in Ancient and Medieval Rhetoric*, ed. Anne King and Helen North (Ithaca: Cornell University Press, 1970); George Kennedy, *The Art of Persuasion in Greece* (London: Routledge and Kegan Paul, 1963), esp. pp. 152–203, and his *The Art of Rhetoric in the Roman World* (Princeton: Princeton University Press, 1972); and Helen North, "The Use of Poetry in the Training of the Ancient Orator," *Traditio*, 8 (1952), 1–33.

3. See, e.g., O. B. Hardison, Jr., *The Enduring Monument: A Study of the Idea of Praise in Renaissance Literary Theory and Practice* (Chapel Hill: University of North Carolina Press, 1962); A. Leigh DeNeef, "Epideictic Rhetoric and the Renaissance Lyric," *The Journal of Medieval and Renaissance Studies*, 3 (1973), 203–31; Barbara Kiefer Lewalski, *Donne's Anniversaries and the Poetry of Praise: The Creation of a Symbolic Mode* (Princeton: Princeton University Press, 1973); James D. Garrison, *Dryden and the Tradition of Panegyric* (Berkeley: University of California Press, 1975). Bernard Weinberg gives less emphasis to the relationship between oratory and poetry, but he nonetheless recognizes its importance, *A History of Literary Criticism in the Italian Renaissance*, 2 vols. (Chicago: University of Chicago Press, 1961), e.g., pp. 4–5, 147–48, 205–6, 723–24. See also the volumes Weinberg edited, *Trattati di poetica e retorica del Cinquecento*, Scrittori d'Italia, Nos. 247, 248, 253, 258, 4 vols. (Bari: Laterza, 1970–74). Michael Baxandall explicitly treats epideictic in relationship to poetry in *Giotto and the Orators: Humanist Observers of Painting in Italy and the Discovery of Pictorial Composition, 1350–1450* (Oxford: Clarendon Press, 1971).

4. John M. McManamon has studied, in relationship to epideictic oratory, the funeral orations for the Renaissance popes and the orations delivered to the cardinals just before they entered conclave to elect a new pope. Though these orations pertain to the broad category of sacred rhetoric, they do not fall within the category of sermons *coram papa inter missarum solemnia*. The orations before conclave are in part deliberative and in part demonstrative. All these orations will be utilized esp. in Chapter VI. See McManamon's "The Ideal Renaissance Pope: Funeral Oratory from the Papal Court," *Archivum Historiae Pontificiae*, 14 (1976), 9–70.

5. I refer to Girolamo Tiraboschi, *Storia della letteratura italiana*, 4 vols. (Milan: N. Bettoni, 1833), esp. vol. III; Alfredo Galletti, *L'eloquenza (Dalle origini al XVI secolo)* (Milan: F. Vallardi, 1938); and Vittorio Rossi, *Il Quattrocento*, ed. Aldo Vallone (Milan: F. Vallardi, 1964). Whatever interest these authors show in sacred eloquence in the Quattrocento is restricted, for practical purposes, to the sermons of the friars, with special attention to Bernardine of Siena. I have examined a number of the sermons of the friars who receive extended treatment in these histories, including St. Bernardine, and none of those I have seen is epideictic. This is true, despite the title, even for Roberto da Lecce's *Sermones de laudibus sanctorum* (Naples: M. Moravus, 1489), Hain #4480. Though an understanding of these preachers is important for an understanding of the Renaissance, we should be aware that in form, content, and purpose the sermons they preached present us with nothing that would substantially

the first step in trying to show that the revival of the *genus demonstrativum* and its application to sacred oratory as practiced at the papal court is the key to understanding that oratory. It is of critical significance also for understanding the theology, the style of religion, and the ideals of reform proposed during the Renaissance on a regular basis by preachers to the pope and his court.

In the next chapter I will examine a number of preachers as "cases" to illustrate in somewhat more detail the course of the *genus demonstrativum's* revival and its application to sacred subjects. We will engage in a kind of rudimentary *Formgeschichte*. In this chapter I will speak in more general terms, and, indeed, I hope to construct two models to use as instruments of exploration and comparison. One model will be constructed from the medieval "thematic," or so-called "university," sermon and the other from the demonstrative or epideictic sermon. The models and the individual sermons from which they are derived provide an opportunity to trace the transformation of a literary genre from a form in which it was imbued with the principles of Scholasticism to a form in which it was imbued with principles of the revived rhetoric of classical antiquity, a rhetoric integral to Renaissance Humanism. If that Humanism is a "pursuit of eloquence," we can determine in this instance precisely what eloquence Humanism pursued.[6] If Renaissance theology is a "rhetorical theology," we can determine in this particular instance just what the

---

distinguish them from their thirteenth- and fourteenth-century predecessors.

Tiraboschi does show appreciation for Aurelio Brandolini, even for his sacred orations, III, 206–8, 277. Galletti's treatment of sacred eloquence is rife with questionable presuppositions. Though all of the orations in Karl Müllner's collection are epideictic, none is a sacred oration; see *Reden und Briefe italienischer Humanisten* (Vienna: A. Hölder, 1899). Works like Jerrold E. Seigel's *Rhetoric and Philosophy in Renaissance Humanism: The Union of Eloquence and Wisdom, Petrarch to Valla* (Princeton: Princeton University Press, 1968), Cesare Vasoli's *La dialettica e la retorica dell'Umanesimo: "Invenzione" e "Metodo" nella cultura del XV e XVI secolo* (Milan: Feltrinelli, 1968) and Nancy S. Struever's *The Language of History in the Renaissance: Rhetoric and Historical Consciousness in Florentine Humanism* (Princeton: Princeton University Press, 1970) treat aspects of rhetoric which do not lead them into a discussion of the *genera*. On the other hand, Quirinus Breen makes a brief but illuminating application of the three *genera* to Calvin's *Institutes* in his "John Calvin and the Rhetorical Tradition," reprinted in the collection of his studies entitled *Christianity and Humanism: Studies in the History of Ideas*, ed. Nelson Peter Ross (Grand Rapids, Mich.: Eerdmans, 1968), pp. 107–29, esp. 114–19.

6. The term, of course, is Hanna Gray's, "Renaissance Humanism: The Pursuit of Eloquence," *Journal of the History of Ideas*, 24 (1963), 497–514. This important article, like the works of Seigel and Vasoli cited above, does not explicitly treat the three *genera*.

rhetoric of rhetorical theology was and how it functioned.[7] But first we must understand something about the rhetoric of classical antiquity which the Renaissance revived and for which it felt such impassioned enthusiasm.

Classical rhetoric was intimately related to civic needs, and, taken in the strict sense, it dealt exclusively with oratory. For oratory, it commonly recognized only three types or *genera*: the *genus iudiciale*, the *genus deliberativum*, and the *genus demonstrativum* or epideictic. Each of these *genera* had its own purpose and more or less well defined civic setting. The first, judicial oratory, was intended for the courtroom, and its purpose was to win conviction or acquittal of the person charged with crime. It was the *ars accusandi et defendendi*, the lawyers' art. This was the *genus* which received most attention in classical treatises. The second *genus* was meant for a deliberative assembly like a senate, and the purpose was to persuade the assembly to take a definite course of action, such as going to war or not going to war. Thus deliberative oratory was defined specifically as the art of persuasion and dissuasion—*ars suadendi et dissuadendi*, the politicians' art.

The third *genus* was considerably broader in scope than the judicial and deliberative. In general, it was intended for a ceremonial occasion, and its purpose was to arouse the sentiments of appreciation or disgust appropriate for some given person, event, or institution. Its characteristic technique was the distribution of praise or blame as circumstances required. It was the *ars laudandi et vituperandi*, the rhetoric of congratulation and the rhetoric of reproach.

In practice this third *genus* often transgressed the limits set for it in a strict interpretation of classical theory. Whatever did not fall into the first two more clearly defined *genera* pertained to the demonstrative or epideictic. A distinguished modern student of classical rhetoric contrasts epideictic with the other two by stating that, whereas in judicial and deliberative causes the speaker tries to move his listeners to a decision or to a specific course of action, in epideictic he tries by means of his art simply "to impress his ideas upon them, without action as a goal."[8] "To impress ideas" is certainly a broad definition.

That definition does, nonetheless, suggest some further qualities which

7. This time the term is Charles Trinkaus's, *In Our Image and Likeness: Humanity and Divinity in Italian Humanist Thought*, 2 vols. (Chicago: University of Chicago Press, 1970), I, 126–28, 141–42, 305–7, etc.

8. Harry Caplan in his edition for the Loeb series of the *Rhetorica ad Herennium* (Cambridge: Harvard University Press, 1954), p. 173.

obtained, supposedly, in true epideictic. First of all, epideictic was considered "display" oratory in the sense that the artful construction of the oration was almost an end in itself. The listener was to a large extent reduced to a passive role, where his function was to appreciate the beauty of the oration rather than to make any decision. The element of display theoretically intrinsic to epideictic oratory often earned for it a bad name in antiquity and a bad name that has associated it with "flatterers" and pretentious windbags ever since. What needs emphasis here, however, is that the aesthetic quality which "display" implies is more integrally related to epideictic than to either of the other two *genera*. Epideictic enjoyed in fact an affinity with poetry and even with song. As the oratory peculiar to ceremonial occasions, it required pleasurable form and sound.

Secondly, epideictic is "dogmatic" oratory. That is to say, it assumes agreement on the point at issue, and its purpose is to arouse deeper appreciation for an accepted viewpoint. Pericles' oration in 431 B.C. over those fallen in the first year of the Peloponnesian War offers an example of such oratory from antiquity, and Lincoln's Gettysburg Address provides an example nearer to hand. Pericles was not trying to prove these men had done well in giving their lives for Athens, and Lincoln was not trying to prove that those who died at Gettysburg had died in a just cause. Both men hoped, rather, to heighten appreciation for what was at stake.

Finally, epideictic had a problem with invention, discovery of materials for the oration, which was peculiar to itself. The other two *genera* supposedly dealt with more immediate and pressing issues. Although classical theory proposed *topoi* or commonplaces for these two *genera*, certain problems of invention were taken care of simply "by the facts of the case." The occasional and ceremonial nature of epideictic often deprived it of obviously immediate issues. Where does one begin, for example, to search for materials or to "get an idea" for a "Fourth-of-July" speech?

The classical treatises elaborated sets of *topoi* for certain epideictic situations, especially for panegyrics of great men and also for praise of inanimate objects like cities. In a panegyric of a great man, these *topoi* were by and large a listing of the individual's deeds, virtues, and achievements. In every instance, comparison would be a particularly important device for invention and amplification. Thus deeds and examples, assumed to have more power to move to appreciation than abstract arguments, played a large role in epideictic oratory as that oratory developed. The impact of deeds and examples would be increased by comparison with other, similar deeds and examples. Epideictic thus relied heavily on history. The *res* or materials that the epideictic orator utilized for his *amplificatio* were often the *res gestae*. The deeds of history were the means through which the orator strove to distribute the appropriate praise and blame. The peculiar nature of the problem of invention in much epideictic, further-more, caused it to be less rigid than the other two *genera* in following the structure of the five or six parts that theory prescribed for a proper oration.

Ancient theory and ancient practice allowed for a blurring of lines among the three *genera*, and praise and blame were surely expected to enter into any judicial or deliberative oration. Moreover, since classical treatises on rhetoric concentrated more heavily on the judicial and de-liberative *genera*, they emphasized that orations were to deal with specific and immediate issues. They were not to deal with general or abstract questions, such as under what conditions guilt can be established or under what circumstances war is justified. These orations would deal, instead, with whether *this* man is guilty and whether *this* war is justified. Is the war, for instance, honest, useful, necessary and, therefore, to be *waged*? Classical oratory rejected the academic ("scholastic") *quaestio* in favor of a practical *decisio*. This restriction to specific and immediate issues would be much less firmly observed in demonstrative oratory, where the orator might simply try to "impress his ideas" upon the audience. But it was still somewhat operative, since it was supposed to characterize all oratory. By dealing with a specific occasion, a specific celebration, a spe-cific individual or city, by the use of specific examples and comparisons and by never losing sight of the orator's responsibility to "move" his lis-teners, epideictic strove to participate in the immediacy of the other two *genera*.

To put oratory's insistence on immediacy into terms that are easily understood and that were actually used in the Renaissance, we need simply recall that a lecture is not a speech.[9] This distinction between lec-ture and oration is partially based upon the distinction between dialectics and rhetoric, as well as upon the different audiences which discourse de-riving from these two disciplines envisioned. The former was appropriate for a learned audience, skilled in technical materials and interested in a

9. See Aurelio Brandolini, *De ratione scribendi libri tres* (Cologne: A Birckmannus, 1573), p. 95, ". . . ut oratio, non lectio aut disputatio, videatur." This book will be discussed later in the chapter.

thorough discussion and resolution of some academic question, whereas the latter was intended for a more general audience and looked to action or appreciation. The former appealed to the head, while the latter appealed to the will and to the emotions. Thus, Aristotle taught that the syllogism was the form of argumentation in dialectics but the enthymeme was the characteristic form in rhetoric.[10]

This brings us to the thematic sermon, a style of preaching that first appeared in the late twelfth and early thirteenth centuries.[11] Its birth roughly coincides with the birth of Scholasticism, and it is unintelligible apart from the scholastic enterprise. Perhaps nowhere is the distinction clearer between medieval preaching and preaching based more immediately upon classical rhetoric than in the use of the syllogism in the thematic sermon. Despite the influence of classical rhetorical theory during the Middle Ages and its influence on the thematic sermon itself, the use of the syllogism in thematic sermons unmistakably betrays that different principles are operative.

As the syllogism indicates, these principles assign a special importance to proof. Due allowance must be made, of course, for the exhortatory and admonitory element integral to the medieval theory of preaching. Nevertheless, a characteristic aim of a thematic sermon was to raise questions and to prove one's answer to them. These questions could be very academic, such as the nature of hellfire and its effects on damned souls—a sharp contrast to the more immediate issues with which classical oratory was supposed to deal.

In Scholasticism, academic questions tended to become ever more refined and technical, as appropriate to a technically skilled clientele who had spent years "in the schools." Insofar as these questions were refined and technical, they were subject to disputation and hence had to be proved.

10. For an application to a "Renaissance" text of this distinction between syllogism and enthymeme (a "syllogism" with only two members), see Breen's "John Calvin," pp. 119–24. Breen's point is stated succinctly, p. 122: "There is a logic in the *Institutes*. In fact, it is full of logic. But the logic is not syllogistic. It is rhetorical logic. Syllogistic logic uses induction and the syllogism; rhetorical logic uses example and the enthymeme." See also A. Brandolini, *De ratione scribendi*, pp. 35–39.

11. See Caplan, *Eloquence*; Th.-M. Charland, *Artes Praedicandi: Contribution à l'histoire de la rhétorique au Moyen Age*, Publications de l'Institut d'Études Médiévales d'Ottawa, No. 7 (Paris: J. Vrin, 1936); and now esp. James J. Murphy, *Rhetoric in the Middle Ages: A History of Rhetorical Theory from Saint Augustine to the Renaissance* (Berkeley: University of California Press, 1974), as well as his *Medieval Rhetoric: A Select Bibliography* (Toronto: University of Toronto Press, 1971). See also J. W. Blench, *Preaching in England in the Late Fifteenth and Sixteenth Centuries: A Study of English Sermons 1450–c.1600* (New York: Barnes and Noble, 1964), esp. pp. 71–320.

The "disputatious" character of this learning contrasts markedly with the "dogmatic" character of epideictic oratory.[12] Medieval preachers, like many preachers before and since, tended to repeat in the pulpit what they had learned or taught in the classroom. In their sermons, consequently, they did not in principle shirk handling "disputed questions."

Two cautions are immediately called for. First, the thematic sermon was by no means the only form of preaching employed in the Middle Ages. For instance, the "ancient" form of the sermon, descended from the patristic homily, was known and practiced.[13] I here adduce the thematic sermon as one of the two models because it is so different from the epideictic and also because it was the actual rival with which epideictic had to compete at the papal court. Secondly, the thematic sermons are described as they now exist, although there is reason to believe that as these sermons were committed to writing they were changed from the form in which they were delivered.

The internal dynamics of the thematic sermon especially distinguished it from the revived epideictic of the papal court. The new oratory of the Renaissance introduced a significant broadening of purpose. In practice, the thematic sermon's principal concern, despite a theoretical importance accorded to persuasional ends, was often simply *to teach*.[14] This emphasis

---

12. The "disputatious" nature of discourse based on dialectics was explicitly recognized in classical theory; see Howell, *Poetics, Rhetoric, Logic*, p. 147.

13. See Blench, *Preaching in England*, esp. pp. 71–86. On other medieval sermon types, see Gerald R. Owst, *Preaching in Medieval England: An Introduction to Sermon Manuscripts of the Period c.1350–1450* (Cambridge: Cambridge University Press, 1926); Charles Smyth, *The Art of Preaching: A Practical Survey of Preaching in the Church of England, 747–1939* (London: SPCK, 1940); Anscar Zawart, *The History of Franciscan Preaching and of Franciscan Preachers (1209–1927): A Bio-Bibliographical Study*, Franciscan Studies, No. 7 (New York: Jos. Wagner, 1928), pp. 241–596; Daniel R. Lesnick, "Preaching Illusion and Reality: Social Transformation in Early Trecento Florence," to be published in *Memorie Domenicane*.

14. See, for instance, the treatise of 1478 by Lorenzo Guglielmo Traversagni adapting Ciceronian rhetoric to the Christian orator, "In novam rhetoricam," BAV cod. Vat. lat. 11441, fol. 26ʳ: ". . . oratores, ambaxiatores sive legati coram principibus perorantes . . . [intendunt] ea ad quae missi sunt suadere. . . . Scholastici vero potissimum docere nituntur, deinde persuadere. Ad secundum vero minime pervenitur absque primo. Itaque prius eis necessarium est distincte quasque partes dividere, deinde vero illas confirmare et confutare, ut tandem ad persuasionis intentum perveniant, quod raro assequuntur moderni quidam scholastici, ..." The Vatican codex is an autograph according to José Ruysschaert, "Lorenzo Guglielmo Traversagni de Savone (1425–1503), un humaniste franciscain oublié," *Archivum Franciscanum Historicum*, 46 (1953), 195–210, esp. 206–7. This important but neglected work was published twice in the fifteenth century, *Rhetorica nova* [Westminster: W. Caxton, 1479/80], Cop. #5270, and under the same title (St. Albans, 1480), Hain #14327. It was also known as *Margarita eloquentiae*. James J. Murphy argues for the medieval character

on teaching was more especially observed in sermons intended for distinguished and learned audiences rather than in sermons for the general populace. For these audiences teaching generally took the form of abstract argument and logical proof. Epideictic, even as it taught by "impressing ideas" upon its listeners, was intensely concerned *to move and to please*, thereby more effectively fulfilling the prescriptions of the indivisible triad of classical theory—*docere, movere, delectare*. The difference in preaching style between the Middle Ages and the Renaissance is thus seen to be far more radical than the adoption of a classicizing vocabulary and far more radical than the abandonment of the structure of the thematic sermon.

The structure of the thematic sermon, however, is important for our purposes, and a word should be said about it. From the time the thematic sermon first appeared, its structure was already established, and it did not thereafter change significantly. The sermon always began with a quotation from Scripture, known as the "theme." This theme was followed by a "protheme," a short section designed to capture attention through wonder, alarm, and so forth, and the protheme was closed by a prayer invoking divine help for preacher and listener alike. The theme was then repeated, followed by a concise summary of its import. Next was announced the division of the sermon into its three parts. If possible, especially for more learned audiences, this division should correspond to the words of the theme itself. Each of the parts of the sermon would be developed by arguments, authorities, and examples according to eight modes for amplification commonly proposed in the *Artes Praedicandi*. The preacher might or might not conclude with a brief summary or admonition.

Perhaps the most important effect this structure had upon the sermon was to diminish any literary unity it might otherwise have had. In the words of a distinguished student of this form, the threefold division, which might contain further subdivisions, resulted in "a series of minisermons."[15] Each part or subpart tended to be a discrete unit unto itself.

After this brief review of classical and thematic oratory, we can begin our examination of the sermons from the *cappelle*. We have excellent assistance in the examination from what would seem at first glance to be a very unlikely source—a treatise on letter writing. Sometime before 1485,

of the work, "Caxton's Two Choices: 'Modern' and 'Medieval' Rhetoric in Traversagni's *Nova Rhetorica* and the Anonymous *Court of Sapience*" in *Medievalia et Humanistica*, NS No. 3 (Cleveland: Case Western Reserve Press, 1972), 241–55.

15. Murphy, *Rhetoric in the Middle Ages*, p. 316.

the Florentine humanist Aurelio "Lippo" Brandolini composed at the papal
court his *De ratione scribendi libri tres*, and he dedicated it to Cardinal
Francesco Piccolomini.[16] The book was not printed until about the middle
of the sixteenth century. Though it has been ignored by modern scholars,
its importance for an earlier era is shown by the fact that, once it was
printed, it ran through a number of editions, the last of which was published in Rome in 1735.[17]

The purpose of Brandolini's treatise is to apply the principles of classical oratory to the art of letter writing. Such an approach was by no means
unique.[18] Brandolini's treatise, however, has four qualities which render
it especially germane to our purposes. First of all, it is a long treatise, in
the course of which Brandolini communicates at least as much about his
understanding of oratory as he does about how to write letters.[19] Brando-

---

16. On Brandolini (c.1454–97), see the article by Antonio Rotondò in the DBI, with
the appended bibliography. To that bibliography should now be added the sections of
Trinkaus's *Image and Likeness* that deal with Brandolini: I, 297–321; II, 601–13.

17. As I indicated above, I will use the Cologne, 1573, edition. Other editions are
listed by Rotondò in his article on Brandolini in the DBI, where he follows the mistaken tradition that there was an edition in Basel in 1498. Though the Basel, 1549,
edition indicates that the book is a work "numquam antea in lucem editi," Rotondò
lists an edition in Basel in 1543. To Rotondò's listing must be added the London edition
of 1573, published by Henricus Middletonus. The date of composition is ascertained
by internal evidence; see Federico Patetta, *Venturino de Prioribus: Umanista ligure
del secolo XV*, Studi e Testi, No. 149 (Vatican City: BAV, 1950), pp. 73–74, n. 3. What
is probably the dedication copy in the Bibl. Com., Siena, cod. H.VII.13, is of no help
in further specifying the date of composition. Tiraboschi considers this Brandolini's
best work, and he describes it, *Storia*, III, 208, ". . . scritta con singolare eleganza,
e in cui si espongono i precetti intorno allo scrivere con metodo e con precisione
superiore a quel secolo. . . ." Since Tiraboschi's day, however, it has been neglected.
A. Gerlo, for instance, does not mention it in his "The *Opus de Conscribendis Epistolis* of Erasmus and the Tradition of the *Ars Epistolica*," in *Classical Influences on
European Culture, A.D. 500–1500*, ed. R. R. Bolgar (Cambridge: Cambridge University
Press, 1971), pp. 103–14.

18. See Gerlo, "*Opus de Conscribendis Epistolis*" and the works referred to in
the following note.

19. Brandolini's treatise runs 253 pages in the Cologne, 1573, edition. The
Epistolare of Giovanni Maria Filelfo contains only about fourteen folios of "precepts"
(Bologna: Bacilerius de Bacileriis, 1489), Hain #*12975. Giovanni Sulpizio's *De
componendis et ornandis epistolis* (Rome: S. Plannck, 1491), Hain #15159, contains
twenty-five folios. Francesco Negro's *Opusculum scribendi epistolas* (Venice: Her-
manus Liechtenstein, 1488), Hain #*11863, is a series of twenty epistolary *genera*,
each with a definition, some rules and an example—much different from Brandolini's
discursive treatment and much shorter. The section "De componendis epistolis" of
Niccolò Perotti's *Rudimenta grammatices* (Venice: Gabrielis Petrus de Tarvisio,
1475), Hain #12648, does not treat the *genera*. Traversagni's *Ars seu modus episto-
landi* was first published in Cologne or Paris in 1480 and republished many times;
see Hain #8221, #8222, #8223, #*8224, and esp. Ruysschaert, "Traversagni," pp.
200–201. It is a short tract, containing only eight folios in the Paris, 1498, edition by

lini seems to have had a keener sense for the practical possibilities of oratory in his own day than did some others who wrote on rhetoric. He states baldly that, regarding oratory in Latin, there is no real possibility of practicing it in the judicial and deliberative *genera* where the vernacular or a crabbed Latin had won the day.[20] Therefore, he gives greater attention to the *genus demonstrativum* than did either the classical treatises or their Italian counterparts in the Quattrocento, with what seems to be the singular exception of the "In novam rhetoricam" by the Franciscan, Lorenzo Guglielmo Traversagni, written at Cambridge in 1478.[21] In actual

---

G. Marchant, Cop. #2855. Though in a very general way it relates letter writing to oratory, it does not do so in terms of the *genera*.

20. See *De ratione scribendi*, pp. 5–6, 215, and esp. 105: "Ac de universo quidem demonstrativo genere diximus satis. Quod quidem copiosius quam ceteri scriptores executi sumus, tum quod aetate nostra vel solum vel maximum est in quo latina versetur oratio, tum . . . ." See also his "De laudibus beatissimi patris Sixti IV pontificis maximi libri," BAV cod. Urb. lat. 739, fol. 59ʳ⁻ᵛ. On this point he is in substantial agreement with Bartolomeo Fazio, *De viris illustribus*, ed. Laurentius Mehus (Florence: J. P. Giovannelli, 1745), p. 7, as well as with Traversagni, "In novam rhetoricam," BAV cod. Vat. lat. 11441, fol. 47ᵛ. See also Erasmus, *Ciceronianus*, ASD, I.2, 654, and Galletti, *L'eloquenza*, pp. 571–72.

21. The originality of Brandolini's and Traversagni's emphasis on demonstrative oratory emerges only by comparison with other treatises and commentaries from Italy in the Quattrocento. George of Trebizond (Trapezuntius), for example, seems to have allowed the classical emphasis on the other two *genera* to blind him to what was happening in his own day, for he notes that "temporibus nostris" demonstrative is rarely employed except as incorporated into judicial and deliberative. *Rhetoricorum libri quinque* (Lyons: S. Gryphius, 1547), pp. 305–6. On Trebizond, see John Monfasani, *George of Trebizond: A Biography and a Study of His Rhetoric and Logic*, Columbia Studies in the Classical Tradition, No. 1 (Leiden: Brill, 1976), esp. pp. 261–89. Galletti, *L'eloquenza*, p. 556, might leave one with the impression that Antonio Loschi's popular *Inquisitio super XI orationes Ciceronis*, written in 1392 and published several times (see Hain #1885, #*1886, #*1887, #10349), gave special importance to the demonstrative. An examination of the *Inquisitio* shows this not to be the case. Of the eleven orations, Loschi classifies nine as principally judicial, one as demonstrative, and one as mixed deliberative and demonstrative. Giovanni Sulpizio's *Commentariolus in Quintilianum de compositionis parte* (Rome: E. Silber, 1487), Hain #*15166, does not deal with the *genera*. Guillaume Fichet's *Rhetoricorum libri III* (Paris: Gering, Kranz and Freiburger, [c.1471]), Hain #7057, follows the standard classical emphasis. Valla does not discuss the *genera* in the *Elegantiae* and only very briefly in the attack on Antonio Rho. I have examined some other commentaries and treatises on rhetoric and oratory, such as those by Francesco Maturanzio and Agostino Dati, but I have found nothing similar to Brandolini and Traversagni. Tommaso "Fedra" Inghirami's "Rhetorica," BAV cod. Ottob. lat. 1485, runs less than thirty folios, and it has nothing distinctive on the *genera*, despite the fact that Inghirami was one of the orators at the court and most certainly employed the epideictic form. The volume of the *Archivio di Filosofia* entitled *Testi umanistici su la retorica* (Rome: Bocca, 1953) yields nothing for our purposes. On Traversagni, see note 14 above. The *Praecepta artis rhetoricae* (Basel: J. Amerbach, [not after 1488]) ascribed to Aeneas Silvius Piccolomini (Pius II) is really an edition of Albrecht von Eyb's *Margarita poetica*; see Hain #*211 and GKW #9542.

fact, most of the Latin oratory which has survived from the Italian Renaissance is demonstrative. Brandolini makes the observation that the ancients wrote less about demonstrative precisely because they knew it so well and had such skill in it.[22]

The second reason Brandolini's treatise is so valuable is that he explicitly comments on the sacred oratory of the papal court, where he was engaged as a poet and writer from about 1480 until 1488. These comments he makes briefly and in passing, but they are extremely informative.[23] Furthermore, what he relates about the theory of epideictic so perfectly corresponds with what is actually found in many of the sermons that his treatise becomes a contemporary commentary on the oratory of the court. At points he makes specific applications of classical theory to the Christian situation.[24] In comparison with the lengthy and earlier "In novam rhetoricam" of Traversagni, Brandolini makes this application to the Christian orator almost by way of *obiter dicta*. Nonetheless, he is one of the first in the Renaissance to formulate the application, and he indicates some awareness of his originality in the importance he assigns to the *genus demonstrativum*.[25] Along with Traversagni, he thus antedates the treatises on preaching of Reuchlin, Erasmus, and Melanchthon.[26] More particularly, his *De ratione scribendi* is a helpful guide for interpreting the theory and rationale which underlies the sacred oratory of the court.

Thirdly, there is one instance in which Brandolini presents an especially helpful key for unlocking that theory and rationale. After his general introduction to epideictic, he begins to apply it to specific situations, viz. to persons, cities, and so forth. Like other Renaissance theorists who tried to adapt epideictic to the Christian pulpit, Brandolini considers panegyrics of the saints and funeral orations. Though he takes care to indicate how the Christian panegyric in these instances will differ from its classical antecedents, he would have found the adaptation easy and natural.[27] But what seems not to have been so easy and what is striking and significant

---

22. See *De ratione scribendi*, p. 105.

23. See *ibid.*, e.g., pp. 6, 64–65, 94–97.

24. See *ibid.*, pp. 94–101.

25. *Ibid.*, p. 97: "Quam quidem partem sum paulo latius executus, quoniam et res ipsa, quippe quae nova sit, usque ad hoc tempus intacta fuerat, et hoc tempore magno Romae in usu est."

26. Johann Reuchlin, *Liber congestorum de arte praedicandi* (Pforzheim: Anshelm, 1504); Erasmus, *Ecclesiastes sive concionator evangelicus*, LB, V, 767–1100; Philipp Melanchthon, *Rhetorices elementa* (Lyons: S. Gryphius, 1539).

27. See *De ratione scribendi*, pp. 97–101.

about his adaptation of epideictic to Christian purposes is his application of epideictic first of all to God.[28] In other words, the first object to which the praise of the demonstrative oration is directed is God himself.

In a sense it is true that here again is a simple application of something which had already appeared in classical theory, for that theory listed "the gods" as proper objects for panegyric. Nonetheless, this was an application which other theorists like Reuchlin, Erasmus, and Melanchthon failed to make, or at least failed to emphasize.[29] For these theorists, once "the gods" were perforce excluded, epideictic was applied to men and to things. Brandolini's insistence on the application of panegyric to the Christian God is as significant as the others' failure so to insist. Erasmus, for instance, sees the Christian preacher as a teacher and persuader. In effect he locates the teaching office in the *genus deliberativum*, through which the preacher expounds and persuades people to accept the "edicts, prom-

28. See *ibid.*, pp. 94–97, esp. 94–95: "Demonstrativum genus consumitur in laudem et vituperationem. Sed quoniam et potior laudandi pars est, et ex laudis contrariis locis vituperatio constat, de ea potissimum dicemus. Laus igitur aut a personis aut a rebus sumitur. Personae in deos et homines distribuuntur. Deum ipsum laudare ob eius magnitudinem vox humana non potest, sed singulos eius actus laudamus, ut potentiam, sapientiam, providentiam, mansuetudinem, ordinem et cetera eius generis, quae ex eius operibus consideramus. Ea praeterea quae ab homine satis intelligi non possunt admiratione et veneratione prosequimur, ut creationem mundi, coniunctionem humanae divinaeque naturae, trium personarum in eadem essentia (sic enim loqui necesse) distinctionem, et quae sunt eius generis, quibus de rebus dicere qui volet eas, quas dixi, partes amplificabit hominesque in earum admirationem contemplationemque adducet. Hoc loco mihi error eorum indicandus est qui cum divinum aliquid in concione laudaturi sunt ea de re partim disputant, partim praecipiunt ac docent quasi in schola apud discipulos, non in templo apud populum, verba faciunt. Quae ratio tum a loco, tum a tempore, tum a personis maxime aliena est. In quod quidem vitium plerique eorum incidunt qui Romae apud Pontificem festis diebus concionantur. Quod quidem mihi dicendum putavi, non ut eos reprehenderem qui in ceteris disciplinis docti sunt, hanc facultatem omnino non attigerunt, sed ut hi, qui oratores haberi volunt, id vitium et plane cognoscerent et quantum possent evitarent. Sed ut ad institutum redeamus, ita divinae res tractandae sunt, si publice dicamus, ut oratio, non lectio aut disputatio, videatur."

29. Though Erasmus makes some provision for the application of demonstrative oratory to the deity, he gives scarcely any attention to it and, for practical purposes, limits his treatment of demonstrative to panegyrics of the saints. See his *Ecclesiastes*, LB, V, 880–86. Special mention must again be made of Traversagni. He does not apply demonstrative oratory to the "deeds" of God explicitly, but he does include all sacred oratory under that *genus*. Moreover, he explicitly mentions certain religious doctrines as examples of the materials with which demonstrative oratory deals. "In novam rhetoricam," BAV cod. Vat. lat. 11441, fol. 54r: "Qualis profecto res esset loqui de cultu Dei, de misericordia illius, clementia, longanimitate erga genus humanum, de gloria vitae aeternae, de providentia, potentia, maiestate divina, de dignitate et excellentia sacrae Eucharistiae et aliorum sacramentorum, de sublimitate sapientiae et philosophiae moralis aliarumque liberalium artium. . . ."

ises and will" of God.[30] A late sixteenth-century treatise on preaching by Ludovico Carbone, while allowing epideictic in the pulpit, insists that the *genus deliberativum* be the *genus* "maxime frequens" for the Christian preacher, since the preacher always has some persuasion in mind.[31]

Brandolini indicates that what man praises most especially in God are his works and deeds.[32] Put in other words, man praises him and his attributes through what he knows, and what man knows are God's deeds, his accomplishments, his acts. In practice this means that the sermons at the court evince a tendency to look upon Scripture more as a history of God's actions and less as a manual of doctrinal proof-texts or a book of artfully disguised philosophical principles. For the preachers these actions are generally interpreted as actions for us men, as *beneficia* to which the only response is gratitude, love, and praise.

Brandolini asserts further that the orator sometimes holds up for veneration and contemplation what is beyond man's comprehension. To a large extent, this is what sacred oratory is concerned with. The specific objects that Brandolini lists as being beyond man's understanding are the Trinity, Creation, and the Hypostatic Union of two natures in the one person of Christ. The orator must avoid the mistake, he warns, of those who from the pulpit would lecture on these subjects as if they were in a classroom. The orator's purpose is not to lecture and dispute but through praise to lead men to admiration and contemplation of divine mystery. Thus in a relatively few words Brandolini has depicted how a literary genre is transformed from an exercise in instruction into an exercise in praise.[33]

In the fourth and final place, Brandolini's treatise is of special signifi-

30. See *Ecclesiastes*, LB, V, e.g., 769–70, 774, 877–79, and esp. 858–59. See also James Michael Weiss, "*Ecclesiastes* and Erasmus: The Mirror and the Image," *Archive for Reformation History*, 65 (1974), 83–108.

31. *Divinus orator vel de rhetorica divina libri septem* (Venice: Societas Minima, 1595), esp. p. 125. This Ludovico Carbone (d. 1597) is not to be confused with the fifteenth-century humanist of the same name (Carbone or Carbo).

32. See *De ratione scribendi*, pp. 94–95 (quoted in note 28 above).

33. See also Traversagni, who like Brandolini places all sacred oratory in the *genus demonstrativum* and who, accordingly, places the strictly thematic sermon there. Traversagni distinguishes the thematic sermon from the "oratorical" (classical) and from the popular sermon on the basis of the audiences for which the sermons are intended. In the case of the thematic sermon the audience is particularly specialized. It is to be given, that is to say, "coram doctoribus et scholasticis." See "In novam rhetoricam," BAV cod. Vat. lat. 11441, fol. 26ʳ, as well as fol. 48ʳ. He insists, however, that the purpose of the thematic sermon cannot ultimately be divorced from some form of persuasion, though he admits "modern scholastics" rarely move beyond "teaching." *Ibid.*, fol. 26ʳ; see note 14 above.

cance because sometime later he became a preacher at the papal court, and his celebrated sermon before Pope Alexander VI for Good Friday, 1496, has survived in eight editions printed between the year it was delivered and 1869.[34] This printing history, extraordinary for any sermon and unique for those from a *cappella pontificia*, in itself tells us we must reckon with Brandolini. We have, besides, his panegyric at the Minerva in honor of Aquinas and a hitherto unexamined oration on Holy Thursday, 1491, delivered in Florence.[35] The fact is that, despite Brandolini's sometimes harsh words about the friars and his criticism of them for not knowing the difference between a lecture and an oration, he himself joined the Augustinian order in 1491 and became a renowned preacher in Rome and elsewhere in Italy during the last years of his life.[36] The three extant sacred orations provide an opportunity to see how he combined theory with practice, and the orations will be examined from that point of view in the next chapter. In anticipation it might simply be stated that each of these orations is unambiguously epideictic and that each is thus an excellent model against which to test other orations from the period.

Meanwhile, I propose a six-point scheme for analyzing the orations from the *cappelle* and for illustrating precisely what constitutes an epideictic sermon when that form is fully achieved. The foil for comparison, as I have indicated, will be the thematic sermon. The categories of analysis are the following: (1) Latin style, (2) sources, (3) structure, (4) unity, (5) *res* or materials preached about, (6) purpose. Though some of these

34. *Oratio de virtutibus domini nostri Iesu Christi* [Rome: J. Besicken, after April 1, 1496], GKW #5017. Burchard records that the sermon was received "cum magna omnium laude," *Liber Notarum*, I, 601–2. Brandolini's dedicatory letter to Alexander VI recounts that the pope several times expressed his pleasure with the sermon personally and through messengers, fol. [1ʳ]. Tiraboschi calls it, ". . . la migliore cosa che in genere di eloquenza sacra latina si vedesse a que' tempi." *Storia*, III, 208. The editions I have examined or found references to are as follows: *Latin*—Rome, 1496, 1596, 1735; Cracow, 1568; Cologne, 1645; Mainz, 1869; *Italian*—Venice, 1596; Rome, 1767.

35. *Oratio pro sancto Thoma Aquinate* [Rome: E. Silber, 1485/90], GKW #5016; "Oratio in cena Domini," Bibl. Com., Siena, cod. H.VI.30, fols. 120ʳ–124ᵛ. The arguments favoring the attribution of the panegyric on Aquinas to Aurelio's brother, Raphael, are not convincing; see my article, "Renaissance Panegyrics of Aquinas," esp. pp. 176–77, n. 12. John McManamon has now prepared an edition of the latter oration, "Renaissance Preaching: Theory and Practice. A Holy Thursday Sermon of Aurelio Brandolini" *Viator*, 10 (1979).

36. See, e.g., the enthusiastic reaction of Matteo Bosso to Brandolini's sermons and extemporaneous poetry that he heard in Verona, *Familiares et secundae Matthaei Bossi epistolae* (Mantua: V. Bertochus, 1498), GKW #4956, ep. LXXV.

categories slightly overlap in actual practice and others, e.g., devices for *amplificatio*, could be added, I believe these six are adequate for our purposes.

1. Latin Style

Even those sermons most obviously influenced by the thematic form and scholastic doctrine almost without exception adopt a classicizing style. That is to say, they attempt to adopt the vocabulary, the syntax, and the prose rhythm that we find in classical and patristic literature and that we do not find in typically scholastic prose. Moreover, technical scholastic expressions like "materia prima," "potentia absoluta," "actus et potentia," and "actus purus" occur only rarely. When they do occur, however, they invariably point in the direction of a more thematic sermon. In even the most classicizing sermons, on the other hand, there is no reluctance to use ecclesiastical words like "cardinales," "schisma," "apostolus," and "propheta" for which there is no strictly classical precedent. Occasionally a classical alternative or circumlocution might be substituted for such words, but these are not what is generally encountered. The practice of referring to the Church as "imperium" or "res publica Christiana" does not seem to have had any prescriptive significance.

On this issue of classical precedent, the sermons could pass the standards that Erasmus establishes in the *Ciceronianus*, where he lashes out at a rigid adherence to classical vocabulary as a Ciceronianism foreign to the true spirit of Cicero.[37] According to Erasmus, such an adherence is

---

37. *Ciceronianus*, ASD, I.2, e.g., 641–42. On the bitter controversy over Ciceronianism in the fifteenth and sixteenth centuries, see Monfasani, *Trebizond*, pp. 289–94; Remigio Sabbadini, *Storia del Ciceronianismo e di altre questioni letterarie nell'età della Rinascenza* (Turin: E. Loescher, 1885); Izora Scott, *Controversies over the Imitation of Cicero*, Columbia University Contributions to Education, No. 35 (New York: Columbia University Press, 1910), which contains an English translation of the *Ciceronianus* of Erasmus; Émile V. Telle's introduction and commentary in *L'Erasmianus sive Ciceronianus d'Étienne Dolet (1535)*, Travaux d'Humanisme et Renaissance, No. 138 (Geneva: Droz, 1974); Morris W. Croll, *Style, Rhetoric, and Rhythm: Essays by Morris W. Croll*, ed. J. Max Patrick et al. (Princeton: Princeton University Press, 1966). None of the figures notably involved in the controversy were preachers at the court with the exception of Battista Casali; see Silvana Seidel Menchi, "Alcuni atteggiamenti della cultura italiana di fronte a Erasmo (1520–1536)," in *Eresia e riforma nell'Italia del Cinquecento*, Biblioteca del "Corpus Reformatorum Italicorum," ed. Luigi Firpo and Giorgio Spini (Florence: Sansoni, 1974), pp. 69–133. See also John Francis D'Amico, "Humanism and Theology at Papal Rome, 1480–1520," Diss. University of Rochester, 1977, esp. Chapter Three, "Towards a Definition of Roman Humanism: Ciceronianism and Religion," pp. 140–80, and Chapter Four, "Cicero as Theologian," pp. 181–253.

even more abhorrent to the spirit that should animate a Christian sermon. Ironically enough, his criticisms were directed against Roman humanists just a few years beyond the period we are considering.

Brandolini's standards anticipate Erasmus's to a startling degree. The sermons, therefore, satisfy Brandolini's directives, especially when he counsels the orator that, while he must eschew the technical vocabulary of "recent" theologians, philosophers, and lawyers, he should not try to speak "as if he were born in some other age."[38] Unusual and difficult words, says Brandolini, should be avoided, lest the orator not be understood. Indeed, he should speak in such a manner that he cannot *not* be understood.[39] Clarity was highly prized by Brandolini, and it seems to have been equally prized by the preachers. The syntax of the sermons, for instance, reflects a concern for intelligibility in its relative simplicity and straightforwardness. Long periods are rare, though syllogisms are even rarer. On the level we have so far been discussing, therefore, style in itself is not a very helpful criterion for identifying a fully epideictic sermon. For instance, while Cajetan was the procurator general of the Dominicans, he preached before Alexander VI and Julius II. His Latin style can be elegantly classical in the sense just described, yet his sermons are not strictly epideictic.

A more technical and detailed analysis of the stylistic characteristics of these sermons would doubtless reveal many useful distinctions. What figures of thought and diction were employed, for instance, and how self-consciously? Fortunately, we have Paul Oskar Kristeller's edition of Guillaume Fichet's oration for Sixtus IV on the feast of Saint Stephen, 1476. This edition gives us, through Fichet's own annotations, indication of detailed and self-conscious use of figures in constructing the oration.[40] Similar studies are required, however, before we can expect to move beyond a few major and relatively obvious points.

For the present there are only two characteristics I would point to as helping to distinguish thematic from epideictic style. The first is a certain lyrical quality, or at least certain lyrical moments, which are often

---

38. See *De ratione scribendi*, pp. 217–19, as well as the *Ciceronianus*, ASD, I.2, 636–37, 643–44. Like Erasmus, Brandolini does not accept Cicero as exclusively normative even among authors from antiquity, but he does unquestionably favor him, *De ratione scribendi*, pp. 212–13, 251–53. See the *Ciceronianus*, 642–43, 657–61, 705.

39. See *De ratione scribendi*, pp. 22, 210–11, 221, 240–44.

40. "An Unknown Humanist Sermon on St. Stephen by Guillaume Fichet," in *Mélanges Eugène Tisserant*, VI, Studi e Testi, No. 236 (Vatican City: BAV, 1964), 459–97.

found in epideictic but rather rarely in thematic. Exclamations of joy, wonder, and dismay are the most obvious and frequent ways in which this emotional element is manifested. The preachers were aware of the distinction between poetry and oratory, and a flowery and versifying style of oratory was unacceptable both in theory and in the practice of the court.[41] Nevertheless, epideictic's traditional relationship to poetry and song appears in some of the sermons. Even a sober canonist like Domenichi refers on occasion to his oration as "mea carmina."[42] More often the relationship appears simply in the more lyrical quality of the style, when that quality seems required by the message. One of the most striking examples of this stylistic tendency is the long congratulation which Agostino Filippi has God or Christ "sing" to the Christian soul as part of his peroration for the sermon on Trinity Sunday, 1513.[43]

The second characteristic consists in the different ways various sacred and profane sources are utilized. In some instances these sources are quoted, and quoted in such a way that they are, or come close to being, a litany of more or less artfully disguised proof-texts. Though in syntax and vocabulary these sermons otherwise avoid the stylistic characteristics of the thematic sermon, they succumb to this one. A litany of proof-texts has significance beyond the question of style, since it points towards a thematic purpose—proof. Nonetheless, the quotations do tend to break the rhythm of the prose and, hence, have stylistic import.

On this question of direct and explicit quotations, it is possible to generalize: the fewer such quotations a sermon contains the more likely it is

41. See De ratione scribendi, pp. 207–13, and de Grassis, "Diarium," Jan. 1, 1512, BAV cod. Vat. lat. 12269, fol. 486^r, and fourth Sunday of Lent, 1516, BAV cod. Vat. lat. 12275, fol. 168^v. There was, moreover, a concern that the verba be determined by the res, and not vice versa. See De ratione scribendi, pp. 203–4, and Andreas Brenta's prefatory letter to Oliviero Carafa for his sermon on Pentecost, 1483, In pentecosten oratio [Rome: E. Silber, after May 18, 1483], GKW #5100, fol. [1^v]. On the distinction between oratory and poetry in antiquity, see North, "Use of Poetry"; Howell, Poetics, Rhetoric, Logic, pp. 45–72; Wesley Trimpi, "The Ancient Hypothesis of Fiction: An Essay on the Origins of Literary Theory," Traditio, 27 (1971), 1–78; Louis Laurand, Études sur le style des discours de Cicéron, 4th ed. (1936–38; rpt. Amsterdam: A.M. Hakkert, 1965), esp. pp. 117–231. On the distinction in the Renaissance, see O. B. Hardison, Jr., "The Orator and the Poet: The Dilemma of Humanist Literature," The Journal of Medieval and Renaissance Studies, 1 (1971), 33–44.
42. "Oratio pro victoriis Christianorum," Aug. 30, 1469, BAV cod. Ottob. lat. 1035, fol. 82^v.
43. "Oratio dominica de Trinitate," in Orationes novem coram Iulio II et Leone X (Rome: J. Mazochius, 1518), fol. [6^r]. Raphael Brandolini's "De musica et poetica opusculum," Bibl. Casan. cod. 805, fols. 31^r–33^v, 68^{r-v}, treats of the interrelationship of poetry, music, oratory, and theology.

to appropriate the other qualities we associate with an epideictic oration. In other words, contrary to what might have been expected, explicit quotation even of classical authors already suggests that the oration will in other ways be less classical.

Beryl Smalley showed long ago that in certain English friars of the fourteenth century quoting classical authors in sermons was no proof of a classical inspiration for them.[44] Further precision is now possible: often enough, quoting classical or any other authors, if done explicitly and with some frequency, is a first indication the sermons are *not* fully classically inspired. The preachers who avoid such quotations are following, probably wittingly, the example of Cicero himself.[45] They utilize, but do not explicitly quote, their sources. The allusions, paraphrases, and even the actual quotations are woven into their text in such a way that they fit the rhythm and do not attract attention to themselves.

2. Sources

From what has just been said, it is clear that critical editions are required if the question of sources is to be pursued with exactitude. Dionisio Vázquez in his Ash Wednesday sermon for Julius II in 1513 nowhere indicates that he is quoting Pico della Mirandola, nor does Agostino Filippi indicate that he is quoting him in his oration for Leo X on Passion Sunday about a year later.[46] Antonio Lollio and Stephanus Thegliatius do not reveal that they are quoting a passage they thought to be from

44. *English Friars and Antiquity in the Early Fourteenth Century* (New York: Barnes and Noble, 1960). See also Blench, *Preaching in England*, pp. 209–27. There is a great propensity to quote poets from antiquity and the Renaissance by the famed "Renaissance" preacher, Paolo Attavanti (Paulus Florentinus), but his *Quadragesimale utillimum de reditu peccatoris* (Milan: U. Scinzenzeler and L. Pachel, 1479), Hain #*7166, is in almost every respect thoroughly thematic. This work is the so-called *Quaresimale Dantesco*.

45. See North, "Use of Poetry," esp. pp. 24–33, and H. D. Jocelyn, "Greek Poetry in Cicero's Prose Writing," *Yale Classical Studies*, No. 23 (Cambridge: Cambridge University Press, 1973), pp. 61–111.

46. See my critical edition of the Vásquez text, "An Ash Wednesday Sermon on the Dignity of Man for Pope Julius II, 1513," in *Essays Presented to Myron P. Gilmore*, ed. Sergio Bertelli and Gloria Ramakus, 2 vols. (Florence: Nuova Italia, 1978), I, 193–209. For the quotation in Filippi compared with Pico's text, see my "Preaching for the Popes," in *The Pursuit of Holiness in Late Medieval and Renaissance Religion: Papers from the University of Michigan Conference*, ed. Charles Trinkaus with Heiko Oberman, Studies in Medieval and Reformation Thought, No. 10 (Leiden: Brill, 1974), p. 428, n. 2.

Saint Bernard in the perorations of their sermons on Good Friday.[47] Examples of quotations and allusions that the preachers chose to weave into their texts without identifying them for their listeners could be considerably multiplied. Therefore, what I have to say under the category of "sources" will necessarily be somewhat impressionistic, and to a large extent it will rest on what is now seen to be a very insecure base, viz., the sources to which the preachers choose to call their audience's attention.

For the Bible, however, greater independence from the preachers' explicit signals is possible, simply because of the Bible's familiarity. And for that source it can be stated that the sermons abound in direct quotation, paraphrase, and allusion.[48] From the description in Chapter One about what was expected of an oration *inter missarum solemnia*, we should not be surprised that this is true. Within the Bible itself, the New Testament is referred to more often than the Old, and the Pauline epistles enjoy some special favor. Two verses from John's Gospel are cited so frequently that they already suggest some of the major doctrinal issues and reform concerns with which the sermons will deal, as we shall see in later chapters: "Et Verbum caro factum est" (1:14) and "Pacem meam do vobis, pacem meam relinquo vobis" (14:27).

It should be noted immediately that these verses are liturgical texts and were repeated in the Mass. The Prologue of John's Gospel in which the "Verbum-caro-factum" occurs was often recited at the end of the Mass, just after the final blessing of the congregation, and the expression was paraphrased in the "homo-factus-est" of the Creed. The peace-text was part of a prayer recited for the so-called kiss of peace just before the distribution of the Sacrament. This correlation suggests that the liturgy helped focus attention on certain scriptural texts.

In at least one important instance, the liturgy supplied a text of its own that recurs in a number of sermons and that is of special importance as indicating a framework of interpretation that consistently came into

47. Lollio, *Oratio passionis dominicae* [Rome: S. Plannck, 1486?], Hain #*10181, fol. [9ᵛ]; Thegliatius, *Oratio de passione Domini* [Rome: S. Plannck, 1496], Hain-Cop. #15457, fol. [11ʳ].

48. In treating "amplificatio," A. Brandolini gives first place to the use of "authorities"—especially Scripture and the saints, *De ratione scribendi*, p. 68: "Amplificatio est oratio ex communibus locis sumpta ad rem augendam vel exaggerandam. Loci communes sunt qui ad omnes causas accommodari possunt. Hi plurimi sunt. Nos paucos et ad institutionem nostram maxime necessarios proferamus. Ex his primus ac praecipuus est ab auctoritate Dei imprimis et eorum quos sanctos appellamus, deinde . . . ."

play when man's Redemption was in question. The text is the prose-hymn from the Holy Saturday service, the *Exultet*. This hymn of high lyric quality, whose author was possibly Saint Ambrose, calls upon all creation to rejoice in its Redemption, and it employs the term "happy fault" to describe Adam's Fall—"happy" for it brought so great a Redeemer.[49] As we shall see, references to the *Exultet* sometimes occur in contexts where we would least expect them and where they act as an important clue to a religious mood.

The Latin Fathers are frequently mentioned, especially Augustine and Jerome, but here again critical editions must eventually come to our aid. What would be especially interesting would be to see what impact the translations of the Greek Fathers by Ambrogio Traversari, George of Trebizond, and others had upon the preachers.[50] Pope Nicholas V was an important instigator of the patristic revival in the Quattrocento, and that fact already suggests that the preachers of the court might have derived some of their doctrinal positions from Greek theology. At any rate, citation of the Fathers is frequent and far outstrips that of any other source except the Bible.

Bernard contends with no real rival among medieval figures. It seems to have been just as bad form to mention a scholastic as to use technical scholastic jargon, for scholastics are rarely referred to by name.[51] Cajetan,

---

49. The most celebrated and frequently quoted lines are the following, *Missale Romanum*, "Sabbato Sancto": "O mira circa nos tuae pietatis dignatio! O inaestimabilis dilectio caritatis: ut servum redimeres, filium tradidisti! O certe necessarium Adae peccatum, quod Christi morte deletum est! O felix culpa, quae talem ac tantum meruit habere redemptorem!" The doctrine of the "felix culpa" in the writings of John Milton has received a certain amount of attention. The most important article dealing with it is Arthur O. Lovejoy's "Milton and the Paradox of the Fortunate Fall," in *Essays in the History of Ideas* (Baltimore: The Johns Hopkins University Press, 1948), pp. 277–95, an article first published in 1937. See also Clarence C. Green, "The Paradox of the Fall in *Paradise Lost*," *Modern Language Notes*, 53 (1938), 557–77, and William G. Madsen, "The Fortunate Fall in *Paradise Lost*," *ibid.*, 74 (1959), 103–5. The most widely ranging study of the doctrine is by Herbert Weisinger, *Tragedy and the Paradox of the Fortunate Fall* (East Lansing: Michigan State College Press, 1953). For a Renaissance controversy on the crucial verses, see Jean-Pierre Massaut, *Critique et tradition à la veille de la Réforme en France*, De Pétrarque à Descartes, No. 31 (Paris: J. Vrin, 1974), pp. 101–5, 159–77.

50. See Charles Stinger, *Humanism and the Church Fathers: Ambrogio Traversari (1386–1439) and Christian Antiquity in the Italian Renaissance* (Albany: State University of New York Press, 1977).

51. One of the more notable exceptions to this tendency would be the thoroughly scholastic sermon of the Franciscan Nicolaus Valla for Alexander VI, second Sunday of Advent, 1502; *Oratio de unione hypostatica Christi* [Rome: J. Besicken, after Dec. 4, 1502]. Valla utilizes Scotus, Pierre d'Ailly, Bonaventure, Aquinas, Ockham, and others.

one of the most noted commentators on Aquinas in the history of Thomism, only once mentions Saint Thomas in the five sermons that survive from his procuratorship. Whenever a preacher does adduce scholastic authorities, however, he has invariably constructed a sermon thematic in purpose.

Plato and Aristotle, Vergil and Ovid, Livy and Sallust, and of course Cicero, as well as other authors from classical antiquity, are cited with some regularity, but notably less frequently than Scripture and the Fathers.[52] The attitude underlying citation of such authors coincides with traditional Christian usage in the patristic and medieval periods and in no instance remotely hints at a global identification of Christian teaching with the teaching of those authors.

Incidents from Roman and Greek history are sometimes adduced to illustrate a particular point. The use of classical examples is almost invariably an instance of *amplificatio* by use of the device of comparison. For that reason, these examples occur with greater frequency in the more epideictic sermons, where there is also greater interest in historical *exempla* and in their power to move to *admiratio*. The Christian is compared to his pagan counterpart, and then it is argued "by how much the more" (*quanto magis*) he should excel for being a Christian. The Christian should "outdo" those with whom he is compared.[53]

The phrase "quanto magis" recurs often. It was a biblical phrase, and a phrase also found in classical authors.[54] It was thus easily incorporated into the rhetorical theory of comparison and into the purposes of the

52. See my "Preaching for the Popes," pp. 408–40. A specific and independent confirmation of my assessment is found in David Gutiérrez, "Testi e note su Mariano da Genazzano (†1498)," *Analecta Augustiniana*, 32 (1969), 117–204, esp. 194–97, where he shows that, in spite of the fact that there is no basis in the sermons of Mariano which survive, the traditional assertion that Mariano's preaching was filled with quotations from the ancient classics is repeated even today.

53. On "outdoing" as a figure of speech, see Ernst Robert Curtius, *European Literature and the Latin Middle Ages*, trans. Willard R. Trask, Bollingen Series, No. 36 (New York: Pantheon, 1953), pp. 162–65. Reuchlin explicitly treats it as a mode of comparison in his short *Liber congestorum*, fol. [9ʳ]. Brandolini states, *De ratione scribendi*, p. 104: "Omnis autem non modo deliberatio, ut Quintilianus affirmat, verum etiam laus comparatione mihi maxime continere videtur. Illa enim sive res, sive persona commendatur quae ceteris sui generis praestare maxime demonstratur." The sensitivity of at least one preacher on the question of *exempla* from pagan history is seen in Agostino Filippi's apology for introducing Philip of Macedon into his sermon "Oratio de veritate," Passion Sunday, 1514, in *Orationes novem coram Iulio II et Leone X*, fol. [10ᵛ].

54. There are about thirty instances of its use, or a close equivalent, in the Vulgate, e.g., Heb. 9:13–14. In Cicero it occurs, e.g., Acad. 1.3.10.

preachers. It was in frequent use from the early days of Lorenzo Valla's panegyric of Aquinas in 1458 until well beyond the period we are considering.[55] As the phrase is actually employed, it perfectly encapsulates a point the preachers tried so often to make: the special excellence of the Christian situation.

3. Structure

The structure of the thematic sermon was precisely defined. The structure of the epideictic was considerably looser, except in the case of a panegyric of an individual. The basic rhetorical principle of adapting the oration to the particular exigencies of persons, occasion, and subject matter encouraged greater variety in epideictic than in the other two *genera* because of the less closely defined function of epideictic oratory. An exordium, possibly indicating the magnitude of the orator's task for the situation and suggesting how inadequate human speech was for it, was indispensable.[56] Also indispensable was a peroration summarizing the oration and attempting to lift the audience to a final appreciation for what had been treated. Somewhere after the exordium an indication of the *topoi* to be dealt with was desirable, and in the sermons at the court it often occurs. The most satisfactory procedure in handling the problem of structure, therefore, is simply to indicate how far the orations depart from what was prescribed for thematic.[57] Obviously, I am here omitting consideration of those rare sermons at the court where an altogether different structure obtained, like the homiletic structure in one of Massari's sermons for Pope Paul II.[58]

55. "Encomium sancti Thomae Aquinatis," ed. J. Vahlen, reproduced in the *Opera omnia*, Monumenta Politica et Philosophica Rariora, ed. Luigi Firpo, Ser. I, No. 5, 2 vols. (I=rpt. Basel, 1540; Turin: Bottega d'Erasmo, 1962), II, 340–52, esp. 347. See also Giovanni Antonio Campano's panegyric of Aquinas in *Opera a Michaele Ferno edita* (Rome: E. Silber, 1495), GKW #5939, fol. [91ᵛ]. On Campano, see Flavio di Bernardo, *Un Vescovo umanista alla Corte Pontificia: Giannantonio Campano (1429–1477)*, Miscellanea Historiae Pontificiae, No. 39 (Rome: Pontificia Universitas Gregoriana, 1975).

56. Brandolini warns the orator about exaggerating his inadequacy, which would be "adolescentium . . . proprium. *De ratione scribendi*, p. 21.

57. With great lucidity John McManamon outlines and contrasts the structure of a thematic oration with that of a classicizing eulogy in "Ideal Renaissance Pope," pp. 29–32. Salvatore I. Camporeale expertly analyzes Valla's use of the classical structure enjoined by Quintilian's *Institutes* and describes its significance. "Lorenzo Valla tra Medioevo e Rinascimento: Encomion s. Thomae (1457)," *Memorie Domenicane*, NS 7 (1976), 11–194, esp. 28–62.

58. "Omelia super capitulo XIᵒ Lucae evangelistae," Bibl. Estense cod. Alpha

A relatively small number of our sermons adheres in detail to the thematic structure. A larger number departs from it completely. That is to say, this latter group omits the opening theme from Scripture, omits the protheme and repetition of the theme, omits the scholastic style of division, and even omits the prayer for divine aid.[59] This latter group invariably contains, on the other hand, a classical exordium and a peroration.

The majority of the sermons that survive, however, fall somewhere between these two extremes. Many sermons that are thematic in subject matter and purpose begin with a classicizing exordium. These also tend to add some kind of peroration and thus not end abruptly, as thematic sermons often do. On the other hand, an even larger majority of the sermons show a decided reluctance to abandon the initial announcement of a scriptural theme and considerable reluctance to abandon the prayer.[60] The latter, indeed, had a classical equivalent. The exordium of Valla's encomium of Aquinas takes pains to justify the prayer as a Christian adoption and adaptation of an ancient practice fallen into desuetude.[61] In any case, the prayer had a natural correlation with an exordium stressing the sacred and exalted character of the celebration and the speaker's human inadequacy for it.

Whenever a preacher employs a strictly thematic structure, he has invariably constructed a sermon that also in subject matter and purpose is thematic.[62] Whenever the preacher completely departs from the thematic structure, he has composed an epideictic oration. The problem comes, of course, with the mixed or hybrid structures. On occasion the elements of thematic structure that remain are obviously only vestigial and therefore cause no confusion. Whether, and in what way, the scriptural theme functions, if there be such a theme, can help determine the character of an oration. But such an analysis is already leading us into the *res* with which the oration deals. In these cases, it is to *res* and purpose that we must

Q.6.13, fols. 79ᵛ–91ᵛ, date and occasion unspecified. See also, e.g., Philippus Mucagata, *Oratio in die epiphaniae* [Rome: E. Silber, after Jan. 6, 1488], Hain #11625.

59. Traversagni briefly describes how the structure of the sermon should be accommodated to the three audiences he envisions—secular or ecclesiastical princes, scholastics and doctors, the people. "In novam rhetoricam," BAV cod. Vat. lat. 11441, fols. 25ᵛ–26ʳ.

60. Jacopo Gherardi informs us, for instance, that the omission of the "theme" in the sermon for the feast of St. John, 1481, was criticized by some members of the court. *Il diario romano*, ed. Enrico Carusi, RIS, 23.3 (Città di Castello: S. Lapi, 1904), 85.

61. "Encomium," II, 346–47. See also Erasmus, *Ecclesiastes*, LB, V, 872–74.

62. An exception, for instance, is Domenico de' Domenichi's "Oratio pro pace Italiae," Ascension Thursday, 1468, BAV cod. Ottob. lat. 1035, fols. 46ʳ–52ᵛ.

turn. By so doing we discover in some instances that a sermon with a mixed form has a mixed purpose that pervades the whole oration.

4. Unity

The threefold division and the lack of concern about a conclusion already indicate that a strictly thematic sermon placed little emphasis on literary unity. In relating the divisions of the sermon to the words of the theme, the preacher did bind the sermon to a point of reference, which had certain advantages for him and for his audience, at least as a mnemonic. A more extrinsic form of unity, however, is difficult to imagine. If the division were based more closely on the intrinsic nature of the question proposed, a certain logical unity would be operative. But there was no urgent concern for marshaling the three logical steps into a single conclusion that would be adequately articulated and impressed on the listeners.

Classical oratory, in contrast, always had a single point to make: the guilt of the accused, the necessity of the war, the praiseworthiness of the hero. A wide variety of *topoi* was offered to aid in driving the point home, but it was always a single point that was being driven home.[63] The preachers at the papal court who were most profoundly influenced by classical rhetoric, therefore, had a sense for literary unity that other preachers did not share.[64] The classicizing preachers self-consciously employed digression in a manner that evinces their appreciation of literary unity. The conclusion is inevitable: those sermons that are more unified literarily are the sermons that are most classicizing and epideictic. Sermons where purpose is most clearly stated at the beginning tend to be more or less unified depending on whether that purpose is epideictic or thematic.

In practice, of course, assessment of the literary unity of a piece of literature is difficult, and assessments of the sermons are not exempt from that difficulty. The general norm is clear, however, and our attention at this point need be directed to only one particular, the use of a conclusion or peroration. As I mentioned earlier, most of the sermons at the court have a conclusion of some sort. But the logical and literary relationship of this conclusion to the body of the sermon is sometimes remarkably tenuous. Exhortatory, admonitory, and, frequently enough, even deliberative

---

63. A. Brandolini states the principle succinctly in *De ratione scribendi*, p. 66: "Oratio enim unum aliquod sibi dicendum proponit. . . ."
64. See *ibid.*, pp. 204–7.

perorations can be appended to a sermon which has in no way prepared us for such a turn. Anxiety about the Turkish threat made the proposal of an "expedition" a dramatic concluding word that was difficult to resist.[65] In these anti-Turk conclusions we sometimes have a microcosmic use of the *topoi* for deliberative oratory—the enemy is weak, the allies are strong, the injury is insufferable, the time is ripe, the cause is just, and God is on our side.

For instance, Battista Casali, a Roman humanist thought by Erasmus to be so thoroughly imbued with the principles of classical oratory that he attacked him for it, changes subject for the peroration of his sermon on "circumcision of heart" for Julius II on January 1, 1508. In that peroration Casali abruptly directs Julius's attention to the shambles to which the Turks have reduced the Christian *oikoumene*, and then he extols the papal library founded by Sixtus IV, Julius's uncle.[66] The disappearance of the idea of circumcision of heart in the last minutes of Casali's oration alerts us to the problem that these conclusions or perorations sometimes present.

5. Res

An epideictic oration is a "dogmatic" exercise and hence it does not dispute "disputed questions." Though we must make some exception for the question of the immortality of the soul and treat it in a later chapter, the fact is that extremely few surviving sermons from the *cappelle* professedly treat materials "disputed" during the era. Massari's sermon before Sixtus IV in S. Maria del Popolo on December 8, 1472, is noteworthy not only for day and place, but also because its subject is the Immaculate Conception.[67] Burchard reveals what he considered the machinations of the procurator general of the Franciscans to avoid showing his sermon

65. See, e.g., Marco Maroldi, *Sententia veritatis humanae redemptionis* [Rome: S. Plannck, after March 25, 1481], Hain #*10778; Rodericus de S. Ella, *Oratio in die parasceve* [Rome: S. Plannck, 1480?], Hain #*13933 (=*13931); Martinus de Viana, *Oratio in die sanctissimae Trinitatis* (Rome: [S. Plannck], 1494), Cop. #6196; Stephanus Basignanas Gorgonius, *Oratio de animae immortalitate* [Rome: n. publ., after Dec. 20, 1517]; and two orations by Battista Casali, "Oratio in die cinerum," Feb. 9, 1502, and "Oratio in die veneris sancti," March 29, 1510, Bibl. Ambr. cod. G.33.inf., fols. 303^v–308^v (pars prima), 2^r–7^r (pars altera). Henceforth this separate foliation will be referred to simply by use of Roman numerals.

66. See my article, "The Vatican Library and the Schools of Athens: A Text of Battista Casali, 1508," *The Journal of Medieval and Renaissance Studies*, 7 (1977), 271–87.

67. *Oratio de conceptione Virginis* [Rome: S. Plannck, c.1480], Hain #*5686(?).

for the second Sunday of Advent, 1486, to the Dominican Master of the Sacred Palace because it proposed the Scotistic rather than the Thomistic opinion on the Virgin's conception, but this sermon has not, to my knowledge, survived.[68] We have, therefore, only one sermon from this period that professes to deal with this question. More interesting still, we have no sermon or part of a sermon that deals with the question whether the blood of Christ shed in his passion and reassumed in his resurrection was united to his divinity during the three days his body was in the tomb— a question which we know exercised the papal court, especially during the pontificate of Pius II.[69] There was, no doubt, reluctance to raise issues during a *cappella* over which the orders represented there were divided. Such reluctance would find comfort in the dogmatic character of epideictic.

Aside from subjects which can be relegated to the "disputes among the schools," there was an even more fundamental line of demarcation between materials congenial to a thematic sermon and materials congenial to an epideictic one. The simple words metaphysics and history denote those materials. No *res* is more general than metaphysics and none more particular than history. As applied to God, this results in a distinction between what God *is* and what he *does*. If a sermon announces that it is dealing with God's *facta, opera, gesta, magnalia*, or *beneficia*, it is inevitably leading into epideictic. When Cristoforo Marcello described the four evangelists for Julius II as the "rerum gestarum scribae," he could not have chosen a more telling phrase to indicate that he viewed the Scriptures as a book of history.[70] When a few years later, before Leo X, Agostino Filippi exclaimed in echo of the psalm, "Fecit mirabilia magna!" he in three words had captured the essence of the epideictic mode.[71]

We thus begin to compose what we might call an epideictic vocabulary,

---

68. *Liber Notarum*, I, 173. The issue is raised briefly on another occasion by the Dominican Master of the Sacred Palace, Marco Maroldi, in his sermon on the Annunciation before the Franciscan pope, Sixtus IV. Maroldi's words can be interpreted as subscribing to the position of Scotus and Bonaventure, which may have been the politic thing to do. *Sententia veritatis humanae redemptionis*, fol. [2^r].

69. Nicolò Palmeri, for instance, did not preach on it, but he twice discussed it publicly for the benefit of the cardinals and people during the pontificate of Pius II, who was present for his discussion, and during the pontificate of Paul II. See BAV cod. Vat. lat. 5815, fols. 126^r–129^r, 135^v–139^r. On the dispute, see Pastor, III, 286–88.

70. *Oratio in die omnium sanctorum* [Rome: M. Silber?, after Nov. 1, 1511], fol. [6^r].

71. "Oratio de multiplici adoratione," Epiphany, 1515, in *Orationes novem coram Iulio II et Leone X*, fol. [12^v]: "Hic, inquam, verus est Deus et non aestimabitur alius ab illo, quippe qui fecit mirabilia magna solus, et profecto solus mirabilia fecit." Cf. Pss. 135(136).4, and 71(72).18.

and the words I have just mentioned can be the first entries. To discover further sets of epideictic words, we must again advert to the fact that epideictic wants as far as possible to present us with works and deeds, and these works and deeds are presented not for a metaphysical analysis but quite literally for viewing. The epideictic preacher consistently invites his distinguished audience at the papal court to "look," to "view," to "gaze upon," and to "contemplate"—*intueri, videre, aspicere, ante oculos ponere, contemplari*! The frequency and consistency with which these verbs are repeated are striking, and such repetition is of great importance for our analysis. It marks a conversion from the cerebral to the visual. "Look," demands Lodovico da Ferrara, the Dominican procurator general, "for I cannot *explain*."[72] What is at stake is clearly seen in the meaning which the verb *contemplari* always conveys in the epideictic context. It never means "to think" or "to consider" or "to meditate." It always means "to gaze upon."

These verbs of seeing relate directly to actions and deeds. Though one may eventually reflect upon an action, one must first see it with one's own eyes or hear it described in words. And, of course, it is possible to describe an action in words. This is what the epideictic preachers tried to do.[73] It was thus that their *res* received its appropriate *amplificatio*. If we should say they were trying "to paint a word-picture," we would be more accurate than that worn expression would at first lead us to believe. They were using the rhetorical device technically known as ekphrasis.

"Ut pictura, poesis" is Horace's famous expression, but the analogy

72. "Sermo de suprema die," in *Orationes quinque* [Rome: n. publ., after 1492], Hain-Cop. #6983, sermon for first Sunday of Advent, 1492, fol. [13ʳ], describing the joy of the saved in the Last-Judgment scene: "Inde clarissimam lucem, immortalem vitam, incredibilem levitatem corpus accipiet. Ardeo equidem omnem eorum felicitatem explicare, sed me conantem superat rei magnitudo. Tantum ergo vos admonuisse liceat: Ponite ante oculos praeclarum hoc et insigne spectaculum!"

73. This *topos* is briefly described by A. Brandolini, *De ratione scribendi*, p. 70: "Alius locus est per quem negotium breviter ponimus ante oculos, ut geri videatur, et quae vel bona vel mala consequi eam rem soleant enumeramus, ut earum rerum enumeratione negotium ipsum augeatur." In speaking of the technique proper to the *genus demonstrativum*, without in any way referring it to sacred oratory, Fichet says in his *Rhetoricorum libri III*, fol. [144ʳ]: " . . . ita commode verbis exprimimus, ut geri denuo coram oculis negotium magis quam per se dici videatur, quae res ad amplificandum et narrandum plurimum prodest." See Erasmus's "De demonstrativi generis epistolis" in his *De conscribendis epistolis*, ASD, I.2, 513–16, as well as his *Ecclesiastes*, LB, V, 940. See also Poliziano's "Praefatio in Suetonii expositionem," *Opera* (Basel: N. Episcopius, 1553), p. 499, where a similar point is made for history, which is implicitly related to epideictic. On the relationship between rhetoric, historical narrative, and artistic illusion, see Struever, *Language of History*, pp. 63–82.

considerably antedates his *Ars Poetica*.[74] There is a basis for it and for its application to the three *genera* of oratory in Aristotle's *Rhetoric*.[75] Recent scholarship has shown that this intersensory metaphor was operative in Quattrocento Italy, that Nicholas V's Alberti was influenced by it, and that it was specifically related to epideictic.[76] This scholarship has been principally concerned, however, with the impact that the metaphor had on painting. What we are now trying to do is to reverse the question to see what impact it had in the other direction, on verbal expression—specifically, on the sacred oratory of the papal court.

Even if there were no more direct evidence that the analogy was operative on that oratory, the future Pius II's well-known statement in 1452 would be grounds for suspecting it: "Amant enim se artes hae [eloquentia et pictura] ad invicem."[77] But, in fact, there is extant an early sixteenth-century commentary on the *Ars Poetica* almost certainly written by one of the preachers, Tommaso "Fedra" Inghirami. In that treatise the analogy between painting in colors and painting in words is several times discussed: the painter is nothing other than a mute poet, and the poet is a painter who speaks.[78]

This treatise, whether written by Inghirami or not, articulates an understanding of the epideictic orator's task that occurs in Inghirami's own oratory with unmistakable clarity. The exordium for his panegyric at the Minerva in 1495 in honor of Thomas Aquinas is explicit. In explaining why the Church annually celebrates the feasts of the saints, he says that

74. A.P. 361.

75. See esp. Wesley Trimpi, "The Meaning of Horace's *Ut Pictura Poesis*," *Journal of the Warburg and Courtauld Institutes*, 36 (1973), 1–34. Cf. Arist. Rhet. III.12.5–6.

76. See Baxandall, *Giotto and the Orators*, as well as Rensselaer W. Lee, *Ut Pictura Poesis: The Humanistic Theory of Painting* (New York: Norton, 1967), a reprint of an earlier article; John R. Spencer, "Ut Rhetorica Pictura: A Study in Quattrocento Theory of Painting," *Journal of the Warburg and Courtauld Institutes*, 20, (1957), 26–44; Ernst H. Gombrich, "Vasari's *Lives* and Cicero's *Brutus*," *ibid.*, 25 (1960), 309–11; Svetlana Alpers, "*Ekphrasis* and Aesthetic Attitudes in Vasari's *Lives*," *ibid.*, 190–215. For an easily available example of a defense of rhetoric wherein the analogy between painting and eloquence abounds, see Philipp Melanchthon's reply (1558) to Pico's famous letter (1485) to Ermolao Barbaro, *Corpus Reformatorum*, IX (1842; rpt. New York: Johnson, 1963), 687–703, available in English translation, with introduction, in Quirinus Breen's "Three Renaissance Humanists on the Relation of Philosophy and Rhetoric," in his *Christianity and Humanism*, pp. 1–68, esp. 39–68.

77. Letter to Niklas von Wyle, c. July, 1452, *Der Briefwechsel des Eneas Silvius Piccolomini*, III Abt., ed. Rudolf Wolkan, Fontes Rerum Austriacarum, No. 68 (Vienna: A. Hölder, 1918), p. 100, n.

78. Without title, inc. "Poeticam caelo ortam et ab diis," BAV cod. Vat. lat. 2742, fol. I^r. See esp. fols. 8^r, 9^{r-v}, 93^v. See Chapter IV, "The Mute Poet," in John Pope-Hennessy's *Raphael* (London: Phaidon, n.d. [1970?]).

it is done "so that their memory, which has begun like a beautiful painting to fade with the lapse of time, might be renewed each year through praise as if with new colors."[79]

The analogy between the art of words and the plastic arts recurs explicitly in the other preachers as they describe their aims.[80] The boldest application of the analogy is that of Hieronymus Scoptius in his oration on the feast of All Saints for Sixtus IV. Scoptius applies it to Christ's preaching of the Sermon on the Mount. Christ speaks like "an expert in the art of painting," who in that marvelous Sermon restored the true image of our souls as if with a new portrait.[81]

79. *Panegyricus in memoriam divi Thomae Aquinatis* [Rome: E. Silber, c. 1495], Hain-Reichling #9186, fol. [2ʳ]: "Inter cetera quae ad bene beateque vivendum sancta mater ecclesia nobis ostendit, patres amplissimi, illud salubre et frugiferum existimatur quod ultra tot praeclara instituta, tot sacrosanctas leges, tot divini humanique iuris praecepta sanctum est ut eorum qui in hac nostra re publica Christiana claruerint et ob merita in divorum numero relati sint solemnia natalesque dies singulis quibusque annis stato tempore celebrarentur, eam praecipue ob causam ut eorum memoria veluti pictura egregia, sed vetustate evanescens, novis quasi coloribus annua laudatione renovaretur, qua totiens repetita mortales expergefactis animis tamquam sagittarii ad metam invitarentur omnique conatu illis similes evadere niterentur. Acriori enim animo ac fiducia ad ea ferimur imitanda quae ab aliis hominibus facta esse cognoscimus quam ad ea sequenda impellamur quae ne ipsi quidem faciunt qui praecipiunt et quae videntur exercendae linguae potius quam vitae instituendae gratia tradidisse, quique eam habendam sapientiam praedicant quam adhuc mortalium consecutus est nemo. Spectamus etenim potius quae fiunt in vita communi quam quae finguntur aut optantur, ut solent pictores qui novos discipulos praestantissimis propositis imaginibus potius quam arte erudire contendunt, vel quia plus oculis quam auribus credunt, vel quia longum iter est per praecepta, breve autem et efficax per exempla." See also his "In laudem omnium sanctorum oratio," Bibl. Guarn. cod. LIII.4.8, fol. 39ʳ.

80. See, e.g., Raphael Brandolini, *Oratio de obitu Dominici Ruvere* [Rome: E. Silber, 1501], fol. [2ᵛ]; Agostino Filippi, *Oratio die epiphaniae MDXX* [Rome: S. Guileretus, 1520], fols. [1ᵛ, 5ʳ]; Anon., "Oratio in funere pontificis maximi [Calixti tertii]," BAV cod. Vat. lat. 4872, fol. 41ʳ.

81. *Oratio in die festo omnium sanctorum* [Rome: E. Silber or S. Plannck, after Nov. 1, 1489], Hain-Cop. #14541, fol. [4ʳ⁻ᵛ]: "Verum postquam pulchritudo illa quae in imagine consistebat peccati sordibus obsolevit et inquinata est, venit qui nos ea turpitudine liberaret atque illis sordibus ablueret propria aqua et viva et saliente in vitam aeternam ut, sublata atque deleta ea contaminatione ac labe in quam propter peccatum incideremus [sic], rursus in nobis beata renovaretur et restitueretur forma. Atque, ut in picturae arte dixerit peritus ad rudes illam pulchram esse effigiem quae ex talibus sit partibus constituta cuius et coma talis et oculorum orbes et superciliorum lineamenta et generum status ceteraque omnia quibus omni ex parte expletur et perficitur pulchritudo, sic et modo Christus Iesus ad illius quod solum beatum est imitationem animam nostram rursus illinit orationem atque describit, et ait imprimis: Beati pauperes spiritu. . . ." The limitations of the painter's and sculptor's art is a recurring theme in Nicoletto Dati's *Oratio die Trinitatis habita* [Rome: J. Besicken and S. Mayr, after June 11, 1503], delivered for Julius II; see GKW, VII, 327.

Practice strove to correspond to theory. With one example can be illustrated how totally different a thematic treatment of a Christian mystery is from an epideictic treatment. The example is taken from the feast of the Ascension. This feast typically provided the scholastic preacher with an occasion to discuss proofs for the afterlife, why and how man is glorified in the next world, and similar questions.[82] Preachers like Massari and the noted Neapolitan humanist Pietro Gravina who chose to treat it epideictically described, instead, with all the color their vocabulary could muster, Christ's entry into heaven. It was a triumphal procession. Christ is greeted by the awaiting angels, and he is joyously accompanied by all his saints. Each category of these blessed souls receives its proper description as the eye of the imagination sweeps along the magnificent scene. This glorious march into heaven is obviously reminiscent of what the preachers imagined a Roman triumphal procession to have been, but *quanto magis* did the heavenly procession surpass even the most glorious earthly counterpart.[83] Some years later Marcello would use the same device for the feast of All Saints.[84]

We understand, therefore, why certain passages believed to have been written by Saint Bernard might appeal to the preachers. The passage mentioned earlier that was quoted by Lollio and Thegliatius occurs as well in at least three other sermons dealing with Christ's suffering and death.[85]

82. See, e.g., Guglielmus Ioseph, *In Christi ascensione adhortatio* [Rome: E. Silber, after May 24, 1487], Hain-Reichling #9448; Rodrigo Sánchez de Arévalo, "Sermo in die ascensionis," prob. 1456, BAV cod. Vat. lat. 4881, fols. 237ʳ–239ᵛ.

83. Massari, "Oratio pulcherrima de ascensione Christi," Bibl. Estense cod. Alpha Q.6.13, fols. 218ᵛ–229ʳ; Gravina, *Oratio de Christi ad caelos ascensu* [Rome: S. Plannck, 1493], Hain-Cop. #7925.

84. Marcello, *Oratio in die omnium sanctorum.*

85. Carlo Alessandri, *Sermo in die parasceve* [Rome: U. Han, after March 25, 1475], GKW #1225, fol. [10ᵛ]; Martinus de Azpetia, *De passione Domini oratio* [Rome: G. Lauer or E. Silber, after 1492], Hain #2238, fol. [7ᵛ]; Martinus Nimireus, *Sermo de passione Domini* [Rome: E. Silber, after April 3, 1494], Hain-Cop. #11889, fol. [9ᵛ]. For Lollio and Thegliatius, see note 47 above. For some indication of the career of Bernard and his contemporaries during this period, see the two articles by Giles Constable, "The Popularity of Twelfth-Century Spiritual Writers in the Late Middle Ages," *Renaissance Studies in Honor of Hans Baron*, ed. Anthony Molho and John A. Tedeschi (DeKalb, Ill.: Northern Illinois University Press, 1971), 3–28, and "Twelfth-Century Spirituality and the Late Middle Ages," in *Medieval and Renaissance Studies*, ed. O. B. Hardison, Jr., No. 5 (Chapel Hill: University of North Carolina Press, 1971), pp. 27–60; Carl Volz, "Martin Luther's Attitude toward Bernard of Clairvaux," in *Studies in Medieval Cistercian History Presented to Jeremiah F. O'Sullivan*, Cistercian Studies Series, No. 13 (Spencer, Mass.: Cistercian Publications, 1971), pp. 186–204; A. N. S. Lane, "Calvin's Sources of St. Bernard," *Archive for Reformation History*, 67 (1976), 253–83; Charles Stinger, "St. Bernard and Pope Eugenius IV (1431–1447)," in *Cistercian Ideas and Reality*, ed. John R. Sommerfelt, Cis-

We are invited to *look* at the body hanging on the cross—with its arms extended to embrace us, with its head inclined to kiss us, with its heart opened to love us.[86] This author, presumably without the same immersion in classical theory as the preachers, was able to direct the eyes to a poignant scene.

Inghirami utilizes the passage attributed to Bernard in an even more striking way than do the other five preachers. His oration for Good Friday, 1504, fulfills the criteria for Renaissance epideictic. In the closing words Inghirami does not quote Pseudo-Bernard verbatim, but he paraphrases him in a classicizing style, and he addresses the words directly to Julius II. The style would have pleased his hearers, while leaving no doubt in their minds as to the venerable source of which Inghirami's words were more than reminiscent.[87]

In a sense what the preachers were trying to do was re-present the stories, the scenes, and the *res gestae* of the Bible, particularly as these were narrated or suggested by the four Gospels. This results in an interesting correlation between epideictic oratory and the Gospels. Indeed, if the Gospels had to be described in terms of the three classical *genera*, without any recourse to other categories of literary criticism, they would have to be described as pertaining principally to epideictic. This would surely be true of what seems to be the oldest tradition of the Gospels, the so-called Passion-Narratives of the three synoptics. These narratives tell the story and paint the scene. To my knowledge none of the preachers made this correlation explicitly.[88] But the fact that a sixteenth-century Lutheran treatise on preaching emphatically located the four Gospels in

tercian Studies Series, No. 60 (Kalamazoo: Cistercian Publications, 1978), pp. 329–43. See also Erasmus, *Ciceronianus*, ASD I.2, 660, and *Ecclesiastes*, LB, V, 857.

86. With some variation in the five sermons in which this passage is quoted or paraphrased, the Latin text is as follows: "Quis enim, ut Bernardus refert, non rapiatur ad spem impetrandae salutis qui eius attenderit corporis dispositionem? Caput habet inclinandum ad osculandum, manus extensas ad amplectendum, pedes confixos ad nobiscum permanendum, totum denique corpus expositum ad nos redimendum." Even with the generous assistance of Dom Jean Leclercq and of P. H. Dal of the Kartoteek Bernard-Konkordans, I have been unable to locate this quotation in the authentic works of Bernard.

87. "De morte Iesu Christi oratio," BN Paris cod. lat. 7352B, fol. 236^r: "En dispessas habet manus ut te excipiat. En caput deflexit ut osculum porrigat. En apertum latus ostentat ut introducat. En sanguinem aquamque spargit ut abluat. En pedes fixos habet ut expectet. Plura ne dicam, lacrimae me impediunt."

88. There is, however, the suggestive observation of Erasmus, *Ecclesiastes*, LB, V, 983: "Siquidem scriptura similis est insigni picturae, quam quo diutius contemplere, hoc plus videas quod admireris."

the *genus demonstrativum* shows that the correlation is not farfetched.[89]

Of course, not all subjects that the Christian orator wanted to treat lent themselves to the same graphic description as did events from the life of Christ. The medieval treatises on how to preach a thematic sermon, the *Artes Praedicandi*, compiled lists of such subjects. One of these *Artes*, the *Tractatulus solemnis de arte et vero modo praedicandi*, is a representative work. It was compiled by a Dominican under the influence of Aquinas, probably in the late fourteenth or early fifteenth century. It prescribes ten topics as "the principal material of all sermons": God, the devil, the heavenly city, hell, the world, the soul, the body, sin, penance, and virtue.[90] Bernardine of Siena's list, obviously quoted from the Rule of Saint Francis, is shorter and moralistic in emphasis: vices and virtues, punishment and glory.[91]

When we examine the sermons at the papal court, we sense a very different emphasis. In his treatise on letter writing, Brandolini mentions three mysteries that "surpass our understanding" but that certainly must be handled by the preacher: Creation, the Trinity, and the Hypostatic Union.[92] Giles of Viterbo and Ambrogio Massari similarly present us with subjects like these for the Christian theologian and preacher.[93] An anal-

---

89. David Chytraeus, *Praecepta rhetoricae inventionis illustrata multis et utilibus exemplis ex sacra scriptura et Cicerone sumptis* (Wittenberg: J. Crato, 1558), fol. [21ʳ].

90. [Nuremberg: Fr. Creussner, n.d.], Hain #*1358, fol. [3ʳ]. On the *Tractatulus*, see Caplan, *Of Eloquence*, pp. 40–78.

91. "Prologus" of the *Quadragesimale de evangelio aeterno* in *Opera omnia*, III (Quaracchi: Collegium S. Bonaventurae, 1956), 18: "Quae maxime in his quatuor, quae sunt vitia et virtutes, poena et gloria, manifeste comprehenduntur." Chapter IX of the Franciscan Rule (1223) is "De praedicatoribus," in *Seraphicae Legislationis Textus Originales* (Quaracchi: Collegium S. Bonaventurae, 1897), p. 44. St. Francis here prescribes: "Moneo quoque et exhortor eosdem fratres ut in praedicatione quam faciunt sint examinata et casta eorum eloquia, ad utilitatem et aedificationem populi, annuntiando eis vitia et virtutes, poenam et gloriam, cum brevitate sermonis, quia verbum abbreviatum fecit Dominus super terram."

92. See *De ratione scribendi*, p. 95, quoted in note 28 above.

93. See Giles's oration opening the Fifth Lateran Council, 1512, Mansi, 32, 670, now in the critical edition by Clare O'Reilly, " 'Without Councils We Cannot Be Saved': Giles of Viterbo Addresses the Fifth Lateran Council," *Augustiniana*, 27 (1977), 166–204, esp. 188: "Verum quod ratione dicimus, ut etiam experimento probemus, cogitandum nobis est tres esse credendarum rerum radices, e quibus universa ecclesiae fides manat. Prima divinae naturae unitas est; altera eadem in natura parentis, sobolis, amoris felicissima Trinitas; tertia in Virginis utero prolis divinae conceptio. In quibus, veluti in altissimis apicibus ac sanctissimis montibus, et reliquae fidei partes novem et pietas universa fundata est." See Massari's Commentary on the third "Rule" of St. Augustine in his *Vita praecellentissimi ecclesiae doctoris divi Aurelii Augustini. Commentarii super regula sancti Augustini* (Rome: G. Herolt, 1481), Hain #*5683, fol. [209ᵛ], where he singles out the Trinity and the Incarnation as the special

ysis of the actual sermons discloses that the preachers tended to concentrate on the great mysteries of the Christian religion, viz., Creation, the Fall, the Incarnation and Redemption, Providence or God's harmonious governance of the universe. Many of the subjects listed by the *Tractatulus* disappear, and the rest are articulated much differently.

Other subjects like purgatory, papal primacy, Mariological issues, and so forth receive no particular attention. The sacraments themselves are rarely treated *in extenso*, though Baptism and the Eucharist are often dealt with in passing. Certain subjects for which the medieval friars were famous, even notorious, for all practical purposes do not occur. I refer to things like relics, indulgences, pilgrimages, and miracle stories. The preachers eschewed "the obscure" and "the disputed" and secondary questions in order to embrace what was in their opinion central and essential.[94] In actual fact, the doctrines that so often engaged the preachers' attention constitute the central Christian mysteries as found in the New Testament and especially as they were propounded by the Fathers and the councils of the Early Church. If Humanism's well-known "weakness for general ideas" is operative here, it is in this instance a weakness that functioned in a way that many Christians could applaud.

But how could great mysteries "surpassing our understanding" be treated in epideictic fashion? Apart from those related to Creation and to the life of Christ, they are abstract and even metaphysical. In actual fact, these mysteries often could not be treated in an epideictic style insofar as that style implied an analogy with the painter's art. The orators at the court endeavored to make these mysteries immediate and relevant to their listeners, but, at the same time, they generally had to resort to standard theological doctrine in treating them. The treatment was different, how-

---

mysteries of the Christian religion. For Traversagni's list, see note 29 above. Trinkaus points out, *Image and Likeness*, I, 142, that Lorenzo Valla judged that "God's benefits in particular to man which are manifested through the Scriptures" were "Divine Providence, the Incarnation and Atonement, Salvation." Melanchthon, in contrast, removes these mysteries, at least in their scholastic mode, from the materials proper to the Christian theologian and preacher, and emphasizes much different ones in his *Loci communes* of 1521. See *Melanchthons Werke in Auswahl*, ed. Robert Stupperich, II.1 (Gütersloh: C. Bertelsmann Verlag, 1952), 5–8.

94. See, e.g., Filippi, "Oratio dominica de Trinitate," 1513, in *Orationes novem coram Iulio II et Leone X*, fol. [4^{r-v}], and Campano, "De Spiritu sancto," undated, in *Opera*, fol. [82^v]: " . . . ita de Spiritu sancto putavi disserendum ut quae alta atque obscura videantur relinquens, aperta explorataque complectar." Paul of Rome's (Paulus de Roma, O.E.S.A.) undated sermon for a *cappella* on the origin and nature of the devils' power is a notable exception as regards subject matter, ["De origine, natura et potestate daemonum"], BAV cod. Ross. 685, fols. 134^r–137^v.

ever, from a thematic treatment. According to Brandolini, the epideictic preacher's treatment was different because his purpose was different.[95] He was not trying to expound these mysteries as in a classroom, nor was he trying to refute heretical adversaries to them. By his orthodox, yet attractive, presentation, he was trying to move his listeners to wonder, to love, to admiration, and to praise. He ascended the pulpit to celebrate the truth, not to prove it.

6. Purpose

Purpose, therefore, is the most important of our categories of analysis, for it is purpose which orders and gives direction to all the other elements which constitute an oration. This point certainly need not be labored. Perhaps the most helpful service which can be performed at this point is to complete the vocabulary of epideictic words by listing the verbs of purpose.

These verbs are critically important, for they set the mood as well as the purpose of epideictic—*venerari, admirari, gratulari,* and *laudare.* The psychological relationship between admiration, gratitude, love, and praise is explicitly touched upon by Brandolini's treatise and assumed by the preachers.[96] In different but related ways they are all reactions to *beneficia.*

They are reactions which spark a further reaction—*gaudere* and *delectari.* The truth of God's great deeds, a truth undisputed and conveying a message of love, moves the listener to enjoyment and delight, to *fruitio* and to *voluptas.*[97] Thus is evoked the final epideictic emotion, the desire

95. See *De ratione scribendi,* pp. 94–97, quoted in part in note 28 above.

96. See *ibid.,* e.g., pp. 122, 124, 167–72. Typical examples of these correlations are found in Domenichi, "Epistola ad Hermolaum Barbarum," BAV cod. Ottob. lat. 1035, fol. 36ʳ⁻ᵛ, and "Oratio ad clerum et populum Brixiensem," *ibid.,* fol. 42ʳ⁻ᵛ.

97. One of the strongest expressions of this emphasis on *gaudium, fruitio,* etc., occurs in A. Brandolini's "De laudibus beatissimi patris Sixti IV pontificis maximi libri." Brandolini makes the point that, whereas in earlier times men had to search for the truth and dispute about it, in the Christian era men are to enjoy it. BAV cod. Urb. lat. 739, fols. 64ᵛ–65ʳ: "Huc accedit sanctissima religio nostra et immortalis Dei verissima certissimaque notitia, qua una re et hi qui caruerunt miserrimi et nos quibus perfrui concessum est haberi possumus felicissimi. Hinc enim virtutum omnium fructus dignissimus uberrimusque percipitur, hinc certa malorum bonorumque scientia, hinc illa quam tanto studio, tot praeceptis, tam multis voluminibus, tam multis saeculis veteres indagavere felicitas, hinc denique illa de qua prisci tantopere dubitabant, de qua tam multis cum argumentis tum rationibus sententiisque disserebant, quam et illi invenire magnopere cupiebant et mortales omnes cupere atque optare summo studio debent, hinc illa inquam immortalitas certissima comparatur." Massari in his *opusculum* "De animae dignitatibus," dedicated to Francesco Piccolomini, makes a similar point. Though he could use arguments and authorities to prove the soul's immortality, he will in the present instance let them delight him

to imitate what is loved and seen as beautiful and beneficent—*imitari*. Under the influence of the *ars laudandi*, the Christian begins to practice the most perfect art of all—the *ars bene beateque vivendi*.[98] In the practice of this art, he brings to fulfillment his own great dignity, "the dignity of man." *Dignitas* and *praestantia* close the vocabulary.

When the words just mentioned occur in some conjunction with each other, the preachers have in mind an epideictic purpose, and they are trying to create an epideictic mood. When words like *docere, probare, explicare,* and *disputare* occur, the preachers reveal that the sermon is thematic. Sometimes the preachers do not so clearly betray what they hope to accomplish in their sermons, and they may use neutral expressions like *verba facere*. Often enough in these cases the purpose is mixed, even confused, and at times it is difficult to determine it with any final certitude. The crucial importance of attempting to determine it, however, should be obvious by now, at the end of our six-point analysis.

The analysis can perhaps best be completed by a synthetic description of the "model epideictic." By reviewing each of the six points and extracting from them those qualities that seem most characteristic of the epideictic form, the model is constructed. The "perfect epideictic" will be an oration whose purpose is to evoke sentiments of admiration, gratitude, and praise, which in turn will lead to a desire for imitation. The materials most appropriate for exciting such sentiments are great deeds, especially the great deeds of God done on man's behalf, and these should be presented to the listener in the most visual and graphic fashion possible. But whatever the materials presented, they should be important in themselves and made relevant to the lives of the listeners. Since the whole oration is directed to these clear purposes, it will enjoy the literary unity which is required by them and, for this reason as well as others, it will abandon the thematic structure. The high purposes of epideictic mean that its vocabulary and syntax will be dignified, but its congratulatory mood allows, even enjoins, at least moments of lyric. In all its moments,

---

"ad persuadendum." That is to say, "In eis gloriari conabor." Bibl. Ang. cod. lat. 835, III, fol. 17^{r-v}.

98. Cf. Cicero, *Off.* I.6.19: ". . . ad bene beateque vivendum." Cf. also *Tusc.* V. 1ff. Cicero makes an explicit connection between epideictic's "praise and blame" and "honorable living" in *Part. Or.* 70: "Ac laudandi vituperandique rationes, quae non ad bene dicendum solum sed etiam ad honeste vivendum valent, exponam breviter atque a principiis exordiar et laudandi et vituperandi." See Donald Lemen Clark, *Rhetoric in Greco-Roman Education* (New York: Columbia University Press, 1957), esp. pp. 133-36.

however, as it seeks to give pleasure to the senses by its sound, it will seek to give pleasure to the soul by its message.

This "model epideictic" accomplishes, it is to be hoped, one of the initial tasks I proposed: the creation of an instrument to test the relationship between Scholasticism and Humanism as illustrated in the sacred oratory of the court. The point-by-point analysis, meanwhile, has begun to reveal what in actual fact Scholasticism and Humanism meant in one specific set of circumstances and how they functioned. Later chapters will provide further details. Meanwhile, it is important to understand why it was the epideictic form that won approval at the court.

First of all, it is inconceivable that the Renaissance revival of ancient rhetoric would not have an impact on preaching at the court, where so many persons were enthusiastic about it. At times the preachers protest that they do not want to distort the simple Christian message by the orator's art, but this protestation is generally lip service paid to a familiar misgiving.[99] Inghirami wards off objections to rhetoric with the traditional argument that Ambrose, Augustine, and Jerome used it. Then comes his most telling point: not to use it, but to rely on the Holy Spirit to perform the orator's task for him, would be superstitious.[100] His apologia would fall on willing ears.

Rhetoric, then, but why epideictic rhetoric? Why not the "persuasion" of deliberative oratory? The preachers knew that deliberative oratory's persuasion was meant for a deliberative body. It looked to a communal decision —indeed, to a communal decision in a political setting. The sacred orators at the court did not hesitate to apply the principles of deliberative oratory, for instance, when they addressed the cardinals about to enter conclave. But this was not the kind of persuasion in which they were engaged *inter missarum solemnia.* The chapel was not a senate or a council chamber.[101] The preachers therefore judged that classical theory left them only

99. See, e.g., Martino de Viana, *Oratio in die cinerum* [Rome: S. Plannck, 1496], Cop. #6198, fol. [1ᵛ]; de Viana, *Oratio in festo divi Thomae de Aquino* [Rome: S. Plannck, 1496], Cop. #6199, fol. [1ʳ]; de Viana, *Oratio de Christi ad caelos ascensione* [Rome: n. publ., 1494], Cop. #6197, fol. [1ᵛ]; Mathias de Canali, *Oratio cinerum* [Rome: J. Besicken, 1503/4], fols. [1ʳ, 2ᵛ]. For the ancient roots of the problem, see James J. Murphy, "Saint Augustine and the Debate about a Christian Rhetoric," *Quarterly Journal of Speech,* 46 (1960), 400–410, and Erich Auerbach, "Sermo Humilis," in *Literary Language and Its Public in Late Latin Antiquity and in the Middle Ages,* trans. Ralph Manheim (London: Routledge and Kegan Paul, 1965), pp. 25–66.

100. See "Rhetorica," BAV cod. Ottob. lat. 1485, fol. 10ᵛ.

101. Traversagni's statement is apposite, "In novam rhetoricam," BAV cod. Vat. lat. 11441, fol. 48ʳ: "Demonstrativum vero genus, quamquam nullum determinatum locum sibi vendicet, tum in ecclesiis frequentissime exercetur . . . ."

epideictic oratory for a *cappella*. If "persuasion" is understood in the generic sense of simply "to move," then it applies to epideictic (and judicial) oratory as well as to deliberative. Thus the preachers engaged in the art of persuasion, though not in the technically more restricted "persuasion" of the second *genus*.

One of the great advantages of epideictic oratory, as a matter of fact, was the very breadth of its scope. In that I have until this point somewhat minimized the instructional element in epideictic, I have been doing the *genus* a disservice. "Impressing ideas," after all, can be taken as almost synonymous for some forms of teaching. Moreover, epideictic theory made generous provision for exhortation, for the giving of counsel, and, of course, for admonition. Blame was to be distributed as well as praise. This aspect of epideictic has important repercussions, obviously, for the question of reform. In brief, the preachers judged that their use of epideictic accorded with the theory of the three *genera*. More important, they knew that epideictic oratory offered them the broad scope needed in the art of preaching.

The preachers' adaptation differs, nonetheless, from Erasmus's location of preaching principally in the *genus deliberativum* and from the understanding he seems to have as to how Christian "persuasion" functions. The insistent importance he attaches to teaching and to exhortation was surely a point well scored. The decision-provoking nature of deliberative oratory's rationale could stand the Christian preacher in good stead. Moreover, Erasmus could find some basis for his position in the most revered of all handbooks for Christian preachers, Augustine's *De Doctrina Christiana*.[102]

102. See *De Doctr. Christ.*, IV.12–13 (27–29), where Augustine emphasizes the persuasive element in preaching, without speaking explicitly of the *genera*. On the other hand, he clearly provides a place for demonstrative oratory for "praising God in himself and in his works," *ibid.*, IV.19 (38). See also *ibid.*, IV.26 (57). It is important to note that Augustine uses the notion of "persuasion" in a broad sense to apply to teaching and to "praising and blaming," as well as to an oration which has moving to an action as a goal. *Ibid.*, IV.25 (55). In context, Augustine is trying to correlate the plain, moderate, and grand styles of speaking to the three purposes of sacred oratory: teaching, praising and blaming, moving to action. On Augustine, Erasmus, and a general tendency of sixteenth-century theory on preaching in northern Europe to emphasize teaching and dialectics, see John S. Chamberlin, *Increase and Multiply: Arts-of-Discourse Procedure in the Preaching of Donne* (Chapel Hill: University of North Carolina Press, 1976), esp. pp. 18–34, 67–91. The general study of Augustine's influence on Erasmus is Charles Béné's *Érasme et Saint Augustin, ou Influence de Saint Augustin sur l'Humanisme d'Érasme*, Travaux d'Humanisme et Renaissance, No. 103 (Geneva: Droz, 1969), esp. pp. 372–425 on the *De Doctrina Christiana* and *Ecclesiastes*. Also to be consulted, however, is André Godin, "Érasme et le

The weakness of Erasmus's adaptation is that it tends to focus the preacher's attention on instructional, moralistic, and exhortatory purposes. Aside from the question of how faithfully his adaptation corresponds to classical theory, it situates the sermon in a narrower and less expansive context than does demonstrative oratory. In some ways it is close to the intents of thematic preaching. Without entering into further discussion about whether the more authentic adaptation of classical theory to the Christian pulpit lay in deliberative or demonstrative oratory, we should simply recognize that in both instances we have an *adaptation*. We must also recognize that the variation in these and similar adaptations tells us something about the theological viewpoint and religious feelings of those making the adaptation. It might also relate to the kind of biblical sources the preacher especially favored, e.g., the arguments of the Pauline epistles or the stories of the Gospels.

As regards "moving" the Christian to a better way of life, the theory of demonstrative oratory rested to a large extent on the premise that its techniques were devised precisely to facilitate such a process. Raphael Brandolini, Aurelio's younger brother and also a figure at the court, merely gave expression to traditional theory when he observed the impact that praise of an individual could have in moving him to virtue, even when the individual may not in every respect deserve the praise he received. Praise was sometimes thinly disguised blame, as the individual was made to see the ideal of what he ought to be.[103] Aurelio, in his turn, realized the psychological advantages that the desire to praise and speak well of others could have for the preacher or writer himself. We are much too prone, he noted, to criticize and to find fault.[104] Praise, in other words, is a healthy corrective even for the person giving expression to it. Some preachers correlated the practice of praise with the Christian message of God's love and of the love that therefore should exist among men.[105]

But the defensiveness of the preachers on the whole question of "flattery" demonstrates that they were aware of the pitfalls of insincerity and

---

modèle origénien de la prédication," in *Colloquia Erasmiana Turonensia*, ed. J.-C. Margolin, 2 vols. (Toronto: University of Toronto Press, 1972), II, 807–20.

103. "De musica et poetica opusculum," Bibl. Casan. cod. 805, fols. 81^v–82^r. See also, e.g., Domenichi, "Oratio ad clerum et populum Brixiensem," BAV cod. Ottob. lat. 1035, fol. 42^r, and esp. Erasmus's letter to John Desmarais, 1504, in *Opus Epistolarum*, ed. P. S. and H. M. Allen, I (Oxford: Clarendon, 1906), 398–403, and the discussion of the theory in Garrison, *Dryden*, esp. pp. 46–63.

104. See *De ratione scribendi*, pp. 104–5, 120.

105. See, e.g., Domenichi, "Epistola ad Hermolaum Barbarum," BAV cod. Ottob. lat. 1035, fol. 36^v.

servility that abounded in the art of praise.[106] Outside the liturgy, the atmosphere of the court seems to have done little to safeguard its members from these pitfalls and, as in most monarchies, it extended to epideictic oratory a welcome suspiciously warm. Furthermore, epideictic blunted the drive for decision typical of the other two *genera*. Confrontation was hardly its first impulse. And this could have repercussions even for sermons. With ease and good grace the preacher could skirt hard issues. Most dangerous of all, he might skirt them without even realizing that the literary form he adopted had dulled his sensibility about his duty to face them.

In the preachers' minds, however, whatever dangers might lurk in the art of praise were exorcised when that art turned to God. He is the object upon which the sermons *inter missarum solemnia* lavished their praise. In that setting the ambitions of Nicholas V and his successors to adorn their court with all that was dignified and beautiful would be fulfilled in the most fitting way, as the best oratorical form, i.e., a form sanctioned by classical antiquity, was employed in the most solemn and dignified situation, the sacred liturgy.

If we wish to add a further reason why the preachers might turn to epideictic oratory as to their appropriate *genus*, we should recall the convergence in mood of epideictic and the liturgy. The liturgy was a celebration and, more emphatically, a celebration which was thanksgiving—Eucharist.[107] "Lift up your hearts," the celebrant sang as he began the most sacred part of the service. Why? In order to "give thanks to the Lord, our God." The traditional description of the Mass as a "sacrifice of praise," a description recited in the Canon of every Mass, was employed by some of the preachers, and the appropriateness of an oration of praise in a ceremony of praise would not be lost on them.[108] The lyrical and

106. See, e.g., A. Brandolini, *De ratione scribendi*, pp. 107–8, 118–19, 126, 168; de Viana, *In die cinerum*, fol. [1ᵛ]; Alexis Celadoni, *Oratio ad sacrum cardinalium senatum* [Rome: J. Besicken, 1503], fol. [1ʳ], now in a modern edition by John McManamon, "Ideal Renaissance Pope," pp. 62–70, esp. 62.

107. See Joseph A. Jungmann, *The Mass of the Roman Rite: Its Origins and Development (Missarum Solemnia)*, trans. Francis A. Brunner, 2 vols. (New York: Benziger Brothers, 1951–55), and by the same author, *The Early Liturgy to the Time of Gregory the Great*, trans. Francis A. Brunner (Notre Dame, Ind.: Notre Dame University Press, 1959); S. J. P. van Dijk and J. Hazelden Walker, *The Origins of the Modern Roman Liturgy: The Liturgy of the Papal Court and the Franciscan Order in the Thirteenth Century* (Westminster, Md.: The Newman Press, 1960).

108. See, e.g., Nicolò Palmeri's sermon for a pope sometime in the 1450's or 1460's, ["De sacrificio"], BAV cod. Vat. lat. 5815, fols. 45ʳ, 46ᵛ; Dominichi, "Oratio in laudem beatissimae Catherinae de Senis," BAV cod. Ottob. lat. 1035, fols. 18ᵛ–19ʳ; B. Carvajal,

artistic element in epideictic harmonized with the mood of a Solemn Mass, where so much of the ceremony was sung. The Gospel passage, upon which the sermon in one way or another was supposed to be based, was itself set to music.

Epideictic, finally, solved some practical problems. It provided an alternative to the highly criticized thematic sermons, which were displeasing not only because of their "barbarous" Latin but also because they were simply boring. Even the uninspired Franciscan procurator general during the pontificate of Paul II—whom we shall have to call Francis of Assisi because that was his name—saw the problem. It was pointless, he stated, to discourse on the mysteries of the Christian religion before the professed Christians of the papal court. It was senseless to waste time persuading believers to belief. In effect Francis was saying that there was no profit in instructing the learned men of the court in the same lessons in theology year after year.[109] Francis's solution to the problem was to launch into tiresomely moralistic exhortations. But there is evidence, if we need any, that as early as Francis's day scolding the listeners and deploring the calamities of the times wearied the court as much as a lecture in theology.[110] Epideictic oratory was, therefore, a needed and welcome relief from the tedium seen as almost inherent in the traditional forms of preaching. As should be clear by now, however, its novelty possessed other, much more profound dimensions.

Oratio de eligendo summo pontifice [Rome: E. Silber, c.1493], GKW #6152, fol. [6ʳ⁻ᵛ]. As Kustas says so well about ekphrasis, *Byzantine Rhetoric*, p. 58: "The opportunity which the ἔκφρασις offered for evoking the inner experience of the beholder before the sacred objects of his religion made it a popular literary form in Byzantium. It is received early into the homily, and whole sermons are in form actually ἐκφράσεις of a new church or an especially beautiful set of icons or mosaics. If we recall that the homily is part of the liturgical drama, we can appreciate the contribution which the ἔκφρασις made to the beauty of the divine service and its effect on the emotions of those participating in it."

109. "Oratio de iustitia servanda," for Paul II, second Sunday of Advent, year unspecified, BAV cod. Vat. lat. 14063, fols. 21ᵛ–22ᵛ.

110. See Gherardi, *Diario*, second Sunday of Lent, 1481, p. 40: "Omeliam eius diei oravit Petrus a Vigevano Insubrorum oppido, ex Minorum religione et sui ordinis in Romana curia procurator. Cum attentione fuit auditus, quippe qui graviter et ornate admodum dixit, nec, ut plerumque accidit, nimius in dicendo fuit, nec praesentium temporum calamitatem deploravit, nec in nostros corruptos mores invectus est, quae plurimum audientibus molesta esse consueverunt."

CHAPTER THREE. ORATORS AND PREACHERS: IN HOC DICENDI MUNERE

Though epideictic oratory had considerable significance at the papal court during the Renaissance, it was imported there from elsewhere. The *genus* was first revived outside Rome and first applied to sacred subjects outside Rome. Before we begin the "case studies" of the preachers, we might try to gather together some information on that revival and its Christian adaptations. The information will provide a sense of location in the larger culture of the Quattrocento. It will be a modest, but in some instances a corrective, supplement to major studies of the history of oratory in Italy like Galletti's. This information will also suggest some of the avenues by which epideictic arrived at the papal court.

Epideictic oratory flourished in Italy in the Quattrocento. We have in print and in manuscript a truly vast number of orations given on ceremonial occasions like weddings, funerals, and the opening of the academic year. The best known example of epideictic literature in the early part of the century is Leonardo Bruni's *Laudatio* in praise of Florence, now dated 1403–4 by Hans Baron. Despite the large volume of epideictic works surviving from the Quattrocento, Bruni's is one of the very few to have aroused any scholarly interest. This interest has been directed, however, almost exclusively to content and not to the epideictic form, even though scholarship has long recognized that the *Laudatio* was inspired by the epideictic oration *Panathenaicus* of the sophist Aelius Aristides composed in the middle of the second century.[1]

1. See Baron's *Humanistic and Political Literature in Florence and Venice at the Beginning of the Quattrocento: Studies in Criticism and Chronology* (Cambridge: Harvard University Press, 1955); *The Crisis of the Early Italian Renaissance: Civic Humanism and Republican Liberty in an Age of Classicism and Tyranny*, rev. ed. (Princeton: Princeton University Press, 1966); and *From Petrarch to Leonardo Bruni: Studies in Humanistic and Political Literature* (Chicago: University of Chicago Press, 1968), which contains the edition of Bruni's *Laudatio* to which I shall refer, pp. 232–63. An edition of the *Laudatio* is also contained in Vittorio Zaccaria, "Pier Candido Decembrio e Leonardo Bruni (Notizie dall'epistolario del Decembrio)," *Studi medievali*, 3 ser., 8 (1967), 504–54, esp. 529–54. There is now an English translation, with an introduction by Ronald G. Witt, in *The Earthly Republic: Italian Humanists on Government and Society*, ed. Benjamin G. Kohl et al. (Philadelphia: University of Pennsylvania Press, 1978), pp. 119–75.

The form of the *Laudatio* deserves examination. If the *Laudatio* is subjected to the test of the epideictic vocabulary compiled in the last chapter, it responds positively in every instance. If it is compared with the coronation oration of Petrarch in 1341, it immediately manifests how much change had been wrought in the practice of eloquence since the day the Father of Humanism received the laurel wreath. Petrarch's oration reveals strong thematic influences, whereas Bruni's *Laudatio* reveals none.[2]

Pier Candido Decembrio's *Panegyricus* of Milan was influenced by Bruni's *Laudatio*, though not written until 1436 and used to counter it.[3] Like the *Laudatio*, it is thoroughly epideictic. It thus differs very much from the *De magnalibus urbis Mediolani* written by Bonvesin della Riva in 1288. Della Riva's *De magnalibus* tries to prove Milan's greatness, and the thematic verbs of proving and explaining appear throughout the text.[4] I submit that the medieval character of this work, in contrast with the Renaissance character of the works by Decembrio and Bruni, is as effectively shown by such an analysis as by an analysis of content.[5]

Unlike della Riva, Decembrio and Bruni do not search for proofs. They invite us to gaze upon and contemplate the beauty of their respective cities and the deeds of their great men. The excellence of Milan and Florence does not need to be argued.[6] The very sight of them and their citizens authenticates their *dignitas*, their *pulchritudo*, their *amoenitas*. Praise is evoked by this vision of beauty and virtue. Here is the critical point where

2. The Latin text is available in *Scritti inediti di Francesco Petrarca*, ed. Attilio Hortis (Trieste: Lloyd, 1874), pp. 311–28. Ernest Hatch Wilkins provides an English translation in his *Studies in the Life and Works of Petrarch* (Cambridge: Mediaeval Academy of America, 1955), pp. 300–13.

3. See Giuseppe Petraglione, "Il 'De laudibus Mediolanensium urbis panegyricus' di P. C. Decembrio," *Archivio Storico Lombardo*, ser. IV, vol. VII [anno XXXIV] (1907), 5–45, which contains the text on pp. 27–45. See also Zaccaria, "Decembrio e Bruni."

4. "De magnalibus urbis Mediolani," ed. Francesco Novati, in *Bollettino dell'Istituto Storico Italiano*, No. 20 (Rome: Istituto Storico Italiano, 1898).

5. See, e.g., Antonio Stäuble, "Due panegirici di città tra Medioevo e Rinascimento," *Bibliothèque d'Humanisme et Renaissance*, 38 (1976), 157–64. Stäuble sees the difference between della Riva and Bruni as political and contentual, and while acknowledging the influence of Aristides on Bruni, describes the form of della Riva's and Bruni's compositions without qualification as "un genere letterario diffuso nell' Antichità come nel Medioevo e nel Rinascimento," p. 157. On the other hand, for the impact of epideictic and ekphrasis on medieval literature, see Ernst Robert Curtius, *European Literature in the Latin Middle Ages*, trans. Willard R. Trask, Bollingen Series, No. 36 (New York: Pantheon, 1953), pp. 68–69, 154–59, 176–202.

6. Bruni, *Laudatio*, p. 240: "Haec quidem omnibus nota sunt et ante oculos exposita, nec demonstratione ulla indigent."

a correlation between the sacred eloquence of the *cappelle* and the secular eloquence of Decembrio and Bruni is verified.

The question recurs: whence this Renaissance emphasis on vision and contemplation? Michael Baxandall sees Manuel Chrysoloras as the transmitter to the West of the rhetorical principles of Hermogenes of Tarsus, the most widely studied authority on rhetoric in Byzantium. He indicates that it was from this source that interest was first aroused in ekphrasis, that is, in Hermogenes' words: "An account with detail; it is visible, so to speak, and brings before the eyes that which is to be shown. . . . The style must bring about seeing through hearing."[7] Bruni studied Greek with Chrysoloras, of course, and so did Guarino of Verona.[8] Decembrio's father had been a disciple of Chrysoloras. But no matter what role the Byzantine emphasis on ekphrasis played in helping focus attention on the painting-oratory analogy of the classical tradition, Baxandall has clearly demonstrated that that analogy was operative on a broad scale among humanists in the first half of the Quattrocento.

By means of this somewhat circuitous route of Bruni, Decembrio, and Guarino, we are beginning at any rate to approach the papal court. Decembrio was called to Rome in 1450 by Nicholas V as a "magister brevium," a position he held well into the pontificate of Calixtus III. Much earlier, in 1405, Bruni had been appointed a papal secretary by Innocent VII, and he served in that office for ten years, though we are only slightly informed about his professional duties in the Curia during that period.[9]

7. *Giotto and the Orators: Humanist Observers of Painting in Italy and the Discovery of Pictorial Composition, 1350–1450* (Oxford: Clarendon Press, 1971), esp. pp. 62–96. The quotation from Hermogenes occurs on p. 85. On Hermogenes, see George Kustas, *Studies in Byzantine Rhetoric*, Analecta Vlatadon, No. 17 (Thessalonica: Patriarchal Institute, 1973), pp. 5–26, and on George of Trebizond's important role in the diffusion of his teaching, see John Monfasani, *George of Trebizond: A Biography and a Study of His Rhetoric and Logic*, Columbia Studies in the Classical Tradition, No. 1 (Leiden: Brill, 1976), pp. 17–18, 248–99, 322–27. See also Annabel M. Patterson, *Hermogenes and the Renaissance: Seven Ideas of Style* (Princeton: Princeton University Press, 1970). Chrysoloras's *laudatio* of Rome and Constantinople, in the Latin translation of 1444, is permeated with the idea that it is the beauty of the two cities that evokes admiration and, hence, praise. "Urbis Romae et Constantinopolis laudatio ab Francisco Aleardo Veronensi in latinum conversa," BAV cod. Reg. lat. 807, fols. 24ʳ–59ᵛ.

8. Ian Thompson questions whether Guarino brought back from Constantinople the large number of Greek manuscripts usually assigned him. "Some Notes on the Contents of Guarino's Library," *Renaissance Quarterly*, 29 (1976), 169–77.

9. See Gordon Griffiths, "Leonardo Bruni and the Restoration of the University of Rome (1406)," *Renaissance Quarterly*, 26 (1973), 1–10.

We do know, on the other hand, that his *Laudatio* influenced the young Aeneas Silvius Piccolomini in the composition of his second description of Basel in 1438. It is likely that the future pope at the same time also had a copy of Decembrio's *Panegyricus*.[10]

In the previous year, 1437, Aeneas Silvius had delivered during the Council of Basel a panegyric in honor of Saint Ambrose.[11] Although there are in this oration certain "Christian" modifications of the classical *topoi*, the structure, purpose, and vocabulary are otherwise thoroughly classical, without a suggestion of any thematic features. The oration is professedly "joyful" and meant "to be heard with joy," as Ambrose is congratulated and his praises recounted. It surely comes as no surprise that Aeneas Silvius was at this early date already adept at both secular and sacred epideictic, but simply mentioning the description of Basel and the oration on Ambrose lends specificity to those gifts of eloquence for which he was so much esteemed by his contemporaries. It was these gifts and these

10. See Berthe Widmer, "Enea Silvios Lob der Stadt Basel und seine Vorlagen," *Basler Zeitschrift für Geschichte und Altertumskunde*, 58–59 (1959), 111–38.

11. "Oratio II. Habita Basileae in divi Ambrosii celebritate," in *Pii II P. M., olim Aeneae Sylvii Piccolominei Senensis, orationes politicae et ecclesiasticae*, ed. Giovanni Domenico Mansi, 2 vols. (Lucca: P. M. Benedinus, 1755–57), I, 38–52, henceforth *Orationes*. Jacob Burckhardt calls attention to this panegyric in *The Civilization of the Renaissance in Italy*, trans. S. G. C. Middlemore, 2 vols. (New York: Harper and Row, 1958), I, 240: "It struck the non-Italian members of the Council of Basel as something strange that the Archbishop of Milan should summon Aeneas Sylvius, who was then unordained, to deliver a public discourse at the feast of St. Ambrogius; but they suffered it in spite of the murmurs of the theologians, and listened to the speaker with the greatest curiosity." For further information on the sermons at the Council, see Johannes Baptist Schneyer, "Baseler Konzilspredigten aus dem Jahre 1432," in *Von Konstanz nach Trient: Festgabe für August Franzen*, ed. Remigius Bäumer (Munich: Schöningh, 1972), pp. 139–145, and Adolar Zumkeller, "Der Augustinermagister Nicolinus von Cremona und seine Septuagesimapredigt auf dem Baseler Konzil," *Annuarium Historiae Conciliorum*, 3 (1971), 29–70. For the Council of Constance, see Paul Arendt, *Die Predigten des Konstanzer Konzils: Ein Beitrag zur Predigt- und Kirchengeschichte des ausgehenden Mittelalters* (Freiburg: Herder, 1933); Heinrich Finke, *Acta Concilii Constanciensis* (Münster: Regensberg Buchh., 1923), II, 367–545; Johannes Baptist Schneyer, "Konstanzer Konzilspredigten: Eine Ergänzung zu H. Finke's Sermones- und Handschriftenlisten," *Zeitschrift für die Geschichte des Oberrheins*, 113 (1965), 361–88; and Adolar Zumkeller, "Unbekannte Konstanzer Konzilspredigten der Augustiner-Theologen Gottfried Shale und Dietrich Vrie," *Analecta Augustiniana*, 33 (1970), 5–74. According to Arendt, pp. 33–60, the sermons for Sundays and feast days at Constance were invariably thematic in form. However, the Fathers of the Council certainly were exposed to the revived epideictic in Poggio Bracciolini's funeral eulogy of Cardinal Zabarella, Sept. 27, 1417. For that oration, see *Opera omnia*, Monumenta Politica et Philosophica Rariora, ed. Luigi Firpo, Ser. 2, No. 6, 2 vols., (I=1538; rpt. Turin: Bottega d'Erasmo, 1964–66, ed. Riccardo Fubini), I, 252–61. By early the next year, Guarino had a copy of this eulogy, *ibid.*, II, 10.

standards of oratorical excellence he would bring to Rome with him as pope in 1458.

We have from this great humanist, however, no oration applying epideictic to God, and his oration to his flock at Asbach in the diocese of Passau, 1445, bears no resemblance to "model epideictic."[12] This oration is a discourse on the Christian life, with heavy moral emphasis. Aeneas obviously viewed his pastoral care in traditional terms of promoting the virtues and eradicating the vices of his flock. The content of this oration corresponds by and large to the "vices and virtues" which Bernardine of Siena proposed as the preacher's materials.

Aeneas's most celebrated oration is the one he as pope addressed to the Congress of Mantua in 1459 urging a war against the Turks.[13] The oration is conceived as pertaining to the *genus deliberativum*, as the *divisio* indicates beyond any doubt. Though not epideictic, this oration is an indisputable example of a classical *genus* self-consciously used by a pope.

But when a few years later in 1461 he delivered his brief oration at the canonization of Catherine of Siena, he began with what might be designated three thematic or scholastic "questions": (1) what does the word sanctity mean? (2) why was canonization introduced into the Church? (3) is Catherine worthy of the honor of canonization?[14] In answering the last question, Pius describes her sanctity principally in terms of monastic virtues and "contempt of the world." Only at the end is there a call to rejoice, addressed first of all to Catherine's fellow citizens of Siena. As sacred oratory is examined in detail, therefore, it begins to reveal discrepancies from anticipated patterns.

Guarino of Verona's name leads us along a different path. After he had at Chrysoloras's inspiration spent his years in Constantinople, and at Bruni's urging taught in Florence, he went to Venice to teach there from 1414–19. During these years in Venice he had a number of students who would later distinguish themselves in various ways, but one of the names associated with Guarino during these Venetian years is particularly significant for the sacred oratory of the papal court—Pietro del Monte.

Del Monte, born in Venice of an important family just after the turn of the century, was a student of Guarino's for several years, beginning in

12. "Oratio III. In Haspach Pataviensis dioecesis," *Orationes*, I, 53–106.
13. "Oratio II. In conventu Mantuano," *Orationes*, II, 9–29.
14. "Oratio habita in canonizatione beatae Catherinae Senensis," *Orationes*, II, 136–44.

1415. In 1433 he received a doctorate in canon and civil law from Padua. He became an apostolic prothonotary at the court of Eugene IV, bishop of Brescia in 1442, and governor of Perugia in 1451. He died in Rome on January 12, 1457. His was a varied career, in which he exemplified the Renaissance ideal of a combination of public office and dedication to learning. Though he wrote principally on canonical topics, especially in defense of the authority of the pope against the claims of councils and emperors, he was influential in bringing the humanist movement to England during his sojourn there as Papal Collector, 1435–40. He has attracted some attention from modern scholars,[15] and his importance for his own era is demonstrated by the publication of major works like his *Repertorium utriusque iuris* and the *De potestate Romani pontificis et generalis concilii*.[16]

His importance for oratory, however, consists in the fact that his oration for Passion Sunday is the earliest example at the papal court, as far as I know, of a fully epideictic sermon on a Christian mystery. The sermon was probably delivered before Nicholas V in 1450 or 1451, and three manuscript versions of it exist in the Vatican Library.[17] It is remarkable

15. See Agostino Zanelli, *Pietro Del Monte* (Milan: L. F. Cogliati, 1907); *Piero da Monte: Ein Gelehrter und päpstlicher Beamter des 15. Jahrhunderts: Seine Briefsamm-lung hrsg. und erläut. von Johannes Haller*, Bibliothek des deutschen historischen Instituts in Rom, No. 19 (Rome: W. Regenberg, 1941); Agostino Sottili, *Studenti tedeschi e umanesimo italiano nell'Università di Padova durante il Quattrocento: I. Pietro del Monte nella società accademica Padovana (1430–1433)*, Contributi alla storia dell'Università di Padova, No. 7 (Padua: Antenore, 1971); Roberto Weiss, *Humanism in England during the Fifteenth Century* (Oxford: Basil Blackwell, 1957), esp. pp. 24–28.

16. *Repertorium* (Rome: S. Marco, 1476), Hain #*11587; (Nuremberg: A. Frisner de Wunsidel and J. Sensenschmid, 1476), Hain #11588; (Padua: J. Herbort, 1480), Hain #*11589; (Lyons: N. Pistoris and R. de Argentina, 1480), Hain #11590; *De potestate* [Rome: L. Gallus, c.1476], Hain #*11591.

17. "Oratio in dominica quadragesimae quae dicitur de passione," BAV cod. Vat. lat. 2694, fols. 301ʳ–308ᵛ, which is the version I will use; Vat. lat. 373, fols. 83ʳ–94ʳ; Vat. lat. 4872, fols. 334ʳ–348ʳ. Haller, *Piero da Monte*, p. *109, gives 1450 or 1451 as the date. In this last codex there is an oration for the first Sunday of Lent, with many cancellations, insertions, marginal additions, etc., fols. 1ʳ–13ʳ. The *incipit* and the first five folios of this oration correspond very closely to sections of the oration for Passion Sunday. Perhaps del Monte was invited to preach for the first Sunday of Lent, and then the day was later changed to Passion Sunday. He delivered another oration at the court, of which two copies are extant in the BAV, "Oratio in die sancto parasceves," cod. Vat. lat. 4872, fols. 15ʳ–27ʳ, and with corrections, fols. 28ʳ–37ᵛ. This Good Friday oration completely abandons the thematic structure, but the purpose is less clearly epideictic than the oration on Passion Sunday. A number of orations, letters, and other works of del Monte are contained in BAV cod. Vat. lat. 2694. Some of these works are also found in BAV cod. Ottob. lat. 675. Of particular interest is his "De vitiorum inter se differentia et comparatione," written while he was a prothonotary and dedicated to Humphrey, Duke of Gloucester, BAV cod. Vat. lat. 1048. Del Monte did not deliver the funeral oration on the death of Calixtus III,

for fulfilling what is required for "model epideictic." It attempts to present for viewing and for admiration God's great deeds on man's behalf, as the exordium states. The oration itself begins with man's creation in God's image and likeness, and then, after a brief lament over the Fall, it moves to a long consideration of the marvelous mystery of man's restoration when the Word became flesh. As Christ ascends the cross the mystery is completed, and he "draws all things to himself" (John 12:32).[18] "Holy Church," del Monte observes, "is forced to exclaim to God: 'O how marvelous is your care for us, how unlimited your love for us—to redeem a servant you handed over your son.' "[19] The exclamation put into the mouth of the Church is a verbatim quotation from the *Exultet*.

The *Exultet* initiates the Easter season. Here it appears in a Lenten sermon. That fact is important. This early example lucidly demonstrates how epideictic form influences the presentation of Christian mystery. The form conditions the preacher to focus on those mysteries, or on those aspects of the mysteries, that are conducive to exciting sentiments of admiration, gratitude, love, and joy, as is manifested in this sermon dealing with man's Redemption. It is no exaggeration to state that this Lenten sermon, where Adam's Fall and Christ's suffering are treated, is a call to joy. The Fall is subordinated to the theme of man's dignity in his creation as God's image and likeness and to his restoration when the Word became flesh. The cross is presented not as a sign of how grievously sin offends God so as to require such expiation but of how immense is God's love for man and of how excellent is Christ's victory over sin and death. Moreover, the materials with which del Monte deals would satisfy the subject matters proposed by Aurelio Brandolini, Ambrogio Massari, and Giles of Viterbo.

Did Pietro del Monte learn the form from Guarino and also learn from him to apply it to God's deeds? There is at present no conclusive evidence one way or the other, but an affirmative answer to the first part of the question has some likelihood.[20] Regarding the second part, the earliest

---

BAV cod. Vat. lat. 4872, fols. 39ʳ–51ᵛ; see John McManamon, "The Ideal Renaissance Pope: Funeral Oratory from the Papal Court," *Archivum Historiae Pontificiae*, 14 (1976), 9–70, esp. 12–13.

18. BAV cod. Vat. lat. 2694, fol. 306ʳ.

19. *Ibid.*, fol. 307ʳ.

20. Guarino's interest and proficiency in the *genus demonstrativum* has been established by Remigio Sabbadini, *La scuola e gli studi di Guarino Guarini Veronese* (Catania: N. Giannotta, 1896), pp. 59–71, 184–86. There are no sacred orations by Guarino, though he did deliver an inaugural address "De civitate Dei"; see *ibid.*, pp. 67, 139. See also "Oratio in laudibus Augustini de civitate Dei" by the student of

example I have found of such an oration is one on the Circumcision by Gasperino Barzizza.[21]

The oration on the Circumcision is undated. It has never been published or studied, although its existence has long been known.[22] It survives in at least three manuscript versions now found in Venice, Florence, and Rome, and this fact indicates some interest and diffusion.[23] It was written by Barzizza to be delivered by another, by "a certain [Franciscan] friar." The oration is thoroughly epideictic, but less obviously and less exuberantly so than the oration by del Monte. Barzizza's oration conveys the message that Christ is the great victor, who by shedding his blood at his circumcision and on the cross has overcome evil and the devil and thus has set us free. The oration congratulates Christ on his triumph, which is compared with military triumphs from Roman antiquity. The materials covered by Barzizza are obviously less ambitious than those covered by del Monte. Also, applying epideictic to certain events in the life of Christ is less novel than del Monte's application of it to mysteries like Creation and the Incarnation.

The only other sacred oration securely attributed to Barzizza that has come down to us is his panegyric of Saint Francis of Assisi, again written to be delivered by another.[24] It is epideictic, even if it does not follow the chronological *topoi* classical theory suggested. The oration is disappointing, in fact, from the viewpoint of content, since it tells us very little about

---

Guarino, the "adolescens" Bernardus de Lombardis, BAV cod. Ottob. lat. 1267, fols. 180ᵛ–182ʳ (new foliation in pencil, 183ᵛ–185ʳ). See esp. fol. 180ᵛ, where he states Guarino set the subject for his oration. Ludovico Carbone names in his funeral oration for Guarino several preachers, including Bernardine of Siena, who were "ab eo artificiose praedicandi ratione instructos," in Karl Müllner's *Reden und Briefe italienischer Humanisten* (Vienna: A. Hölder, 1899), p. 99. On the preachers mentioned by Carbone, see Sabbadini, *op. cit.*, pp. 140–44. Among them was Timoteo Maffei, who wrote a treatise dedicated to Pope Nicholas V entitled "In sanctam rusticitatem litteras impugnantem."

21. See the article in the DBI by G. Martellotti, with the bibliography indicated there.

22. See Remigio Sabbadini, "Lettere e orazioni edite e inedite di Gasparino [sic] Barzizza," *Archivio Storico Lombardo*, 13 (1886), 828 (#24).

23. "Oratio in circumcisione Domini," Bibl. Marc. cod. lat. XI.21 (3814), fols. 42ʳ–45ᵛ; Bibl. Ang. cod. lat. 1139, fols. 27ᵛ–30ᵛ; Bibl. Ricc. cod. 779, fols. 41ᵛ–43ᵛ. Sabbadini was unaware of the version in the Riccardiana, which appears in the codex without indication of author. I was able to identify it through the *incipit* supplied by Kristeller, *Iter*, I, 201.

24. "Oratio de laudibus beati Francisci ab alio pronunciata," in *Gasparini Barzizii Bergomatis et Guiniforti filii opera*, ed. Giuseppe A. Furietti, 2 vols. in one (Rome: J. M. Salvioni, 1723), I, 45–50.

Francis. Whatever importance it has consists in its being an early example of Christian adaptation of the *genus demonstrativum* by a humanist of note. Since Gasperino died in 1431, this oration certainly antedates the panegyric of Ambrose by Aeneas Silvius Piccolomini in 1437.

In the Biblioteca Angelica in Rome there is an oration addressed to a pope which is without date, title, or indication of author. A date early in the Quattrocento seems likely from the other documents in the codex whose provenance has been established, and many years ago Remigio Sabbadini suggested Barzizza as the author.[25] The orator or preacher, whoever he was, was told by the pope to use the Gospel from the Mass of the day for his material, and from this fact, as well as from other evidence in the text, it is clear that the occasion was the fourth Sunday of Lent.[26] The passage from the Gospel is the feeding of the multitude with five loaves and two fish (John 6:1–14), and in those sections of the oration where it is treated the audience is invited to contemplate and admire the deed.[27] The oration, however, seems largely motivated by admiration of the pope or gratitude to him for some benefit bestowed, probably the "golden rose" which was traditionally conferred on some individual, city, or church on that Sunday in recognition of achievements in favor of the Church.[28] It is thus questionable whether the oration was delivered as a liturgical sermon *inter missarum solemnia*. The orator spends considerable time describing and praising the papal office. The oration, in any event, is almost certainly the earliest, from those I have seen, that attempts *coram papa* to apply the new rhetoric to a text of the Gospels.

The orations in honor of Saint Jerome composed in Padua probably sometime between 1390 and 1397 by the renowned humanist Pier Paolo

---

25. Bibl. Ang. cod. lat. 1139, fols. 4ʳ–6ᵛ, inc. "Verba sunt quantum ego existimo, beatissime pater." See Sabbadini, "Barzizza," p. 831 (#66). The codex, which contains other works certainly composed by Barzizza, was unknown to Furietti when he compiled Barzizza's *Opera*. See Enrico Narducci, *Catalogus codicum manuscriptorum praeter Graecos et Orientales in Bibliotheca Angelica* (Rome: L. Cecchini, 1893), pp. 475–81.

26. Bibl. Ang. cod. lat. 1139, fol. 4ᵛ. Both Sabbadini and Narducci are mistaken when they describe the oration as being about St. Philip. The saint's name appears early in the text simply because of the role he plays in the pericope from the Gospel for the Sunday. See Sabbadini, "Barzizza," p. 831 (#66) and Narducci, *Catalogus*, p. 475 (#2).

27. Bibl. Ang. cod. lat. 1139, fol. 5ʳ: "Verum nescio quid hodie plus vel aedificare possit vel oblectare quam si rem ipsam uti gesta est referente evangelio contemplemur, seu taciti miremur tantae potentiae magnitudinem, seu toto ore unanimes ac devote caelestis gratiae liberalitatem praedicemus."

28. See *ibid.*, fol. 6ᵛ.

Vergerio are the earliest adaptations in the Renaissance of classical panegyric to a Christian saint that I have examined.[29] During these years Vergerio, along with Guarino and Vittorino da Feltre, frequented the circle of Giovanni di Conversino da Ravenna, under whose tutelage Vergerio perfected his understanding of rhetoric. Vergerio's orations honoring Jerome were the fulfillment of a kind of vow, and they helped inaugurate among humanists a tradition of panegyrics of that saint.[30]

There is, for instance, the panegyric of Jerome by Nicolaus Bonavia of Lucca, delivered at Padua in 1410 *inter missarum solemnia* in the presence of the bishops of Padua and Florence as well as the archbishops of Patras and Corfu.[31] Barzizza had begun teaching at Padua in 1407, but he is not numbered by the preacher among his "praeceptores."[32] Vergerio had, of course, left Padua earlier and even spent some years, 1404–9, in the papal curia. Bonavia's panegyric is an example of the tradition honoring

29. These orations were called to my attention by Professor Kristeller and Professor Eugene F. Rice, Jr., of Columbia University. Mr. John McManamon supplied me with some useful information concerning them. They are described by Leonardo Smith in his edition of the *Epistolario di Pier Paolo Vergerio*, Fonti per la Storia d'Italia, No. 74 (Rome: Istituto Storico Italiano per il Medio Evo, 1934), pp. 91–93n. The principal codices in which the orations are contained are: (1) Bodleian Libr. cod. Canon. misc. lat. 166, fols. 141^r–158^v; (2) Museo Civico, Padua, cod. B.P. 1287, fols. 35^r–41^r; (3) *ibid.*, cod. B.P. 1203, pp. 204–25; (4) an unnumbered codex of Vergerio's works in the Archivio Gravisi-Barbabianca of Capodistria, fols. 55^r–70^r; see Smith, *op. cit.*, pp. xxx–xlvii. The oration beginning, "Sanctissimum doctorem fidei nostrae," is in PL 22, 231–36. The oration beginning, "Hodie mihi, fratres carissimi," was published by Domenico Mauro Salmaso, *De d. Hieronymo opuscula* (Padua: Vulpiana, 1767), pp. 7–19. The oration in Bodleian Libr. cod. Canon. misc. lat. 166, fols. 149^r–152^v, beginning "Quotiens reverendi patres," is not listed by Smith and does not appear in either of the Paduan manuscripts. It is dated, fol. 152^v, "Senis 1408."
30. See Smith's edition of the *Epistolario*, Letter XXXXII, pp. 91–92, "quasi voto quodam constitutum." Professor Rice is preparing a book on St. Jerome in the Renaissance.
31. BAV cod. Vat. lat. 5994, fols. 3^r–7^v. According to Kristeller, *Iter*, I, 309, there is another copy of this oration at the Bibl. Ambr., cod. R.92 sup. Nicolaus Bonavia gave an oration in praise of logic in Siena, 1406, contained in BAV cod. Vat. lat. 5223, fols. 156^r–158^v, and there is an oration of his at the Biblioteca Laurenziana, Florence, cod. Ashbur. 201, according to Kristeller, *Iter*, I, 83.
32. BAV cod. Vat. lat. 5994, fol. 7^v: " . . . coram . . . praeceptoribus meis peritissimis Rapphaele Fulgosio Placentino, Rapphaele Raimundo Cumano, Signorino Homodeo Mediolanensi et universo scholasticorum coetu." On these individuals, see Mario Emilio Cosenza, *Biographical and Bibliographical Dictionary of the Italian Humanists and of the World of Classical Scholarship in Italy, 1300–1800*, 6 vols. (Boston: G. K. Hall, 1962–67), II (1962), 1767; IV (1962), 3009. For a study of cod. 70 of the archiepiscopal library of Udine, which contains a number of sacred and secular orations from Padua in the Quattrocento, see Ludwig Bertalot's "Eine Sammlung paduaner Reden des XV. Jahrhunderts," now reprinted in *Studien zum italienischen und deutschen Humanismus*, ed. Paul Oskar Kristeller, Raccolta di Studi e Testi, Nos. 129–30, 2 vols. (Rome: Storia e Letteratura, 1975), II, 209–35.

Jerome, but it is especially important because it allows the inference that adaptation of the *genus demonstrativum* to Christian saints was a standard exercise in rhetoric at Padua by the beginning of the Quattrocento.

As the century wore on, ever more examples of appropriation of the classical *genus* appear. Of some significance for the papal court is another panegyric of Jerome, composed and delivered in Siena by the Sienese humanist Agostino Dati no later than September 30, 1446. In early 1447 an illuminated copy of this oration was sent to Viannisius de Albergatis (Albergati) of Bologna.[33] Albergati was appointed a papal prothonotary a few weeks later, shortly after the election of Nicholas V, and he, presumably, retained possession of this altogether classicizing panegyric in its expensive membrane codex during his many years in papal service.[34] I mention this manuscript simply as a detail in what must be the extremely complicated story of the arrival of the Christian adaptation of the *genus demonstrativum* at the papal court. What is clear from this oration and especially from Pietro del Monte's, nonetheless, is that no later than the pontificate of Nicholas V "sacred epideictic" had arrived there.[35]

This arrival coincides with the return to Rome in 1448 of Rome's greatest humanist, Lorenzo Valla. We must assume that the general reform of theology which Valla advocated and which derived from his understand-

33. "Oratio de laudibus sancti Hieronymi," BAV cod. Vat. lat. 13738. The prefatory letter of Vangelistas Salvius is dated viii Kl. Martias, 1447. Dati delivered a panegyric at Siena sometime during the pontificate of Calixtus III (fol. 10ᵛ), "Concio in honorem sancti Calisti martyris infra missarum solemnia," BAV cod. Vat. lat. 3699. This panegyric is also classicizing.

34. On Albergati, see Bruno Katterbach, *Referendarii Utriusque Signaturae a Martino V ad Clementem IX et Praelati Signaturae Supplicationum a Martino V ad Leonem XIII*, Studi e Testi, No. 55 (Vatican City: BAV, 1931), pp. 35–36.

35. Jean Jouffroy prepared his "In Ioannis evangelistae laudes oratio" for Eugene IV (fol. 171ʳ), found in BAV cod. Ross. 685, fols. 171ʳ–174ᵛ. This panegyric is certainly influenced by classical principles, as is his oration for the funeral of Nicholas V, BAV cod. Vat. lat. 3675, fols. 30ʳ–37ʳ. On this latter oration, see McManamon, "Ideal Renaissance Pope," pp. 12 and passim. On Jouffroy, whom Nicholas nominated bishop of Arras in 1453 and whom Pius II created a cardinal in 1461, see Charles Fierville, *Le cardinal Jean Jouffroy et son temps, 1412–1473* (Paris: Coutances, 1874).

Another sermon showing classical influences and prepared for Eugene IV, but seemingly never delivered, is "Sermo presbyteri Laurentii Pisani," BAV cod. Vat. lat. 3706. The sermon preached for Eugene IV by Franciscus Florentinus (seu Paduanus) in Florence in the basilica of S. Maria Novella on Holy Thursday, year unknown, adopts a classicizing Latin style, but is thematic in purpose and content, "Pro divinissima eucaristia oratio," BN Florence cod. Landau 152, fols. 56ʳ–59ᵛ.

There is an anonymous "Sermo in epiphania Domini" for a pope, Bibl. Marc. cod. lat. XI.100 (3938), fols. 54ʳ–58ʳ. According to Kristeller, *Iter*, II, 255, it was composed before 1454. This *sermo* abandons the more obvious characteristics of thematic structure, but in its use of sources, its purpose, etc., it must be classified as thematic.

ing of the controlling function of rhetoric in such a reform had some impact on the court. Recent studies have expertly analyzed that reform,[36] although the degree and precise nature of Valla's impact upon the papal court is yet to be determined. As far as we know, moreover, Valla never preached at a papal liturgy.

On the other hand, there are two sacred orations that Valla delivered in Rome towards the end of his life. These orations at least provide further evidence that sacred epideictic was in use in Rome by the middle of the Quattrocento. The *sermo* on the mystery of the Eucharist, delivered somewhere in Rome probably on Holy Thursday, 1456, first argues for the credibility of Transubstantiation. The second and final part of the *sermo* is in praise of the Eucharist, and especially in praise of the dignity and excellence the sacrament works in those who receive it.

The panegyric on Aquinas, delivered in S. Maria sopra Minerva on March 7, 1457, the year of Valla's death, is justly celebrated.[37] Valla's bold and clever turning of the oration into an apologia for his own humanistic style of theology against the scholastic style of Aquinas is unique for the genre. But otherwise this panegyric and the second part of the *sermo* on the Eucharist do not modify the patterns for epideictic oratory.

During the pontificates of Nicholas and Calixtus when Valla was last active in Rome, relatively few sermons survive which can be securely identified as preached before the popes *inter missarum solemnia*. Among these few are several by Nicolò Palmeri. With Palmeri, therefore, the case studies might formally begin. He was an Augustinian friar who later

36. See Charles Trinkaus, *In Our Image and Likeness: Humanity and Divinity in Italian Humanist Thought*, 2 vols. (Chicago: University of Chicago Press, 1970), I, 103–70; II, 571–78, 633–38; Mario Fois, *Il pensiero cristiano di Lorenzo Valla nel quadro storico-culturale del suo ambiente*, Analecta Gregoriana, No. 174 (Rome: Pontificia Universitas Gregoriana, 1969); Giovanni di Napoli, *Lorenzo Valla: Filosofia e religione nell'Umanesimo italiano*, Uomini e dottrine, No. 17 (Rome: Storia e Letteratura, 1971); Salvatore I. Camporeale, *Lorenzo Valla: Umanesimo e teologia* (Florence: Istituto Nazionale di Studi sul Rinascimento, 1972).

37. See my "Some Renaissance Panegyrics of Aquinas," *Renaissance Quarterly*, 27 (1974), 174–92; Paul Oskar Kristeller, "Thomism and the Italian Thought of the Renaissance" in his *Medieval Aspects of Renaissance Learning*, ed. and trans. Edward P. Mahoney, Duke Monographs in Medieval and Renaissance Studies, No. 1 (Durham, N. C.: Duke University Press, 1974), pp. 63–64; and now esp. Salvatore I. Camporeale, "Lorenzo Valla tra Medioevo e Rinascimento: Encomion s. Thomae (1457)," *Memorie Domenicane*, NS 7 (1976), 11–194. Both of these orations are reprinted in Valla's *Opera omnia*, Monumenta Politica et Philosophica Rariora, ed. Luigi Firpo, Ser. I, No. 5, 2 vols. (I=Basel, 1540; rpt. Turin: Bottega d'Erasmo, 1962), "Sermo de mysterio eucharistiae," II, 63–72; "Encomium sancti Thomae Aquinatis," ed. J. Vahlen, II, 340–52.

became bishop of Catanzaro and bishop of Civita Castellana and Orte.[38] He was teaching in Rome during the pontificate of Nicholas.[39] Five of his sermons certainly preached before popes sometime between that period and his death in 1467 are extant, and there is a sixth which probably was preached *coram*.[40] For only one of these six has the pope been identified with certainty, and that is Pius II.[41]

Since Palmeri was a member of the Augustinian order, he had, presumably, a scholastic theological training.[42] This presumption is confirmed by the responses he accords three scholastic *quaestiones* he undertook to answer publicly, one each during the pontificates of Nicholas V, Pius II, and Paul II.[43] But the presumption is especially confirmed by the six sermons. They are all thematic. One of them we can entitle "De pacis dignitate."[44] The sermon is of some interest because it handles this typically epideictic subject thematically. It is also of interest because it is one of the rare instances in which the papal office with its prerogatives and functions is professedly discussed in the sermons: papal headship of the Church guarantees unity and peace.

Despite Palmeri's protestation of proceeding "sermone simplici" while preaching before Pius II, he certainly employed the new rhetoric in some of his other orations.[45] He delivered the eulogy for the first day of the obsequies for Nicholas V in 1453.[46] That oration shows the influence of

38. See G. B. Vaccaro, "Nicolò Palmeri: Vescovo di Orte e Civita Castellana, 1402–1467," *Bolletino Storico Agostiniano*, 12 (1935–36), 83–86, and Kristeller, *Medieval Aspects*, p. 148.

39. This fact is established from BAV cod. Vat. lat. 5815, fol. 102^r, which indicates that the *quaestio* that follows was presented in the church of Aracoeli, Rome, in 1450, the jubilee year, fols. 102^r–111^v.

40. These orations, as well as other works by Palmeri, are all in BAV cod. Vat. lat. 5815. The orations *coram* are listed in the Appendix. Though I have not examined the codex in the Biblioteca Nazionale of Florence (Magl. VIII.1434), the description in Kristeller, *Iter*, I, 134, seems to indicate it contains nothing not in the Vatican codex.

41. BAV cod. Vat. lat. 5815, fol. 111^v.

42. On the course of studies in the order, see David Gutiérrez, "Los estudios en la Orden agustiniana desde la edad media hasta la contemporánea," *Analecta Augustiniana*, 33 (1970), 75–149.

43. BAV cod. Vat. lat. 5815: (1) on the conception of Christ, for cardinals, prelates and the people of Rome, church of Aracoeli, 1450, fols. 102^r–111^v; (2) whether the blood of Christ shed on the cross was conjoined to his divinity after the resurrection, "coram Pio II," fols. 135^v–139^r; (3) same question as in 1450, for cardinals and people, during the pontificate of Paul II, Pantheon ("sanctae Mariae rotundae"), fols. 126^r–129^r.

44. *Ibid.*, fols. 84^v–101^v.

45. *Ibid.*, fol. 113^r.

46. *Ibid.*, fols. 3^r–12^v. See McManamon, "Ideal Renaissance Pope," pp. 12, 40, and passim.

classical rhetoric, but not immediately or consistently. His funeral eulogy for Cardinal Domenico Capranica in 1458 and the one for Cardinal Prosper Colonna in 1463, on the contrary, are thoroughly imbued with the principles that classical epideictic prescribed for such occasions, and they are reasonably representative of the oratory produced by other preachers for the funerals of cardinals from 1450 until 1521.[47] In this funeral oratory, the classical *topoi* condition the formulation of an ideal of Christian virtue in somewhat the same way the epideictic form influences the presentation of dogma.[48] This influence of the *topoi* will be discussed in Chapter Five. Palmeri's funeral oratory, moreover, alerts us to a certain versatility, a certain ability to switch back and forth between "Scholasticism" and "Humanism" that characterizes some of the preachers.

Besides del Monte's and Palmeri's sermons, the only others I have discovered from this early period are those by Rodrigo Sánchez de Arévalo: two each for Nicholas V, Calixtus III, and Pius II.[49] We also have his panegyric of Aquinas from about 1450, probably delivered at the Minerva.[50] Arévalo was a Spaniard, trained in canon law.[51] Like the other

47. For Capranica, BAV cod. Vat. lat. 5815, fols. 13^r–32^v; for Colonna, *ibid.*, fols. 119^r–126^r. See Pastor, II, esp. 483–95.

48. The interest at the court in funeral oratory is indicated in many ways, e.g., in Andrea Brenta's "Oratio funebris Lysiae per Andream Patavinum in latinum traducta," dedicated to Oliviero Carafa, BAV cod. Vat. lat. 6855, fols. 1^r–23^r. In the dedicatory letter to Carafa, Brenta clearly indicates he understands the function of this oratory, esp. fol. 4^{r-v}. Brenta preached on Pentecost, 1483, for Sixtus IV.

49. These are all contained in BAV cod. Vat. lat. 4881, and they are listed in the Appendix.

50. BAV cod. Vat. lat. 4881, fols. 234^r–237^r. In dating the orations of Arévalo, I follow Trame (see next note) when the date is not otherwise clear.

51. He has aroused a fair amount of scholarly interest, which has led to two books: Richard H. Trame, *Rodrigo Sánchez de Arévalo, 1404–1470: Spanish Diplomat and Champion of the Papacy* (Washington: Catholic University Press, 1958), and Juan María Laboa, *Rodrigo Sánchez de Arévalo, Alcaide de Sant'Angelo* (Madrid: Seminario Nebrija, 1973). There have been, besides, a number of articles: José López de Toro, "El primer tratado de pedagogía en España (1453)," *Boletín de la Universidad de Granada*, 5 (1933), 259–75; 6 (1934), 154–72, 361–87; 7 (1935), 195–217; Hayward Keniston, "A Fifteenth-Century Treatise on Education by Bishop Rodericus Zamorensis," *Bulletin Hispanique*, 32 (1930), 193–217; Hubert Jedin, "Sánchez de Arévalo und die Konzilsfrage unter Paul II," *Historisches Jahrbuch*, 73 (1953), 95–119; Teodoro Toni, "La realeza de Jesucristo en un tratado inedito del siglo XV," *Estudios eclesiásticos*, 13 (1934), 369–98; Antonio García García, "Un opúscolo inédito di Rodrigo Sánchez de Arévalo: *De libera et irrefragabili auctoritate Romani pontificis*," *Salmanticensis*, 4 (1957), 474–502; and two studies by Robert B. Tate, "Rodrigo Sánchez de Arévalo (1404–1470) and His *Compendiosa Historia Hispanica*," *Nottingham Medieval Studies*, 4 (1960), 58–80, and "An Apology for Monarchy: A Study of an Unpublished 15th-Century Historical Pamphlet," *Romance Philology*, 15 (1961–62), 111–23.

figures so far encountered, he combined a life of public activity with writing and was a person to be reckoned with in his own day, especially during
the pontificate of Paul II. He was an absentee bishop who resided in
Rome for most of his adult life; he was at one time procurator at the
papal court for Henry IV of Castile; and, finally, he was prefect of the
Castel Sant'Angelo. During the pontificate of Paul II he had the dubious
honor of holding prisoner humanists like Platina and Pomponio Leto
who Paul II thought were plotting against him.

If Arévalo's sermons are for the moment excluded, his writings can be
said to focus on two areas: morals and political theology. His political
theology expounds an extreme form of papal plenitude of power. This
theology found a ready ear in Paul II and helped strengthen papal resistance to the idea of a council during the last quarter of the century. The
politico-theological aspect of Arévalo's writings has been carefully studied.
Less attention has been given to his moral concerns, in spite of the fact
that he wrote what must be the most popular moralistic treatise of his
day, the *Speculum vitae humanae*. This book was first published in 1468
and dedicated to Paul II. In just a little over thirty years, it underwent
at least twenty-six editions, including translations into German, French,
and Spanish, and was still being printed in the seventeenth century.[52]
Arévalo also wrote a treatise on education,[53] a treatise on the reform of
the Church dedicated to Bessarion,[54] a commendation of arms written in
response to Platina's treatise in praise of peace,[55] a treatise on the poverty
of Christ and the apostles done at the request of Paul II,[56] and other
works as well. We will have occasion to utilize some of these writings
later. The sermons, though often concerned with morals and occasionally
with reform, also treat of doctrinal matters like the Incarnation, the Trinity, and Redemption, and do this with a certain competency. His views on
the papacy, however, do not appear in them.

The two sermons before Nicholas V and the panegyric of Aquinas
from the same period betray classical influences on the structure and pur-

---

52. I will use the Michael Soly edition, Paris, 1656.

53. Published by Keniston in the article cited above, note 51.

54. "Libellus de remediis afflictae ecclesiae," BAV cod. Barb. lat. 1487, fols. 107ʳ–
156ᵛ.

55. "Commendatio armorum militarium," in *Cremonensium monumenta Romae
extantia*, ed. Thomas Augustinus Vairani, 2 vols. in one (Rome: G. Salomoni, 1778),
I, 67–106.

56. "Libellus de paupertate Christi et apostolorum," BAV cod. Vat. lat. 969, presentation copy to Paul II.

pose. But the unsteady nature of the influence is demonstrated by the protracted preliminaries in the "Sermo in die Petri et Pauli," 1448 or 1450. The mixture of thematic and classical elements prolongs the introduction to this basically devotional sermon to the point of tedium before the preacher finally begins the first part of the body of the sermon. These preliminaries consume so much time that he has to omit the third part altogether, the part which was to deal with Paul.

The two sermons for Calixtus are more thematic than the earlier ones. We might be tempted to explain this "regression" by speculating that perhaps the Spanish pope was less sensitive to the new developments in sacred oratory and perhaps less sympathetic to them than was Nicholas. But such an explanation does not suffice to explain why the two sermons preached before Pius II some years later are the most thematic of them all.

The process observed in Arévalo is reversed in his contemporary and fellow bishop, Domenico de' Domenichi. Upon his arrival in Rome, Domenichi moved from thematic to epideictic oratory. Born in Venice in 1416, teaching philosophy at Padua by 1437, nominated bishop of Torcello by Nicholas V in 1448—these are the highlights of his early career.[57] Jedin has argued that although humanist skills were a definite part of Domenichi's early education, his theological works remained untouched by Humanism and show an orientation towards Thomistic positions. While bishop of Torcello, Domenichi preached of course in Venice, but he also preached in Florence and even in Neustadt before Emperor Frederick III and his wife.[58] All these early sermons are in every respect thematic, even in vocabulary and syntax.

During the pontificate of Calixtus III he began to spend time in Rome. In 1458 he delivered the oration to the cardinals before they entered the conclave where Pius II was elected successor to Calixtus.[59] Although this oration must be classified as substantially thematic, evidences of a classicizing influence appear in the style, syntax, use of an exordium, and so

57. See Hubert Jedin, "Studien über Domenico de' Domenichi (1416–1478)," *Abhandlungen der Mainzer Akad. d. Wiss. u. d. Lit., Geistes- u. sozialwiss. Kl.*, No. 5, 1957 (Wiesbaden: F. Steiner, 1958), pp. 177–300. This extremely careful study treats Domenichi's sermons very briefly and has practically nothing on the sermons and orations composed after his arrival in Rome, contained in BAV cod. Ottob. lat. 1035.

58. These sermons are found in BAV cod. Ross. 1037, as well as in the codices of the other libraries listed by Jedin, "Studien," pp. 292–93. Jedin was unaware of the BAV codex.

59. BAV cod. Ottob. lat. 1035, fols. 1ʳ–9ᵛ. See McManamon, "Ideal Renaissance Pope," p. 16 and passim.

forth. The oration Domenichi delivered upon the death of Pius in 1464 for the election of his successor is much more classicizing.[60] Within a loose thematic structure he fits a panegyric of Pius and an adaptation of the *genus deliberativum* as he tries to persuade the cardinals to a course of action, viz., to an honest and canonical election. The sermons and other orations he gave in Rome during the pontificates of Pius II and Paul II appropriate even more securely elements of classical epideictic.

In 1476, just two years before his death, Roman citizenship was conferred upon Domenichi. On that occasion he addressed to the magistrates and people an oration in praise of the city.[61] It is epideictic, without a trace of thematic form. The oration does not employ ekphrasis, but it is filled with examples and comparisons from history to illustrate Rome's greatness. Ten years earlier, when he was nominated bishop of Brescia by Paul II, he delivered an oration to his clergy and people which contained a panegyric of that city showing his control by that date of the classical *genus*, including the device of ekphrasis.[62] This oration also demonstrates the easy harmonizing found in many of the preachers between the *ars laudandi* and the religious impulse to praise God.[63] We must not be ungrateful for God's benefits, advises Domenichi as he is about to review the merits of Brescia. As far as possible, every moment of our lives should be engaged in the praise of God. Thus we can say with the psalmist: "Benedicam Dominum in omni tempore; semper laus eius in ore meo" (Ps. 33:2[34:1]).[64]

But what is particularly interesting about Domenichi's oratorical career is that not only two, but three stages can be discerned in it. In his oration in 1463 honoring Catherine of Siena and in his oration on peace for Paul II in 1468, he discloses an interesting fact. He is now "rusty" in the *dicendi studia*. He has not practiced, now these many years, what he had once learned.[65] In other words, as a boy or young man he had studied the orator's art. As bishop of Torcello, however, he had consistently employed the thematic form. Now in Rome Domenichi is trying to learn the art once again, and he asks indulgence for not being more proficient in it.

60. BAV cod. Ottob. lat. 1035, fols. 10ʳ–18ᵛ. See McManamon, "Ideal Renaissance Pope," p. 16 and passim.

61. BAV cod. Ottob. lat. 1035, fols. 83ʳ–87ᵛ.

62. *Ibid.*, fols. 42ʳ–45ᵛ.

63. The preachers could find a basis for such a correlation suggested in Augustine, e.g., Sermo 67, PL 38, 433–37.

64. BAV cod. Ottob. lat. 1035, fol. 42ʳ⁻ᵛ.

65. *Ibid.*, fols. 19ᵛ and 46ᵛ, "quasi robiginem quamdam contraxerat."

This apology suggests that epideictic, in the terms we have been describing it, was not yet widely perceived as appropriate or adaptable to the pulpit even by prelates who had the skills to employ it.

The oration in praise of Catherine of Siena was delivered at the Minerva shortly after her canonization, in the presence of Pius II and at his invitation.[66] Like the pope himself, Domenichi emphasizes the ascetical and mystical aspects of Catherine's life, though her career would surely provide good scope for somebody wishing to highlight the virtues of public service. In his oration on peace, Domenichi indicates more awareness of virtues exercised in the service of others, especially by persons in public office.[67] This difference in emphasis is doubtless due to many factors, but it is not unrelated to the firmer grasp of classical oratory in the second instance—the hero classical rhetoric envisioned was a man serving his fellow citizens. It is worth noting, moreover, that that second oration was delivered on the feast of the Ascension. As in the sermons of Massari and Gravina for the same feast, the listeners are invited to raise their eyes heavenwards to gaze upon and contemplate the heavenly scene. Domenichi's art in painting that scene, however, falls short of the art of Massari and especially that of Gravina.

Domenichi was a close collaborator with Pius II, and for Pius he composed a treatise on the reform of the Church. While supporting the papacy against those who would try to diminish its true prerogatives, he differed from people like Arévalo who took an extreme position. He consistently advocated a papacy moderated by its duty to consult and to take the advice of the cardinals gathered in consistory. As we have seen, though he was influenced by certain elements of what we consider Renaissance culture, he also underwent typically medieval influences. All these facts suggest the name of another great collaborator with Pius II—Cardinal Nicholas of Cusa.

Cusa and his sermons demand some consideration. Cusa never preached *coram papa*, it is true. Yet he did preach four sermons in Rome to the canons of the major basilicas during his reform visitation as Pius II's vicar for the city in 1459.[68] These sermons form only a minuscule per-

---

66. *Ibid.*, fols. 18ᵛ–28ʳ.
67. *Ibid.*, fols. 46ʳ–52ᵛ.
68. All four are contained in BAV cod. Vat. lat. 1245: (1) in St. Peter's, "Dum sanctificatus fuero in vobis," fols. 279ᵛ–281ᵛ; (2) again in St. Peter's, "Sic currite ut comprehendatis," fols. 281ᵛ–282ᵛ; (3) in the Lateran, "Audistis, fratres, Pium secundum," fols. 282ᵛ–284ʳ; (4) in S. Maria Maggiore, "Sicut nuper dum synodum," fols. 284ʳ–286ʳ. See chapter two, "Legatus Urbis," of Erich Meuthen's *Die letzten Jahre des*

centage of the over three hundred we still possess today in the *corpus* of Nicholas's writings.

Cusa's sermons have been utilized by two contemporary scholars— Rudolf Haubst and James E. Biechler—in their studies of his theology, but otherwise they have been almost completely neglected.[69] Except for the portions in the sixteenth-century edition of Cusa's works by Lefèvre d'Étaples, they have for the most part never even been printed.[70] Since the two great codices of these sermons now in the Vatican Library were prepared in Rome under Cusa's own supervision during the precise period he was active at the court and participating in its liturgies, they invite comparison with the sermons of the *cappelle*.[71] The fact that these codices were prepared with meticulous care and at what must have been enormous expense reveals that Nicholas thought them important.

Scholarship is in general agreement that Nicholas's impact on his own age, on Italy, and on the Rome of Pius II was not great.[72] Nevertheless, his outline for the reform of the Church did influence Pius II and the future

---

Nikolaus von Kues: Biographische Untersuchungen nach neuen Quellen, Wissenschaftliche Abhandlungen der Arbeitsgemeinschaft für Forschung des Landes Nordrhein-Westfalen, No. 3 (Cologne: Westdeutscher Verlag, 1958), pp. 28–52.

69. See Biechler, *The Religious Language of Nicholas of Cusa,* American Academy of Religion, Dissertation Ser., No. 8 (Missoula, Montana: Scholars Press, 1975), and the books by Haubst, *Die Christologie des Nikolaus von Kues* (Freiburg: Herder, 1956) and *Das Bild des Einen und Dreieinen Gottes in der Welt nach Nikolaus von Kues,* Trierer theologische Studien, No. 4 (Trier: Paulinus, 1952), as well as Haubst's articles: "Nikolaus von Kues als theologischer Denker," *Trierer Theologische Zeitschrift,* 68 (1959), 129–45; "Nikolaus von Kues über die Gotteskindschaft," in *Nicolò da Cusa: Relazioni tenute al convegno interuniversitario di Bressanone nel 1960* (Florence: Sansoni, 1962), pp. 29–46; "Nikolaus von Kues und die Theologie," *Trierer Theologische Zeitschrift,* 73 (1964), 193–210; "Die leitenden Gedanken und Motive der cusanischen Theologie," in *Das Cusanus-Jubiläum,* ed. Rudolf Haubst, Mitteilungen und Forschungsbeiträge der Cusanus-Gesellschaft, No. 4 (Mainz: Matthias-Grünewald, 1964), pp. 257–77; "Thomas von Aquin in der Sicht des Nikolaus von Kues," *Trierer Theologische Zeitschrift,* 74 (1965), 193–212; "Der Leitgedanke der Repraesentatio in der cusanischen Ekklesiologie," in *Nikolaus von Kues als Promotor der Ökumene,* ed. Rudolf Haubst, Mitteilungen und Forschungsbeiträge der Cusanus-Gesellschaft, No. 9 (Mainz: Matthias-Grünewald, 1971), pp. 140–59; "Theologie in der Philosophie—Philosophie in der Theologie des Nikolaus von Kues," in *Nikolaus von Kues in der Geschichte des Erkenntnisproblems,* ed. Rudolf Haubst, Mitteilungen und Forschungsbeiträge der Cusanus-Gesellschaft, No. 11 (Mainz: Matthias-Grünewald, 1975), pp. 233–60.

70. The Heidelberg Academy has undertaken the publication of the sermons as part of its complete critical edition of Cusa's works. The first fascicule appeared in 1970, and several more have followed. The magnitude of the work which lies ahead is suggested by the fact that only four sermons were edited in the first fascicule.

71. BAV cod. Vat. lat. 1244 and Vat. lat. 1245.

72. See, e.g., Eugenio Garin, "Cusano e i Platonici italiani del Quattrocento," in *Nicolò da Cusa: Convegno di Bressanone,* pp. 75–100, esp. 76–77.

Pius III.[73] Moreover, a number of his works were written, copied, or retained in Rome.[74] The two codices of sermons, for instance, were in the Vatican Library by 1481.[75] Rome was not, therefore, totally insulated from this major figure.

An examination of Cusa's sermons reveals that the theological themes which Cusa consistently propounded correlate with some of the themes which emerge from the *cappelle*. While this correlation is probably only correlation, not influence one way or the other, nonetheless a review of the religious message of Cusa's sermons can provide another valuable point of reference for locating the sermons of the *cappelle* in the culture of the Quattrocento.

The doctrines to which Cusa consistently recurs in his preaching tally almost point for point with the doctrines that Brandolini, Massari, and Giles of Viterbo proposed and that actually emerge in the *cappelle*—the Trinity, the Incarnation-Redemption, man's elevation to divine sonship, and the harmony or concord of the universe. Lest I be suspected of forcing Cusa into the Roman mold, I must point out that this interpretation of his sermons was anticipated by Haubst some years ago.[76] Moreover, Haubst

73. See, e.g., Stephan Ehses, "Der Reformentwurf des Kardinals Nikolaus Cusanus," *Historisches Jahrbuch*, 32 (1911), 274–97; Guido Kisch, "Nicolaus Cusanus und Aeneas Silvius Piccolomini," in *Cusanus Gedächtnisschrift*, ed. Nikolaus Grass (Innsbruck: Universitätsverlag Wagner, 1970), pp. 35–43; Erwin Iserloh, "Reform der Kirche bei Nikolaus von Kues," in *Das Cusanus-Jubiläum*, pp. 54–73; Rudolf Haubst, "Der Reformentwurf Pius' des Zweiten," *Römische Quartalschrift*, 49 (1954), 188–242; and Alfred A. Strnad, *Francesco Todeschini-Piccolomini: Politik und Mäzenatentum im Quattrocento*, Sonderdruck of *Römische Historische Mitteilungen* (Graz: H. Böhlaus, 1966), esp. pp. 181–82.

74. See Rudolf Haubst, *Studien zu Nikolaus von Kues und Johannes Wenck: Aus Handschriften der vatikanischen Bibliothek*, Beiträge zur Gesch. d. Phil. u. Theol. d. Mittelalters, No. 38.1 (Münster: Aschendorff, 1955), esp. pp. 11–15, 32–33; Paul Wilpert, "Die handschriftliche Überlieferung des Schrifttums des Nikolaus von Kues," in *Nicolò da Cusa: Convegno di Bressanone*, pp. 1–15; Gerhard Kallen, *Die handschriftliche Überlieferung des Concordantia Catholica des Nikolaus von Kues*, Cusanus-Studien VIII, Sitzungsberichte d. Heidelberger Akad. d. Wissenschaften, Philoshistor. Kl., Jahrgang 1963, 2 Abh. (Heidelberg: C. Winter, 1963), esp. p. 17; Hans Gerhard Senger, *Zur Überlieferung der Werke des Nikolaus von Kues im Mittelalter*, Cusanus-Studien IX, Sitzungsberichte d. Heidelberger Akad. d. Wissenschaften, Philos-histor. Kl., Jahrgang 1972, 5 Abh. (Heidelberg: C. Winter, 1972), esp. pp. 18–25.

75. See Haubst, *Studien aus der vatikanischen Bibliothek*, pp. 11–13.

76. See *Christologie*, p. 39; "Nikolaus und die Theologie," pp. 194 and 207; "Gedanken und Motive," p. 259; "Die Gotteskindschaft." Cusa provides us with his own summary of the content of his preaching, a "summa evangelii," in his "De aequalitate" ("Vita erat lux hominum"), BAV cod. Vat. lat. 1245, fol. 262ᵛ: "Sed erat lux vera, ipsum Verbum Dei, quae lux illuminat omnem hominem ratione vigentem, in hunc mundum venientem. . . . illis dedit potestatem, quamvis essent homines, ut

indicated that the basic scriptural text out of which Cusa's theology originates is the Johannine Prologue.[77] With these judgments of Haubst there can be no cavil.

Still another feature of Cusa's sermons correlates them with those of the *cappelle*. The interpretation he gives to his favorite doctrines is extremely positive and optimistic. This interpretation is surely derived in part from the influence upon him of Saint Bonaventure.[78] The world, for instance, is a theophany. Cusa sees it as a reflection of the heavenly world, participating in the unity and concord that is the Trinity. In describing the world he on occasion uses the Bonaventurian theme of the world as God's book, a book wherein the honest and believing eye can discern God himself. Man in a special way is God's image and likeness. Moreover, through the Holy Spirit the charity of God has been poured into man's heart. Through that charity men are united to one another, to Christ, and to God.

When Cusa describes man's Redemption, he generally does so in terms of man's enlightenment by Christ the teacher. Even Christ's death on the cross is interpreted as an act "testifying to the truth" (John 18:37) rather than as expiation.[79] Though at times Cusa makes use of the Anselmian idea of satisfaction for sin, he much more frequently thinks of Christ's death simply as the supreme moment of his mission of "enlightening every man."[80] Cusa may on occasion lament men's sins, but he has little indeed

fierent filii Dei per gratiam, sicut ipse erat per naturam. . . . Quod quidem Verbum est caro factum, quia filius Dei factus est filius hominis. . . . Quibus omnibus manifestissime ostendit Iesum esse filium Dei, qui verba patris sui, qui verax est, locutus est et eius opera fecit, cuius verba sunt stabiliora quam caelum et terra, et promissa maxima, scilicet resurrectionis ad immortalem vitam, quam solus Deus possidet, cuius possessionis haeres est ipse Christus et credentes in eum corde et opere cohaeredes. Et fiunt haec omnia in homine per Spiritum sanctum, . . . qui est caritas Dei. Quae dum diffunditur per corda fidelium facit eos Deo gratos propter inhabitantem Spiritum sanctum, et unit eos nexu insolubili Christo capiti, . . . ut in unitate corporis Christi, Spiritu Christi vegetati, cohaeredes sint regni immortalitatis et vitae aeternae possessores felicissimi. Haec est summa evangelii in variis sermonibus meis infra positis varie explanati secundum datam gratiam, magis obscure dum inciperem in adolescentia. . . ."

77. *Christologie*, pp. 22–30.

78. See Francis N. Caminiti, "Nikolaus von Kues und Bonaventura," in *Das Cusanus-Jubiläum*, pp. 129–44.

79. See, e.g., "In parasceve," BAV cod. Vat. lat. 1244, fol. 69[r–v]; "Dicite filiae Sion," *ibid.*, fol. 79[v]; "Responsio," *ibid.*, fol. 83[v].

80. My interpretation here coincides with that of Biechler, *Religious Language*, pp. 105–38, and it differs from Haubst's emphasis, which sees Redemption for Cusa in Anselmian terms. *Christologie*, esp. p. 84. There is no doubt, on the other hand, that Cusa on occasion spoke in explicitly Anselmian terms, e.g., "Oportuit pati Christum," BAV cod. Vat. lat. 1244, fol. 74[r].

to say about hell or the Devil. He has little to say about the Fall except
in relationship to man's elevation to divine sonship and his transformation into the likeness of Christ and God.

The materials—the *res*—that Cusa treats in his sermons correspond,
therefore, in a general way to the materials that the preachers often treat.
But there the similarity definitely ends. As far as I can discover, not a
single sermon of Cusa's manifests any significant influence of classical
rhetoric in the terms in which I have been describing it. Though he has
materials that in themselves are eminently adaptable to epideictic purposes, he does not use them epideictically. In structure and purpose, his
sermons bear no resemblance to the "Renaissance" sermons of the
cappelle.

Cusa's sermons usually have a loose thematic structure, at least as
they begin, and he occasionally even speaks of his "theme." In actual
fact, some of the sermons are homilies, or turn into homilies, that is, a
verse-by-verse exegesis of a scriptural passage.[81] Others tend to ramble,
following some favorite idea wherever it might lead.[82] Others engage in a
question-answer dialogue between Cusa and an imagined interrogator.[83]
The language tends to be abstract and even metaphysical. Scripture is
often quoted or paraphrased, and that practice does introduce a more
concrete vocabulary. However, Cusa's penchant for interpreting Scripture allegorically infuses a mystical and remote quality into the language
of the sermons even when Scripture is being commented upon.[84] Etymology is important for him, and it occurs in some of the sermons.[85]
Numerology is also important.[86] Cusa only rarely descends to practical
issues, even in his reform sermons in Rome and elsewhere. When he does

81. For example, "Volo mundare," BAV cod. Vat. lat. 1245, fols. 211ᵛ–213ᵛ, or
"Loquimini ad petram," *ibid.*, fols. 235ʳ–238ᵛ. The second part of "Loquimini" is a
comment on the "thema," fol. 238ᵛ; the "thema" is also mentioned in "Domine adiuva
me," *ibid.*, fol. 229ʳ.
82. See, e.g., "Respice Domine," *ibid.*, fols. 107ᵛ–110ᵛ.
83. See, e.g., "In die parasceves," *ibid.*, fols. 174ᵛ–176ʳ; "Sic currite ut comprehendatis," *ibid.*, fol. 282ᵛ.
84. See, e.g., "Sic nos existimet homo," *ibid.*, fol. 197ʳ⁻ᵛ; "Sermo in parasceve,"
ibid., fol. 248ʳ; "Domine adiuva me," *ibid.*, fols. 229ᵛ–230ʳ; and esp. "Loquimini ad
petram," *ibid.*, fols. 235ʳ–238ᵛ.
85. See, e.g., "Ostendite mihi numisma," *ibid.*, fol. 186ʳ⁻ᵛ, and "Sic currite ut
comprehendatis," *ibid.*, fol. 282ᵛ.
86. See, e.g., "Spiritu ambulate," *ibid.*, fol. 115ᵛ, and "Loquimini ad petram," *ibid.*,
fol. 235ʳ.

so descend, he often enough inculcates the need for obedience and for conformity to the rules for one's state in life.[87]

This style of preaching did not escape criticism even in Cusa's own
day. In a sermon in Brixen on the feast of the Annunciation, 1457, Cusa
notes that some of his flock are "murmuring" that the things he preaches
are "too deep" for them.[88] He tries to ward off the criticism by comparing
himself with Christ teaching the Samaritan woman at the well (John 4).
Though Christ's disciples who stood by did not understand him, he was
revealing to the woman "profound and secret" truths. What, then, did
Cusa conceive the purpose of preaching to be?

In 1457 at a synod of his diocese of Brixen, Cusa attempted during a
sermon to answer a priest he imagines asking him how "to evangelize so
that Christ be known."[89] Cusa's response delimited the materials the
preacher was to preach about. These consist equivalently of three major
categories. First, he must preach Christ's birth, his miracles, his death and
resurrection. From this base he moves to faith that Christ was the Son of
God, to be believed and obeyed. Thirdly, he instructs his flock in Christ's
doctrine and commandments, and he teaches how Christ was the exemplar
for our lives. He also teaches how Christ "opened the Scripture" (Luke
24:32).

It was Cusa's practice of trying to "open the Scripture" that seemed
to earn for him the criticism of his flock. He believed the Gospel was "full
of most precious revelations,"[90] and under the influence of numerology,
etymology, and allegory he tried to disclose these revelations. Even
though he contained his exegesis within the limits of the great themes
enumerated above and used these themes as verifiers for his deeper understanding, we need not wonder that he at times left his flock somewhat be-
fuddled. We must also note that Cusa's view of Scripture as a book of
secret revelations is far removed from the view of some of the preachers
at the court that Scripture was a book of history.

On another occasion Cusa described the preaching of Christ, thus by
implication describing the ideal for all preachers. This time he deals not

---

87. See, e.g., "Dominus Iesus misit me," *ibid.*, fol. 36ᵛ; "Domine adiuva me,"
ibid., fol. 229ʳ⁻ᵛ; "Loquimini ad petram," *ibid.*, fol. 237ᵛ; "Sic currite ut comprehendatis," *ibid.*, fol. 282ᵛ; and "Respice Domine," *ibid.*, fols. 107ᵛ–110ᵛ, esp. 109ʳ⁻ᵛ.
88. "Loquimini ad petram," *ibid.*, fol. 235ʳ.
89. "Ministrat nobis fratres," *ibid.*, fol. 263ᵛ.
90. "Loquimini ad petram," *ibid.*, fol. 235ʳ.

with the materials of preaching but with its purpose and the effect it should have. Cusa could not be clearer about purpose. A sermon is to teach and to prescribe or command.[91] The prescribing or commanding he in this instance practically equates with exhortation, and it seems therefore to regard morals. But the preacher's prescriptions, commands, or exhortations will be effective only insofar as they proceed from the charity and sanctity of the preacher, as Cusa insists was the case with Christ and with Saint Bernardine of Siena. Ultimately the words should penetrate to the heart and kindle it.

Kindling the heart is an effect of preaching that is not alien to epideictic. The preachers at the papal court, moreover, would not deny the base of charity and sanctity out of which the sacred orator must move. Even classical theory insisted no one could be a good orator unless he were a good man. *Quanto magis* for the Christian orator! The preachers' quarrel with Cusa would be that he neglected a middle step between the sanctity of the preacher and the kindling effect the words should have. That middle step was the orator's art, rightly practiced.

As has already been suggested, many theorists in the history of Christianity have denied the necessity of that art's mediation.[92] Some have even seen it as an impediment to unadorned truth's power to penetrate and to transform. Cusa does not seem professedly to have subscribed to that view. He seems to have ignored the issue rather than explicitly taken sides on it. In practice, however, he did not exercise the orator's art as it was known in his day. In this regard his years as a student at Padua seem to have had no discernible influence on him.[93] Despite the effect he believed preaching should ultimately have, in his own sermons he consistently describes what he is doing as teaching, explaining, and revealing. Brandolini would say Cusa expected a lecture to accomplish what only an oration can do.

91. "Volo mundare," *ibid.*, fol. 211ᵛ, " . . . praedicatio Iesu fuit simul docens et imperans."

92. See the references in note 99 of Chapter II, as well as Kustas, *Byzantine Rhetoric*, pp. 27–45.

93. Professor Paul Oskar Kristeller has quite correctly called attention to Cusa's relationships to various humanists, and he judges Cusa to be "deeply imbued with the humanist culture of his time." See "A Latin Translation of Gemistos Plethon's de fato by Johannes Sopianus Dedicated to Nicholas of Cusa," in *Nicolò Cusano agli inizii del mondo moderno* (Florence: Sansoni, 1970), pp. 175–93, esp. 182. See also Biechler, *Religious Language*, pp. 11–36. Insofar as Humanism is related to the art of oratory, however, the degree of Cusa's personal appropriation of humanistic culture was negligible. Biechler would seem to support this conclusion, pp. 105–6.

Cusa's understanding of the purposes of sacred oratory is similar to Augustine's in the *De Doctrina Christiana* and to Erasmus's in the *Ecclesiastes*.[94] All three of these thinkers believed in the utility, even the necessity, of the allegorical interpretation of Scripture—under the surface there often lies a deeper truth.[95] With each of these men, the deeper truth almost invariably and inevitably was reducible to some philosophical or theological proposition. In other words, the deeper truth tended to be at least one step removed from the "deeds" and "actions" that were often the burden of the literal sense. The contrast with "model epideictic" is once again highlighted: teaching the "philosophy of Christ" is something quite different from celebrating God's great deeds.

Cusa contrasts in many ways with another prolific preacher who was active at the court of Pius II and continued to preach for the popes through the next two pontificates—those of Paul II and Sixtus IV. His name is Ambrogio Massari, already mentioned several times.[96] Elected prior general of the Augustinian friars in 1476 (or 1477), he held that office until he was incarcerated in the Castel Sant'Angelo by Pope Innocent VIII in 1485. The pope believed some calumniators of Massari within the order, but even today it is not clear just what the supposed offense was. Though Massari did not have a long imprisonment, he was broken in body and spirit by the time he was released, and he died shortly afterwards.[97] Such an incident abruptly returns us to the sometimes harsh realities of life in Renaissance Rome.

Until 1485 Massari's career seems to have been one of steady recognition and accomplishment, and it gave every promise of ending happily. He was born of a humble family at Cora, near Rome, and entered the Augustinians at a young age. By June of 1452 he was studying in Florence,

---

94. See *De Doctr. Christ.*, e.g., IV.1–4; 12–13; *Ecclesiastes*, LB, V, e.g., 770, 774, 775, 778, 790, 796.

95. See *De Doctr. Christ.*, e.g., II.6, III; *Ecclesiastes*, LB, V, e.g., 1028–51.

96. There has been no study of Massari, but Tomás de Herrera, *Alphabetum Augustinianum*, 2 vols. (Madrid: G. Rodriguez, 1644), provides some reliable dates and biographical information, I, 41. I have tried to supplement the information in Herrera and other standard Augustinian reference works with Massari's registers in Aug. Gen. Arch., Dd. 7 and Dd. 8, as well as an earlier register, Dd. 6. Also helpful is the manuscript book in the Archives by Tommaso Bonasoli (d. 1801), "Notizie della religione agostiniana e della provincia romana." See also Kristeller, *Medieval Aspects*, p. 146.

97. See Herrera, *Alphabetum*, I, 41, and esp. Bonasoli, "Notizie," pp. 90–91. See also Aug. Gen. Arch., Dd. 8, fol. 7ʳ, for Massari's letter to the various provinces and congregations of the order commending the recently elected Innocent VIII to the prayers of the brethren, Sept. 12, 1484.

probably at the convent of Santo Spirito.[98] As is clear from his writings and the fact that he held at least twice the position of a "regent" within the order (a teacher of major courses in theology with the right of supervision of other teachers), he had a scholastic training. But perhaps at Santo Spirito he had his first exposure to the new oratorical culture.

In 1466 and again in 1470 he was elected provincial of the Roman Province of the Augustinians, and in 1470 he also assumed the office of procurator general at the papal court. He had, however, already preached a panegyric on Saint Augustine in the presence of Pius II. Once elected prior general, he continued his efforts to reform the order in which he had already been engaged as provincial. He, in fact, favored the observant movement within the order.

Massari composed a large number of orations for various occasions, including at least nine preached before popes. He wrote a life of Saint Augustine,[99] a commentary on each of Augustine's three "Rules,"[100] a defense of the Augustinian friars against the calumnies of the Augustinian canons,[101] a scholastic commentary on the Liber sex principiorum attributed to the twelfth-century theologian Gilbert of Poitiers,[102] and a treatise on the "dignities of the soul" dedicated to Francesco Piccolomini,[103] as well as other works.[104] Until now these writings have, for all practical purposes, never been examined, and they deserve in their own right a separate study.

What is of interest for the moment are Massari's sermons. The pane-

---

98. See Aug. Gen. Arch., Dd. 6, fol. 169ᵛ.

99. The "Vita" is contained in *Vita praecellentissimi ecclesiae doctoris divi Aurelii Augustini. Commentarii super regula sancti Augustini* (Rome: G. Herolt, 1481), Hain #*5683, fols. [2ʳ–14ᵛ].

100. These commentaries are contained in the *Vita Augustini*, fols. [15ᵛ–232ᵛ].

101. *Defensorium ordinis heremitarum s. Augustini* [Rome: G. Herolt, not before 1482, despite Hain #*5684]. Massari's little manuscript, ["Epistola ad Canonicos Regulares Congregationis Phrisonariae"], Bibl. Ang. cod. lat. 12, fols. 61ʳ–62ᵛ, seems to have been intended as a preface to the *Defensorium*.

102. ["Commentarii in librum sex principiorum Giliberti Porretani"], Bibl. Ang. cod. lat. 12, fols. 1ʳ–60ᵛ.

103. "De animae dignitatibus," Bibl. Ang. cod. lat. 835, with separate foliation within the codex, III, fols. 1ʳ–32ᵛ.

104. See esp. Bibl. Estense cod. Alpha Q.6.13 (formerly 894), which seems to be the fullest collection of Massari's unpublished works. I have not examined the BN Paris cod. lat. 5621, but Professor Walter Principe kindly communicated to me a description of its contents. This codex contains many of the works in the Modena codex, but it seems less complete. I have been unable to locate, in particular, the oration "De laudibus urbis Romae" which Massari supposedly wrote.

gyric of Augustine for Pius II was delivered in 1463.[105] It is a valiant attempt to utilize the classical *genus*, but the oration is contentually so vapid and the praise so unrestrained as to make this piece a caricature of what a panegyric is supposed to be. The panegyric of Augustine for Paul II is worse.[106] With one exception, his other sermons tend to be more thematic than classical, but they are generally not without their epideictic parts or moments.

The most interesting of these sermons is the panegyric of John the Evangelist for Paul II.[107] Though to a markedly less degree than the sermon by Fichet studied by Professor Kristeller, this panegyric contains in print some rubrics explaining what the orator is doing. The oration is composed of two parts, which professedly correspond to what are called two *genera*. What is noteworthy is the meaning attached to these *genera*. The first part of the oration pertains to the *genus* where the "life" and "deeds" of John are related. The second part or *genus* is a "disputation" on the respective merits of the active and contemplative lives in which Massari "demonstrates" the superiority of the latter through definitions, arguments, and authorities. Both by Massari's description of the second *genus* and by what he does when he employs it, he without doubt meant it to mean what I have been referring to as thematic, and he clearly distinguishes this from a *genus* that deals with "life" and "deeds."

The exception to the generally thematic nature of Massari's sermons for the popes is the "Oratio pulcherrima" for the feast of the Ascension, delivered probably before Paul II or Sixtus IV.[108] From the conventional thematic framework the oration retains only the verse from Scripture at the beginning and the prayer. The epideictic purpose is clearly stated in the exordium: to narrate and to praise the Ascension. As I noted in the last chapter, Massari describes Christ's entrance into the heavenly court in terms of a great procession or reception. The *laus* due the Ascension is compared with the *dignitas* of the Incarnation. The Ascension is not found wanting. Through the Incarnation Christ descended to redeem

105. "Oratio de laudibus eiusdem sancti [Augustini] coram Pio secundo, pontifice maximo, et toto cardineo coetu," in *Vita Augustini*, fols. [233ʳ–237ᵛ].

106. "Oratio de laudibus eiusdem sancti [Augustini] coram Paulo Veneto secundo, pontifice maximo, et coetu cardineo," in *Vita Augustini*, fols. [241ᵛ–247ᵛ].

107. *Oratio de Ioannis apostoli et evangelistae laudibus* [Rome: B. Guldinbeck, n.d.], Hain #*5688.

108. "Oratio pulcherrima de ascensione Christi," Bibl. Estense cod. Alpha Q.6.13, fols. 218ᵛ–229ʳ.

man; today he ascends to glorify human nature. In the Incarnation salvation began; today it attains its full perfection. In the Incarnation Christ began to fulfill the promises of old; today the benefits that were promised are attained.[109] In the peroration Massari insists that today are received through the ineffable grace of Christ greater and more ample gifts than those once lost in the Fall through the Devil's envy.[110]

Pietro Marsi was a younger contemporary of Massari.[111] He was a cleric, a canon of the church of San Lorenzo in Damaso. At least by 1481 he was teaching rhetoric at the *Studium Urbis*.[112] Though he had earlier studied under Johannes Argyropulus, he considered himself to some extent a disciple of Pomponio Leto, whose funeral eulogy he delivered in 1497. In that eulogy he relates that Leto came to Rome in order to study with Valla, a fact by which Marsi implicitly establishes his own intellectual genealogy reaching back to Valla.[113] Besides some poetry, commentaries on Cicero and Terence, and some other minor works, he preached at least four times before Innocent VIII—two panegyrics of Saint Stephen, a panegyric

109. "Oratio pulcherrima," Bibl. Estense cod. Alpha Q.6.13, fol. 219[r-v]: "Non enim est minor ascensionis laus quam incarnationis dignitas. Incarnatio enim, ceu a doctorum principe Aurelio Augustino accepimus, terris dedit salvatorem, sed ascensio caelis reddidit glorificatorem. . . . Per incarnationem nos redempturus descendit, sed hodie humani generis naturam clarificaturus ascendit. In illa salutis nostrae incohatio, in hac perfectio continetur. In illa promissa incepit, in hac beneficia consummavit."

110. "Oratio pulcherrima," Bibl. Estense cod. Alpha Q.6.13, fol. 228[r]: "Hodie non solum paradisi possessio[ne] firmati sumus, sed super angelorum in Christo penetravimus sedes. Hodie ampliora per ineffabilem Christi gratiam suscepimus dona quam per diaboli perdideramus invidiam. Hodie mortis et corruptionis nostrae mutata est sententia."

111. There is some biographical information on Pietro Marsi in Arnaldo della Torre, *Paolo Marsi da Pescina: Contributo alla storia dell'Accademia Pomponiana* (Rocca S. Casciano: L. Cappelli, 1903), esp. pp. 97–98, 224–25, and in Egmont Lee, *Sixtus IV and Men of Letters*, Temi e Testi, No. 26 (Rome: Storia e Letteratura, 1978), pp. 189–90.

112. On the *Studium*, see Lee, *Sixtus IV*, pp. 151–92, and D. S. Chambers, "Studium Urbis and *Gabella Studii*: The University of Rome in the Fifteenth Century," in *Cultural Aspects of the Italian Renaissance: Essays in Honor of Paul Oskar Kristeller*, ed. Cecil H. Clough (New York: Zambelli, 1976), pp. 68–110. Of the teachers listed by Chambers, 1482–84, at least four preached at the court: Pietro Marsi; Andrea Brenta, professor of Latin and Greek, whose sermon on Pentecost, 1483, has survived; Guillelmus Bodivit, O.M., ("sacrae theologiae doctor") whose orations on the Annunciation, 1484, and on Trinity Sunday, 1485, have also survived; and Tito Veltri, bishop of Acquapendente and lecturer on the Codex, whose several orations *coram* I have not been able to locate. On Veltri's preaching at the court, see Jacopo Gherardi, *Il diario romano*, ed. Enrico Carusi, RIS, 23.3 (Città di Castello: S. Lapi, 1904), e.g., 15, 33, 39.

113. *Funebris oratio in obitu Pomponii Laeti* [Rome: E. Silber, 1497], Hain #10792. See esp. fols. [1[v], 2[v]].

of John the Evangelist, and an oration on the feast of the Ascension.[114]

The eulogy for Leto is altogether classicizing. A panegyric of Saint Augustine dedicated to Ferdinand and Isabella of Spain is notably less so.[115] Further, the sermons before Innocent are much more thematic in structure and purpose than we would have expected from Marsi's background. In varying degrees this is true even of the three panegyrics before the pope, but it is especially true for the oration on the Ascension.[116] In that oration Marsi avows that his purpose is praise. But he engages, rather, in trying to prove the soul's immortality, sometimes by means of a chain of proof-texts. He quotes or refers to Aquinas, Averroes, Avicenna, and Nicholas of Lyra by name. The first part of the oration refutes the idea that "the philosophers" knew the soul was immortal. The second part adduces theological arguments to prove its immortality, and the third part presents Christ's Ascension as confirmation of it. Several times the dignity of man is expounded, and the *Exultet* is quoted.[117] But this oration is very different from Massari's for the same feast some years earlier.

We might now look in succession at three Dominicans who exercised the office of procurator general of their order from the time of Innocent VIII through the pontificate of Julius II. The first of these is Lodovico Va-

114. These orations are listed in the Appendix. The similarity of the titles must not be allowed to obscure the fact that there are two distinct orations on Stephen, Hain #*10785 (and #*10784) and #10786.

115. *Panegyricus in memoriam sancti Augustini* [Rome: E. Silber, n.d.], Hain #10787.

116. In the first oration on St. Stephen, he speaks of himself as "novus in hoc genere dicendi et in spatiis Romani gymnasii hactenus versatus." *Oratio in die sancti Stephani* [Rome: S. Plannck, n.d.], Hain #*10785, fol. [1ᵛ]. I am not certain precisely what interpretation can be given those words, but the fact is that the second panegyric (Hain #10786) on Stephen, delivered probably in 1487 (Burchard, *Liber Notarum*, I, 216), is less thematic than the first. Marsi's words, at the very least, indicate that his own training in rhetoric and his teaching of it are not grounds for inferring practice in sacred epideictic, with perhaps the exception of funeral eulogies. Marsi is one of the few preachers at the court on whom Pastor specifically comments. He states that in the panegyric on St. John, "The wealth of classical reminiscences which the reader encounters stands in singular contrast to the subject of the oration, praise of John the Evangelist." It is ironical that Pastor elected such a traditional preacher for his implied criticism. He suggests that Marsi's style, as he incorrectly interprets it, was the rule at the court. See *Geschichte der Päpste*, 4ᵗʰ ed. (Freiburg: Herder, 1899), III, 250–51; this section does not appear in the English edition; translation is mine. Pastor was incorrect in assigning this oration to 1487; see Burchard, *Liber Notarum*, I, 216. It seems, rather, to be the one Burchard describes for Dec. 27, 1485, I, 136: "Sermonem fecit quidam discipulus Pomponii absque omnium laude."

117. *Oratio in die ascensionis de immortalitate animae* [Rome: E. Silber, n.d.], Hain-Cop. #*10790.

lentia da Ferrara (Ludovicus de Valentia Ferrariensis).[118] He was born in
Ferrara towards the middle of the century, and he decided early to follow
in his father's footsteps by pursuing a degree in law. At the age of twenty-
two, however, he entered the Dominican order at Bologna, where four
years later he was already a "lector philosophiae ac theologiae." After another four years, the Duke of Ferrara, Ercole d'Este, by means of an
Apostolic Brief, had him transferred back to his home town to teach
philosophy there. Six years later the Venetian Senate engaged him to
teach theology at the University of Padua, and eventually, through the
offices of Oliviero Carafa, he was appointed procurator general in 1491.
He held that office until his death in 1496. He supposedly debated with
Pico della Mirandola "in aula pontificis" sometime during his life; if
there is any truth in that assertion, the debate would have taken place
in 1487, the year Pico presented his theses to Innocent VIII.[119] During the
course of Lodovico's career, he wrote a treatise on the Eucharist, compiled
an *enchiridion* of Aristotle's ethics, and wrote commentaries on Lombard
and Aquinas, as well as other works. His eloquence was praised by Pietro
Marsi, who according to the conceits of the times compared him with
Demosthenes and Cicero.[120] The preacher of his funeral eulogy, Timotheus
de Totis of Modena, pronounced a considerably more measured judgment: in his day he was regarded as the best orator at the *cappelle
pontificie*.[121]

---

118. The best source for information on Lodovico is his funeral eulogy by a fellow
Dominican, Timotheus de Totis of Modena, *Oratio de funere Ludovici de Ferraria*
[Rome: E. Silber, 1496], Cop. #5843. Timotheus was himself a preacher for the
cappelle, and two of his sermons have survived in the same printing as the eulogy,
Cop. #5843: (1) before Alexander VI for the feast of the Ascension, *Sermo quod
omnino datur ultimus finis creaturae rationalis*, and (2) for the same pope, first Sunday
of Advent, *Sermo qualiter possimus Iesum Christum induere*. There is another printing of these two sermons, Cop. #5844. Like the sermons of Lodovico, these sermons
of Timotheus are representative examples of how elements of thematic and epideictic
could be effectively combined. Timotheus was born about 1462. He was ordained a
priest in Rome in 1486. By 1489 he was teaching at the Dominican convent at Ferrara
with the title of Bachelor of Sacred Scripture, and by 1499 he was a Master of Sacred
Theology. See Tommaso Kaeppeli, "Domenicani promossi agli ordini sacri presso la
Curia Romana (1426–1501)," *Archivum Fratrum Praedicatorum*, 34 (1964), 173.
    119. See Timotheus de Totis, *Oratio de funere Ludovici de Ferraria*, fol. [5ʳ].
    120. This encomium is appended to Timotheus's eulogy, fol. [5ʳ]. See Quint. X.1.
108–9, as well as X.1.76–79, 82; see also McManamon, "Ideal Renaissance Pope," p.
37, and my "Renaissance Panegyrics of Aquinas," pp. 184–85.
    121. *Oratio de funere Ludovici de Ferraria*, fol. [4ʳ]: "Primus enim, pace aliorum
dixero, orator cappellae pontificis hoc tempore habebatur."

Five of his sermons from the *cappelle* survive.[122] They deserve some attention because they are good examples of how an effective compromise between thematic and epideictic preaching could be accomplished. As I indicated in the last chapter, it is this compromise-form or mixed-form that tends to dominate at the court particularly from about the time of Sixtus IV and Innocent VIII. What this means regarding structure is that the sermons open with a verse from Scripture. This is followed by an exordium, which often indicates a twofold or threefold division, and it ends with a prayer. Then there is the body of the sermon, which closes with a peroration. The fragmenting effect of the division is often mitigated by the indication of some leading idea or virtue or sentiment that will pervade the whole oration.

Within such a structure various purposes could be accomplished: while generally avoiding overly technical matters, theological doctrines could be reviewed. These doctrines at some point are seen as *beneficia* and are held up for admiration. It is such a double purpose we find in Lodovico's first oration on the Incarnation and in his second on Christ's temptation in the desert. In the fourth, on grace, he reverts to a much more thematic or scholastic treatment of the subject, and under the surface one even catches a glimpse of the scholastic dispute about the precise relationship between grace and charity. The fifth sermon is an exercise in looking up to the Church triumphant and the heavenly hierarchy to see the model for the Church on earth. Not surprisingly, Pseudo-Dionysius is referred to by name. Ekphrasis is employed in this oration in a modified and restrained way.

The third oration on the Last Judgment is more epideictic in character than any of the others. When speaking of the Last Day, Lodovico tries to depict the solemn scene where Christ sits as judge with all mankind gathered round him. The scriptural basis Lodovico uses for this scene is the twenty-fifth chapter of Matthew, where entrance into heaven is conceded not on the basis of faith or religious practices but solely on the basis of works of mercy—I was hungry and you fed me, I was thirsty and you gave me to drink, I was naked and you clothed me. The peroration directs a pointed reminder to Alexander VI, then probably in the first year of his pontificate, that on that Last Day he will have to render an account not only for himself but also for the entire flock confided to his

122. *Orationes quinque* [Rome: n. publ., after 1492], Hain-Cop. #6983.

pastoral care. Unlike some preachers in the late Middle Ages who dealt with eschatological subjects, Lodovico has nothing to say about the Devil and never threatens his listeners with the terrifying thought that the end might be nigh.

Cajetan's career is the best known of all the court preachers.[123] He exercised the office of procurator from 1501 until 1508, and left that office only to be elected, again with the strong support of Carafa, master general of the Dominican order. The one further bit of biographical information that might be especially pertinent is that, while master general, Cajetan worked for the reform of the order.[124]

Five sermons survive from his procuratorship.[125] The first of them, delivered on the first Sunday of Advent, 1501, before Alexander VI, deserves a somewhat careful examination. In the exordium Cajetan notes that the "Senate" expects great oratorical art in its preachers. He tries in fact to respond to this expectation by means of a Latinity which is among the most classicizing and difficult in the sermons at the court. Brandolini's canon of easy intelligibility suffers a setback from this distinguished scholastic theologian, who here tries sedulously to avoid scholastic terminology despite a subject matter that almost demands it. The classicizing intent of the Latin style is incontrovertibly clear from a summary he offers of the passage from Luke's Gospel (11:5–8) about the importunate friend. Cajetan's summary paraphrases the passage into altogether classical vocabulary and syntax. When we set this summary alongside the passage from Luke, we dispel any doubt about Cajetan's determination to appropriate a classicizing style and to eschew, whenever he thought appropriate, even the Latin of the Vulgate.[126] On the other hand, whenever

123. Some recent studies on Cajetan, which contain further bibliographical information, are: Marvin O'Connell, "Cardinal Cajetan: Intellectual and Activist," *The New Scholasticism*, 50 (1976), 310–22; Anton Bodem, *Das Wesen der Kirche nach Kardinal Cajetan: Ein Beitrag zur Ekklesiologie im Zeitalter der Reformation*, Trierer theologische Studien, No. 25 (Trier: Paulinus, 1971); Olivier de la Brosse, *Le pape et le concile: La comparaison de leurs pouvoirs à la veille de la Réforme*, Unam Sanctam, No. 58 (Paris: Cerf, 1965); Jared Wicks, "Thomism between Renaissance and Reformation: The Case of Cajetan," *Archive for Reformation History*, 68 (1977), 9–32, and *Cajetan Responds: A Reader in Reformation Controversy* (Washington: The Catholic University of America Press, 1978).

124. In particular, see Gabriel M. Löhr, "De Caietano Reformatore Ordinis Praedicatorum," *Angelicum*, 11 (1934), 593–602.

125. The edition I will use is found in Cajetan's *Opuscula omnia* (Lyons: G. Rovillius, 1588), pp. 181–89. The sermons are ably analyzed by Wicks, "Thomism."

126. The text of the Vulgate is as follows: "Et ait ad illos: Quis vestrum habebit amicum, et ibit ad illum media nocte et dicet illi: Amice, commoda mihi tres panes, quoniam amicus meus venit de via ad me, et non habeo quod ponam ante illum;

he actually quotes Scripture verbatim, he quotes the Vulgate accurately and precisely.

The purpose of this oration is to "please" both the understanding and the affections. Such a purpose is preeminently consonant with epideictic. But the sermon is in fact an appeal to the head, and that appeal is in terms of proving a point. Except for the *oblectare* of the exordium, the epideictic verbs are absent. Instead we find *disputare, disserere, docere,* and *demonstrare.* A very brief peroration takes notice of the "collapsed" condition of religion, and it therefore exhorts to prayer.

The ostensible subject of the sermon is, as a matter of fact, the efficacy of prayer and divine cult, "De vi cultus divini et orationis efficacia." Cajetan turns this subject into a disquisition on man's causality. The basic argument is that prayer is truly an efficient cause. Since prayer is the prayer of man, however, man is thus vindicated as a true cause. God desires in his goodness that man participate in the divine prerogatives as much as possible, and he has devised that man share even in his causality. In Cajetan's words, God has communicated to man "agendi virtutes."[127] The "deification" of man, the elevation of men to be "divinae consortes naturae" (2 Pet. 1:4), consists in fitting him for action.[128] Man is thereby made a cooperator with God and a co-cause with him, a "friend." In one of the few emotional passages in the sermon, Cajetan marvels at how God has dignified his servants with such exalted powers.[129]

By an exposition of standard Thomistic doctrine on secondary causality and on man's "participation in the divine nature," Cajetan has established the Renaissance themes of man's dignity and the emphasis on action that we associate with Jacob Burckhardt. Burckhardt would be surprised, however, to see these themes grounded in an orthodox Christian theology.

---

et ille deintus respondens dicat: Noli mihi molestus esse, iam ostium clausum est, et pueri mei mecum sunt in cubili; non possum surgere et dare tibi. Et si ille perseveraverit pulsans, dico vobis, etsi non dabit illi surgens eo quod amicus eius sit, propter improbitatem tamen eius surget et dabit illi quotquot habet necessarios." Cajetan's summary in the "Oratio de vi cultus divini et orationis efficacia" reads, *Opuscula,* p. 183: "Clausis ostiis intempesta nocte se puerisque suis somnum capientis evangelicus amicus post negatum mutuum, post increpatam molestiam improbitate pulsantis victus, quotquot opportuni fuerant panes elargitus est." Note esp. the substitution for the Vulgate's "media nocte" the classical expression "intempesta nocte" (cf. Cic. Phil. 1.3; id. Pis. 38; Verg. A. 3.587; id. G. 1.247), for "mecum sunt in cubili" the expression "somnum capientibus" (cf. Cic. Tusc. 4.19.44; Plaut. Mil. 3.1.115).

127. "Oratio de vi cultus divini et orationis efficacia," in *Opuscula,* p. 182.
128. *Ibid.,* pp. 182–83.
129. *Ibid.,* p. 183.

This sermon well exemplifies the complexity of the relationship between Scholasticism and Humanism in these sacred orators of the court.

The other four sermons seem to become ever more scholastic in purpose and treatment as we move along chronologically. However, especially in the second and third, the idea of man's dignity recurs implicitly or explicitly, and a fundamentally optimistic view of human nature prevails. The subject of the fourth sermon, it might be noted, is the immortality of the soul.[130] The fifth is on the professedly "conjectural" subject of how the damned souls suffer from physical fire in hell. The treatment is dispassionate and objective. This sermon is the most thematic of the five, and it seems to be a unique example of this subject in the sermons of the *cappelle*.

The oration Cajetan delivered before Julius II and the Fifth Lateran Council in 1512, conceived against the background of the tense ecclesio-political crisis of the Pisan Schism, invites the council to turn its eyes heavenwards if it wishes to find the true exemplar of the Church.[131] Against that exemplar it can test the inauthenticity of the "Pisan Church," and it can see what is required in the reform of "our Church." It is not wholly fanciful to detect all three of the classical *genera* operative in this oration: judicial—the "Pisan Church" stands in the dock, accused of crime;[132] deliberative—the Fathers must be persuaded to take the right course of action in the Lateran Council; demonstrative—Cajetan "impresses his ideas" on them about the true model of the Church.

Cajetan's successor in 1508 as procurator was Nicolaus Splenger a Schomberg (Schönbergt).[133] Born of a noble family of Swabia in 1472, he came to Italy at an early age for his studies. At Pisa he received his doctorate "in utroque iure." By 1495 he had met Savonarola and taken him as

---

130. "Oratio de immortalitate animorum," in *Opuscula*, pp. 186–88. This sermon has been translated into English by James K. Sheridan under the title, "On the Immortality of Minds," in *Renaissance Philosophy*, ed. Leonard A. Kennedy (The Hague: Mouton, 1973), pp. 46–54.

131. I will use the edition in the *Opuscula*, pp. 189–92, because of the defects in the Mansi edition to which Nelson H. Minnich has called attention, "Concepts of Reform Proposed at the Fifth Lateran Council," *Archivum Historiae Pontificiae*, 7 (1969), 239–41. On the Mansi edition, see also Clare O'Reilly, " 'Without Councils We Cannot Be Saved': Giles of Viterbo Addresses the Fifth Lateran Council," *Augustiniana*, 27 (1977), 166–204, esp. 179–81.

132. Erasmus notes in his *Ecclesiastes*, LB, V, 894: "Rarum est autem concionatorem in genere iudiciali versari, sed tamen ab hac specie non multum abest cum e suggesto disserit adversus Iudaeos, haereticos aut schismaticos, aut etiam paganos."

133. See Pastor, VII, 167, 219, 238, 458, and Daniel-Antonin Mortier, *Histoire des Maîtres Généraux de l'ordre des Frères Prêcheurs*, V (Paris A. Picard, 1911), 154.

his spiritual guide. Within two years he entered the Dominican order at the convent of San Marco in Florence, and in 1506 he became prior there. One of Cajetan's first acts as master general was to appoint this one-time disciple of Savonarola his successor in the procuratorship. When Schomberg left that office in 1512, he continued an active career in the order and, like Cajetan, ended his days a cardinal. These two distinguished members of the Order of Preachers are buried almost side by side at the entrance to the Church of the Minerva in Rome.

Five of Schomberg's sermons before Julius II were published at Leipzig in 1512 and republished there in 1684.[134] In these sermons Schomberg employs the mixed structure described above, or at least a structure that is only vestigially thematic. There is a persistently moral emphasis in the sermons. But, apart from these two factors, all the sermons are otherwise epideictic. They are brief, to the point, and, even in those dealing with sin and the trials of this life, ultimately positive in outlook.[135] The last two sermons deal with two subjects we encounter elsewhere in sermons at the court: Providence or the order of the universe and the immortality of the soul.

We associate Schomberg with Savonarola. Two friars who arrived at the court at just about the time he left the procuratorship in 1512 we can associate with the name of Pico della Mirandola. The first of these is a Servite by the name of Agostino Filippi (Augustinus Philippus Florentinus). He was presumably a Florentine by birth. He was procurator general of the order from 1512 until his death in 1521, and he left ten sermons preached before Julius II and Leo X. Outside these lean facts, nothing else is known about him at present.[136] The ten sermons retain some elements of the thematic structure, but they almost without exception turn their materials to an epideictic purpose, which sometimes is announced.

---

134. *Orationes vel potius divinorum eloquiorum enodationes* (Leipzig: W. Stöckel, 1512); *Orationes V Romae* (Leipzig: D. Fleischerus, 1684).

135. I am here revising the opinion of Schomberg's orations I proposed in "Preaching for the Popes," in *The Pursuit of Holiness in Late Medieval and Renaissance Religion: Papers from the University of Michigan Conference*, ed. Charles Trinkaus with Heiko Oberman, Studies in Medieval and Reformation Thought, No. 10 (Leiden: Brill, 1974), p. 413.

136. See Alessio Rossi, *Manuale di storia dell'ordine dei Servi di Maria (MCCXXXIII–MCMLIV)* (Rome: S. Marcello, 1956), p. 799, and Arcangelo Maria Giani, *Annalium sacri ordinis Fratrum Servorum Beatae Mariae Virginis*, 2 vols. (Florence: C. Junta, 1618–22), II, fol. 81ʳ. The sermons are found in two publications: *Orationes novem coram Iulio II et Leone X* (Rome: J. Mazochius, 1518) and *Oratio die epiphaniae MDXX* [Rome: S. Guileretus, 1520].

This is true, for instance, even of somewhat unpromising materials like the sacraments, or especially like "truth" in the sermon "De veritate." Recurring in these sermons are various articulations of the idea of the dignity of man and descriptions of the different processes by which men are spiritually "transformed." "Contemplation," in the epideictic sense, often reappears as one of those processes.

Perhaps the most intriguing aspect of Filippi's sermons, however, is his use of Pico della Mirandola's "Oration on the Dignity of Man." In the sermon "De veritate," he in effect continues the discussion of Pico's views on man's indeterminacy that had been raised some months earlier in the sermon on Ash Wednesday, 1513, by the Spanish Augustinian, Dionisio Vázquez. What we must advert to is that both preachers, with certain implicit qualifications, subscribe to Pico's views and actually quote him. They are not the only preachers for the Renaissance popes to do so.[137] We verify in the incorporation of Pico's "Oration" into the sermons at the court a good instance of the interaction between secular and sacred oratory in the Renaissance.

Besides the Ash Wednesday sermon in 1513, Vázquez preached a sermon on the Hypostatic Union for Leo X on the third Sunday of Advent, 1517. For a further analysis of these two sermons, I refer the reader to the recent editions of them, and about the second I will simply state that it is perhaps somewhat more thematic in purpose and treatment.[138] But a word must be said here about Vázquez's career.[139] He was born in Toledo in 1479 and entered the Augustinians when he was about nineteen. He early won the favor of Charles of Hapsburg. When in 1522, for instance, he accepted the appointment to the new chair of Scripture at Alcalá, Charles imposed one condition: he must continue as Lenten preacher in the pulpit of his palace. Vázquez supposedly introduced the new humanistic exegesis into Alcalá, where he lectured on Romans and John's Gospel. He also introduced the "new style" of preaching, i.e., a classicizing substitute for the thematic sermon. More interesting still, on March 28,

137. Others, for instance, would be Inghirami and Hieronymus Arzius. See the next chapter and also my "Preaching for the Popes," pp. 425–29.

138. *Oratio in die cinerum* (Rome: J. Mazochius, 1513), now critically edited by me, "An Ash Wednesday Sermon on the Dignity of Man for Pope Julius II, 1513." The second oration is *De unitate et simplicitate personae Christi in duabus naturis oratio* (Rome: J. Mazochius, 1518), now in the modern edition by Quirino Fernandez, "Fray Dionisio Vázquez de Toledo, orador sagrado del Siglo de Oro," *Archivo Agustiniano*, 60 (1976), 105–204, esp. 158–78.

139. See the article by Fernandez referred to in the previous note.

1527, he defended Erasmus against the charges of the Spanish Inquisition, and Marcel Bataillon numbers him among Erasmus's more ardent allies in Spain.[140]

These case studies might now be concluded by a composite examination of the orations of three preachers at the court who without any ambiguity can be described as humanists—Aurelio Brandolini, Tommaso Inghirami, and Battista Casali. If we wish to apply a negative criterion to the term humanist in these instances, we can simply affirm that the three preachers never studied philosophy, theology, or law "in the schools." If we wish to speak more positively, we can say that their writings and their occupations were those the Renaissance conventionally assigned to men dedicated to the cause of good letters.

Brandolini, the Florentine, belongs to an earlier generation than the other two, and he presumably associated with Leto and Platina during his years at the court of Sixtus IV and Innocent VIII. A portion of his career has already been described, and there is no need to repeat here a chronology of his life, which is easily available elsewhere.[141] A brief listing of some of his writings, however, will be useful because of their importance for the rest of the book. Besides his sacred orations and the treatise on letter writing, Brandolini composed verses in praise of the accomplishments of Sixtus IV,[142] a treatise retelling in a humanistic style the story of the Old Testament,[143] a comparison of monarchies and republics dedicated to Lorenzo the Magnificent,[144] a dialogue on the human condition dedicated to King Matthias Corvinus of Hungary, in whose court he spent several years,[145] and towards the very end of his life another treatise on the condition of man entitled *Christiana paradoxa*, in obvious imita-

---

140. *Érasme et l'Espagne: Recherches sur l'histoire spirituelle du XVIe siècle* (Paris: Droz, 1937), pp. 255, 319, 373, 476, 522, 606.

141. See note 16, Chapter Two.

142. "De laudibus beatissimi patris Sixti IV pontificis maximi libri," BAV cod. Urb. lat. 739. Some excerpts were published by Eugène Müntz, *Les arts à la cour des papes pendant le XVe et le XVIe siècle*, 3e partie (Paris: E. Thorin, 1882), pp. 56–60.

143. "Epitoma in sacram Iudaeorum historiam," BAV cod. Ottob. lat. 438.

144. "De comparatione rei publicae et regni ad Laurentium Medicem Florentinae rei publicae principem libri tres," in *Irodalomtörténeti emlékek. II: Olaszországi XV századbeli íróknak Mátyás királyt dicsöitö müvei*, ed. Ábel Jenö (Budapest: 1890), pp. 77–183. The treatise has been analyzed by Lynn Thorndike, *"Lippus Brandolinus De Comparatione Reipublicae et Regni*: A Treatise in Comparative Political Science," in *Science and Thought in the Fifteenth Century* (New York: Columbia University Press, 1929), pp. 233–60.

145. *De humanae vitae conditione et toleranda corporis aegritudine* (Basel: R. Winter, 1543).

tion of Cicero's *Paradoxa Stoicorum*.[146] Though hardly an original think-er, Brandolini for that reason reveals in his writings all the more about the mentality and values which obtained among his contemporaries.

Inghirami and Casali were active at the court from the days of Alex-ander VI. Inghirami was born in Volterra in 1470 of a family that had connections at the papal court.[147] As a young man he studied under Leto in Rome, where he was active as secretary, poet, and orator until his death there in 1516. In 1503 Alexander VI conferred upon him a canonry in the Lateran. In 1505 Julius II named him prefect of the Vatican Library and later made him a canon of Saint Peter's, and he also conferred other honors on him.

Inghirami delivered a sermon *coram papa* on the feast of All Saints, 1497, which Burchard described as received "cum magna omnium laude."[148] Though we have a number of orations by Inghirami delivered in Rome, including the funeral eulogy for Julius II, the only other sermon for a *cappella* that has been found is the one for Good Friday, 1504.[149] There has been some speculation that Inghirami was the paganizing orator whom Erasmus supposedly heard on Good Friday during his visit to Rome in 1509 and whom he has Bulephorus criticize so mercilessly in the *Ciceronianus*.[150] But there is no basis in the date or in the contents of this oration to support such a thesis, and no solid evidence has been adduced in favor of it.

Casali was a member of a somewhat important Roman family, and like Inghirami he studied poetry and eloquence under Leto.[151] In 1496 at the early age of twenty-three, he began teaching Latin at the *Studium Urbis*. On Ash Wednesday, 1502, he delivered his first sermon at the papal court in the presence of Alexander VI, who was displeased with the

146. Rome: F. Minitius Calvus, 1531.

147. On Inghirami, see McManamon, "Ideal Renaissance Pope," pp. 14–15, 30–33, passim; Isabella Inghirami, "Notizie dei codici, degli autografi e delle stampe riguar-danti le opere dell'umanista volterrano Tommaso Inghirami, detto Fedro," *Rassegna Volterrana*, 21–23 (1955), 33–41; Annamaria Rugiadi, *Tommaso Fedra Inghirami: Umanista volterrano (1470–1516)* (Amatrice: Scuola Orfanotrofio, 1933); Paul Künzle, "Raffaels Denkmal für Fedro Inghirami auf dem letzten Arazzo," in *Mélanges Eugène Tisserant*, VI, Studi e Testi, No. 236 (Vatican City: BAV, 1964), 499–548.

148. Bibl. Guarn. cod. LIII.4.8 (formerly 5885), fols. 38ʳ–50ʳ; *Liber Notarum*, II, 58.

149. BN Paris cod. lat. 7352B, fols. 221ʳ–236ʳ.

150. See the references in Silvana Seidel Menchi, "Alcuni atteggiamenti della cul-tura italiana di fronte a Erasmo (1520–1536)," in *Eresia e riforma nell'Italia del Cinquecento*, Biblioteca del "Corpus Reformatorum Italicorum," Miscellanea I, ed. Luigi Firpo and Giorgio Spini (Florence: Sansoni, 1974), p. 106, n. 169.

151. On Casali, see Seidel Menchi, "Alcuni atteggiamenti," pp. 89–116.

preacher. The sermon is extant, and its contents offer no particularly obvious reason to explain why the pope was "valde turbatus," unless Alexander was annoyed by the unusually long peroration demanding from him a campaign against the Turks. The inference easily drawn from Burchard's comments is that Alexander was perturbed because of Casali's long hair and secular dress. At any rate, Casali's poetry and eloquence won for him the favor of both Julius II and Leo X. In 1508 Julius created him a canon of the Lateran, and in 1517 Leo conferred upon him the more lucrative benefice of a canonry in Saint Peter's. A number of Casali's letters and other works survive, including an "Invectiva in Erasmum" from 1524 in defense of the Roman humanists against Erasmus's criticisms. Besides the Ash Wednesday sermon for Alexander VI, three other sermons before Julius II and a fourth preached probably for Leo X are also extant in the Biblioteca Ambrosiana of Milan.[152] Casali died in 1525.

The sacred orations of these three humanists abandon all features which characterize the structure of a thematic sermon. Inghirami's sermon for Good Friday is extraordinarily long, and its style is somewhat difficult, even inflated. The style of the other sermons is elegant but readily intelligible. Almost all the sermons are sustained by a broad dogmatic base consisting of Creation, Fall, and Redemption. This last doctrine sometimes leads the preachers into paradoxical encomia that are typically Christian, such as Casali's in praise of death in his sermon for the feast of the Ascension and in praise of Christ's cross on Good Friday. But the basic Christian doctrines are taken for granted in these sermons rather than proved or explained.

On the other hand, in almost all the sermons there is a decided tendency to review the great events of sacred history from the Old Testament, the life of Christ, and the early centuries of the Church. This means Scripture is interpreted in its "literal" or "historical" sense, and for all practical purposes allegory, numerology, etymology, and mystical meanings are not utilized. Moreover, Scripture is not employed principally as a source from which to develop doctrinal issues, much less as a chain of proof-texts. Christ's life, in particular, is presented as a series of *exempla* for our admiration and imitation, and his virtues are especially effectively treated by Brandolini. Christianity's moral superiority to the ethics of

152. They are all found in "Io. Baptistae Casalii epistolae, orationes, libelli supplices et alia id generis," Bibl. Ambr. cod. G.33 inf., I, fols. 303ᵛ–308ᵛ; II, fols. 2ʳ–22ᵛ. The first of these, I, fols. 303ʳ–308ᵛ, is the Ash Wednesday sermon preached for Alexander VI; see Burchard, *Liber Notarum*, II, 318.

the Romans and the events leading to its triumph over the Empire and the Emperors are several times recounted and celebrated at length.

Four of Casali's sermons have something to say about the threat of the Turks. In several instances he moves into some relatively abstract considerations of issues in moral philosophy that sound vaguely Neoplatonic. He also shows more interest in a general kind of natural philosophy than do the other two. Aside from some qualifications like these, the sermons of the three humanists have the humanistic bias we would expect—they are historical in their approach.

Our study of these fifteen or so selected "cases" is now completed, and it has merely skimmed the surface of what are often fascinating stories, most of which have yet to be explored in any detail by scholars. Moreover, we have sampled only a relatively small number from the approximately seventy preachers whose sermons from the *cappelle* I have been able to locate. I hope the review has conveyed some sense of the careers of the preachers, some sense of chronological movement, and some sense of the complexity of the questions under discussion. I chose these particular preachers because of the number of sermons and other works some of them wrote that are pertinent to our purposes and because of the diversity of their backgrounds and their special relationship, in some instances, to larger issues in Italy in the Quattrocento and early Cinquecento.

For other preachers very brief descriptions will have to suffice: Stephanus Thegliatius (d. 1515), made archbishop of Antivari in 1473 and transferred to Patras and Torcello in 1485, whose whole career was dominated by the problem of the Turk and who left four sermons *coram*;[153] Marco Maroldi, O.P. (d. 1495), who is the only Master of the Sacred Palace whose sermons have survived and who, in that office, dealt with Pico's case in 1487;[154] the Augustinian procurator, Giovan Battista Signori, who in 1487 sat on the commission investigating Pico;[155] Bernardino Carvajal

153. On Thegliatius (Teglatius, Tagliacci, Taleazzi, Taleazzo), see Minnich, "Concepts of Reform," pp. 198–201, and Bernardino Feliciangeli, "Le proposte per la guerra contro i turchi presentate da Stefano Taleazzi vescovo di Torcello a papa Alessandro VI," *Archivio della R. Società Romana di Storia Patria*, 40 (1917), 5–63.

154. Little is known about him. He is listed as "Marcus Maroldi della Bella" by Innocentius Taurisano, *Hierarchia Ordinis Praedicatorum*, 2nd ed. (Rome: Manuzio, 1916), pp. 48–49. He was a Neapolitan, and he held the office of Master from 1481 until 1490. He left the office on being elected bishop of Reggio Calabria. For the commission which examined the Pico case, see Giovanni di Napoli, *Giovanni Pico della Mirandola e la problematica dottrinale del suo tempo* (Rome: Desclée, 1965), p. 91.

155. He held the office of procurator from 1486 until 1488 according to N. Racanelli, "La Gerarchia Agostiniana: I Procuratori Generali dell'Ordine (1256–1931)," *Bollettino Storico Agostiniano*, 10 (1934), 142.

(d. 1523), whose sermons and orations are among the most thoroughly thematic to have come down to us from the period, who was eventually created a cardinal by Alexander VI in 1493 at the request of Ferdinand of Aragon and who in 1511 became a leader in the Pisan Schism against Julius II;[156] Pietro Galatino, O.M. (d. 1540), who wrote a number of cabalistic-Joachimite treatises on the reform of the Church, who looked desperately for the "Angelic Pastor" who would effect that reform, and whose *De archanis catholicae veritatis* defended Reuchlin in 1518, eventually running through at least seven editions before 1672;[157] Antonio Lollio of San Gemignano (d. 1486), secretary to Francesco Piccolomini, whose oration on the Circumcision Poliziano described as "golden" and whose oration on Passion Sunday of 1486 is permeated with anti-Semitic sentiments;[158] Cristoforo Marcello (d. 1527), apostolic prothonotary and then archbishop of Corcyra, *bête noire* of Paris de Grassis for his liturgical publications, mortal enemy of the "pagan" Aristotelians and of Martin Luther, victim of the Sack of Rome;[159] Tommaso Radini Tedeschini, O. P. (d. 1527), who over the objection of de Grassis was appointed "substi-

156. On Carvajal, see McManamon, "Ideal Renaissance Pope," pp. 16–17, 29–30, passim; Pastor, V, VI and VII passim; Strnad, *Todeschini-Piccolomini*, pp. 124, 241, 352, 386, 389. On the relationship of his oration on All Saints to Cosimo Rosselli's fresco in the Sistine Chapel, "The Sermon on the Mount," see L. D. Ettlinger, *The Sistine Chapel before Michelangelo: Religious Imagery and Papal Primacy* (Oxford: Clarendon, 1965), pp. 89–90; *Sermo in die omnium sanctorum* [Rome: G. Herolt, after Nov. 1, 1482], GKW #6154.

157. On Galatino, whose name is sometimes given as Pietro Colonna, see Arduinus Kleinhans, "De Vita et Operibus Petri Galatini, O.F.M., Scientiarum Biblicarum Cultoris (c.1460–1540)," *Antonianum*, 1 (1926), 145–79, 327–56. Galatino's sermon on Jan. 1, 1515, listed in the Appendix, deals with the question of man's Redemption, God's fidelity to his promises, the necessity of circumcision of heart, etc. Though some of the parts of it are fanciful, it does not adduce any cabalistic texts, nor does it indulge in apocalyptic speculation. In other words, it is more sober and conventional than Galatino's other works. Kleinhans lists another oration by Galatino for Good Friday, 1522, supposedly printed that same year, p. 179. Like Kleinhans, I have been unable to find a copy of it.

158. On Lollio, see Strnad, *Todeschini-Piccolomini*, esp. pp. 333–34, 370–71. Among his writings there are "De institutione pontificis," "De coelibatu sacerdotum," and a "Vita sanctae Eugeniae." The principal codices containing his writings are: Bibl. Ang. cod. lat. 1077, BAV cod. Vat. lat. 8092, and BAV cod. Chigi F.IV.83.

159. On Marcello, see Minnich, "Concepts of Reform," pp. 181–83, and Joaquim Nabuco's introduction to *Le Cérémonial Apostolique avant Innocent VIII: Texte du manuscrit Urbinate Latin 469 de la Bibliothèque Vaticane établi par Dom Filippo Tamburini*, Bibliotheca "Ephemerides Liturgicae," Sectio Historica, No. 30 (Rome: Edizioni Liturgiche, 1966), pp. 34*–38*. Marcello published in 1521 his *De auctoritate summi pontificis* (Florence: P. Junta, 1521), defending papal supremacy over a council and refuting various positions of Luther. Moreover, in the peroration of his "De laudibus Ioannis evangelistae" for Pope Clement VII, delivered shortly after Clement's election, he mentions the "Lutheran plague," BAV cod. Vat. lat. 3644, fol. 10ʳ.

tute" to Prierias as Master of the Sacred Palace in 1521 and who had already written against Luther in the previous year;[160] Baptista Mantuanus, O.Carm. (d. 1516), religious poet esteemed by Pico, prior general of his order and advocate of reform, whom Pope Leo XIII in 1885 officially declared a "blessed" of the Church.[161] Neglect will have to be the fate of the careers of other preachers, even of important figures like Gravina, Campano, Mithridates, Mariano da Genazzano, and others who have already been mentioned earlier.

At this point, some general conclusions about the materials reviewed in this chapter might well be stated. First of all, certain relationships between sacred epideictic and its secular counterpart have emerged, especially concerning the device of ekphrasis. Some instances of the early adaptation of epideictic to Christian purposes have been indicated, and the suggestion has been made that the adaptation to funeral eulogies and to panegyrics of the saints was earlier, easier, and more frequent than the adaptation to Christian mysteries. Not surprisingly, Padua, Venice, and Florence were the foci of interest for the first half of the Quattrocento.

It was then possible to document the fact that by the time of Nicholas V, and seemingly not before then, sacred epideictic was in use in the papal chapel in Rome. Through the next few pontificates, however, the thematic sermon was the usual form for the *cappelle,* employed even by preachers who we know could construct funeral eulogies and other orations according to the precepts of classical rhetoric. Why this situation prevailed is subject to conjecture—the weight of tradition favoring the

160. See Giuseppe Berti's introduction to Radini's *Orazione contro Filippo Melantone,* ed. Flaminio Ghizzoni (Brescia: Paideia, 1973). Paris de Grassis describes Radini as a person "qui aliquando in cappella oravit tam eleganter," "Diarium," Palm Sunday, 1521, BAV cod. Vat. lat. 12275, fol. 393[r]. The only one of his orations from the *cappelle* which seems to have survived is for All Saints, 1520, Bibl. Ricc. cod. 904, fasc. 8, fols. 87[v]–92[r]. This oration is not mentioned by Berti, and he seems not to have known of it.

161. There is considerable literature on Mantuanus. See Edmondo Coccia, *Le edizioni delle opere del Mantovano,* Collectanea Bibliographica Carmelitana, No. 2 (Rome: Institutum Carmelitanum, 1960); Graziano di S. Teresa, "Ramenta Carmelitana, 13: Nuova cronologia della vita del b. Battista Mantovano," *Ephemerides Carmeliticae,* 9 (1958), 423–57. See now esp. Kristeller, *Medieval Aspects,* pp. 65–71, where extensive bibliographical information is provided; Rodolfo Girardello, "Vita e testi inediti del beato Battista Spagnoli," *Carmelus,* 21 (1974), 36–98; and Romano Rosa, "Tomismo e antitomismo in Battista Spagnoli Mantovano (1447–1516)," *Memorie Domenicane,* NS 7 (1976), 227–64. I am very much indebted to Professor Nelson Minnich of the Catholic University of America for obtaining and checking bibliographical information for me at the Carmelitana Collection in Washington, D. C. I am also indebted to Rev. Joachim Smet, O. Carm., of the Institutum Carmelitanum, Rome, for similar assistance.

thematic form, failure to perceive how epideictic would be adapted to doctrinal subject matter, lack of materials illustrating how to adapt it. At any rate, from about the time of Sixtus IV and Innocent VIII, the impact of classical rhetoric is broadly evidenced by the frequent use of the mixed form, especially in preachers from the mendicant orders. In these instances, the sermons tend to be less visual and less historical in approach than the fully epideictic sermons by humanists like Aurelio Brandolini, Inghirami, and Casali; but typically Renaissance themes, like the dignity of man, recur in them.

A certain versatility is observable in many of the preachers, an ability to use either the thematic or the epideictic form, and caution must be exercised in designating a preacher or his sermons as thematic or epideictic. For instance, Cajetan exemplifies that a classicizing style is no sure indication that a sermon is in other ways characteristically humanistic, and Marsi shows that even a teacher of classical rhetoric may be reluctant to apply his principles to an oration *coram* if he is treating a mystery like the Ascension, or he may indeed even be incapable of doing so.

In brief, what this chapter has tried to accomplish is to provide some evidence about the origins of sacred epideictic in the Renaissance and provide, at the same time, some evidence suggesting how it arrived at the papal court and how it fared there until the death of Leo X.[162] Now, before closing the chapter, we might for a moment look away from the court to see how that style of preaching fared elsewhere in the second half of the Quattrocento and the early years of the Cinquecento. What I am offering, obviously, is merely a few pieces for an interlocking puzzle whose hundreds of details have yet to be gathered.

First of all, there is no evidence that sacred epideictic had any immediate impact on popular preaching in Rome itself during the second half of the Quattrocento. Bernardino da Feltre preached in Rome during Lent of 1482, and he is said to have attracted "prelates and cardinals and have merited the praises of Sixtus IV."[163] Roberto da Lecce preached there in

---

162. The most convenient point to begin a study of the history of preaching at the court for the remainder of the century would be the collection of sermons made by Paolo di Francis, O.P. (Paulus de Francis), *Orationes selectae in sacello apostolico infra missarum solemnia, coram summo pontifice sacroque purpuratorum patrum senatu habitae* (Rome: A. Zannettus, 1606). Unfortunately, di Francis decided to omit the names of the preachers, and he does not provide dates for the sermons. Despite its defects, it is valuable as the only collection of sermons *coram* that exists. There is a copy of this somewhat rare book at the Bibl. Ang.

163. See Alfredo Galletti, *L'eloquenza (Dalle origini al XVI secolo)* (Milan: F. Vallardi, 1938), p. 267, with no source indicated.

1492, and he, too, supposedly was very well received.[164] But the sermons of these two preachers as we now have them show no impact of the new rhetoric. The same is true of the sermons of Paolo Attavanti, who possibly preached in Rome in the 1460's.[165] Ambrogio Spiera, procurator general of the Servites, preached Lenten series in the church of San Marcello in 1453 and 1454.[166] Unlike the other three preachers, Spiera would have been present at the *cappelle*, but he seems to have made no application of the new style to his own preaching. In other words, the meager evidence we presently have is negative.

Preachers of the court were known and appreciated outside Rome, as we have already seen for Mariano da Genazzano and Aurelio Brandolini. Matteo Bosso was a great admirer of Brandolini and possibly imitated him in his Good Friday oration in Latin, 1495.[167] This sermon by Bosso makes effective use of the epideictic genre. Bosso had been a procurator in Rome for the canons regular of the Lateran congregation from 1486 until 1488, so he would have heard other preachers besides Brandolini using the classical style.[168]

Giovanni Pontano, admirer of both Mariano da Genazzano and Giles of Viterbo, composed a "Sermo Aegidii ad Populum" to illustrate how a worthy successor of Mariano should preach.[169] The little sermon on the excellence of Christ and on the benefits he confers on mankind bears no

---

164. See Galletti, *L'eloquenza*, p. 274. Erasmus's wicked story about Roberto's sermon *coram* is probably false, certainly exaggerated; see *Ecclesiastes*, LB, V, 985–86. On Roberto, see also *ibid.*, 982. For an instance of a popular preacher in Rome, "natione incognitus," who in 1491 predicted dire events and the eventual appearance of the "angelic pastor," see Stefano Infessura, *Diario della città di Roma*, ed. Oreste Tommasini, Fonti per la storia d'Italia (Rome: Istituto Storico Italiano), pp. 264–65). On the problem of the "angelic pastor," see Pastor, V, 224–25; Friedrich Baethgen, *Der Engelpapst*, Schriften der Königsberger gelehrten Gesellschaft, Geisteswiss. Kl., 10 Jahr, Hft. 2 (Halle: M. Niemeyer, 1933), pp. 75–119; Bernard McGinn, "Angel Pope and Papal Antichrist," *Church History*, 47 (1978), 155–73. Erasmus at least twice asserts he heard at Rome a preacher who claimed the gift of prophecy; see *Ecclesiastes*, LB, V, 798, 954. The Fifth Lateran Council tried to deal with the problem of apocalyptic preaching in its decree, "Supernae maiestatis praesidio," Dec. 19, 1516.

165. See Galletti, *L'eloquenza*, pp. 300–302, and the unsigned article on him in the DBI.

166. On Spiera, see Ronald M. Rentner, "Ambrosius Spiera: A Fifteenth-Century Italian Preacher and Scholar," *Church History*, 43 (1974), 448–59.

167. *In Iesu Christi salvatoris passione flebilis et devotissimus sermo* (Bologna: Plato de Benedictis, 1495), GKW #4960 (another printing, GKW #4961).

168. See the article in the DBI by C. Mutini.

169. The "Sermo" is part of Pontano's "Aegidius," found in *I dialoghi [di Pontano]*, ed. Carmelo Previtera (Florence: Sansoni, 1943), pp. 241–84.

resemblance to thematic sermons, and it fulfills the general criteria established for epideictic, though not so obviously as some of the other sermons we have discussed. The Latin oration on the Incarnation given at Bergamo in 1463 by the humanist Giovanni Michele Alberto Carrara, in contrast, is classicizing in style and structure but thoroughly thematic in intent.[170]

Poliziano read Lollio's sermon, and he esteemed the preaching of Mariano.[171] More important, we have three little vernacular sermons composed and recited by him as a boy or young man in one of the Florentine confraternities for the laity.[172] The third of these is of some interest. By the time Poliziano wrote it, he was probably in his late teens or even early twenties. In purpose, vocabulary, and general treatment of God's "maravigliose opere e virtù," he generally fulfills what is required for an epideictic sermon.[173]

Vázquez, we are told, was influential on sacred oratory in Spain. The first wave of his influence, presumably, was in courtly and academic circles, but a collection of his sermons in Castilian has fortunately survived and been published.[174] The fact that he preached in the vernacular indicates a wider audience for his sermons than his career in court and

170. *Opera poetica, philosophica, rhetorica, theologica,* ed. Giovanni Battista Giraldi (Novara: Istituto Geografico de Agostini, 1967), pp. 155–66. My judgment is based on the selection from the oration and the summary contained in this edition.

171. On Poliziano and the preachers, see Ida Maïer, *Ange Politien: La formation d'un poète humaniste,* Travaux d'Humanisme et Renaissance, No. 81 (Geneva: Droz, 1966), pp. 426 (Lollio), 428 (A. Brandolini), 431 (Mariano da Genazzano), 434–35 (Bosso). In her *Les manuscrits d'Ange Politien,* Travaux d'Humanisme et Renaissance, No. 70 (Geneva: Droz, 1965), p. 393, n. 2, she mentions Poliziano's letter to Francesco Piccolomini praising the "golden" oration of Lollio, found in Poliziano's *Opera* (Basel: N. Episcopius, 1553), p. 110. She also reproduces a letter from Lollio to Poliziano describing a sermon on the cross of Christ by Giovanni Lorenzi, pp. 393–94. Lollio thought the sermon would soon be published, but I have not been able to find it in print or in manuscript.

172. *Prose volgari inedite e poesie latine e greche edite e inedite,* ed. Isidoro del Lungo (Florence: Barbèra, 1867), pp. 3–16. Zelinda Zafarana's article shows, on the other hand, that Florentines continued to hear more traditional sermons, moralistic in emphasis, "Per la storia religiosa di Firenze nel Quattrocento: Una raccolta privata di prediche," *Studi medievali,* Ser. 3, 9 (1968), 1017–1113.

173. On these sermons, see Galletti, *L'eloquenza,* pp. 299–300, whose judgment even on the third is somewhat negative. The youthful sermons to Florentine confraternities of Giovanni Nesi do not resemble the epideictic sermons of the papal court. These sermons of Nesi, certainly influenced by classical theory, are for the most part moralistic exhortations to virtue. For the texts along with an illuminating correlation with changes in Florentine culture and politics, see Cesare Vasoli, "Giovanni Nesi tra Donato Acciaiuoli e Girolamo Savonarola: Testi editi e inediti," *Memorie Domenicane,* NS 4 (1973), 103–79.

174. *Sermones,* ed. Félix G. Olmedo, Clásicos castellanos, No. 123 (Madrid: Espasa-Calpe, 1943).

university implies. Dominicus Crispus of Pistoia, who delivered the panegyric on Aquinas at the Minerva in 1493, preached an elegant and thoroughly epideictic oration in Latin on the Ascension at the court of Vladislav II, King of Hungary and Bohemia (1490–1516).[175]

As we have seen, by 1504 Reuchlin was trying to adapt classical principles to the Christian pulpit in Germany, and Schomberg's sermons were first published in Leipzig in 1512. But earlier than any of these instances in Germany is the oration delivered on Christmas Day, 1484, at Heidelberg. The orator is Rudolf Agricola.[176] The oration itself, addressed to "doctissimi viri," is as epideictic in style, subject matter, structure, and purpose as any I have examined. God's great deed is extolled and praised. God became man that he might make us sons of God. We must rejoice, therefore, and be glad. The oration was not published until 1527.[177] What influence it had before that date is yet to be established, but we know at least that sacred epideictic had a distinguished exponent outside Italy as early as the time Brandolini was writing his treatise in Rome at the papal court.

175. A presentation copy of this oration is now in the Library of the Serail, Istanbul, Ahmet III Collection, cod. 46. Professor Paul Oskar Kristeller kindly allowed me to use his microfilm of the oration.

176. *Oratio de nativitate Christi* (Paris: C. Wechelus, 1536). The sermon also appears in the second volume of Agricola's *Opera*, entitled *Lucubrationes aliquot lectu dignissimae* (Cologne: I. Gymnicus, [1539]), pp. 118–25, with the detailed analysis of its rhetoric in the "Scholia" by Alardus of Amsterdam (Aemstelred), pp. 125–37.

177. Tübingen: U. Morhardus, 1527. See H. E. J. M. van der Velden, *Rodolphus Agricola (Roelof Huusman): Een nederlandsch Humanist der vijftiende Eeuw* (Leiden: A. Sijthoff, n.d.), p. 234, n. 6.

CHAPTER FOUR. CHRISTIAN DOCTRINE: NUNC PACEM HABENT LITTERAE CHRISTIANAE

From the diaries of the Masters of Ceremonies, from Brandolini's treatise, and from the sermons themselves, the subject matter to which the preachers were to address their orations is clear. The preachers were to treat "divine things" and the great mysteries that surpass our understanding. However, as is clear from the history of Christian theology, the doctrines and beliefs of the Christian religion allow for considerable variety of interpretation and emphasis. Some ages and cultures have been preoccupied by one or other doctrine and have accorded it a practical or theological centrality that other ages and cultures have denied it. Moreover, particular theological methods or cultural presuppositions can impart to the same doctrine and can elicit from the same text a significance different from what it would have under different circumstances. It is precisely this phenomenon that we are now about to investigate as it manifests itself in the sacred orators of the papal court during the Renaissance.

I propose, therefore, to examine the general problem of the theological viewpoint advocated by the preachers of the *cappelle*. What doctrines did they emphasize, out of what presuppositions did the emphasis come, and what vision of reality was thereby projected? My purpose, ultimately, is to reconstruct the religious world view that animated the preachers and that to a greater or lesser degree they shared. From this world view we shall move in the following two chapters to two closely related questions: what ideal of the virtuous or reformed life did the preachers propose, and what elements comprised their ideal for a reformed Church and society?

The first problem every orator faces is the problem of "invention," i.e., what to speak about. To be told to speak about divine things and the mysteries of the Christian religion eliminated for the preachers at the court, if all went well, the temptation to turn a sacred discourse into a political harangue or a too obvious panegyric of the prince. But considerable scope for the preacher's ingenuity still remained. At the papal court that scope began to be narrowed through the influence on the sermon of certain principles of classical rhetoric. Concurrently, the expectations of the audience also gradually began to change. A lecture, many members of the court came to know well, is not a speech. From the pontificate of Nicholas V forward, these new rhetorical principles and these new audience-expecta-tions influenced even those sermons that still retained thematic features. They also influenced other writings of the preachers at the court—their poetry, their treatises, and of course their non-liturgical orations.

In other words, certain points of departure for the sacred orators at the court had been explicitly and self-consciously expounded as the classiciz-ing oration confronted the thematic sermon in the same arena of the papal liturgies. These points of departure can now be summarily stated. First of all, the sermon was to focus on the great truths, agreed upon by all, and it was to avoid technical and disputed questions. Secondly, insofar as the sermon was influenced by the *genus demonstrativum*, it was to focus on those truths that would excite sentiments of wonder, gratitude, love, and desire for imitation.

In the third place, the truths must be made relevant to the lives of the listeners. The sermons were expected to be doctrinally sound and theo-logically learned. At the same time they were not meant to be academic. The preacher's learning and all his proficiency in the art of oratory were to be directed to the single goal of aiding his listeners in their efforts to mas-ter the most important art of all—the art of good and blessed living. "Ars bene beateque vivendi" was Cicero's expression, but it was given a Chris-tian interpretation by the sacred orators of the court. No phrase brings us closer to what "humanist theology" or "rhetorical theology" was con-cerned with. None more sharply distinguishes that theology from the theology of the schools and the schoolmen.

The preacher's art was in no respect more difficult, however, than in this endeavor to relate learning to living, to relate doctrine to action. The success of the preacher could indeed be measured in terms of his ability to conjoin these two aspects of his art, as well as in his skill at not sacri-ficing one for the other. Though the sermons had to relate to man's con-cerns, they were to be about God and his message. These sermons at the court are, therefore, doctrinal sermons. The preachers meant to teach as well as to move and to please. They meant to move and to please by means of their teaching. The Renaissance preachers for the popes are not the Renaissance "preachers of repentance" whom Burckhardt and Pastor admired.[1] They are preachers of the Christian mysteries.

As the preachers of the court approach their task, many of them give

1. See Pastor, V, 175–80; Jacob Burckhardt, *The Civilization of the Renaissance in Italy*, trans. S. G. C. Middlemore, 2 vols. (New York: Harper and Row, 1958), II, 450–63.

evidence that they were aware of these points of departure. There were also other factors operative in the preachers' approach to their materials that were even more deeply imbedded in their consciousness. We have so far been discussing assumptions that in some way related to rhetoric and to rhetoric's proper function in sacred oratory. These other assumptions can be described as philosophical. They were concerned with the ultimate constitution of reality.

For the sake of brevity and clarity, I shall reduce the preachers' philosophical assumptions, as I see them, to nine general propositions: (1) reality is ordered; (2) reality is, consequently, coherent, and its parts interlock to form an harmonious totality; (3) the order and coherence of reality are discoverable, at least partially, by the human mind; (4) the discovery of order and coherence in its earthly expression discloses a divine exemplar that has impressed its own order and coherence upon earthly reality; (5) the order and coherence of earthly reality—the intelligibility of earthly reality—reflects the exemplar, as that exemplar is made known through a study of its earthly reflection and through the exemplar's direct revelation of itself; (6) thus, a study of the exemplar compels, in its turn, a study of the reality of the world; (7) earthly reality in fact participates in certain qualities of the exemplar; (8) besides the qualities of order and coherence in which earthly reality participates, the divine exemplar's quality of stability or immutability is of particular importance; (9) the order, coherence, and stability discovered in the universe have aesthetic implications, since they are the components of that aspect of reality known as beauty.[2]

These assumptions were so deeply imbedded in the preachers' consciousness that there was no clear perception that there might be alternatives to them. They seem to have been broadly accepted and taken for granted, though some of them were perhaps more explicit and firm for preachers trained in the scholastic tradition than for those who were not. Though they were sometimes articulated, they were articulated as statements of fact. Though they had an immense impact on how the preachers

---

2. A suggestive foil for these assumptions is provided by the second chapter, "The Cultural Background of the Current Situation," in Langdon Gilkey's *Naming the Whirlwind: The Renewal of God-Language* (Indianapolis: Bobbs-Merrill, 1969), pp. 31–71. Other books describe, in very different ways, the mentality implied by the assumptions I have listed, e.g., Peter L. Berger, *The Sacred Canopy: Elements of a Sociological Theory of Religion* (Garden City, N.Y.: Doubleday Anchor, 1969), esp. pp. 111–23; Eric Voegelin, *Order and History*, 3 vols. (Baton Rouge: Louisiana State University Press, 1956–57), esp. I, ix–xiv, 1–45, 452–81.

preached, they were not professedly correlated with any of the functions preaching was meant to serve.

Despite the fact that some of the preachers at the court may not have had much training in metaphysics or even had much patience with it, these assumptions are patently metaphysical in their scope. As such, they provided in their coherent form nothing less than a framework of interpretation through which the preachers viewed the universe. Consequently, these metaphysical assumptions can be translated into hermeneutical correlates. That is to say, these metaphysical assumptions prompted the preachers to fit what they saw, studied, and experienced into a prefabricated scheme of how they already knew reality was constituted.

Before descending to a more detailed examination of some of the assumptions and their implications, we might observe that they are compatible with certain Christian doctrines and that in the sermons and other writings of the preachers at the court they frequently find their most impressive formulation in terms of these doctrines. Providence is the doctrine that perhaps best captures the viewpoint underlying several of the assumptions. Though only a few sermons deal professedly with Providence as their principal subject matter, Providence is a belief that permeates them all, and it on occasion puts in a dramatic appearance at the crucial moment.[3] The conviction, namely, that God created and continues to govern the universe according to principles in accord with reason and goodness pervades the thinking of the preachers. In addition to Providence, the preachers occasionally use Christian beliefs like the Incarnation of Christ, the Redemption of man, the Creation of the world, the nature of the Church, or the final reckoning of the Last Day as vehicles for expressing some of the assumptions I have enumerated.

Nonetheless, these assumptions cannot be simply identified with Christian doctrine. In the terms in which I have described them, they actually derive more directly from various philosophies of classical antiquity. As such, they only coincide or are rendered consonant with specifically Christian beliefs.

I will not make an attempt at isolating the influence on the preachers of particular philosophies and philosophers. It would be a task of immense difficulty, not least of all because of the large number of individuals in-

---

3. See, e.g., Petrus Terasse, *Oratio de divina providentia* [Rome: S. Plannck, after March 9, 1483], Hain-Cop. #*15369, and Nicolaus Schomberg, "Quarta oratio. Nox praecessit," in *Orationes vel potius divinorum eloquiorum enodationes* (Leipzig: W. Stöckel, 1512), fols. [9ʳ–12ᵛ].

volved and because of the synthetic mind-set which often obtained. Far less would I venture to disentangle the relationship between "Hellenism" and "the Gospel" as it manifests itself in the preachers. We must be aware, above all, that the orators of the court drew upon patristic and scholastic sources where "Hellenism" and "the Gospel" interpenetrated each other. Finally, without in any way minimizing the seriousness with which the preachers generally distinguished philosophy from Christian revelation and without minimizing the significance of the perceptions some of them had of the Bible as a book of history, we must be aware that the question of the relationship between "Hellenism" and "the Gospel" in its modern formulations never occurred to them.

It never occurred to them, moreover, that the world might be ugly or absurd in any radical way. Though the preachers were keenly aware of certain contingent deformities due to the corrosive influence of "men and the times," they did not see that influence as touching the fundamental constitution of the universe. The preachers lived in an ordered, harmonious, stable, and beautiful world, a fitting reflection of the divine exemplar. Order, harmony, and beauty were constitutive of the reality of the world. Order was especially important. It provided the structure from which harmony and beauty derived. As Augustine had long ago propounded, it was the unconditioned condition required for all stability and peace.[4]

Of absolutely critical importance for understanding the theology and the ideals of reform of the preachers, consequently, is an understanding of their view of reality as ordered and an understanding of the extremely high rank they assigned order in their scale of values. In some ways order seems actually to have been their ultimate value, or at least their ultimate measure for value. Conversely, chaos was the ultimate evil, or the hallmark of that which was ultimately evil. Confusion was synonymous with Babylon, the evil city.

This appreciation of the value of order permeates the sermons and other writings of the preachers to such a degree that all I can hope to do is call attention to a few significant expressions of it. In Aquinas himself, wisdom is described in terms of its ordering powers—"sapientis est ordinare";[5] and it is in Cajetan, among the preachers, that the supreme value

4. Cf. Aug. Civ. Dei. 19.13.
5. See *Summa Theologiae*, I.1.6, referring to Aristotle's *Metaphysics*, I.11. On the centrality of the idea of order in Aquinas, see John H. Wright, *The Order of the Universe in the Theology of St. Thomas Aquinas*, Analecta Gregoriana, No. 89 (Rome: Pontificia Universitas Gregoriana, 1957). See also Herman Krings, *Ordo: Philo-*

of order and its relationship to wisdom surface most impressively. The prefatory letter to the first volume of his commentary on Aquinas's *Summa Theologiae,* completed in 1507, is addressed to Oliviero Carafa. In the elegant Latin of that short letter, Cajetan takes the relationship of order to wisdom as his theme.[6] He cites Aristotle to the effect that order is the greatest accomplishment of divine wisdom. He might very well have coordinated the assertion attributed to Aristotle with what was, at least for this early period of his life, perhaps his favorite verse from the Old Testament: "Attingit igitur [sapientia] a fine usque ad finem fortiter, et disponit omnia suaviter" (Wisd. 8:1). That verse is quoted in Cajetan's first sermon for the *cappelle* and paraphrased in his oration for the Fifth Lateran Council.[7] It appears in each instance at a critical juncture. In his *De comparatione* and his *Apologia,* both written in repudiation of the Pisan Schism at about the same time as the oration for the council, the same verse appears four more times, always to emphasize the disposing and ordering power of wisdom.[8] The threat of Pisa was a threat to order.

Schomberg, Cajetan's successor in the procuratorship, paraphrases the verse from Wisdom in his sermon for Julius II on divine Providence.[9] Another Dominican, Raynaldus Mons Aureus, also quotes it for Alexander VI, and he depicts God as "ex ordine et dispositione sapiens."[10] The Dominicans had no monopoly on a preoccupation with order. Petrus Terasse, the Carmelite bachelor of theology who later became superior general of his order, called Sixtus IV's attention to the two goods that Aquinas taught that God imparted to his creation. The first was ontological goodness, viz., goodness "secundum substantiam." The second was the good of

---

sophisch-historische Grundlegung einer abendländischen Idee (Halle: M. Niemeyer, 1941), esp. pp. 50–78.

6. "Praefatio in expositionem Primae Partis Summae sancti Thomae Aquinatis," in *Opera omnia iussu impensaque Leonis XIII P. M.,* IV (Rome: S. C. de Propaganda Fide, 1888), 3–4.

7. "Oratio de vi cultus divini et orationis efficacia," in *Opuscula omnia* (Lyons: G. Rovillius, 1588), p. 183, and "Oratio de ecclesiae et synodorum differentia," *ibid.,* p. 192.

8. *De Comparatione Auctoritatis Papae et Concilii cum Apologia eiusdem Tractatus,* ed. Vincentius M. Iacobus Pollet, Scripta Theologica, No. 1 (Rome: Angelicum, 1936), pp. 91, 207, 211, 298.

9. "Quarta oratio. Nox praecessit," in *Orationes vel potius divinorum eloquiorum enodationes,* fol. [10ʳ]. He opens this oration on Providence with the words, fol. [9ᵛ]: "Naturae ordine et legibus sanctum ac dispositum est, beatissime pater, ut certi et stati rerum effectus non a promiscuis communibusve causis, sed maxime suis ac propriis oriantur."

10. *Oratio de visione Dei* [n.p.: n. publ., after Dec. 26, 1496], Hain #*11548, fol. [2ᵛ].

order or "bonum ordinis."[11] Lodovico de Bagnariis (Ludovicus Imolensis), a Franciscan, explicitly correlates the idea of order with Creation, Redemption, and Providence.[12]

Domenichi, too, manifests a love for order and a fear of the primordial chaos,[13] but his sentiments pale in comparison with those of his contemporary, Nicholas of Cusa. In Cusa's sermons and other writings, order dominates in a truly extraordinary degree as a test for authenticity and as a goal for practical action. He puts his conviction succinctly: whatever is from God is ordered—"Quae a Deo sunt ordinata sunt."[14] The sacred orators of the *cappelle* shared that conviction.

The very mention of Cusa's name suggests another of the assumptions I enumerated: the coherence of reality, its *concordia* or *concordantia*. The order that provides a place for everything in the universe is not sufficient. Every reality must, further, be linked with every other reality by bonds that result in an harmoniously conjoined totality.[15] This harmony or concord of the universe invites an analogy with music. The aesthetic aspect of the analogy was not lost on the preachers, especially on those from the humanist tradition like Andrea Brenta, Giovanni Antonio Campano, Cristoforo Marcello, and Raphael Brandolini.[16] Brenta, for example, alludes to Aristotle and Quintilian as witnesses to the symphony and harmonious concord of the heavens. According to Cusa, who does not represent the humanist tradition, the universe is bound together, and each part bound with every other part, by a "loving connectedness."[17]

11. *Oratio de divina providentia*, fol. [1ᵛ]. Cf. *Summa Theologiae*, I.22.1.

12. *Oratio in die sancti Stephani* [Rome: S. Plannck, after Dec. 26, 1481], Hain-Cop. #*9162, fol. [4ʳ]; "Oratio de Christi passione," BAV cod. Vat. lat. 11542, fol. 17ʳ⁻ᵛ.

13. See, e.g., "Oratio pro pace Italiae," BAV cod. Ottob. lat. 1035, fol. 50ᵛ.

14. "Haec est voluntas Dei," BAV cod. Vat. lat. 1245, fol. 145ᵛ.

15. On this question, see James E. Biechler, *The Religious Language of Nicholas of Cusa*, American Academy of Religion, Dissertation Ser., No. 8 (Missoula, Montana: Scholars Press, 1975), esp. pp. 154–60, as well as Leo Spitzer, "Classical and Christian Ideas of World Harmony," *Traditio*, 2 (1944), 409–64; 3 (1945), 307–64; and S. K. Heninger, Jr., *Touches of Sweet Harmony: Pythagorean Cosmology and Renaissance Poetics* (San Marino, Calif.: Huntington Library, 1974).

16. Brenta, "In disciplinas et bonas artes oratio," in Karl Müllner's *Reden und Briefe italienischer Humanisten* (Vienna: A. Hölder, 1899), p. 78, (Arist. de caelo, II. 9, 290b; Quint. I.10,12); Campano, "Initio studii MCCCCLV Perusiae oratio," in *Opera a Michaele Ferno edita* (Rome: E. Silber, 1495), GKW #5939, fol. [71ᵛ]; Marcello, *Oratio in die omnium sanctorum* [Rome: M. Silber?, after Nov. 1, 1511], fol. [2ᵛ]; Brandolini, "De musica et poetica opusculum," Bibl. Casan. cod. 805, fols. 13ʳ⁻ᵛ, 19ᵛ–22ᵛ.

17. *De Docta Ignorantia*, ed. Ernestus Hoffman and Raymundus Klibansky, Opera omnia iussu et auctoritate Academiae Litterarum Heidelbergensis ad codicum fidem edita, I (Leipzig: F. Meiner, 1932), p. 98 (II.10). For a classic formulation of the

Whence is this "loving connectedness" derived? It is derived from the divine exemplar. Charles Trinkaus has shown the determinative role the image-and-likeness theme played in the religious thought of a number of Italian humanists.[18] That theme is no less pervasive in the sacred orators, perhaps especially in those trained in Scholasticism. Though the image-and-likeness verse is applied in Genesis directly to man, the preachers follow the tradition of employing it as a clue for interpreting all created reality. Man may be the creature upon whom God has impressed his image and likeness, but all creation somehow reflects the deity. The triplet of measure, number, and weight (Wisd. 11:21) according to which the universe was created might be seen, for instance, to correspond to the Father, Son, and Holy Spirit of the Trinity.[19] All reality is incised with vestiges of God, who creates according to the image or "Word" in the divine mind.[20] Thus a theme emerges once again from the Johannine Prologue: "In the beginning was the Word, and the Word was with God. . . . All things were made through him, and without him was made nothing that was made" (John 1:1–3).

Even when dealing with Creation, therefore, the preachers seem to have been as conscious of exemplary as they were of efficient causality. The image must respond to its exemplar. This is preeminently true of man, but it is also true of everything else in the universe. Earth is a reflection of heaven. By "looking around" us, we contemplate vestiges of God everywhere.

But man is capable of discovering the divine vestiges in the world around him and of discovering the image and likeness according to which he was made only if he raises his eyes to heaven. He must "look up." The preachers often invite their listeners to do just that. They are urged to

philosophical questions suggested by the mind-set I am here describing, see Arthur O. Lovejoy, *The Great Chain of Being: A Study of the History of an Idea* (New York: Harper and Row, 1960), esp. 3–98.

18. In *Our Image and Likeness: Humanity and Divinity in Italian Humanist Thought*, 2 vols. (Chicago: University of Chicago Press, 1970), esp. I, xiv.

19. See, e.g., Mons Aureus, *Oratio de visione Dei*, fols. [2ᵛ–3ʳ], and my *Giles of Viterbo on Church and Reform: A Study in Renaissance Thought*, Studies in Medieval and Reformation Thought, No. 5 (Leiden: Brill, 1968), p. 22.

20. See, e.g., Thomas Capitaneus, *Oratio in die omnium sanctorum* [Rome: S. Plannck, after Nov. 1, 1483], GKW #6023, fols. [2ᵛ–3ʳ], and esp. Agostino Filippi, "Oratio de veritate," in *Orationes novem coram Iulio II et Leone X* (Rome: J. Mazochius, 1518), fol. [9ʳ]: "Ex rebus autem increata sunt quaedam—ut solus Deus. Reliqua vero omnia ab eodem et facta et creata dicuntur, cuius esse quoque participant. Haec igitur quatenus exemplari divino, quam vocamus ideam secundum quam ex tempore condidit illa Deus, quadrant et respondent vera dicuntur et sunt."

look up to contemplate a heavenly scene or a divine reality. When this invitation comes from preachers representing the humanistic tradition, it often means to open a scene of the heavenly court that is the exemplar for the earthly court and that is man's final destiny. When the invitation comes from preachers representing the scholastic tradition, it often calls to a contemplation of the divine nature.[21] In both cases the underlying presupposition is the same: in some way earth corresponds to heaven. With that principle securely in mind, we are now ready to study the first of the three great mysteries that surpass our understanding—the mystery of the Trinity.

No subject seems more unlikely for preachers who wanted to abandon the abstractions of the classroom to say something immediately meaningful for the lives of their listeners. But the preachers were compelled to deal with this topic. One of the feasts on which they preached was Trinity Sunday. Moreover, anyone who comprehended the barest rudiments of theology knew that this mystery was central to Christianity as interpreted by the Fathers and scholastics, and it had been the object of great controversy in the councils of the early Church. No matter how metaphysical the mystery was and no matter how difficult to handle in the pulpit, it could not be slighted.

The Trinity in the sermons of the preachers at the court is the critical test for our own powers of historical imagination. For us, nothing perhaps could be more remote from life, more academic and abstruse, than speculations about how three are one. For them, the speculations were imbued with considerable relevance. The Trinity was not a doctrine which one merely recited in a creed or to which one gave a merely notional assent. It provided the theological framework in which the mysteries of Creation and Redemption were comprehended, and thus it was inseparable from them. It was, therefore, a key for interpreting man and his world. It was a central Christian doctrine from which cosmology, anthropology, and political science could be derived.

Only in the next two chapters will the wide-ranging implications the preachers found in the nature of the deity, especially for politics and ecclesiology, become clear. But already perceptible is how the diversity

---

21. This distinction is not always maintained; humanists, too, call for a contemplation of the divine nature. See, e.g., Brenta, *In pentecosten oratio* [Rome: E. Silber, after May 18, 1483], GKW #5100, fols. [9ʳ–10ʳ], and Platina's "Tractatus de laudibus pacis," in *Cremonensium monumenta Romae extantia,* ed. Thomas Augustinus Vairani, 2 vols. in one (Rome: G. Salomoni, 1778), I, 90–91.

in the universe might be seen to correspond to the diversity of the three Persons. The diversity and grades of being in the universe, however, are not discrete units in a world without plan. All is coordinated into one harmonious song, just as the three Persons are only one God. The Trinity is the final reconciliation of the problem of the one and the many, and the universe reflects that reconciliation.[22] As Brenta says about the interaction of the three Persons: "Among them there is no discord nor the vicissitude of war. There all three think the same, there all three foreknow the same. . . . From there is all heavenly and earthly harmony constituted."[23]

It is an easy step, therefore, from the great mystery of the Trinity to the mystery of Creation. Before contemplating the world around them, the preachers already had an idea of what they would find there. The world would be harmonious and beautiful, as was its Creator. In describing this product of divine creativity, the preachers addressed a subject more congenial to their art than was the Trinity, but not a subject distinct from it. Massari sees the harmony of the world as intimating the "peace" that reigns among Father, Son, and Holy Spirit and that binds all grades of creation together.[24] Cusa sees the same relationship.[25] The universe enjoyed an ontological "pax et concordia" which reflected its triune Creator.

Inghirami speaks in more humanistic terms when he depicts the universe. In his sermon for All Saints, 1497, he describes it epideictically, as if he were speaking in praise of a city or a Renaissance church.[26] When God constructed the universe, he constructed a magnificent temple. He

22. This reconciliation is particularly important for Cusa. See, e.g., *De Pace Fidei*, ed. Raymundus Klibansky and Hildebrandus Bascour, Opera omnia iussu et auctoritate Academiae Litterarum Heidelbergensis ad codicum fidem edita, VII (Hamburg: F. Meiner, 1959), p. 21 (VII). The idea did not die in the Renaissance. See, e.g., Joseph Ratzinger, *Einführung in das Christentum: Vorlesungen über das Apostolische Glaubensbekenntnis* (Munich: Deutscher Taschenbuch, 1971), pp. 122–23.

23. *In pentecosten oratio*, fol. [9ʳ⁻ᵛ]: ". . . Deus Pater, Deus Filius, Deus Spiritus sanctus. Non est illic ulla discordia, non est belli vicissitudo. Omnes idem sentiunt, una omnium praecognitio. . . . ex quo terrestrium caelestiumque rerum harmonia constituitur."

24. "Oratio de pace," Bibl. Estense cod. Alpha Q.6.13, fols. 76ᵛ–77ʳ.

25. See, e.g., "Vidi civitatem sanctam," BAV cod. Vat. lat. 1244, fol. 119ᵛ.

26. "In laudem omnium sanctorum oratio," Bibl. Guarn. cod. LIII.4.8, fol. 39ᵛ: " . . . et etenim cum Deus mundi hanc machinam divinitatis augustissimum templum fabrefecerit, supercaelestem regionem mentibus decoravit, aethereos globos aeternis animis vegetavit, inferioris mundi quisquilias omnigena animalium turba complevit, ut esset qui tanti operis rationem inspiceret, pulchritudinem admiraretur, magnitudinem obstupesceret. . . ." Cf. Pico, "Oratio de hominis dignitate," in *De Hominis Dignitate, Heptaplus, De Ente et Uno*, ed. Eugenio Garin, Edizione Naz. dei Classici del Pensiero Italiano, No. 1 (Florence: Vallecchi, 1942), p. 104.

then decorated it with such skill that all who gaze upon it admire its beauty and wonder at its magnitude. Inghirami is closely paraphrasing, without acknowledgment, Pico's "Oration on the Dignity of Man," and he does this before Alexander VI, the pope who lifted Pico's excommunication.

As we might expect, Inghirami then moves immediately from the temple of the universe to that extraordinarily marvelous part of God's creation found therein—man. The Christian doctrine of Creation as proposed under the influence of epideictic purpose and vocabulary leads almost inevitably into the Renaissance theme of man's dignity.[27] The preachers developed that theme with considerable variety of argument. If the *dignitas* of the rest of the universe excites sentiments of wonder and admiration, the *dignitas hominis* excites them all the more. Agostino Filippi affirms that when God created Adam, he endowed him with an excellence and perfection that defies our earthly categories.[28] He enjoins that, after we contemplate the presence of God in the world around us, we turn our thoughts upon ourselves to recognize our own "excellence."[29]

The beauty and harmony of man's body is where the preachers might begin. Pietro Marsi quotes Saint Bernard's injunction to man to consider how noble is his body.[30] Aurelio Brandolini, in his treatise on the human condition for King Matthias of Hungary, invites the king and his queen to look at and contemplate their bodies—the beauty of the contours, the artful disposition of the members, the order of the whole.[31]

27. On this vast theme, see Paul Oskar Kristeller's useful summary, "The Dignity of Man," in his *Renaissance Concepts of Man and Other Essays* (New York: Harper and Row, 1972), pp. 1–21, as well as Trinkaus, *Image and Likeness*, passim.
28. "Oratio de peccato," in *Orationes novem coram Iulio II et Leone X*, fol. [15ʳ]: "Egregia quadam supercaelesti tam perfectione et excellentia humanae sobolis parentem primum magnifice insignavit altissimus."
29. "Oratio in epiphania," in *Orationes novem coram Iulio II et Leone X*, fol. [2ᵛ]: "Sic hominum mentes ignarae, incultae torpore et ignavia obrutae, salvatoris nostri oculos graviter offendentes, eum exclamare compellunt, 'Resipiscite iam, et de profundo somno ad vigiliam excitatae quae in mundo sunt contemplamini. Ex eis Deum diligenter inspicite, et in vosmetipsos conversae vestri excellentiam cogitate.'"
30. *Oratio in die ascensionis de immortalitate animae* [Rome: E. Silber, n.d.], Hain-Cop. #*10790, fol. [4ʳ]: ". . . homo, inquit Bernardus, cogita qualem te fecit Deus, nempe secundum corpus egregiam creaturam, secundum animam magis insignem, rationis participem, beatitudinis aeternae capacem."
31. *De humanae vitae conditione et toleranda corporis aegritudine* (Basel: R. Winter, 1543), p. 107: "Intuemini deinde vos ipsos, vestrum corpus atque animum considerate, et in altero tam insignem figuram, tam pulchram, tam artificiosam membrorum dispositionem, tam inenarrabilem ordinem, tantas et tam incredibiles utilitates. . . ." On this work, esp. as it expounds various arguments for man's dignity, see Trinkaus, *Image and Likeness*, I, 298–306.

The most unusual panegyric of man's body, however, comes from Thomas Capitaneus in his sermon for All Saints before Sixtus IV in 1483. While describing the beauty and order of the universe that leads to a natural knowledge of God, he adduces Hermes Trismegistus as his authority for that part of the universe that is man.[32] Thomas sanctions the tradition that recognized in Hermes the first philosopher, from whom Socrates and Plato were descended. He affirms that Hermes led men to a knowledge of God by means of a consideration of the human body. This Dominican friar then quotes a long section from the *Pimander* describing the skillful construction of the body as an argument for the existence of the Creator. Thomas's intriguing sermon to the Franciscan pope was delivered some twenty years after Ficino had translated the *Corpus Hermeticum* for Cosimo de' Medici.

The dignity of man's body, great though it was, suffered in comparison with his other dignities. The preachers were heirs to the long Augustinian tradition of applying the image-and-likeness verse to man and of finding in man's soul a true image of the Trinity—in man's memory, intellect, and will.[33] Massari's overly enthusiastic application of the image-and-likeness verse to Saint Augustine earned him in fact some criticism at the court to which he felt compelled to respond.[34]

According to Marsi, man's excellence consists in his being created in the image and likeness of God, which means he is immortal, for all things divine are immortal.[35] Man's reason ("ratio") effects his "participation in

---

32. *Oratio in die omnium sanctorum*, fols. [3ᵛ–4ʳ]. Cf. Chapter V of the *Pimander* in Marsilio Ficino, *Opera omnia*, Monumenta Politica et Philosophica Rariora, ed. Luigi Firpo, Ser. 1, Nos. 9–10, 2 vols. (rpt. Basel, 1576; Turin: Bottega d'Erasmo, 1962), II, 1843. For another sermon preached before Sixtus in which Hermes is frequently adduced as an authority, see Leonardo Nogarola, "Oratio in die nativitatis Domini," BAV cod. Ross. 1124, fols. 1ʳ–14ʳ.

33. See, e.g., Marsi, *Oratio in die ascensionis de immortalitate animae*, fols. [3ᵛ–4ʳ]; Marcus Antonius Ticinensis, *In adventu oratio* [Rome: S. Plannck, after Dec. 6, 1500], fol. [4ʳ]; Inghirami, "De morte Iesu Christi oratio," BN Paris cod. lat. 7352B, fol. 223ᵛ; Ambrogio Massari, "De animae dignitatibus," Bibl. Ang. cod. lat. 835, III, fols. 15ʳ– 17ʳ, and esp. 17ʳ: "O, igitur, creaturarum felicissima, de qua tam gloriosa dicta sunt, quae sic ad similitudinem et imaginem Dei facta sis, tu civitas Dei merito es appellanda, cuius mens paradisus est, in qua dum caelestia meditantur quasi in paradiso voluptatis delectaris, tu sponsa Christi propter dilectionem, templum Spiritus sancti propter sanctificationem. . . ."

34. See "Sermo in quo quidem ostendit quod Augustinus est imago Trinitatis," in *Vita praecellentissimi ecclesiae doctoris divi Aurelii Augustini. Commentarii super regula sancti Augustini* (Rome: G. Herolt, 1481), Hain #*5683, fols. [237ᵛ–241ʳ].

35. *Oratio in die ascensionis de immortalitate animae*, fol. [4ʳ].

divinity," affirms Aurelio Brandolini.[36] Timotheus de Totis saw man's excellence in the fact that he thirsts for God, and he assumes that the goodness of God will not allow that thirst to go unquenched. He therefore exclaims: "O marvelous benignity and charity of our Creator! O most excellent dignity of man!"[37]

Important in the story of Creation in Genesis is the fact that all things were made for man and that man himself has the power to command the fishes of the sea and the birds of the air and all the animals that move upon the face of the earth. The preachers utilized this fact to impress upon their hearers man's great worth. As Marcus Antonius Ticinensis says before Alexander VI: "And everything was made for man, as for a single end, and indeed we read that some have even gone so far as to adore him because of his immense dignity."[38] Through the nobility and beauty of the union of body and soul, man was for him a microcosm.[39] For Vázquez he was, as citizen of the heavens and lord of the earth, the true binding force of the universe. In the Ash Wednesday sermon of 1513 for Julius II, Vázquez borrows without acknowledgment Pico's phrase describing man as "mundi copula et hymenaeus," and he here quotes almost verbatim several of Pico's most impressive lines "de humanae naturae praestantia."[40]

Even more significant is the section of this oration that contains Vázquez's long apology for man's basic indeterminacy and his potential "to

36. *De humanae vitae conditione*, pp. 58–59. See also *ibid.*, e.g., pp. 25, 44, and his *Christiana paradoxa* (Rome: F. Minitius Calvus, 1531), fol. [10ʳ].

37. *Sermo quod omnino datur ultimus finis creaturae rationalis* [Rome: E. Silber, 1496], Cop. #5843, fols. [6ᵛ–7ʳ]. On this idea in Brandolini's *Paradoxa*, see Trinkaus, *Image and Likeness*, I, 319–21.

38. *In adventu oratio*, fol. [4ʳ]: "Et propter hominem omnia facta sunt, tamquam propter unum finem, hominem ipsum ob immensam eius nobilitatem aliquos ut deum iam adorasse legimus." This is possibly an allusion to the famous line from Chapter III of Trismegistus's *Asclepius*, in Ficino, *Opera*, II, 1859: "Propter hoc, o Asclepi, magnum miraculum est homo, animal adorandum et honorandum." See also, e.g., Filippi, "Oratio in epiphania," in *Orationes novem coram Iulio II et Leone X*, fol. [2ʳ–ᵛ]; Stephanus Basignanas Gorgonius, *Oratio de animae immortalitate*, [n.p.: n. publ., after Dec. 20, 1517], fol. [4ʳ].

39. *In adventu oratio*, fol. [4ᵛ]. On this idea in the Renaissance, see Trinkaus, *Image and Likeness*, II, 974 (index), and Rudolf Allers, "Microcosmus from Anaximandros to Paracelsus," *Traditio*, 2 (1944), 318–407.

40. See my critical edition of this sermon, "An Ash Wednesday Sermon on the Dignity of Man for Pope Julius II, 1513," in *Essays Presented to Myron P. Gilmore*, ed. Sergio Bertelli and Gloria Ramakus, 2 vols. (Florence: Nuova Italia, 1978), I, 193–209.

be whatever he desires." For Vázquez, man's dignity is superior to the angels', not because of some static excellence, but because of his unlimited capacity to merit grace and to ascend to an ever closer union with God. Although arguments from indeterminacy in Christian theology reach back to the patristic tradition, Vázquez is certainly here dependent upon Pico's "Oration" for his formulation of it. Significantly, he places a stress on grace that is missing from the "Oration." Within a year or so of Vázquez's sermon, Agostino Filippi addressed Pico's thesis in the presence of Leo X. He basically agrees with Pico's view of man as self-determining and multipotential. But this view does not preclude, in his eyes, man's having a proper end prescribed for him by God.[41] Inghirami, in his sermon for All Saints in 1497, used the same arguments from man's indeterminacy to praise God's liberality, as he continued his paraphrase of Pico. God made man to be as if he were his own maker—so much did God put into man's hands![42]

To praise God's liberality through the fact of man's indeterminacy and his power "to be whatever he will" indicates still another reason for man's excellence. In creating man, God imparted to him a share in his own causality. Man is a true cause, made as he is in the image and likeness of the First Cause. When Petrus Terasse raises the question of man's causality, he is dependent like Cajetan upon Aquinas for his phraseology, though he does not mention the saint by name. Terasse follows Aquinas's reasoning when he sees in man's causality an expression of God's abundant goodness and God's desire to share what he has with his creatures.[43]

---

41. "Oratio de veritate," in *Orationes novem coram Iulio II et Leone X*, fols. [8ᵛ–9ʳ]. Cf. Pico, "Oratio de hominis dignitate," pp. 104–6.

42. "In laudem omnium sanctorum oratio," Bibl. Guarn. cod. LIII.4.8, fol. 39ᵛ: " . . . [Deus] hominem excitavit, quem, ut facilius divinam liberalitatem inspiceret, nullis angustiis, nullis praescriptis legibus coercuit, in manu eius posuit quidquid perfiniret tamquam si ipse sui ipsius opifex extitisset, ut in quam ipse maluerit formam sese effingeret. Erant ante oculos bruta caelique, erat mors et immortalitas, ut haberet quod optaret, essetque quod vellet, statimque in quam ipse inclinaret eam consequeretur." Cf. Pico, "Oratio de hominis dignitate," pp. 104–6. In 1531 Hieronymus Arzius, preaching before Clement VII on Ash Wednesday, also utilized Pico's "Oration" in emphasizing the dignity of man, *Oratio de natura, bello et pace utriusque hominis* (Rome: n. publ., 1531), fols. [3ᵛ–4ʳ]. Part of this oration was also inspired by Pico's "Heptaplus," in *De Hominis Dignitate*, p. 304; cf. fol. [5ʳ].

43. *Oratio de divina providentia*, fol. [3ᵛ]: " . . . nec propterea defectus virtutis arguendus in Deo, sed magis suae bonitatis abundantia laudibus extollenda est." Cf. *Summa Theologiae*, I.22.3: " . . . non propter defectum suae virtutis, sed propter abundantiam suae bonitatis, ut dignitatem causalitatis etiam creaturis communicet." See also Terasse, *ibid.*, fol. [1ᵛ]: "O, virtutem indeficientem, quae in communicando causalitatem etiam creaturis tuae bonitatis abundantia maxime clares!"

According to Schomberg, an important aspect of God's image and likeness with which God impressed men is participation in divine freedom.[44]

We have already examined Cajetan's treatment of man as a true cause in his sermon before Alexander VI on the efficacy of prayer. Here it might simply be noted that, in his sermon on the immortality of souls, Cajetan argues that man is different from the other animals because of his indeterminacy. Unlike other animals, man has no defined "operandi modus."[45]

As the doctrine of Creation is translated by the preachers into the theme of man's dignity, therefore, several characteristics of that translation emerge. First of all, there is the persistence and frequency with which the theme occurs. Secondly, the variety of argumentation is considerable. Thirdly, the variety of sources from which the preachers drew is impressive and again indicates how consistently the theme was pursued—Scripture, Augustine, Bernard, Trismegistus, Pico, and Aquinas. There are certainly other sources still to be determined. Finally, only rarely does discourse on the misery of the human condition appear in the sermons.[46] It is a significant fact that three of the Ash Wednesday sermons extant from the court in the early sixteenth century are on the dignity of man.[47] Thus the prototypical instance for a statement on man's abject condition as created from the dust of the earth and destined to dissolution is transformed into an occasion for exalting his excellence. Though the preachers might sometimes deplore their times, they found it difficult to deplore the work of God's hands that was his creation.

When the preachers turned to the third great mystery that engaged their art, they were even more optimistic. For the sake of conciseness, this mystery is best termed the Redemption. Put into scholastic vocabulary with which most of the preachers would be familiar, it could be termed the mystery of the order of grace. It consisted in the restoration

44. "Quarta oratio. Nox praecessit," in *Orationes vel potius divinorum eloquiorum enodationes,* fol. [11^{r-v}].
45. "Oratio de immortalitate animorum," *Opuscula,* p. 187.
46. The preachers were of course capable of this theme, e.g., Martinus de Viana's *Oratio in die cinerum* [Rome: S. Plannck, 1496], Cop. #6198. Aurelio Brandolini discourses on it in his *Paradoxa,* as Trinkaus has shown; see *Image and Likeness,* I, 317–20. Even while discoursing on man's misery, Brandolini gives the theme a somewhat positive turn, a fact that Trinkaus suggests by pointing out the "complementarity of the themes of the misery and dignity of man." *Ibid.,* p. 320.
47. Vázquez, *Oratio in die cinerum* (Rome: J. Mazochius, 1513); Arzius, *Oratio de natura, bello et pace utriusque hominis* (1531); Aegidius Ricardus, "De dignitate hominis oratio," (1537), in his *Orationes decem coram Paulo III* (Venice: F. Bindoneus and Mapheus Pasineus, 1540), fols. 15^{r}–17^{v}.

of man and the world after the catastrophe of the Fall, which had so seri-
ously marred the order and harmony of what God had made. It was a
restoration that was gratuitous, that owed its reality purely and simply
to a free act of God's favor, i.e., to God's grace. It was effected through
the life and deeds of Christ, and it is thereby identical with the christological mystery and related to the trinitarian mystery.

Brandolini seems to be referring to the Redemption when he speaks of
one of the mysteries "surpassing understanding" as the Hypostatic Union,
i.e., the union of the divine and human natures in the one person of
Christ.[48] This seems to be what Giles of Viterbo is referring to when he
speaks of the third of the great mysteries from which the faith of the
Church originates as "the conception of the divine Son in the Virgin's
womb."[49] These two preachers thus immediately direct our attention to one
of the most arresting aspects of the mystery of the Redemption as it was
consistently propounded at the court: a tendency to identify the Redemption with the Incarnation, with the moment when the human and divine
natures were united, with the moment when "the Word became flesh and
dwelt among us."

The attribution of redemptive efficacy to the Incarnation was by no
means an invention of the preachers. The Greek Fathers had effectively
developed that doctrine and joined it to the question of man's deification.[50]
The theology of the Western Church, however, has generally tended to
pinpoint the redemptive act in Christ's death on the cross, or in the conjunction of his suffering, death, and resurrection. The preachers were far
from denying a special efficacy to the three days of Christ's life when he
suffered, died, and rose from the tomb, as the many sermons for Good
Friday that have survived demonstrate. Nonetheless, the preachers tend
to place an emphasis on the Incarnation that is peculiarly recurrent. That
emphasis wants to view all the subsequent events of Christ's life as
articulations of what was already inchoately accomplished in the initial
moment of man's restoration, which was the Incarnation in the Virgin's

48. *De ratione scribendi libri tres* (Cologne: A. Birckmannus, 1573), p. 95," . . . coniunctionem humanae divinaeque naturae."
49. Opening oration at the Fifth Lateran Council, 1512, Mansi, 32, 670, " . . . in
Virginis utero prolis divinae conceptio." See now Clare O'Reilly's critical edition,
" 'Without Councils We Cannot Be Saved': Giles of Viterbo Addresses the Fifth Lateran Council," *Augustiniana*, 27 (1977), 166–204, esp. 188.
50. See Jules Gross, *La divinisation du chrétien d'après les pères grecs: Contribution historique à la doctrine de la grace* (Paris: J. Gabalda, 1938). See also the article
"Grace" in the *Dictionnaire de spiritualité*, VI (1965), esp. 715–21.

womb. Whereas God's first great "deed" was the act of Creation, his second great "deed" was his becoming flesh and dwelling among us.

When the preachers looked at these two deeds, they did not doubt which was the more wonderful. Whatever injury man and the universe had suffered in the Fall was healed in the Redemption. The preachers inculcate this truth. Marsi tells his hearers that grace heals completely.[51] Casali tells them that they have been repaired "in integrum."[52] Thegliatius tells them that when the Word assumed flesh he wished to indicate man's full restoration.[53] Significantly, Thegliatius's statement about the Incarnation appears in his Good Friday sermon. Also significantly, in that same Good Friday sermon he quotes the *Exultet*.[54]

In Thegliatius as in other preachers, the *Exultet* signals that a crucial point is being made: man is in a *better* state now than if Adam had not sinned.[55] With the Redemption, all that was lost in the Fall was restored— and more besides. Pietro del Monte celebrates this truth in that first epideictic oration we possess from the court, and other preachers after him implicitly or explicitly indicate that they share the same belief.[56] Inghirami, for example, does so in his sermon for Julius II on Good Friday, 1504.[57]

51. *Panegyricus in memoriam sancti Ioannis evangelistae* [Rome: S. Plannck, after Dec. 27, 1485?], Hain #*10789, fol. [2ᵛ].

52. "Oratio in die veneris sancti," Bibl. Ambr. cod. G.33 inf., II, fol. 5ᵛ.

53. *Oratio de passione Domini* [Rome: S. Plannck, 1496], Hain-Cop. #15457, fol. [2ʳ⁻ᵛ]: "Unde qui dixit, 'Et Verbum caro factum est,' ex parte maxime corrupta et unione Verbi vivificata totius reparationem significare voluit." See also, e.g., Guillelmus Bodivit, *In die annuntiationis Virginis sermo* [Rome: B. Guldinbeck, after Aug. 12, 1484], GKW #4503, fol. [1ʳ]: "Nunc vero per unionem realem naturae et spiritualem gratiae et gloriae aliarumque virtutum absque mensura omnia reconciliata sunt, et totus homo huius inclitae annuntiationis virtute reparatus est."

54. *Oratio de passione Domini*, fol. [3ᵛ]. He attributes it to Gregory: "Unde . . . Gregorius, magnifico illo spiritu quo repletus erat, voce ecclesiae intonuit: 'O certe necessarium Adae peccatum, quod Christi morte deletum est.'"

55. *Ibid.*, fol. [4ᵛ]: " . . . sic in horto Christi passio inciperet, per quam a malis omnibus liberati via gratiae ad excellentiorem gradum iustitiae restituti essemus."

56. "Oratio in dominica quadragesimae quae dicitur de passione," BAV cod. Vat. lat. 2694, fol. 307ʳ: " . . . multoque magis videtur Deum suo proprio sanguine reparasse singulari caritate id quod perierat quam magna potestate fecisse ab initio quod non fuerat." See also *ibid.*, fol. 305ᵛ.

57. "De morte Iesu Christi oratio," BN Paris cod. lat. 7352B, fol. 226ʳ: " . . . cum uberiorem materiam beneficentiae in nos divinae praestiterit. Nisi enim ille [Adam] peccasset, numquam Deus summittendo se humanum genus tanto opere exaltasset, numquam copiosius quantum nos amaret ostendisset, quorum oblivisci etiam post tot nostra delicta non potuerit, immo quos pretiosius redemerit quam fecisset. Prope itaque est ut exclamem nihil tanti esse ut nolimus non peccatum ab illo, cum causam Deo praestiterit maioris beneficii in nos conferendi quam fuerat ab initio constitutum. An quisquam tam est divinarum rerum expers qui non intelligat ex Christi more non solum in pristinam libertatem nos affectos sed gloriosius quoque exaltatos, cumulatioribus muneribus donatos? . . ."

Once again, the belief is not original with the preachers, as the *Exultet* itself gives evidence. Giovanni Antonio Sangiorgio, in his sermon on Passion Sunday for Sixtus IV, cites Augustine as his authority for the "more perfect" gifts which the Incarnation bestowed.[58] Aquinas and others could be cited as well. The doctrine was standard. The emphasis it received and the persistent tendency to link it to the Incarnation were not standard. In fact, this tendency to link the Redemption with the Incarnation is one among the factors which characterize the religious viewpoint of the sermons during the *cappelle* as peculiarly "incarnational."

In an article published a few years ago, I spoke of the theology of the papal court during the Renaissance as an "incarnational theology," and I have elsewhere tried to illustrate and document certain aspects of that theology or world view.[59] But a fuller and more systematic detailing of what is involved now seems indicated, and I shall here undertake to describe it as it is found in the sacred orators of the court.

First of all, the mystery of the Incarnation receives more explicit attention at the court than either the Trinity or Creation. Secondly, it is seen, as I have been indicating, as in itself redemptive: by the Word's becoming flesh man was restored and made the recipient of even "more perfect" gifts. Thus this mystery tends to usurp or at least to share in the redemptive efficacy usually reserved to Christ's passion, death, and resurrection. Given the prominent role the Crucifixion played in late medieval and Counter-Reformation art, it is worth noting that in the great Christ-cycle of the Sistine Chapel, where so many of these sermons were preached, there is no fresco depicting Christ's suffering and death, if we except the distant and barely perceptible view of Calvary through one of the windows of Cosimo Rosselli's "Last Supper."

---

58. *Sermo in dominica quinta quadragesimae* [Rome: n. publ., c.1480], Hain #7599, fol. [2ʳ]: "Accedit etiam quod hac mirabili incarnatione Verbi Deus humanae naturae perfectiora dona tribuere voluit. . . . Quod Augustinus libro de spiritu et anima dilucide expressit. Propterea Deus, ait, homo factus est ut totum hominem beatificaret, ut in se intus et extra pascua inveniret: intus in deitate creatoris, extra in carne salvatoris." Sangiorgio was bishop of Alessandria and was later made a cardinal by Alexander VI in 1493.

59. "The Discovery of America and Reform Thought at the Papal Court in the Early Cinquecento," in *First Images of America: The Impact of the New World on the Old*, ed. Fredi Chiappelli, et al., 2 vols. (Berkeley: University of California Press, 1976), I, 185–200. See also my "Preaching for the Popes," in *The Pursuit of Holiness in Late Medieval and Renaissance Religion: Papers from the University of Michigan Conference*, ed. Charles Trinkaus with Heiko Oberman, Studies in Medieval and Reformation Religion, No. 10 (Leiden: Brill, 1974), pp. 408–40, and "Man's Dignity, God's Love, and the Destiny of Rome: A Text of Giles of Viterbo," *Viator*, 3 (1972), 389–416.

Some preachers at times simply identify salvation with the Incarnation. Del Monte says: "And through the Incarnation of his only begotten son, God concedes this special gift to us that we become free men from being slaves and that from strangers we are promoted to sons."[60] Palmeri could not be simpler: ". . . in his Incarnation, human nature was justified."[61] Sangiorgio stated for Sixtus IV: "We know the effect of the Incarnation was the restoration of the human race."[62] Sánchez de Arévalo, Carvajal, and Guillelmus Bodivit speak in equally clear terms.[63]

Often the preachers conjoin the two events of the Incarnation and the Crucifixion, as in Thegliatius's sermon for All Saints, 1492: " . . . in the Virgin's womb and on the cross he kissed us and renewed all reality."[64] We find in Marco Maroldi the ancient belief that the day of the Incarnation was the same day as that on which Christ would die on the cross, and such a coinciding of dates suggests a coinciding of significance.[65] Belief in that coincidence can be traced back to Augustine's reporting it in the *De Trinitate*.[66] A certain coinciding of the mysteries was suggested, as a matter of fact, by the liturgical prayers for the feast of the Annunciation.[67] "Annunciation" seems to have been almost a misnomer for a liturgical solemnity which was often construed to be the feast of the Incarnation.[68]

60. "Oratio in dominica quadragesimae quae dicitur de passione," BAV cod. Vat. lat. 2694, fol. 304ᵛ: " . . . et per unigeniti filii sui incarnationem hoc nobis praecipuum munus concessit, ut liberi efficiamur ex servis, et de extraneis provehamur in filios."
61. ["De veteri et novo testamento"], BAV cod. Vat. lat. 5815, fol. 68ʳ: "Nam in incarnatione sua humana natura iustificata est."
62. *Sermo in dominica quinta quadragesimae*, fol. [1ᵛ]: "Et quoniam novimus incarnationis effectum reparationem humani generis extitisse, consonum fuit ut per illum [filium Dei] in adoptionem a Deo reciperemur qui in Trinitate filius erat et permanet."
63. See Sánchez de Arévalo, "Sermo in die annuntiationis," BAV cod. Vat. lat. 4881, fol. 240ʳ; Carvajal, *Oratio in die circumcisionis* [Rome: S. Plannck, 1488/90], GKW #6147, fol. [8ᵛ]; Bodivit, *In die annuntiationis Virginis sermo*, fols. [1ʳ, 4ʳ].
64. *Oratio in die omnium sanctorum* [Rome: S. Plannck, 1496], Hain-Cop. #15459, fol. [2ᵛ]: " . . . proprio ore in Virginis utero ac in cruce deosculans omnia innovavit, iuxta illud 'Ecce, nova facio omnia' [Rev. 21.5]."
65. *Sententia veritatis humanae redemptionis* [Rome: S. Plannck, after March 25, 1481], Hain #*10778, fol. [1ʳ].
66. Trin. IV.5, PL 42, 894. See Maria E. Gössmann, *Die Verkündigung an Maria im dogmatischen Verständnis des Mittelalters* (Munich: M. Hüber, 1957), p. 25.
67. Gössmann makes this point, *Verkündigung*, p. 25, esp. for the Postcommunion prayer for the feast: "Gratiam tuam, quaesumus, Domine, mentibus nostris infunde: ut qui, angelo nuntiante, Christi filii tui incarnationem cognovimus, per passionem eius et crucem ad resurrectionis gloriam perducamur."
68. See Gössmann, *Verkündigung*, esp. pp. 11–26, 286, and Ernst Guldan, " 'Et verbum caro factum est': Die Darstellung der Inkarnation Christi im Verkündigungsbild," *Römische Quartalschrift*, 63 (1968), 145–69, esp. 162. Massari, for instance, identifies

From such vantage points, each event of the life of Christ could be interpreted both as an extension or reflection of the Incarnation and as having redemptive value. The feasts of Christmas and Epiphany are practically identified with the Incarnation. The shedding of blood at the Circumcision adumbrates the Crucifixion. The Resurrection and the Ascension fuse in their specific redemptive effects.[69] Mariano da Genazzano puts it succinctly: "There is nothing in the whole life of Christ, as he is born and as he dies, which is not part of our Redemption."[70] But no deed is recounted more often or excites more outcries of joy and gratitude than the Word's becoming flesh.

This sense of excitement over the Incarnation is surely related to the soteriological values assigned it. The Incarnation was seen as redemptive. If we examine a little more closely the soteriology of the preachers, we will discover there another reason why "incarnational" is an apt term for their religious world view: they propounded an "incarnational soteriology." The repercussions that this incarnational soteriology, like all soteriologies, had for reform will be discussed later. Now it is important to realize not only that the preachers construed the Incarnation as redemptive but also to understand by what action they envisioned Redemption to have been effected. What happened when the Word became flesh?

This question can be approached by way of a comparison that is close to hand—the soteriology of Nicholas of Cusa. For Cusa, Redemption is a liberation from ignorance and an enlightenment by truth. Christ is, above

---

the feast of the Annunciation with the Incarnation, "Sermo de annuntiatione," Bibl. Estense cod. Alpha Q.6.13, fol. 230^{r-v}. See also Girolamo Bordoni's "Oratio in natalitii[s] salvatoris habita in alma urbe in Ara Caeli, 1525," BAV cod. Chigi L.IV.75, fols. 103^v–107^v, and Bodivit, In die annuntiationis Virginis sermo, fol. [1^r].

69. Thegliatius provides an excellent example of the blurring of the distinctions among the various mysteries in his sermon on Good Friday for Innocent VIII, 1492, Oratio de passione Domini, fol. [10^v]: "In hac die tractatum est de origine dignitateque humanae naturae, de eius lapsu, de incarnatione filii Dei, de mundi innovatione, de humani generis restauratione, de diaboli expulsione, de statu, dignitate, auctoritate, sacramentis, desponsatione ecclesiae, de primatu sedis apostolicae, de usu et abusu sedentis in ea. . . . Hodie homo creatus est. Hodie lapsus est. Hodie Christus passus est. Hodie Verbum caro factum est." Maroldi identifies the days of Creation, Incarnation, and Crucifixion with each other. Sententia veritatis humanae redemptionis, fol. [1^r]. See also Cusa, "Loquimini ad petram," BAV cod. Vat. lat. 1245, fol. 235^r: "Solet communiter teneri quod Christus in ea die mortuus est in cruce in qua in Virginis utero conceptus atque quod hic dies sit dies creationis saeculi."

70. Oratio de passione Iesu Christi [Rome: E. Silber, after April 13, 1498], Hain-Cop. #7555, fol. [10^r] " . . . nihil est enim in omni vita nascentis Christi vel morientis quod non pars redemptionis nostrae sit."

all, a teacher. His whole life and even his death are interpreted by Cusa as an act of "testifying to the truth" (John 18:37). For that was he born, and for that did he come into the world. Cusa may at times espouse a theory of satisfaction and expiation, but if we search for the distinguishing characteristic of Cusa's understanding of the Redemption, we must say that it consists in the teaching of the truth by Christ and the appropriation of that truth by the Christian. When the Word became flesh, the great teacher entered the world. Teaching is the redemptive action par excellence.

With accuracy, consequently, Cusa's soteriology can be described as sapiential. Redemption is a revelation and an enlightenment. Christ is the teacher, and the Church is his school.[71] The preacher's task, in imitation of Christ, is to help reveal the revelation, delving ever more deeply into the profound secrets it contains. If Cusa's preaching has an analogue in early Christian writings, that analogue could be some form of didache, i.e., a form of instruction. A correspondence between what Cusa thought Redemption to be and the literary forms in which he discussed that Redemption is certainly discernible. Discourse and dialogue, question and answer, speculation and "revelation"—these are all appropriate to the teacher, to the man who wishes to impart his wisdom.

We have already noted that many of Cusa's favorite theological themes are found in the preaching of the court. Nonetheless, we must realize that a decidedly different soteriological focus was operative in him than in the sermons of the *cappelle*. For the preachers, the Incarnation was an efficient cause and an historical deed. Preachers with a scholastic training might prefer the former phrase and those with a humanistic training might prefer the latter. But at present the distinction is not particularly pertinent. Both traditions would emphasize that because of the Incarnation something "out there" changed. "Reality" is now different. "History" has taken a decisive turn.

How is reality different? *What* turn has history taken? First of all, the universe has been restored and reconciled to God, as Domenichi tells his listeners.[72] As Marsi tells his, Christ's Redemption has made "all things

71. "Missus est Gabriel angelus," BAV cod. Vat. lat. 1245, fol. 148ᵛ: "Caput autem ecclesiae seu scholae rationis est magister unus, scilicet Christus, qui influit spiritum in rationem credentium. . . ." See also "Venite post me," *ibid.*, fol. 192ʳ: "Christus praeest ecclesiae rationabilium, ubi colitur veritas. Satan praeest ecclesiae, congregationi, ubi est contemptus veritatis et dominatur error."

72. See "In nativitate Domini sermo," preached while he was bishop of Torcello for Emperor Frederick III in Neustadt, BAV cod. Ross. 1037, fol. 171ʳ⁻ᵛ.

new" (Rev. 21:5).[73] The world out there, as it here and now is, apart from any action man takes and apart from any new truth he might learn, has a new relationship of friendship with God. The Incarnation caused the universe to change. Once it was fallen, now it is restored.

Secondly, man's nature is different. It has a new dignity. This dignity includes man's appropriation of the teachings of Christ, but it is something more as well. Man is different, and therefore individual men are potentially different from what they would have been had the Word not become flesh. The means are available for men to effect this change in themselves and to appropriate this new dignity. But human nature is different whether individual men take advantage of the situation or not.

Cusa saw Redemption as something the *Incarnate Word* did, viz., give testimony to the truth. Cusa neglects rather than denies the historical character and context of Christ's advent, mission, and testimony to the truth. The preachers saw Redemption as something the *Incarnation* did, viz., once and for all transform certain aspects of created reality through the historical event which united humanity with divinity. For Cusa, a fuller understanding of the truth was made available to the world when Christ entered it and began teaching. For the preachers at the court, the world itself was transformed and was once again made holy at the moment of the Incarnation when the Creator assumed unto himself a created nature. Cusa's soteriology was principally sapiential. The preachers' was ontological and more notably historical.

In the preachers' ontological and historical interpretation of the Incarnation, there is manifested an impressive instance of the reciprocal influence that the concern of metaphysics for the constitution of reality and that the concern of rhetoric for action could have upon one another. The new oratory helped elicit from the scholastic preachers a heightened sense of the Incarnation as an historical act or event, and the traditional theology of the Fathers and the scholastics provided the humanists with a ready vocabulary to describe the cosmic benefits that the event had conferred.[74]

73. See *Oratio in die ascensionis de immortalitate animae*, fol. [5ʳ].

74. For a discussion of patristic and medieval, as well as modern, views on grace, nature, the Incarnation and Redemption, with ample bibliography, see Karl Rahner, "Nature and Grace," in *Theological Investigations*, trans. Kevin Smith, IV (Baltimore: Helicon Press, 1960), pp. 165–88. See also Gross, *La divinisation du chrétien*; Henri Rondet, *Gratia Christi: Essai d'histoire du dogme et de théologie dogmatique* (Paris: Beauchesne, 1948); M.-D. Chenu, *La théologie au douzième siècle* (Paris: J. Vrin, 1957), esp. pp. 289–308; and J. Patout Burns, "The Concept of Satisfaction in Medieval Redemption Theory," *Theological Studies*, 36 (1975), 285–304.

This convergence of the ontological and historical is important for understanding the preachers' conviction that they lived in a reconciled universe.

As the preachers contemplated the Redemption, therefore, they were impressed by the significance of living in the Christian era. Theirs were indeed happy times.[75] The decisive deed had been done. The preachers' new literary form was appropriate for recounting such a deed and for celebrating it. Their task was to make men appreciate it, and their reform efforts would be directed to bringing discordant elements into harmony with it.

This sense of ontological and historical change is, certainly, applicable also to other events from the life of Christ besides the Incarnation, and the preachers from time to time make such an application. This sense is peculiarly incarnational, however, because the Incarnation is the mystery the preachers especially favored and because they saw it as constitutive for all that followed after it. The convergence of that predilection for the Incarnation and the sense of the ontologico-historical change it effected is what gave their soteriology its particular characteristics.

Thus, even when the preachers discoursed on the death of Christ, they relatively rarely emphasized its expiatory character or depicted it as a testimony to the truth. I say "relatively rarely" because these preachers had no preconceived intention of displacing or subverting traditional interpretations of the meaning of Christ's suffering.[76] As they actually present the mystery of his death on the cross, however, they tend to interpret it in the same way they interpret the Incarnation and to blur the distinction between these mysteries.

Here again their selection of scriptural texts provides a useful clue. One of the texts that the preachers often utilize is, as we have by now learned to expect, from John's Gospel: "If I be lifted up, I will draw all things to myself" (12:32).[77] As the Incarnation was an act of drawing the

75. See, e.g., Timotheus de Totis, *Sermo quod omnino datur ultimus finis creaturae rationalis*, fol. [8ʳ]): "Felices ergo nos [text=vos], qui hac aetate nati sumus, qui lumen veritatis agnoscimus, quibus regna caelorum iam patefacta sunt, quae per ante tot saecula incognita clausaque extiterunt." See also Filippi, "Oratio de sacramentis," in *Orationes novem coram Iulio II et Leone X*, fol. [8ᵛ].

76. For a concise and informative study of the traditional teaching, see Burns, "Concept of Satisfaction."

77. See, e.g., del Monte, "Oratio in dominica quadragesimae quae dicitur de passione," BAV cod. Vat. lat. 2694, fol. 306ʳ, and Martinus de Azpetia, *De passione Domini oratio*, [Rome: G. Lauer or E. Silber, after 1492], Hain #2238, fols. [4ᵛ, 8ʳ]. Casali alludes to the verse and develops the idea of Christ as a magnet, "In die ascen-

created into the divine, so is the Crucifixion. The Incarnation joined God to man, the Redemption joins man to God. The two mysteries fuse, becoming almost indistinguishable. Sangiorgio's Lenten *Sermo in dominica quinta quadragesimae*, for instance, speaks mainly about the Incarnation. Moreover, it is a call for praise and an invitation to joy. Thus the Incarnation and the Crucifixion frequently receive the same interpretation. Emphasis on the Crucifixion as an expiation for sin and a satisfaction for a debt is thereby considerably lessened.

In general, therefore, when the preachers treat the Crucifixion, they do not dwell on the enormity of the sin that required such a Redeemer and that affixed him to the cross. They emphasize, instead, the immense love of God that provided such a Redeemer and the wonderful results the Redemption effected. The *Exultet* is a panegyric of that love and its redemptive results. The peregrinations of the *Exultet* through the various mysteries of Christ's life celebrated by the preachers indicates how common to them that very positive perspective was.

As we have seen, that positive perspective was applied to the constitution of the universe and to the history of the human race when these were seen in the light of what the Incarnation accomplished. The final quality I would, therefore, attribute to the preachers' incarnational theology is that it is world-affirming. Despite the fact that the preachers certainly conceptualized in terms of a two-storied universe, they still affirmed the value and beauty of this world. Heaven is our homeland, true, and we have here no lasting city. Earth is a pale reflection of heaven. Men are prone to sin, and the Church needs reform. *Nevertheless*, the world and man, as they here and now are, are redeemed, good, endowed with "more perfect" gifts.

The theology of the preachers was incarnational, therefore, also in the sense that the Incarnation provided a basis for legitimizing the use of the goods of this world and for validating a measure of human fulfillment in man's present state.[78] If this proposition is stated negatively,

---

sionis," Bibl. Ambr. cod. G.33 inf., II, fol. 21ʳ. The verse from John and the idea of Christ as lodestone are favorites of Cusa. See, e.g., "Relictis omnibus," BAV cod. Vat. lat. 1245, fol. 105ᵛ, and "Medius vestrum stetit," *ibid.*, fol. 130ᵛ; *De Docta Ignorantia*, pp. 139–40 (III.7); *De Pace Fidei*, p. 45 (XIV). On the significance of the verse from John in Erasmus, see my "Erasmus and Luther: Continuity and Discontinuity as Key to Their Conflict," *Sixteenth Century Journal*, 5, No. 2 (October, 1974), 47–65, esp. 54.

78. See, e.g., the article "Incarnationism" by D. J. Forbes in *New Catholic Encyclopedia*, VII, 416–17.

it means that the preachers could not with full consistency advocate withdrawal from the world in order to await fulfillment only in the after-life. They could not subscribe to any world-hating mentality that views man's life on earth exclusively or principally as an exile in a vale of tears. It is well known that such a mournful view of man's lot characterized much preaching in the late Middle Ages, as Blench has carefully established for England in the fifteenth and sixteenth centuries.[79] The incarnational theology of the preachers at the court stands in great contrast to that view.

It is true that when the preachers acquired the skills appropriate to epideictic oratory, they learned the art of deploring as well as the art of congratulating. Given the occasion, they knew quite well how to wring their hands in despair and dismay; but their theological viewpoint re-strained their exercise of the art of reproach in a way that it did not re-strain their exercise of the art of praise. Their preaching confirms and further illustrates Charles Trinkaus's assertion that the Renaissance pro-jected "possibly the most affirmative view of human nature in the history of thought and expression."[80] Ultimately, the universe was good, and man was good. Somewhat like the saint whose Gospel they so often cited, the preachers perceived that to a certain degree the *eschaton*—the fulfillment and the final era—had already arrived.[81]

The sympathy many of the preachers felt for scholastic theology helps explain the world-affirming tendency we detect in them. Scholasticism's first task, as it was defined in the historical context of the thirteenth cen-tury, was to answer how Aristotle's philosophy related to Christian doc-trine. Put in broader terms, Scholasticism asked and tried to answer how nature related to grace. This was the question central to the enterprise in its inception.

There is no doubt that the dynamics of Aquinas's solution to this ques-tion consisted in an attempt to reconcile nature and grace. Although Saint

79. J. W. Blench, *Preaching in England in the Late Fifteenth and Sixteenth Cen-turies: A Study of English Sermons 1450–c.1600* (New York: Barnes and Noble, 1964), esp. pp. 228–47. See also, e.g., E. Jane Dempsey Douglass, *Justification in Late Medi-eval Preaching: A Study of John Geiler of Keisersberg*, Studies in Medieval and Refor-mation Thought, No. 1 (Leiden: Brill, 1966), pp. 134–39.

80. *Image and Likeness*, I, xiv.

81. For a concise description of the elements comprising the "realized eschatology" of John's Gospel and of the various positions contemporary scholars have assumed regarding it, see Raymond Brown's "Introduction" to *The Gospel according to John (i–xii)*, The Anchor Bible, No. 29 (Garden City, N.Y.: Doubleday, 1966), pp. cxvi–cxxi.

Thomas wanted to safeguard a clear distinction between the two orders and to protect the gratuity of the order of grace, he also taught that the orders were not inimical to each other.[82] Such a theology contrasts with the sense of alienation discernible in Augustine's theology. Especially as the bishop of Hippo grew older, he became more convinced of how little the City of Man had to offer the City of God.[83]

Although Thomas Aquinas was not the only theologian produced by medieval Scholasticism, he was the scholastic theologian upon whom the preachers at the court most frequently seem to have been dependent. Bonaventure was canonized by Sixtus IV in 1482, but he never enjoyed an annual celebration in his honor like the one for Aquinas at the Minerva. For that matter, neither did any other medieval figure, including Francis of Assisi, enjoy such recognition.

Several reasons could be adduced to help explain the prominence of that celebration at the Minerva, which seems to have been even more prestigious than the one for Saint Augustine at the church named for him just a short distance away. However we explain the liturgical preeminence Thomas enjoyed in Rome, it seems to correspond with the esteem in which his theology was held. Valla is a well-known exception to this generalization, and among the preachers at the court Blessed Baptista Mantuanus launched a noteworthy attack on Saint Thomas.[84] Aside from these two individuals, the admittedly imperfect information presently available points to a broad recognition in Rome of Thomas's achievement even in this pretridentine period.

The reconciliatory impulse we find operative in Aquinas was operative in other scholastics as well, especially in the major figures of the early generations. It seems to have been these figures to whom the preachers had recourse when they based their position on scholastic doctrine. Therefore, even apart from the question of Thomas's theological impact in

82. See Rondet, *Gratia Christi*, pp. 200–34; Rahner, "Nature and Grace," pp. 165–88; A. M. Fairweather, ed., *Nature and Grace: Selections from the Summa Theologica of Thomas Aquinas*, The Library of Christian Classics, No. 11 (Philadelphia: The Westminster Press, 1954).

83. See, e.g., Peter Brown, *Augustine of Hippo: A Biography* (Berkeley: University of California Press, 1969), esp. pp. 299–329.

84. For a general study of Thomas's influence during the Italian Renaissance, see Paul Oskar Kristeller's "Thomism and the Italian Thought of the Renaissance" in the collection of his studies, *Medieval Aspects of Renaissance Learning*, ed. and trans. Edward P. Mahoney, Duke Monographs in Medieval and Renaissance Studies, No. 1 (Durham, N.C.: Duke University Press, 1974), pp. 27–91, esp. 63–71 on Valla and Mantuanus.

Rome, that same reconciliatory impulse was at work. The scholastic assumptions operative in many of the sermons at the court thus contributed to the preachers' positive assessment of the world rather than bridled it.

We shall return to this world-affirming tendency in the next two chapters. Further details will then be provided to illustrate what it meant in concrete circumstances. For the time being it is sufficient to draw the broad distinction between a world-affirming and a world-denying spirituality. This distinction indicates the final argument for applying the term "incarnational" to the religious perspective of the preachers at the court, viz., the preachers' positive assessment of the present redeemed situation. As was true with the doctrine of Creation, this positive assessment is directed especially to man.

We thus encounter once again the theme of the dignity of man in the sermons at the papal court. This time the preachers do not insist on man's excellence as created in God's image and likeness but on his transformation and even deification as redeemed by Christ and subject to the workings of grace. Man becomes more truly a son of God than ever before. He is in fact divinized. In the peroration of his sermon on the Hypostatic Union, Cajetan paraphrases Saint Leo the Great when he demands that the Christian acknowledge his dignity. He then paraphrases the scriptural text so influential upon Aquinas when he supplies the reason for the Christian's dignity: he has become a partaker of the divine nature— "divinae iam consors factus naturae" (2 Pet. 1:4).[85]

For Timotheus de Totis, grace is the "new law," not written on tablets of stone but infused into our souls, whereby we "put on Christ."[86] It is the inner light and warmth by which we are transformed into the Lord, says Filippi.[87] For Maroldi, this internal "erudition" is superior to all external examples.[88] Alexander Cortesius asks Sixtus IV and the rest of the court to consider how much they owe to him who snatched them from the power of darkness and translated them into the kingdom of the son of his love.[89] Thus far the preachers speak in terms which would be especially congenial to Cusa; then they begin to move beyond them.

---

85. "Oratio de unione Verbi cum natura humana," in *Opuscula*, pp. 184–85.
86. *Sermo qualiter possimus Iesum Christum induere* [Rome: E. Silber, 1496], Cop. #5843, fol. [9ᵛ].
87. "Oratio in epiphania," in *Orationes novem coram Iulio II et Leone X*, fol. [4ʳ].
88. *Oratio in epiphania* [Rome: J. Gensberg, after Jan. 6, 1475], Hain #*10779, fols. [9ᵛ–10ʳ].
89. *Oratio in epiphania* [Rome: S. Plannck, after Jan. 25, 1483], GKW #7796, fol. [6ᵛ].

For Lodovico da Ferrara nothing is more conducive to man's dignity than to be able to do those good and just things that others are incapable of doing. This capacity derives from grace and contributes to man's dignity.[90] Through the sacraments, according to Filippi, the charity of God has been poured into our hearts by the Holy Spirit, who now dwells within us (Rom. 5:5).[91] Giles of Viterbo also fastened onto that same verse from Romans, a verse favored by his spiritual father, Saint Augustine.[92] Filippi reminds his listeners in another sermon that God created their souls in love and that through love they will transform themselves into gods.[93] Sentiments like these could be lifted from the sermons of many Christian preachers throughout the ages. The distinctive feature about them in the *cappelle pontificie* is the controlling role they play in the sermon's message.

For the most part, the Incarnation is proposed as the mystery that dignified human nature with this surpassing new excellence. In conveying this idea the boldest formulation was at the same time one of the most traditional: "God became man, that man might become God." The idea can be traced back to Saint Irenaeus, but the concise formulation that became so popular occurs in a sermon of Pseudo-Augustine. Saint Thomas quotes it, and Petrarch paraphrases it.[94] Domenichi, Massari, Filippi, Vázquez, and Thegliatius, among the preachers, do the same.[95]

For Thegliatius, moreover, the Incarnation sealed the nuptials between

90. "Sermo de divina gratia," in *Orationes quinque* [Rome: n. publ., after 1492], Hain #6983, fol. [15ᵛ].

91. "Oratio de sacramentis," in *Orationes novem coram Iulio II et Leone X*, fol. [8ʳ].

92. See my "Man's Dignity," pp. 393–94.

93. "Oratio dominica de Trinitate," in *Orationes novem coram Iulio II et Leone X*, fol. [6ᵛ].

94. Ps. Aug., Sermo spurius 128, PL 39, 1997; "Factus est Deus homo, ut homo fieret deus." This is a simplified version of a formulation which is genuinely Augustinian, e.g., PL 39, 1504, and 38, 909, and esp. 1012: "Deos facturus qui homines erant, homo factus est qui Deus erat." For Aquinas, see *Summa Theologiae*, III.1.2: "Quinto, quantum ad plenam participationem divinitatis, quae vera est hominis beatitudo et finis humanae vitae; et hoc collatum est nobis per Christi humanitatem. Dicit enim Augustinus . . . , Factus est Deus homo, ut homo fieret Deus." The paraphrase in Petrarch is in *De remediis utriusque fortunae*, II.93, in *Opera omnia*, I (Basel: H. Petri, 1554), 211. For Irenaeus, see *Contra haereses*, V, praef., PG 7, 1120: ". . . Verbum Dei, Iesum Christum Dominum nostrum, qui propter immensam suam dilectionem factus est quod sumus nos, uti nos perficeret esse quod est ipse."

95. Domenichi, "In nativitate Domini sermo," BAV cod. Ross. 1037, fol. 184ᵛ; Massari, "De animae dignitatibus," Bibl. Ang. cod. lat. 835, III, fol. 31ᵛ; Vázquez, *Oratio in die cinerum*, fol. [7ᵛ]; Thegliatius, "Oratio in concilio Lateranensi," Mansi, 32.920.

the son of God and "our humanity."[96] Giles of Viterbo develops a similar idea at some length.[97] Carvajal states: "He is called Emmanuel, which means 'with-us.' Thus is designated the cause of our salvation: the union of the divine and human natures in the son of God, through which God is conjoined to us."[98] When Lodovico da Ferrara affirms that by emptying himself, taking the form of a servant, and being born for us Christ restored us to our dignity, we must observe how a Pauline text (Phil. 2:7) dealing with Christ's death on the cross is here paraphrased to make it interpret the Nativity or Incarnation.[99]

Marcus Antonius Ticinensis exclaims about that Incarnation: "O, how immense is the kindness of the eternal Father! How great is the dignity of man! How incomprehensible the sublimity of Jesus Christ, of whom it is truly said and proclaimed that he is perfect God and perfect man!"[100] At the Incarnation, the same preacher informs his hearers, the Lord conferred greater dignity upon human nature than he ever did upon the angels —to the man Christ he conceded the supreme grace, and of Christ's plenitude we have all received (John 1:16).[101]

The Crucifixion and Resurrection of Christ, as well as other events from his life, are also interpreted by the preachers as signifying man's new dignity. A special importance is attributed to the Ascension when the *beneficia* of the Redemption were fully and finally achieved, as Christ took his place at the Father's right hand. It was at that moment, says Marsi, that humanity was exalted above the choirs of angels.[102] It was at

96. *Oratio in die omnium sanctorum*, fol. [2ᵛ]: "Et ideo tamquam sponsus de thalamo suo processit, quia non solus sed coniugatus de Virginis utero exivit, in quo certe utero Dei filius nuptias fecit, uxorem duxit, quia priusquam nasceretur humanitatem nostram sibi coniunxit."

97. See my "Man's Dignity," p. 393.

98. *Oratio in die circumcisionis*, fol. [8ᵛ]: "In eo enim quod dicitur Emmanuel, quod interpretatur nobiscum, designatur causa nostrae salutis, quae est unio divinae et humanae naturae in persona filii Dei, per quam actum est ut Deus esset nobiscum particeps."

99. "Sermo de adventu Christi," in *Orationes quinque*, fol. [3ʳ]: "Parvulus, inquit [Isaias], quia formam servi accipiens semetipsum maiorem in modum exinanivit. Natus est nobis, quia Virgo concepit et peperit filium, qui nostram nobis dignitatem amplitudinemque restituit."

100. *In adventu oratio*, fol. [5ʳ]: "O, ingens igitur aeterni patris benignitas! O, quam magna hominis dignitas! O, incomprehensibilis Iesu Christi sublimitas! De quo vere dicitur et praedicatur quod est perfectus Deus et perfectus homo."

101. *Ibid.*, fol. [4ʳ]: "Nonne humanae naturae plus gratiae plusque excellentiae Dominus concessit quam ipsis angelis? Concessit, inquam, Christo homini summam gratiam ita ut de plenitudine eius accepimus omnes."

102. *Oratio in die ascensionis de immortalitate animae*, fol. [6ᵛ]: " . . . et humanita-

that moment, says Gravina, that human nature took its place above the very stars. The Ascension shows that not only men's souls but also their bodies are immortal.[103] Mortality is thus transferred into the heart and home of immortality: "O, dignity of the human race, dignity never before heard of in all the ages of the world!"[104]

From the question of man's dignity, we move almost imperceptibly to the question of his immortality. In fact, while treating the dignity of man, the preachers often touched upon that live issue of their day, the immortality of the human soul.[105] Though older in origin, the issue became particularly critical and more clearly formulated in Italy in the latter part of the Quattrocento and early Cinquecento. It reached a kind of climax at the Fifth Lateran Council when by the decree "Apostolici regiminis sollicitudo," December 19, 1513, the thesis was condemned that at least according to philosophy the human soul is mortal.

In addition to any number of more or less casual mentions of the soul's immortality, there are some instances where the question is professedly dealt with. Gravina's epideictic oration on the Ascension, 1493, is an instance of a sermon where the issue keeps recurring but is not handled systematically. Though Averroes is mentioned, he is dismissed in one short line. The very fact of the Ascension, according to Gravina, makes it superfluous to seek the testimony of philosophers like Pythagoras and Plato and of prophets like the Sibyls.[106]

---

tem, quae culpa primi parentis depressa iacebat, super choros angelorum exaltavit." The same idea occurs, e.g., in St. Leo the Great, Sermo 73, PL, 54.396.

103. *Oratio de Christi ad caelos ascensu* [Rome: S. Plannck, 1493], Hain-Cop. #7925, fol. [4ʳ].

104. *Ibid.*, fol. [2ʳ]: "Sed quemadmodum se summiserat cum formam servi indueret, ita secum ea sublata ascendit ac superevolavit ad caelum. Quare super excelsa mundi, ut Augustinus canit, terrenum corpus hodie imponitur, et ossa inter sepulchri angustias paulo ante conclusa coetibus angelorum inferuntur, et in gremium immortalitatis mortalis natura transfunditur. O, nullis antea saeculis auditam humani generis dignitatem! O, admirabile divinae mysterium clementiae, quo erexit ex terra inopem et ex stercore elevavit pauperem. . . . Quid enim maius per Deum nobis conferri potuit quam quod caelestibus exaequati dignitate sumus?"

105. The literature on this problem is ample. The most comprehensive study is Giovanni di Napoli, *L'immortalità dell'anima nel Rinascimento* (Turin: Società Editrice Internaz., 1963). See also Étienne Gilson, "Autour de Pomponazzi: Problématique de l'immortalité de l'âme en Italie au début du XVIᵉ siècle," *Archives d'histoire doctrinale et littéraire du Moyen-Age*, 28 (1961), 163–279; Paul Oskar Kristeller, "The Immortality of the Soul," in his *Renaissance Concepts of Man*, pp. 22–42; Edward P. Mahoney, "Nicoletto Vernia on the Soul and Immortality," in *Philosophy and Humanism: Renaissance Essays in Honor of Paul Oskar Kristeller*, ed. Edward P. Mahoney (New York: Columbia University Press, 1976), pp. 144–63.

106. *Oratio de Christi ad caelos ascensu*, fol. [3ʳ].

Massari composed his treatise on the dignities of the soul about 1458, at the beginning of the pontificate of Pius II. He dedicates the long, final part of it to the question of the soul's immortality.[107] As we have already seen, he disclaims he is "disputing" the question. He will adduce "testimonies" to enjoy them and glory in them. This epideictic purpose seemingly gives him license to gather examples, arguments, and authorities from a wide range of sources. He shows little sense of discrimination in this operation, and he does not develop any single line of argument at length. Perhaps he hopes for a cumulative effect. The treatment is of some interest, nonetheless, as an example of how intimately the question of immortality was tied to the theme of the dignity of man.

At least six sermons have survived from the *cappelle* that somewhat systematically deal with the soul's immortality. The first of these is by Francis of Assisi, preached for Paul II; the next is also by a Franciscan, Ioannes de Trevio, delivered before Sixtus IV in 1473.[108] These are unexceptional, thematic sermons that try to prove the soul's immortality from reason, authority, and examples. The third sermon, which has already been described, is Pietro Marsi's, delivered before Innocent VIII probably in 1490. Part of this basically thematic sermon is dedicated to refuting the idea that the philosophers had a correct view of the soul's immortality. Though Marsi does not advocate the view later proscribed by the council that according to philosophy the soul is mortal, he does firmly maintain that philosophy cannot prove the soul's immortality. The philosophers' arguments should not be used even to try to confirm Christian belief in immortality. The Christian doctrine is a divine doctrine. "We say that the perpetuity of the rational soul is not due to anything intrinsic to it but is from a divine ordination."[109] Certainly not all of Marsi's listeners would have shared his viewpoint, but it would have been congenial to anyone in his audience influenced by the opinions of Scotus and Ockham.[110] Marsi, professor of rhetoric at the *Studium Urbis*, proposes his

107. "De animae dignitatibus," Bibl. Ang. cod. lat. 835, III, fols. 17ʳ–28ʳ.

108. Francis of Assisi, "Oratio de immortalitate animorum," BAV cod. Vat. lat. 14063, fols. 12ᵛ–17ᵛ; Ioannes de Trevio, *Oratio de animarum immortalitate* (Rome: J. P. de Lignamine, 1473), Hain #*15610.

109. *Oratio in die ascensionis de immortalitate animae*, fol. [3ʳ]: "Animae rationalis perpetuitatem non per aliquod intrinsecum ipsius esse dicimus, verum ex ordinatione divina, ut non solum in suis naturalibus perseveret, sed propter meritum vel demeritum ita dixerim gloriam sortiatur et poenam."

110. See James K. Sheridan's introduction to his translation of Cajetan's "On the Immortality of Minds," in *Renaissance Philosophy*, ed. Leonard A. Kennedy (The Hague: Mouton, 1973), pp. 41–46.

position, as a matter of fact, in terms of the scholastic distinction "de Dei ordinata potentia."[111]

Cajetan addressed the question on the first Sunday of Advent, 1503, just a few days after Julius II had been elected pope.[112] Cajetan's conviction is that the soul's immortality can be proved philosophically, and he sets out to do just that, borrowing and adapting arguments from Aquinas. In other words, he expounds the standard Thomistic position, sharply opposed to the position held by Marsi. Cajetan later in life, we know, lost this early confidence in the power of philosophy to demonstrate the soul's immortality.[113]

For the same pope some years later, Schomberg again raised the issue. His sermon is principally epideictic in purpose, though the materials he presents are various arguments showing the soul's immortality. He reproves Aristotle for his doubts and ambiguities, and he also mentions the errors of Plato.[114] But Schomberg does not directly confront the issue with which the council would deal. Though more orderly and disciplined, his sermon is similar in spirit to Massari's treatment of the question.

The only sermon on immortality I have discovered after the promulgation of the council's decree is by the procurator general of the Carmelites, Stephanus Basignanas Gorgonius, delivered before Leo X on December 20, 1517.[115] Just two Sundays earlier Leo had asked Paris de Grassis to remind the Master of the Sacred Palace about the fifteen-minute rule. On Gorgonius's sermon, de Grassis observed: "The procurator of the Carmelites delivered the sermon. It was not very good, and it was too long. Many people found fault with it on both counts."[116] At least in this instance, de Grassis exercised restraint in his criticism.

Gorgonius's sermon would be exceptionally long even apart from the fifteen-minute rule. Moreover, though delivered at this late date, it is

111. *Oratio in die ascensionis de immortalitate animae*, fol. [3ʳ].

112. "Oratio de immortalitate animorum," in *Opuscula*, pp. 186–88. See, again, Sheridan's introduction in *Renaissance Philosophy*, pp. 41–46.

113. See, e.g., Emilia Verga, "L'immortalità dell'anima nel pensiero del Card. Gaetano," in *Il Cardinale Tomaso [sic] de Vio Gaetano nel quarto centenario della sua morte*, a special supplement to *Rivista di filosofia neo-scolastica*, 27 (1935), 21–46, esp. 33–35; Etiénne Gilson, "Cajetan et l'humanisme théologique," *Archives d'histoire doctrinale et littéraire du Moyen Age*, 22 (1955), 113–36.

114. "Quinta oratio. Ductus est Iesus in desertum," in *Orationes vel potius divinorum eloquiorum enodationes*, fols. [13ʳ–17ᵛ], esp. [16ᵛ].

115. *Oratio de animae immortalitate*.

116. "Diarium," BAV cod. Vat. lat. 12275, fol. 246ᵛ: "Sermonem habuit procurator Carmelitarum non nimis bonum et satis longum, in utroque a pluribus damnatum."

thoroughly thematic. Even the Latin style shows less classical influence than almost any of the other sermons that are extant from the *cappelle* for the period we are considering. Gorgonius sets out to prove the soul's immortality, gathering his authorities with that end in view. Socrates, Plato, and Aristotle, for instance, knew the soul's immortality. Averroes, however, denied it, and his influence in Italy, sad to say, is immense. In the light of that supposed fact, Gorgonius then assesses the condition of philosophy in his day: "The pernicious contagion of that damnable man has so grown and so extended the branches of its perfidy in almost all the schools of Italy that no one can be considered a good Peripatetic and an accomplished philosopher if he does not dare to sustain with arguments the profane opinion of Averroes."[117] The quality of Gorgonius's assessment of Averroes's influence suggests the other exaggerations with which the sermon abounds and which make it unnecessary to delay over it any longer. It might be noted, however, that Gorgonius makes no effort to link immortality with man's dignity.

At this juncture it is appropriate to ask whether the preachers manifested any particular preoccupation with another question, one which would convulse Europe just as the period under study draws to a close. In other words, did they adopt any significant stance on the important question of Pelagianism and Semi-Pelagianism? Did the religion espoused in these sermons in any way underwrite the save-yourself tenets of Augustine's adversaries in the fifth century, and was there operative in them a Renaissance view of the "autonomy of man" that would contradict the canons of the Council of Carthage and the Second Council of Orange?

The immediate response to these questions is that the problem of the relationship of grace to free will or nature is not often treated *ex professo*. Probably the best instances of such a treatment are Timotheus de Totis's sermon in 1496 about "putting on Christ" and a sermon by Lodovico da

117. *Oratio de animae immortalitate*, fol. [2ᵛ]: "Averroes cum Themistio tam manifesti erroris auctor humanam animam unam intelligentiam abstractam . . . et illam unicam in omnibus hominibus. . . . Cuius damnati viri pernitiosa pestis in omnibus fere Italiae academiis usque adeo excrevit et perfidiae ramos extendit ne peripateticus bonus et consummatus philosophus videatur qui prophanam Averrois sententiam argumentis sustentare non ausit." Giles of Viterbo, in his "Historia XX saeculorum" written during the pontificate of Leo X, offers a similar judgment, specifying "Padua" and Nicoletto Vernia as promoting or tolerating the infection, Bibl. Ang. cod. lat. 502, fol. 96ᵛ: "Coepit sub Sixto quarto Patavii, deinde sub Innocentio octavo, ita virus fundere, Nicoletto Theatino scholas regente, ut paucis his annis omnia infecerit, omnia labefactaverit, fidem undique exagitatam orbe terrarum prope migrare coegerit." See my *Giles of Viterbo*, pp. 47–49.

Ferrara some years earlier on "divine grace." But even in these sermons the grace-freedom relationship is a subordinate theme. The precisions of that relationship, as elaborated by the scholastics, were perhaps too technical for the *cappelle*. Perhaps the focus on what was "objective," ontological, and historical distracted the preachers from the more subjective question of the particular internal processes by which an individual was invested with God's favor. Moreover, though the issue was raised and settled in a generic way during the patristic era, the controversies did not engage the attention of even that era with the same degree of sustained interest as had the trinitarian and christological controversies. We must remember, in fact, that the decrees of the Second Council of Orange against those who would later be known as Semi-Pelagians went unnoticed by theologians during the Middle Ages and would not be recovered until later in the sixteenth century.[118]

On the other hand, the preachers were well aware of the Pelagian heresy, and they had no intention of being identified with it. Palmeri mentions Pelagius by name and compiles a list of scriptural proof-texts to refute him.[119] Both Timotheus de Totis and Lodovico da Ferrara insist upon the insufficiency of "the Law" and of nature for man's salvation.[120] Lodovico, as well as Cajetan, Antonio Lollio, and Martinus de Azpetia, invokes the absolute necessity of grace.[121] Filippi confesses in explicitly Pauline terms that grace would not be grace unless freely given.[122] When Marsi extolled Augustine's "moral philosophy" over that of Socrates, Plato, and Aristotle in his panegyric of the saint, he was being consistent with the position he adopted towards the philosophers on the question

118. See Harry J. McSorley, "Was Gabriel Biel a Semipelagian?" in *Wahrheit und Verkündigung: Michael Schmaus zum 70. Geburtstag*, ed. Leo Scheffczyk et al., 2 vols. (Munich: Schöningh, 1967), II, 1109–20.

119. ["De pacis dignitate"], BAV cod. Vat. lat. 5815, fols. 99ᵛ–100ᵛ.

120. De Totis, *Sermo qualiter possimus Iesum Christum induere*, fol. [11ʳ]; Lodovico, "Sermo de adventu Christi," in *Orationes quinque*, fols. [3ᵛ–5ʳ], and "Sermo de divina gratia," *ibid.*, fol. [14ʳ⁻ᵛ].

121. Lodovico, "Sermo de adventu Christi," in *Orationes quinque*, fol. [4ᵛ]; Cajetan, "Oratio de vi cultus divini et orationis efficacia," in *Opuscula*, p. 182; Lollio, *Oratio circumcisionis dominicae* [Rome: S. Plannck, 1485?], Hain #*10180, fol. [3ᵛ]; de Azpetia, *De passione Domini oratio*, passim.

122. "Oratio in dominica de passione," in *Orationes novem coram Iulio II et Leone X*, fol. [19ʳ]. See also de Totis, *Sermo qualiter possimus Iesum Christum induere*, fol. [9ᵛ]; Vázquez, *De unitate et simplicitate personae Christi in duabus naturis oratio* (Rome: J. Mazochius, 1518), fol. xvʳ, now in the modern edition by Quirino Fernandez, "Fray Dionisio Vázquez de Toledo, orador sagrado del Siglo de Oro," *Archivo Agustiniano*, 60 (1976), 175.

of the immortality of the soul.[123] In his first panegyric in honor of Saint Stephen, furthermore, he rejects the philosophers' belief that they can attain beatitude on their own—philosophers "whose vanity Augustine derided."[124] These statements seem to express, more or less, the convictions of other preachers, even of humanists like Marcello and Aurelio Brandolini.[125]

The preachers, therefore, repudiated Pelagianism, as we surely would expect. But the casual and untechnical nature of their observations about the relationship between grace and nature makes further precision difficult. Some of the statements of Lodovico da Ferrara, for instance, bear a Semi-Pelagian interpretation, and the same can be said of other preachers.[126] In trying to interpret the preachers' meaning in this context, we must be aware that in general they were persuaded that, especially since the Incarnation, grace was abundantly present in the world and abundantly available to men. Perhaps Timotheus de Totis puts this conviction into its most appealing formulation when he asks: "For who is there whom God does not call—that God who affirms through John that he stands always at the door of our soul knocking and seeking entrance?"[127] Indeed,

---

123. *Panegyricus in memoriam sancti Augustini* [Rome: E. Silber, n.d.], Hain #10787, fol. [8ʳ]: "Laudatur moralis philosophiae parens ille Socrates, et merito quidem. Laudatur dives ille Plato, cuius multiplicem doctrinam suspexit antiquitas. Laudatur artifex ille disciplinarum ac immensae subtilitatis Aristoteles. . . . Sed illis longe Augustinum praeponam." See also *ibid.*, fol. [9ᵛ].

124. *Oratio in die sancti Stephani* [Rome: S. Plannck, n.d.], Hain #*10785, fol. [4ʳ]: " . . . et [philosophi] dicentes se esse sapientes, stulti facti sunt. Hoc ideo illis accidit quoniam refugientes gratiae splendorem ipsius naturae perfectionem posuerunt, et a seipsis posse fieri beati opinati sunt, quorum vanitatem deridet Augustinus."

125. Marcello, "Oratio de laudibus Ioannis evangelistae," BAV cod. Vat. lat. 3644, fols. 6ᵛ–7ʳ; Brandolini, *De humanae vitae conditione*, pp. 61–62.

126. See, e.g., "Sermo de divina gratia," in *Orationes quinque*, fol. [16ᵛ]. See also, e.g., Schomberg, "Tertia oratio. Ductus est Iesus in desertum," in *Orationes vel potius divinorum eloquiorum enodationes*, fol. [7ᵛ]; Marcus Antonius Ticinensis, *In adventu oratio*, fol. [6ʳ]; de Totis, *Sermo qualiter possimus Iesum Christum induere*, fols. [10ʳ, 11ᵛ].

127. *Sermo qualiter possimus Iesum Christum induere*, fol. [11ᵛ]: "Nam, teste Paulo, nihil prorsus sufficimus nostra virtute cogitare [nisi] a Deo ipso excitati et adiuti. Quos enim non vocat, qui semper se ad ostium stare et pulsare animum nostrum per Ioannem affirmat [Rev. 3:20]?" See also, e.g., Maroldi, *Oratio in epiphania*, fol. [2ʳ]; Lollio, *Oratio circumcisionis dominicae*, fol. [1ᵛ]; Domenichi, "In nativitate Domini sermo," BAV cod. Ross. 1037, fol. 163ᵛ. On this question, see the perceptive article by Charles Trinkaus, "Italian Humanism and the Problem of 'Structures of Conscience,'" *The Journal of Medieval and Renaissance Studies*, 2 (1972), 19–33, esp. 32. See also his observations on the relationship between the activism inherent in Renaissance rhetoric and the emphasis on God's grace, *Image and Likeness*, I, 32, 46–48; II, 633, 649, and see, as well, his "Erasmus, Augustine, and the Nominalists," *Archive for Reformation History*, 67 (1976), 5–32.

the great emphasis the preachers place on man's freedom, on his true causality, and on his power even "to be whatever he desired" pointed to God's liberality and munificence. That emphasis was meant to tell the audience as much about God as it did about man.

There is no doubt, in any event, that some of the preachers take a notably positive view of the natural goodness of man. This was surely true of Cajetan.[128] Lodovico da Ferrara and Timotheus de Totis are convinced of the harmony between reason and Christ's "law," as we might expect from Dominicans, and they express this harmony in almost identical terms.[129] These positions correlate with the basic presupposition about the order and congenial harmony of the universe discussed earlier. Whether the reconciliatory dynamic inherent in these positions, as well as in the scholastic enterprise as a whole, caused preachers to trangress the limits of orthodoxy, however, must for the moment remain an open question.

Possibly as a consequence of the preachers' relative lack of interest in the grace-freedom relationship, they manifest no particular concern for the problem of predestination. Moreover, the "salvation of the pagan," of those who never had either heard Christ's message or been baptized, is rarely touched upon.[130] On those few occasions when it does receive some attention, the "good pagans" tend to receive gentle treatment. Marsi's harsh judgment about the accomplishments of the ancient

128. See, e.g., Otto Pesch's article, "Thomismus," in *Lexicon für Theologie und Kirche*, X (1965), 157–67, esp. 164.

129. Lodovico speaks about Christ's "law" and "precepts," "Sermo de adventu Christi," in *Orationes quinque*, fol. [3ᵛ]: "In his profecto nihil invenies, postquam diu multumque evolveris cogitaverisque, quod rationi dissonet, quod a veritate divertat, quod a bonis se abducat moribus, quod abs te reprehendi castigarive possit." De Totis also speaks about Christ's "law," *Sermo quod omnino datur ultimus finis creaturae rationalis*, fol. [7ʳ]: " . . . in qua profecto nihil invenies, postquam diu multumque evolveris, cogitaveris, quod rationi dissonet, quod abs te castigari reprehendique possit." De Totis seems deliberately to be quoting the preacher he so much admired and whose funeral eulogy he delivered.

130. For background on this problem, see Biechler, *Religious Language*, pp. 81–92; Louis Capéran, *Le problème du salut des Infideles*, 2 vols. (Toulouse: Grand Séminaire, 1934); Ralph V. Turner, "*Descendit ad Inferos*: Medieval Views on Christ's Descent into Hell and the Salvation of the Ancient Just," *Journal of the History of Ideas*, 27 (1966), 173–94; George H. Williams, "Erasmus and the Reformers on Non-Christian Religions and *Salus Extra Ecclesiam*," in *Action and Conviction in Early Modern Europe: Essays in Memory of E. H. Harbison*, ed. Theodore K. Rabb and Jerrold Seigel (Princeton: Princeton University Press, 1969), pp. 319–70; Hans Baron, "Erasmus-Probleme im Spiegel des Colloquium 'Inquisitio de fide,'" *Archiv für Reformationsgeschichte*, 43 (1952), 254–63. See also the pertinent, but more widely ranging, article by J. Patout Burns, "The Economy of Salvation: Two Patristic Traditions," *Theological Studies*, 37 (1976), 598–619.

philosophers seems to be very much a minority opinion. Signori comes much closer to expressing the appreciation which the preachers felt for "the philosophers" when he speaks of them as holy men, filled with the divine spirit.[131] Massari is even more emphatic.[132]

The preachers felt a special reverence for Plato and Socrates, for Cato and Cicero. Carvajal cites Pseudo-Dionysius to the effect that by angels these men were led to belief in the true God. His own conviction is firm: "Anaxagoras, Zeno, Socrates, Plato, and Aristotle, as well as other upright philosophers who worshiped one God and led lives of virtue—these I would never judge damned to eternal fires."[133]

Agostino Filippi seems to go a step further in his sermon on the Trinity for Leo X, 1513. When he applies the term "learned ignorance" to the mentality with which one should approach the august mystery of the Trinity, he is applying the term to the same mystery to which Cusa applied it in his famous treatise.[134] Filippi maintains that knowledge of the Trinity is achieved only through revelation. Nonetheless, in terms again reminiscent of Cusa, he says that belief in God—in the same God, it would seem—is confessed by "all nations under heaven, with diversity of ceremony and cult."[135] While Filippi tries to uphold the distinctiveness of Christian belief, he also upholds the position that other sincere worshipers, in the past and in the present, are not enemies to that belief. Though these

131. See *Oratio de summo Deo* [n.p.: n. publ., after Dec. 11, 1485], Hain #14732, fol. [5ʳ⁻ᵛ].
132. See his "Commentarius super [tertia] regula divi Augustini," in *Vita Augustini*, fols. [189ᵛ–190ʳ], and "De animae dignitatibus," Bibl. Ang. cod. lat. 835, III, fols. 22ᵛ–26ʳ. See also Raphael Brandolini, "Oratio de obitu Mariani Genazanensis," BAV cod. Vat. lat. 10806, fols. 68ᵛ–69ʳ.
133. *Sermo in die omnium sanctorum* [Rome: G. Herolt, after Nov. 1, 1482], GKW #6154, fol. [2ᵛ]; "Anaxagoram, Zenonem, Socratem Platonemque hisque et Aristotelem addam aliosque observantissimos philosophos qui cultum unius Dei receperunt, sese magnis dedere virtutibus—hos ego numquam opinione mea aeternis incendiis damnatos iudicabo."
134. "Oratio dominica de Trinitate," in *Orationes novem coram Iulio II et Leone X*, fol. [4ʳ⁻ᵛ]: "De creatore curiose minime disputabo, at fatebor ingenue hoc certe scire quod nescio naturam Dei. Neque haec in me ignorantia tristitiam parit, nec quemquam Christiani gregis vel consultissimum ullo modo perturbare debet, si hoc enim sciverimus quod nescimus, naturam Dei ceteris longe amplius scire videbimur. . . . Quanto nos illis [gentilibus] sapientiores! Docta profecto et omni cognitione plena haec ignorantia!"
135. *Ibid.*, fol. [4ᵛ]: "Aliquod esse numen in universo quem Deum nostri dixerunt, non modo sacrorum canonum auctoritas praedicat, . . . non solum insuper omnes quae sub caelo sunt nationes caeremoniarum et cultus diversitate illi sacra canentes confitentur, verum et universa quoque rerum natura proclamat." Cf. Cusa, *De Pace Fidei*, pp. 4–7 (I). Cf. also Ficino, "De Christiana religione," in *Opera*, I, 4.

sincere worshipers are not fully enlightened, they still possess a measure of the truth. Other preachers, without being as explicit as Filippi, approach classical culture, especially, with the same sentiment.

Heretics, not the "good pagans," were the real enemies to the Christian faith. Heretics by definition knowingly and willingly denied the truth, and, hence, their misbelief was criminal. Palmeri's refutation of Pelagius indicates a pattern of argument the preachers frequently adopted when dealing with heresies about the Trinity or the Incarnation. Briefly or at length the insanity of the heresies was exposed, and the classic refutations of them were adduced.

These refutations of the heretics were rhetorical in the sense that they functioned as an appropriate *amplificatio* in praise of the security and orthodoxy of the faith of the Church or as illustrations of how the sins of pride, luxury, and avarice could pervert the human will and intellect. In the latter case, the preachers conveyed an awareness that a resurgence of heresy was always possible. Occasionally, even aside from the pernicious influence of Averroes, they warned that they saw some of the heresies they have just refuted corrupting the Church of their own day.[136] In these instances, however, their warnings are generally vague, and they engender the suspicion that they are not firmly grounded in fact.

What emerges from the sermons, indeed, is a great sense of doctrinal security. Even if heresy should perchance appear once again, its refutations had already been marshaled, standing ready to march into battle. Massari in his *Vita* of Saint Augustine expressed in an exaggerated way a mentality that rather broadly obtained in the preachers. We find in Augustine's writings, according to Massari, refutations for all heretics.[137] Augustine's bequest to future ages was a firm and secure defense against them.

More soberly and in somewhat different terms, Aurelio Brandolini conveys this same sense that the great conflicts of the patristic age had resulted in the triumph of orthodoxy and had finalized that triumph. In his "Epitoma in sacram Iudaeorum historiam," he distinguishes his own age from that of Jerome by the fact that Jerome's had to combat doctrinal doubts and adversaries.[138] Jerome's age laid the doubts and adversaries to rest—for all times, it would seem.

---

136. See, e.g., Mariano da Genazzano, *Oratio habita dominica tertia adventus* [Rome: E. Silber, after Dec. 16, 1487], Hain-Cop. #7554, fols. [4ᵛ–5ʳ].

137. *Vita Augustini*, fol. [13ᵛ].

138. BAV cod. Ottob. lat. 438, fol. 8ᵛ: "Sed quod tunc instantibus adversariis dubiisque rebus nostris necessario faciendum fuit, nunc sublatis illis statuque con-

Lodovico da Ferrara, the learned professor of scholastic philosophy and theology, develops the same idea at greater length and more effectively. He praises the doctrinal achievements of the Church's great teachers— Dionysius, Basil, Chrysostom, and Damascene; Gregory, Jerome, Ambrose, and Augustine; Thomas, Albert, Alexander of Hales, Bonaventure, and Giles of Rome. How many errors they defeated, how many enemies they overcame! There is nobody "in our times" who would, therefore, dare attack the Christian faith—not philosophers, not poets, not orators, not mathematicians, not augurs, not magicians, not heretics. They have all already been conquered by these unconquerable leaders of the Church. Therefore, says Lodovico, "Peace now reigns in Christian doctrine"— "Nunc pacem habent litterae Christianae."[139]

Lodovico voices a sentiment found in most of the preachers. The great truths had been formulated, the great errors had been refuted. The classic truths had received their classic formulation, as had also the classic refutation of the heretics. This classicist mentality was found in both the scholastic and the humanist tradition.[140] It assumed that perduring and stable standards of truth and excellence had been established. Man's present task consisted in trying to conform to them rather than in reexamining them.

We thus return to the considerations with which this chapter began. The sense of perennially valid truth and even perennially valid patterns of behavior converges nicely with the sense of ontological stability in the universe. The "pax theologica" achieved a coordination of the Church's faith with the ontological peace in the universe. Theological peace now reigned, as it should reign. That peace was part of the proper situation of the universe.

With doctrines secure, man had his answers to the fundamental ques-

---

firmato servandum non est. Causa enim sublata, effectus quoque ipse e vestigo tollitur." See also his "De laudibus beatissimi patris Sixti IV pontificis maximi libri," BAV cod. Urb. lat. 739, fols. 64^v–65^r, quoted in note 97 of Chapter II.

139. "Sermo de conformitate ecclesiae militantis ad ecclesiam triumphantem," in *Orationes quinque*, fol. [19^r]: "Sapientiae vero ac doctrinae omnes facile cedunt, victi ab invictissimis ecclesiae ducibus. Nunc pacem habent litterae Christianae. Nunc immensis veterum theologorum laboribus fruimur."

140. For descriptions of some of the elements of what I call a classicist mentality, as manifested in different disciplines, see Bernard Lonergan, *Method in Theology* (New York: Herder, 1972), pp. 300–302; Ernst Robert Curtius, *European Literature in the Latin Middle Ages*, trans. Willard R. Trask, Bollingen Series, No. 36 (New York: Pantheon, 1953), pp. 247–72; R. G. Collingwood, *The Idea of History* (New York: Oxford University Press, 1956), pp. 42–45.

tions of human existence. He knew what he was, where he came from, what he was destined for, what he should resemble. He knew, besides, the basic structure of the world around him, and he knew how to interpret the evidence that his senses and experience presented to him. The preachers thus made doctrine, as such, relevant to the "ars bene beateque vivendi." That is, they provided their listeners with a sense of order, stability, and personal identity in a world where these values were, perforce, under some threat. The sermons were meant to cast light on the mystery of man's life and to equip the listeners with the inspiration they needed to face life's problems.[141]

Classical oratory taught the preachers how to present their doctrine so that it performed these functions. Most of the preachers seemed to learn at least the rudiments of the lesson. The scholastics among them may never have come to believe that their "disputes" were meaningless, and they may never have subscribed to Valla's belittling the use of philosophy for theology, but they tried to keep technical issues out of their sermons and to relate what they had to say to the art of good and holy living.

Martinus de Viana, a professor of scholastic theology, put the matter well. In his sermon for Ascension Thursday, 1494, he at one point lists a number of scholastic questions about Christ's Ascension—did he ascend by his own power, did he ascend by a "violent" or by a "natural" motion, was his ascent proper to his human or to his divine nature, and so forth. These are very subtle matters, de Viana says, and *very much worth knowing.* " But it would be altogether inappropriate to enter into them "here"— "hoc in loco." He will, instead, discourse on man's dignity![142]

141. Thus the preachers performed the function Peter Berger has termed "nomization," *Sacred Canopy*, pp. 22–28. For an essay which discusses the Renaissance in terms of its "profound anxieties," see William J. Bouwsma, "Renaissance and Reformation: An Essay in Their Affinities and Connections," in *Luther and the Dawn of the Modern Era: Papers for the Fourth International Congress for Luther Research*, ed. Heiko A. Oberman, Studies in the History of Christian Thought, No. 8 (Leiden: Brill, 1974), pp. 127–49. The figures Professor Bouwsma discusses, as well as the questions with which he approaches his materials, sharpen the contrast between his interpretation of the Renaissance and what I describe as operative in the preachers at the papal court.

142. *Oratio de Christi ad caelos ascensione* [Rome: n. publ., 1494]. Cop. #6197, fol. [2ʳ]: "Sed plurimum supervacaneum fore arbitror, patres amplissimi, hoc in loco investigare utrum conveniens fuerit quadragesimo post resurrectionem die Christum ad caelos ascendere, et secundum quam naturam ascensio sibi conveniat, et an propria ascenderit virtute, et, cum ascensio quidam sit motus, an fuerit naturalis vel violentus, et . . . quam plurima alia subtilissima cognitioneque dignissima, quae inter viros

The relationship between Scholasticism and Humanism in these sermons is intricately complex, and de Viana here touches on only one aspect of it. But the writings of the preachers of the *cappelle* seem to indicate that a certain peace was established between scholastics and humanists, even though personal and professional jealousies were occasionally in evidence and even though the impact of Humanism on traditional doctrine was producing a new rhetorical mode of theologizing, in contrast to the dialectical mode of Scholasticism. The scholastics and humanists, nevertheless, both borrowed from each other and found in each other some convergence in outlook. Many of the ideas in the preachers on the dignity of man, for instance, were articulated in scholastic theology. But it was the principles of epideictic rhetoric that orchestrated these ideas into a paean. This particular interaction of Scholasticism with Humanism resulted in a religious world view that was resoundingly affirmative. It was affirmative in its view of the constitution of man and the universe, and it was affirmative in its confidence in the impregnable nature of the truth it celebrated.

When Lodovico da Ferrara reviewed the long theological history of the Church, he saw no ugly discontinuities. He saw, rather, an orderly procession, with each great tradition—the Greek Fathers, the Latin Fathers, and the scholastics—contributing to an harmonious culmination. He saw the whole theological enterprise contributing to the healthy doctrinal situation in which he and his contemporaries found themselves. As never before, "Peace now reigns in Christian doctrine! We now enjoy the fruits of the immense labors of the ancient theologians!"

After Lodovico utters these words, he immediately raises a more sobering issue. Although the Christian religion today has many learned teachers, few Christians bring their lives into conformity with its message. The preacher of the *cappelle* could not content himself with providing his listeners with a cosmological and anthropological interpretation of their existence. He had to be relevant to their lives in yet another way. He had to enter into the question of their actions, their morals, and their practical

---

scholasticos disceptari solent, suntque a nobis Parisiis et alibi frequentius disputata. Sat nobis in praesentia erit humanae naturae quam per Christi ad caelos ascensionem adepta est dignitatem attente considerare. Quid enim maius per Deum nobis conferri potuit quam quod caelestibus exaequati dignitate sumus?" Note that the last line quoted here occurs verbatim in the sermon by Pietro Gravina for the same feast just a year earlier, *Oratio de Christi ad caelos ascensu*, fol. [2ʳ]; see note 104 above. On the general problem of the adaptation of style and content to audience, see Paul Oskar Kristeller, "The Scholar and His Public in the Late Middle Ages and Renaissance," in *Medieval Aspects*, pp. 1–25.

values. He did this by praising what he found there as praiseworthy and by reprehending what he found as reprehensible. He thereby constructed an ideal of the virtuous life, and he moved his listeners to engage in the practice of the art of good and holy living. It is to this aspect of the sacred orator's task that we now turn.

CHAPTER FIVE. THE IDEAL OF THE CHRISTIAN LIFE: NON NOBIS SOLUM NATI SUMUS

In his third sermon at the papal court, Lodovico da Ferrara depicted the distribution of merits and demerits on the Last Day exclusively according to the works of mercy men performed for their fellow men.[1] The scriptural basis for such a depiction was impeccably orthodox, and there is nothing in Lodovico's utilization of the twenty-fifth chapter of Matthew's Gospel that need once again detain us unless it points to something beyond a personal preference of the preacher. Does Lodovico's emphasis on works of mercy fit into a more general pattern of piety propounded by the sacred orators of the court?

The answer to that question is affirmative. With truly remarkable consistency, the preachers of the *cappelle* defined Christian piety in terms of man's relationship to his neighbor—helping the needy, forgiving enemies, consoling the afflicted, visiting the sick, and, in general, ministering to others' needs. The practitioner of this piety is not intent on suppressing his own humanity. According to Campano, indeed, man vindicates his right to be called human by obeying the divine impulse within him to show compassion to his fellow human beings and to go to their aid.[2]

Andrea Brenta's sermon for Pentecost, 1483, epitomizes the ideal of the Christian life the preachers espoused: "Our cult of God is a spiritual one, and it consists in thinking honest thoughts, speaking helpful words, doing good deeds, and storing up in heaven a wealth of piety which no accident or evil fortune can snatch away."[3] Some years after Brenta's sermon, Inghirami in his panegyric of Aquinas repeats Brenta's description

---

1. "Sermo de suprema die," in *Orationes quinque* [Rome: n. publ., after 1492], Hain-Cop. #6983, fols. [10ᵛ–13ᵛ].

2. "De Spiritu sancto oratio," in *Opera a Michaele Ferno edita* (Rome: E. Silber, 1495), GKW #5939, fol. [85ʳ]: "Alter alterum diligimus, etiam incognitum. Unde nomen nobis vindicamus ut homines diceremur, non ab 'humo' ut parum eruditi quidam arbitrantur . . . , sed ab humanitate ipsa, quae tota in amore, in benevolentia, in caritate versatur. Ita cum insint nobis semina divini amoris, natura ipsa impellimur ad lacrimas, ad misericordiam, ad opem ferendam, etiam incognitis, quae propria sunt hominis iniecta atque infusa divinitus."

3. *In pentecosten oratio* [Rome: E. Silber, after May 18, 1483], GKW #5100, fol. [2ᵛ]: "Spiritu namque Deum colimus honesta cogitando, bene dicendo, recte agendo et in caelo pietatis thesauros qui nullo fortunae aut casus impetu eripi possint reponendo."

almost verbatim.[4] Aurelio Brandolini expressed similar sentiments—in his *Christiana paradoxa*,[5] in the sermon on Christ's Passion,[6] and even in the treatise on letter writing. In that treatise he lists several specifically Christian virtues which must be added to the virtues for panegyrics listed by the classical authorities. Along with faith, hope, charity, and chastity, Brandolini insists especially on giving succour to the needy and forgiveness to enemies. It is these virtues, presumably, that distinguish the Christian hero from his pagan counterpart.[7]

The eulogies of Catherine of Siena by Pius II and Domenichi that highlighted her acts of austerity and penance stand apart from the other orations of the court in their glaring singularity.[8] At the present moment I cannot indicate another instance of a similar emphasis in the sermons, although the preachers did on occasion speak of works of bodily penance in their other writings. In their orations, however, that particular ascetical tradition is not advocated. Fastings, vigils, hairshirts, and flagellations— one searches without avail for commendations of them.[9]

4. *Panegyricus in memoriam divi Thomae Aquinatis* [Rome: E. Silber, c.1495], Hain-Reichling #9186, fol. [7ᵛ]: "Denique per omnes virtutes honesta cogitando, bene dicendo, recte agendo, et in caelo pietatis thesauros qui nullo fortunae aut casus impetu eripi possunt congregando, ad sapientiam, cui tanto desiderio flagrabat, contendit [Thomas]."

5. Rome: F. Minitius Calvus, 1531, e.g., fol. [5ᵛ]: "At inimicum, quem et natura refugit et voluntas detestatur, diligere—haec summa laus, haec ingens gloria, haec Christiana perfectio est."

6. *Oratio de virtutibus domini nostri Iesu Christi* [Rome: J. Besicken, after April 1, 1496], GKW #5017, fol. [11ᵛ]: "Servemus in proximos atque aequales quam ipse non dubitavit in servum atque hostem servare iustitiam. Caritatem quam ipse usque ad inimicos extendit omnibus veram sinceramque exhibeamus, neque pudeat nos (cum homines simus) hominibus ministrare, quoniam etiam Deus ipse hominibus ministravit. Ne, obsecro, pauperes atque humilis fortunae homines fastidiamus, cum salvator ipse et pauperrimus et humillimus semper fuerit. Remittamus adversariis nostris iniurias. . . ."

7. *De ratione scribendi libri tres* (Cologne: A. Birckmannus, 1573), p. 100: "Quid, pars illa liberalitatis quae egenis succurit, nobis ex divina institutione tradita, quam nos recepto Graeco vocabulo eleemosynam appellamus, quantam nunc hominibus laudem affert, quae veteribus paene incognita fuerat? Clementia erga inimicos, quae nobis item ex divino instituto servanda est, si adsit, magna laude digna erit, quod praecipue in Stephano laudamus martyre; si absit, sacerdotibus praesertim, vitio dari poterit."

8. Pius II, "Oratio habita in canonizatione beatae Catherinae Senensis," in *Pii II P.M., olim Aeneae Sylvii Piccolominei Senensis, orationes politicae et ecclesiasticae,* ed. Giovanni Domenico Mansi, 2 vols. (Lucca: P. M. Benedinus, 1755–57), II, 136–44; Domenichi, "Oratio in laudem beatissimae Catherinae de Senis," BAV cod. Ottob. lat. 1035, fols. 18ᵛ–28ʳ.

9. Cajetan does mention them as a kind of equivalent of prayer. "Oratio de vi cultus divini et orationis efficacia," in *Opuscula omnia* (Lyons: G. Rovillius, 1588), p. 183. Petrus de Vicentia expressly rejects fasting, prayer, "sacrifices" and confes-

Medieval saints are not presented in the sermons as examples of piety. Dominic and Francis, founders though they were, suffer this same impressive neglect. After the sermon by Domenichi honoring her, Saint Catherine of Siena's name does not appear again. All this is in contrast with the veneration expressed for the saints of the Bible and of the patristic era.

On great public and liturgical occasions the precious relics conserved in Saint Peter's were exposed for the faithfuls' devotion, and Pius II considered the reception in Rome of the head of Saint Andrew one of the momentous events of his pontificate. Yet there is hardly a word about relics in the sermons.[10] The traditional miracles associated with the life of Aquinas are indeed recounted in his annual panegyric, but, as was mentioned earlier, miracle stories find little place in the sermons *coram*. There is, besides, no hint in these sermons that pilgrimages, scapulars, indulgences, and vows to saints existed and were flourishing practices.

There is no particular emphasis on the reception of the sacraments as constituting an important element in Christian piety. Although the Eucharist is from time to time eulogized, practically nothing is said by way of direct encouragement to receive or adore it. Issues like the Real Presence and Transubstantiation are not discussed. The Eucharist is seen, rather, as a sign of Christ's abiding love for men and of the love which should reign among his disciples.[11] Once again, what the preachers fail

---

sion of sins as being sufficient for salvation unless one also helps one's neighbor in need. He curiously applies this doctrine to the necessity of supporting a war against the Turks, March 25, 1490, *Oratio pro capessenda expeditione contra infideles* [Rome: J. Besicken, 1490?], Hain #12860, fols. [3ʳ, 7ᵛ–8ʳ].

10. Filippi carefully distinguishes the adoration due to God alone and the veneration which may be paid the saints. "Oratio de multiplici adoratione," in *Orationes novem coram Iulio II et Leone X* (Rome: J. Mazochius, 1518), fol. [12ᵛ]. In a rare example of such interest in the sermons, he then briefly discusses the veneration of images and relics: "Quorum [sanctorum] imagines et quae apud nos remanserunt reliquias eodem quo et illos honore prosequimur et veneramur. Non ea quidem ratione qua sunt res quaedam, utpote colore, ligno, auro et id genus compluribus constitutae, sed qua potius illorum merita, dignitatem, excellentiam et celsitudinem signant et referunt. Hoc namque pacto in utrumque, signum scilicet et signatum, eodem momento est unus animi motus." See Ruth Olitsky Rubinstein, "Pius II's Piazza S. Pietro and St. Andrew's Head," in *Essays in the History of Architecture Presented to Rudolf Wittkower*, ed. Douglas Fraser, et al. (London: Phaidon, 1967), pp. 22–33.

11. See, e.g., Aurelio Brandolini's "Oratio in cena Domini," Bibl. Com., Siena, cod. H.VI.30, fols. 120ʳ–124ᵛ. On this issue, see Creighton E. Gilbert's article, "Last Suppers and Their Refectories," in *The Pursuit of Holiness in Late Medieval and Renaissance Religion: Papers from the University of Michigan Conference*, ed. Charles Trinkaus with Heiko Oberman, Studies in Medieval and Reformation Thought, No. 10 (Leiden: Brill, 1974), pp. 371–402. However, the sermon preached for Eugene IV by Franciscus Florentinus (seu Paduanus) in Florence in the basilica of S. Maria Novella on Holy Thursday, year unknown, does treat of Transubstantiation, the nature of the

to speak about is almost as significant as the themes to which they generally recur.

When the preachers speak about works of mercy and the reconciliation of man with man, however, they do so in earnest. There would be no better occasion to exhort one's listeners to penance and fasting than in an Ash Wednesday sermon. But when in 1496 Martinus de Viana begs his listeners to begin the Lenten season devoutly by performing "works of piety," he says: "Let us put out the fire of our anger, let us put away our hatreds, let us strive to understand each other, and let us anticipate each other's needs through acts of humble service."[12] In his panegyric of Aquinas, de Viana describes the distinguishing marks of the true religion in terms of "visiting orphans and widows in their necessities and keeping oneself immaculate from the world" (James 1:27).[13]

The emphasis on works of mercy cuts across the traditions represented at the court. The friars surely convey this understanding of Christian piety as forcefully and consistently as do the humanists. When Massari describes even for his subjects in the Augustinian order what it means to be a true observer of the "Rule" of Saint Augustine and of the "law" of Christ he does not resort to the minutiae of observances within the cloister. He says it consists in "sharing whatever goods we have with our brothers, the poor, visiting the sick, offering consolation to the suffering and afflicted, and enjoying union, peace, and charity with all."[14] When Lodovico da Ferrara has Christ reproach men from the cross, he has the Savior insist that what he finds reprehensible in men is not their delivering him up to death, but their exercising no mercy or piety towards each other.[15]

These acts of ministering to one's fellow men very often received a specification congenial to the classical tradition. They were specified in terms of public service. Domenichi, in his oration on peace for Ascension Thursday, 1468, paraphrases Cicero's De officiis.[16] Domenichi's point is

---

priest's power to convert the elements, and similar questions. "Pro divinissima eucaristia oratio," BN Florence cod. Landau 152, fols. 56ʳ–59ᵛ.

12. Oratio in die cinerum [Rome: S. Plannck, 1496], Cop. #6198, fol. [6ᵛ].

13. Oratio in festo divi Thomae de Aquino [Rome: S. Plannck, 1496], Cop. #6199, fols. [5ᵛ–6ʳ].

14. Commentary on the "third Rule," in Vita praecellentissimi ecclesiae doctoris divi Aurelii Augustini. Commentarii super regula sancti Augustini (Rome: G. Herolt, 1481), Hain #*5683, fols. [37ᵛ–38ʳ].

15. "Sermo de suprema die," in Orationes quinque, fol. [12ᵛ].

16. I.7.22: " . . . ut praeclare scriptum est a Platone [Epist. IX. 358a], non nobis solum nati sumus ortusque nostri partem patria vindicat, partem amici." Aurelio

that, if praise is due to "private men" who minister to the wellbeing of others, it is all the more due to men whose lives are of public service: "Man is not born for himself alone"—"Quod homo non solum sibi natus sit."[17] Palmeri, in his funeral eulogy for Domenico Capranica, 1458, seems to be alluding to the same source: "Man is born to be of use and service to others."[18] The Franciscan, Ludovicus de Bagnariis, uses almost the same expression in his funeral eulogy in 1478 for Cardinal Pietro Ferrici.[19] Poggio Bracciolini had voiced the identical sentiment many decades earlier in his eulogy for Cardinal Zabarella at the Council of Constance, September 27, 1417.[20]

It is, as a matter of fact, in the funeral eulogies that the ideal of public service most frequently appears. The preachers were eulogizing bishops, cardinals, and popes, whose lives had been public; the classical oratorical models they imitated were meant for civic heroes. More important, the very precepts of rhetoric insisted that eulogies emphasize what the individual did for others rather than what benefited himself. Cicero in the *De oratore* (II.85.346) advises the speaker to concentrate on virtue which was "fructuosa aliis," and Quintilian in the *Institutio* (III.7.16) enjoins that he concentrate on those deeds which were done "aliena potius causa quam sua." No genius was needed to make a correlation between these precepts and the Christian ideals of loving one's neighbor as oneself and being willing to lay down one's life for one's friend.

Indeed, this correlation provides another emphatic demonstration of how classical rhetoric focused attention on certain aspects of the Christian tradition rather than on others. It provides another emphatic demonstra-

---

Brandolini paraphrases the expression in his prefatory letter to Francesco Piccolomini. *De ratione scribendi*, p. 5. On the relationship of rhetoric to "public happiness," see Nancy S. Struever, *The Language of History in the Renaissance: Rhetoric and Historical Consciousness in Florentine Humanism* (Princeton: Princeton University Press, 1970), pp. 101–14.

17. "Oratio pro pace Italiae," BAV cod. Ottob. lat. 1035, fol. 51^v: "Nam si privatis hominibus laudi et honori datur, quod proximorum saluti et utilitati inserviant, quod homo non solum sibi natus sit sed ortus sui causam partim patria partim amici vindicent, quanto magis hoc regibus et principibus decorum et gloriosum putamus . . . ."

18. "Oratio funebris cardinalis Firmani," BAV cod. Vat. lat. 5815, fol. 25^v: " . . . homo vero natus ad ceterorum mortalium utilitatem et commodum."

19. *In funere domini Petri Ferrici oratio* [Rome: n. publ., 1478?], Hain #9160, fol. [2^r]: "Noverat enim vir prudentissimus nullam esse in hominum genere meliorem naturam quam eorum qui se ad usum commodumve multorum natos arbitrarentur."

20. See *Opera omnia*, Monumenta Politica et Philosophica Rariora, ed. Luigi Firpo, Ser. 2, No. 6, 2 vols., (I=1538; rpt. Turin: Bottega d'Erasmo, 1964–66, ed. Riccardo Fubini), I, 253, 255, 259.

tion of how form influenced content. The preachers of the court defined Christian piety principally as good deeds done for others; the precepts of classical rhetoric helped them determine on that definition. These precepts helped fix an attitude that would be operative beyond the formal settings of oratory and that would emphasize charity and service to one's neighbors as central to true religion. Rhetoric added no new doctrines to Christianity, but it threw some doctrines into high relief and thus created from them patterns which were distinctive.

The ideal of public service as a pattern for Christian virtue had, certainly, no rival in the oratory of the court. Campano praised Pius II for it,[21] and Niccolò Capranica did the same for Bessarion.[22] In depicting the "ideal pope" whom the cardinals should elect as successor to Julius II, Pedro Flores insisted on the need for a man who would put the common good above all personal advantage.[23] When Inghirami delivered the funeral eulogy for the same pope just a few days earlier, he said he would bypass those virtues of Julius that are an ornament for the individual who possesses them but are of no service to others. The cynic might respond that in Julius's case this was perhaps a prudent ploy. Inghirami will, in any case, concentrate on those "great and exalted virtues" of Julius which were fruitful for others.[24]

One of Inghirami's most interesting uses of the ideal of public service occurs in his panegyric of Thomas Aquinas, though that saint's academic career would seem little susceptible of such an interpretation. Inghirami argues for the legitimacy and utility of those who engage in the practical "arts" and in public service. He concedes, however, that the pursuit of knowledge is a more blessed activity than the mere administration of temporal affairs. But the happiest condition of all is to combine study with action and public service.[25] This is precisely what Aquinas did, especially

21. "In exequiis divi Pii II oratio," in *Opera*, fol. [103ᵛ]: " . . . ut omnis eius oratio atque vita ad publicam utilitatem omnium et commodum singulorum . . . ."
22. See "Nicolai episcopi Firmani oratio in funere Bessarionis," in *Kardinal Bessarion als Theologe, Humanist und Staatsmann*, ed. Ludwig Mohler, III (Paderborn: F. Schöningh, 1967), 404–14.
23. *Oratio de summo pontifice eligendo* [Rome: n. publ., 1513], fol. [3ᵛ]. For similar expressions, see the oration erroneously attributed to Pietro del Monte on the death of Calixtus III, "Petri episcopi Brixiensis oratio in funere Calixti tertii," BAV cod. Vat. lat. 4872, fol. 47ᵛ. On these funeral orations, see John M. McManamon, "The Ideal Renaissance Pope: Funeral Oratory at the Papal Court," *Archivum Historiae Pontificiae*, 14 (1976), 9–70.
24. "Pro Iulio II funebris oratio," in *Thomae Phaedri Inghirami Volaterrani orationes duae*, ed. Pietro Luigi Galletti (Rome: G. Salomoni, 1777), pp. 81–82.
25. *Panegyricus in memoriam divi Thomae Aquinatis*, fols. [4ᵛ–5ʳ]: "Beati felicesque

by his preaching.[26] Domenichi, many years earlier, held up somewhat the same ideal for the cardinals. Like the Fathers in the golden age of the Church, they should be "ambidextrous," as it were. They should devote part of their time to the study of sacred letters and part to their official duties.[27]

The ideal of public service plays an important role in the writings of Aurelio Brandolini,[28] but we have more actual examples of it in the writings of his brother, Raphael, possibly for no other reason than that more of Raphael's funeral eulogies have survived. (Unfortunately, no copies of his sermons *coram* have been located.) In Raphael's consolatory letter to Cardinal Niccolò Fiesco upon the death of the cardinal's nephew, he twice paraphrases the line from Terence, ". . . humani nil a me alienum. . . ." (*Heaut.* 1.1.25), to describe the ideal of the cardinal's life.[29] In the second instance, he uses the phrase to introduce his commendation of the cardinal's virtues, which put the common and public good above personal and private advantage. This is the ideal for "a public man and a very religious cardinal"—"ut publicum hominem, ut religiosissimum cardinalem."

In his funeral eulogies, Raphael like other preachers praises the building and restoration of churches as acts of piety and public service.[30] On at least two occasions he moves beyond this traditional category to praise public building in general. The first occasion is in the treatise on music and poetry.[31] The second is more dramatic and occurs in his oration on

---

sunt igitur illi qui prudenter, iuste, fortiter, temperate administrant omnia. Beatiores felicioresque tamen illi qui in rerum naturalium indagatione caelestiumque contemplatione versantur. Illi vero beatissimi felicissimique et supra hominem appellandi qui utramque vitam sic tenuerint, in utraque sic se exercuerint, ut cui potissimum adhaeserint cognitu sit difficillimum."

26. *Ibid.*, fols. [11^v–12^r, 15^v].

27. "Tractatus seu quaestio an sit obediendum superiori praecipienti revelationem secreti," BAV cod. Barb. lat. 1201, fol. 73^v.

28. See, e.g., *De ratione scribendi*, pp. 58–59; *Paradoxa*, fol. [9^v].

29. "[Epistola] Raphael Brandolinus Iunior Lippus Nicolao Flisco," Bibl. Ang. cod. lat. 252, fols. 4^v–5^r, 16^r.

30. See, e.g., *Oratio de obitu Dominici Ruvere* [Rome: E. Silber, 1501], fol. [8^{r-v}], where he at the same time implicitly criticizes the cardinal for money spent on buildings which were "privata magis quam publica, sua potius quam aliena, luxuriosa verius quam fructuosa."

31. "De musica et poetica opusculum," Bibl. Casan. cod. 805, fols. 55^v–56^v: "Quare, si ab eis est poetica initiis profecta quibus mortale genus optime continetur, si non unam alteramve disciplinam sed universas expressit nedum praelibavit, si eius nomen praeclarum in terris est habitum, si poetae ipsi populis, regibus ac diis etiam immortalibus vivi mortuique acceptissimi fuere, dubitamus illam omnibus rebus, personis, locis, temporibus oportunam, fructuosam ac necessariam potius iudicare? Magno est enim usui ad assequendam earum quas memoravi doctrinarum cog-

reform intended for the Fifth Lateran Council. He has just urged Leo X to continue the construction of the new Saint Peter's, an act of piety that will redound to Leo's glory and immortal fame. He then calls for the repair of all churches and convents. Finally, he exhorts that "cities be renovated, and all towns be restored."[32]

Raphael's call for the restoration of cities and towns is not typical of the orations at the court, but neither is it inconsistent with them. Nor is it inconsistent with the emphasis on man as the builder of this world, *homo faber*, found in other humanist writings like Giannozzo Manetti's *De dignitate et excellentia hominis.*[33] We have no reason to suspect that the Fathers of the council for whom the call was intended would have found it inappropriate to the purposes for which they were assembled. The sermons *coram*, it is true, do not evidence concern with urban projects, and they do not tie man's dignity to his engagement in them. Nonetheless, they are concerned with the City of Man in terms of constructing a society in which harmony, mutual understanding, and a commitment to assisting one's fellow men in their needs prevail.

An impressive text of Giles of Viterbo captures many of the themes we

---

nitionem, atque imprimis formandae eloquentiae ac mortalium vitae bene beateque instituendae oportuna, quodque omnium videri potissimum debet servandae religioni, constituendis urbibus ac plurimis etiam artibus excolendis maxime necessaria. Quippe quae vel una fuit in causa ut deorum immortalium religio induceretur, coleretur, servaretur. Una inquam fuit in causa ut rudes ac efferati veterum animi, quippe qui in agris ferino victu sine iure, sine lege, sine iudicio agebant ad ius colendum, ad promulgandas leges, ad constituendos magistratus partim poena partimque praemio perquam facile flecterentur, ut moenia sibi constituerent, ut ea et privatis et publicis aedificiis munirent ac exornarent, moribus, institutis, exemplis non solum firmarent, sed longe lateque dilatarent, ut difficillima quaeque moliri facinora non dubitarent."

32. "Oratio ad Lateranense concilium," BAV cod. Ottob. lat. 813, fols. 55ᵛ–56ᵛ: "Fecerunt hoc maiores tui, pientissime pontifex. Observavit magnus ille Cosimus proavus. Non contempsit Petrus avus. Neutri concessit Laurentius pater. Quippe qui non Florentiae modo, sed in plerisque Italiae civitatibus nobilissima templa excultissimaque monasteria partim de integro condidere, partim ab aliis condita refecere. . . . Tuum est hoc opus [St. Peter's], beatissime pater. A te uno deiecta illius sacratissimi templi sacella, nudatae arae, squallentes apostolorum et martyrum effigies, prostrati sanctissimorum pontificum tumuli, exturbati magna ex parte parietes opem auxiliumque deposcunt. . . . Hanc tu, ut potes et debes, totis viribus amplexare, ut tuo stimulo, tuo exemplo, tuo inquam beneficio sacrorum aedificiorum contemptus, squallor ac situs tollatur, ut locorum omnium restitutio et reformatio consequatur. Reformentur singula cunctis in civitatibus fana et cenobia. Constituantur civitates ipsae. Oppida renoventur. Arces ad fidei propugnaculum munitissime aedificentur. Navalia ad aedificandas ornandasque classes erigantur. Ad eas autem tuendas ac recreandas effodiantur portus."

33. See Charles Trinkaus, *In Our Image and Likeness: Humanity and Divinity in Italian Humanist Thought,* 2 vols. (Chicago: University of Chicago Press, 1970), I, 230–58.

have been discussing.[34] This text is in the form of a letter addressed to Giles's friend, Antonio Zoccoli, and to "the Romans." In actual fact, this "letter" much more closely resembles a formal discourse or a sermon, and it surely was intended for the eyes of Julius II. It probably incorporates ideas found in the sermons Giles preached *coram papa inter missarum solemnia*, all of which are lost.

This text deals with man's dignity. It is different from Giles's discussion of that same subject in his commentary on Lombard's *Sentences* in that it does not base man's dignity on his being created in the image and likeness of God. The verse from Genesis dominates Giles's discussion in the commentary, where it probably was suggested to him in Augustinian terms by Lombard himself. In the letter to Zoccoli and the Romans, Giles bases his case not on the dignity with which God endowed man in Creation, but on the outpouring of love which the Incarnation effected and symbolized. Through this love man is transformed into "God" and rendered immortal. The Incarnation, as a work of love, evokes from man a response in love. Thus charity is seen as the principal duty of the Christian life.

As the recipient of God's transforming love, man has a mission to help transform others by means of it. This mission is especially incumbent upon the Romans because of the exalted destiny of their city. In the commentary on Lombard, which was being written at about the same time as the letter, Giles attempted to locate man in the universe by discussing his dignity in relationship to the dignity of the angels, a problem inherited from scholastic commentaries on the *Sententiarum libri*. In the present text such metaphysical comparisons are absent. Man's dignity or, in this instance, man's transformation is not viewed as assigning him a niche in a hierarchy of honors but as imposing upon him a mission. It also imbues him with a holy dynamism that enables him to fulfill his mission. That dynamism derives from the love of God poured into men's hearts.

In Giles's discourse, therefore, we once again see vindicated for religious literature the emphasis on action that Burckhardt discovered in Renaissance secular literature and that Trinkaus sees as generally characteristic of humanist thought on man's dignity. Giles's emphasis was not peculiar to himself. The sermons *coram* of other preachers emphasized man's true causality, as we have noted, and they thereby suggest an activism that would be in accord with the promotion of learning, the restoration

34. The text is contained in my "Man's Dignity, God's Love, and the Destiny of Rome: A Text of Giles of Viterbo," *Viator*, 3 (1972), 389–416.

of churches, and the general adornment of the city, all commended in the other forms of oratory practiced in Renaissance Rome.

Underneath the commendation of public service in this oratory lay the conviction that private wealth should be of benefit to others. Thus Schomberg, in his first sermon *coram* for Julius II, speaks about the obligations of kings and prelates. The use of wealth for the poor, for art and scholarship, and for the building of churches is one of their weapons against the vice of avarice.[35] Moreover, it was one of the ways in which men could imitate the liberality and munificence of their generous God. The God of the preachers was not thrifty. Magnanimity, liberality, and generosity were the hallmarks of God the Creator and Redeemer, who did his utmost to share with his creatures what he had and was.

These same open-handed qualities were also the hallmarks of the great heroes from classical antiquity. Domenichi invokes Jerome's authority when he urges the cardinals about to elect a successor to Calixtus III to put the example of self-sacrifice and public service of ancient Romans like Cato, the Scipios, and the Decii before their eyes.[36] The virtues which Aristotle's *Rhetoric* (I.9) assigns as fit objects for epideictic oratory's praise are the ones esteemed by the preachers at the court—justice, fortitude, temperance, magnificence, magnanimity, liberality, gentleness, prudence, and wisdom. In brief, Christian doctrine, classical *exempla*, and classical theory of rhetoric were interpreted by the orators to make them converge in the construction of an ideal of the virtuous life.

The four cardinal virtues of temperance, justice, fortitude, and prudence, especially, undergirded that ideal. These virtues had been incorporated into the great scholastic syntheses of the Middle Ages, but with the revival of classical rhetoric in the Renaissance the cardinal virtues received a new emphasis. Aurelio Brandolini's treatise on letter writing and Traversagni's on rhetoric show the intimate connection between them

35. "Prima oratio. Ductus est Iesus in desertum," in *Orationes vel potius divinorum eloquiorum enodationes* (Leipzig: W. Stöckel, 1512), fol. [4ᵛ]. See also Hieronymus Scoptius, *Oratio in die festo omnium sanctorum* [Rome: E. Silber or S. Plannck, after Nov. 1, 1489], Hain-Cop. #14541, fols, [1ᵛ–2ʳ]; Tommaso Radini Tedeschini, "In die sanctorum omnium oratio," Bibl. Ricc. cod. 904, fol. 90ʳ.

36. "Oratio die qua intrarunt ad electionem," BAV cod. Ottob. lat. 1035, fol. 7ʳ. For a study related to the matter under discussion here, see Hans Baron, "Cicero and the Roman Civic Spirit in the Middle Ages and the Early Renaissance," in *Lordship and Community in Medieval Europe*, ed. Fredric Cheyette (New York: Holt, Rinehart, and Winston, 1968), pp. 291–314.

and good oratory.[37] Some years earlier Massari related them directly to the exercise of ecclesiastical government, and he describes them as constitutive of "public and civic virtue."[38] Filippi implicitly makes the same correlation.[39]

All virtues, however, were meant to function in the service of charity. In traditionally scholastic terms Marsi reminded his listeners that charity was "the form of all the virtues."[40] When the preachers looked at God's great deeds, they saw them under the formality of his love. When they looked at the life of Christ, they saw it under the same formality.

Aurelio Brandolini's oration in Florence on Holy Thursday, 1491, is here a safe guide for what the preachers meant by the imitation of Christ.[41] Brandolini invites his audience to contemplate the supper which Jesus shared with his disciples in terms of the three actions he performed during it. First, he washed the disciples' feet, a work of love that teaches humility. Then he taught that his precept was the precept of love. Finally, he instituted the Eucharist, which symbolizes both humility and love. The Eucharist—one bread out of many grains of wheat—signifies as well the communion and unity that will reign in Christ's Church. Other preachers from the court urge Christians to admire and emulate those same virtues.[42]

The preachers' emphasis on inner affections and attitudes, as well as the effort to relate these affections and attitudes to Christian mysteries, saves their insistence on works of mercy and charity from unqualified identification with a moral code. The "good works" of the Christian were to be animated by an interiorized religious sentiment.[43] This sentiment

37. See De ratione scribendi, pp. 88–94. See also Traversagni, "In novam rhetoricam," BAV cod. Vat. lat. 11441, fol. 56[r].

38. "De animae dignitatibus," Bibl. Ang. cod. lat. 835, III, fols. 5[r] and 10[v]–11[r]: " . . . quicumque popularem ac civilem virtutem, quam temperantiam ac iustitiam, fortitudinem ac prudentiam vocant exercere . . . ."

39. See Oratio die epiphaniae MDXX [Rome: S. Guileretus, 1520], esp. fol. [4[r-v]]. On the saints' practice of these virtues, see Inghirami, "In laudem omnium sanctorum oratio," Bibl. Guarn. cod. LIII.4.8, fols. 45[v]–46[r].

40. Panegyricus in memoriam sancti Ioannis evangelistae [Rome: S. Plannck, after Dec. 27, 1485?], Hain #*10789, fol. [4[r]].

41. "Oratio in cena Domini," Bibl. Com., Siena, cod. H.VI.30, fols. 120[r]–124[v].

42. See, e.g., del Monte's "Oratio in die sancto parasceves," BAV cod. Vat. lat. 4872, fol. 23[r], and esp. de Viana's description of how Christian piety is superior to that of Plato and Cicero, Oratio in festo divi Thomae de Aquino, fol. [2[r]].

43. See, e.g., esp. de Viana, ibid.; de Totis, Sermo qualiter possimus Iesum Christum induere [Rome: E. Silber, 1496], Cop. #5843, fols. [9[r]–11[v]]; Filippi, "Oratio in dominica de passione," in Orationes novem coram Iulio II et Leone X, fol. [19[v]]; de Canali, Oratio cinerum [Rome: J. Besicken, 1503/4], fol. [2[v]].

related directly to the oratorical form that evoked it. Admiration and gratitude characterize the response to what is in itself beautiful and loving.
From these two sentiments emerges the desire to praise. We have already
called attention to Domenichi's articulation of a sentiment particularly
proper to the Christian: "I will bless the Lord at all times. His praise will
ever be on my lips" (Ps. 33:2[34:1]).[44] A religion in which the praise
of God resounded in the hearts of believers was what the preachers desired to accomplish by their words.

Massari returns to the idea several times that the truly happy man is
the man grateful for God's benefits and the man who sings his praises.[45]
When Filippi describes man as created "for action," what he is referring
to in particular is not the building of the earthly city but the action of
praising God.[46] The panegyrics of the saints were interpreted as acts of
praise of God, and the scriptural text used to justify them was again from
the psalms: "Mirabilis Deus in sanctis suis" (Ps. 67[68]:36).[47]

If we ask by what process one is to bring one's affections into conformity with this ideal, we consistently hear the same response. It is by
"looking," by "contemplating," by holding up the reality to our gaze.
The supposition seems to be that the beauty and attractiveness of the
object will in itself evoke and sustain the inner affections appropriate for
the constant exercise of the art of holy living.

The contemplation which the preachers urged is closely related to another practice they propose, the reading of Scripture and the Fathers of
the Church. They encourage the practice directly by indicating its transforming effects and indirectly by praising it in those they eulogize. Palmeri, Massari, Lodovico da Ferrara, and the Brandolinis are among those

44. "Oratio ad clerum et populum Brixiensem," BAV cod. Ottob. lat. 1035, fol.
42^{r-v}.
45. "De sapientia Christi [oratio]," Bibl. Estense cod. Alpha Q.6.13, fol. 46^r, and
the commentary on the "third Rule," in *Vita Augustini*, fol. [203^r]. See also Ioannes
Sambocius, *Oratio in festo solemni divinae Trinitatis* [Rome: S. Guileretus and E.
Nani, 1514], fol. [3^r]: "Sicut enim nullum est momentum quo non utamur vel fruamur
Dei bonitate ac misericordia, ita nullus dies absque laudibus eius preterire debet,
quo non confiteamur beneficentiam eius in nobis et similitudinem imaginis eius
revereamur nobilitate morum, exercitio virtutum, dignitate meritorum."
46. "Oratio de sacramentis," in *Orationes novem coram Iulio II et Leone X*, fol.
[7^r].
47. See, e.g., Domenichi, "Oratio in laudem beatissimae Catherinae de Senis,"
BAV cod. Ottob. lat. 1035, fol. 19^r; Thegliatius, *Oratio in die omnium sanctorum*
[Rome: S. Plannck, 1496], Hain-Cop. #15459, fol. [1^r]; Massari, *Vita Augustini*, fol.
[2^v].

for whom this practice seems especially important.[48] When Agostino Filippi states that there lies hidden in sacred letters a living and efficacious power to transform the soul into divine love, his ideas resemble ideas found in Erasmus's "Paraclesis," written at about the same time.[49]

In Brenta's formulation of the ideal of Christian piety, he specified not only "speaking helpful words and doing good deeds." He specified as well "thinking honest thoughts"—"honesta cogitando." For Filippi, Inghirami, and Vázquez, thoughts directed to God and heavenly things were one of the sources of man's true, inner dignity.[50] The preachers often insisted that teachers of Scripture and theology conform their lives and their inner aspirations to what they taught.[51] A union of piety and learning was the ideal for which to strive. The "docta pietas" that Filippi enjoins is a correlate for the "docta ignorantia" he also professes.[52] The ideal of "docta pietas" was achieved in the only saints the city of Rome annually

48. See e.g., Palmeri, "Oratio funebris cardinalis Firmani [Domenico Capranica]," BAV cod. Vat. lat. 5815, fols. 16ᵛ, 28ʳ; Massari, commentary on the "third Rule" in Vita Augustini, fols. [146ᵛ–148ʳ]; Lodovico da Ferrara, "Sermo de pugna Christi cum daemone," in Orationes quinque, fols. [8ᵛ–9ʳ]; R. Brandolini, Oratio de obitu G. Perrerii [n.p.: n. publ., 1500?], fol. [9ᵛ]; A. Brandolini, "Epitoma in sacram Iudaeorum historiam," BAV cod. Ottob. lat. 438, fol. 2ʳ⁻ᵛ. See also Casali, "In die ascensionis," Bibl. Ambr. cod. G.33 inf., II, fol. 20ʳ.

49. "Oratio de veritate," in Orationes novem coram Iulio II et Leone X, fols. [9ᵛ–10ʳ]: "Ad illum [Deum] igitur, quoniam dum sumus in corpore plus amare quam cognoscere possumus, ardentissimi amoris pennis advolemus, ut voluntatis in Deum ferventissimus ardor clarissimam eiusdem saltem in caelestibus mentibus nostris intelligentiam sumministret. Idipsum autem facillime consequimur si non cessabimus litteras sacras nocturna versare manu, versare diurna [cf. Hor. A.P. 268]. Latet enim in illis caelestis vis quaedam viva et efficax, quae legentis animum (si modo illas pure humiliterque tractaverit) in amorem divinum mirabili quodam potestate transformat. Id vero longe locupletius assequimur, si post lectionem sacram veterum patrum at praecipue Christi vitam moresque pro virili proposuerimus nobis imitandos. Accommodatior namque ad virtutem via imitatio est quam simplex lectio." Cf. the "Paraclesis," LB, V, 142–44. On the transformational effects of divine action on the soul, see also, e.g., Nicoletto Dati, Oratio die Trinitatis habita [Rome: J. Besicken and S. Mayr, after June 11, 1503], fol. [2ᵛ].

50. See, e.g., Filippi, Oratio die epiphaniae MDXX, fol. [3ᵛ]; Inghirami, Panegyricus in memoriam divi Thomae Aquinatis, fol. [4ʳ⁻ᵛ]; Vázquez, Oratio in die cinerum (Rome: J. Mazochius, 1513), fol. [8ʳ]. Somewhat similar ideas occur in Cusa's sermons, e.g., "De sacramento," BAV cod. Vat. lat. 1244, fol. 114ʳ, and "Domine adiuva me," BAV cod. Vat. lat. 1245, fols. 229ᵛ–230ʳ.

51. See, e.g., R. Brandolini, "Oratio ad Lateranense concilium," BAV cod. Ottob. lat. 813, fol. 53ᵛ; de Viana, Oratio in festo divi Thomae de Aquino, fol. [5ʳ⁻ᵛ], and esp. fol. [4ʳ]: "Sapientia enim nisi in aliquo actu fuerit, quo vim suam exerceat, inanis et frustra videtur."

52. See "Oratio in die epiphaniae," in Orationes novem coram Iulio II et Leone X, fol. [14ʳ].

celebrated with solemn panegyrics outside the *cappelle*—Saint Augustine and Saint Thomas Aquinas.

Two general qualities were expected to pervade the religious sentiments and practices proposed by the preachers. The first was a sense of joy, to which we have already several times alluded. Aurelio Brandolini links joy inseparably with the intent of the *genus demonstrativum* to extend sincere congratulation and praise.[53] The good man takes joy in the achievement of others, and his congratulation is an expression of the joy he shares with them.

The other quality is a sense of moderation, which can be attributed at least in certain instances to the preachers' appreciation for harmony and proportion as constitutive of the order of the universe, as Raphael Brandolini suggests in his treatise "On Music and Poetry."[54] Put into other words: at least regarding the ideal of personal piety, the "violent extremes" which Huizinga found characteristic of late-medieval life and religion in France and Burgundy are lacking.[55]

Massari, for instance, enumerates five reasons for the special excellence of Augustine's "Rule." The first three are the excellence of its author, the excellence of those it proposes for imitation, viz., the apostles, and its antiquity. The fourth reason is the Rule's "argumentum." Whereas other rules for religious orders give detailed attention to fasts, disciplines, and other "corporal observances," Augustine's Rule deals with spiritual values, i.e., love of God and neighbor, union of hearts and minds, and the concord of holy morals. This fourth reason introduces the fifth, which is the "moderation" of the Rule's precepts. What it imposes is neither too light nor too heavy. The Rule of Augustine employs "the mean," and its precepts do not fall into either vicious extreme of exaggerated austerity or laxity. Its precepts, for a fact, can be recognized by their standing "in the middle," where true virtue stands.[56]

Massari's long Commentary on this "third Rule" of Augustine is really a protracted treatise on the Christian life. It is altogether traditional in its doctrine, but it is also marked by notable moderation and balance. The section on the vow of obedience, for example, gives as much attention to

53. *De ratione scribendi*, p. 124.
54. "De musica et poetica opusculum," Bibl. Casan. cod. 805, fols. 32ʳ–33ᵛ.
55. *The Waning of the Middle Ages* (Garden City, N.Y.: Doubleday Anchor, 1954), esp. pp. 9–31.
56. ["Commendatio regulae"], in *Vita Augustini*, fols. [14ᵛ–15ᵛ].

the duties of justice and good example on the part of the superior as it does to the obligations of the subject. The important quality of human compassion, "misericordia," is frequently recommended to all alike throughout the Commentary.[57]

Massari treats the question of fasting at some length in the Commentary.[58] His treatment is a reminder that the failure of the preachers to speak of certain traditional practices in their sermons is not automatically a sign they ignored or contemned them. Though Massari implicitly criticizes other rules for focusing too exclusively on corporal observances, he did not thereby mean to exclude such observances from the life of the Augustinian friars. Indeed, he commends them.

He commends them, however, insofar as they are used with moderation and seen in a larger context. Fasting can be a help in rising to higher values. But it is only a help, not an end in itself. Massari's observations on eating and abstaining from eating thus confirm the balance and sense of proportion evident in the rest of the Commentary.

How the Christian conducted himself at table was, in fact, a matter of some concern to the preachers, especially when they constructed their ideal of the "good cardinal." The life-style of the cardinals elicited considerable criticism in the Quattrocento and early Cinquecento, but it had elicited criticism much earlier, along with attempts to regulate it. At Avignon Popes John XXII and Clement VI tried to impose limits on the cardinals' households and particularly on their tables.[59] John XXII's "Dat normam vivendi" is a good example of such attempts, and it characteristically descends to great detail in describing the number of courses and the kinds of food that were proper for the cardinals' meals. Gluttony was a vice that attracted much attention in the Middle Ages, and it was a vice in which, presumably, the wealthy indulged. This vice continued to attract notice during the Renaissance.

Arévalo, in his long discussion in the *Speculum vitae humanae* about why the popes have such short lives, assigns as the first cause their overindulgence in good food, a vice characteristic of all princes.[60] Massari's Commentary on the "third Rule" leaves one with the impression that

57. *Ibid.*, fols. [15ᵛ–210ᵛ]; on obedience, fol. [161ʳ⁻ᵛ].
58. *Ibid.*, fols. [48ᵛ–52ᵛ].
59. See Norman P. Zacour, "Papal Regulation of Cardinals' Households in the Fourteenth Century," *Speculum*, 50 (1975), 434–55.
60. Paris: M. Soly, 1656, pp. 291–93.

gluttony was one of the most prevalent vices of his day, and his criticisms seem to be directed specifically to prelates.[61] Cusa's reform proposal for Pius II touches on the question,[62] and Domenichi's proposal for the same pope reproaches the cardinals for their luxurious feasting.[63] The reform bull prepared for Sixtus IV imposes certain limitations on the cardinals' tables, without being as detailed as "Dat normam vivendi."[64] Like Domenichi's proposal, the bull briefly indicates the religious spirit that should prevail at the cardinals' meals. In that regard it differs from the document of John XXII, which is simply sumptuary regulation.

The religious spirit appropriate to those meals is described in greater detail by some of the preachers. Their descriptions are of interest not only because of the religious ideal implicit in them but because they also anticipate Erasmus's *Convivium religiosum*. Though much less detailed than Erasmus's famous colloquy, the "godly feasts" depicted by the preachers contain all the essential elements Erasmus later developed so effectively. We find these feasts described in Niccolò Capranica's funeral eulogy for Bessarion and in similar eulogies by Palmeri, Campano, and Raphael Brandolini, as well as in Domenichi's reform proposal.[65] They are found as well in other documents from the period.[66]

The godly feast is typified by a table that is modest and perhaps frugal. The food is attractively served, even on silver plate, but without ostentation or display. Wine is used with moderation. Instead of being entertained with secular music or by actors, the guests listen to reading from Scripture or to lives of the Fathers as the meal begins. Then, either during

61. In his *Vita Augustini*, fols. [53ʳ–61ᵛ].
62. See Stephan Ehses, "Der Reformentwurf des Kardinals Nikolaus Cusanus," *Historisches Jahrbuch*, 32 (1911), 294.
63. *Tractatus de reformationibus Romanae curiae* (Brescia: Baptista Farfengus, 1495), GKW #8638, fols. [11ʳ–12ʳ].
64. "Quoniam regnantium cura non minor," BAV cod. Vat. lat. 3884, fol. 123ʳ.
65. Capranica, "Oratio in funere Bessarionis," in *Bessarion*, III, 411–12; Palmeri, "Oratio funebris cardinalis Firmani [Domenico Capranica]," BAV cod. Vat. lat. 5815, fols. 24ʳ–25ʳ, and ["Oratio in funere cardinalis Prosperi Columnensis"], *ibid.*, fols. 121ʳ⁻ᵛ; Campano, "In funere cardinalis sanctae Susannae Saxoferratensis [Alessandro Oliva da Sassoferrato, O.E.S.A., d.1463] oratio," in *Opera*, fol. [118ʳ]; R. Brandolini, *Oratio de obitu Dominici Ruvere*, fol. [9ʳ]. On the deeper significance of Erasmus's dialogue, see Myron P. Gilmore, "Erasmus' Godly Feast," in *Pursuit of Holiness*, pp. 505–9, and Marjorie O'Rourke Boyle, *Erasmus on Language and Method in Theology* (Toronto: University of Toronto Press, 1977), pp. 129–41. See also Lawrence V. Ryan, "Art and Artifice in Erasmus' *Convivium Profanum*," *Renaissance Quarterly*, 31 (1978), 1–16.
66. See, e.g., the prefatory letter by Iulius Simon Siculus for his *Oratio de poeticae et musarum triumpho ad religiosissimos Romanarum litterarum censores* (Rome: J. Mazochius, 1518), fol. [2ᵛ].

the meal or afterwards, the host and his guests discuss the reading or some other edifying topic. In their discussions they sedulously avoid speaking ill of others—"that vice so natural to the Roman Curia."[67] We are born, after all, to speak blessings and to praise others, not to speak ill of them. Our Savior admonished us to have compassion on our fellow men, not to judge them.

At the end of the meal the host and his guests make certain to give thanks to God and to praise him, through the recitation of psalms or some other prayers. The host then accompanies his guests to the door. The serenity of his countenance reflects the serenity of the meal. He says goodbye to guests who are joyful and satisfied, and he returns to his quarters to spend some time in study.

As the godly feast well illustrates, the ideal of the Christian life which the preachers designed was meant to be as harmonious and humanly attractive as was their depiction of the deeds of God. Religion in its doctrine and in its practice should, if properly presented, entice men to embrace it. If men did so, the world would fully achieve the harmony which Christ had already inchoately restored.

At this point we might, in fact, generalize that the spirituality which the preachers propounded substantially corresponds with the concerns and values inherent in their interpretation of doctrine. Balance and harmony are obvious correlates. The joy that was to sing in the heart of the Christian is another and is what would be expected of a piety exercised in the context of a rhetoric and a religion of praise. If the preachers' theology extolled God's deeds, we should not wonder that their piety extolled man's deeds. We should not wonder that such a piety would make an effort to reconcile itself with man's life as spent amidst other men. The Incarnation rendered holy all that was human. We should, then, anticipate that a piety based on that mystery would demonstrate special appreciation for the humane virtues of generosity, compassion, and service to one's fellows.

Furthermore, the preachers' recourse to antiquity for their theological authorities is consistent with their recourse to the Bible and the Fathers for their examples of piety. Still, the failure to mention medieval saints and to give any real attention to practices we associate with medieval

---

67. Palmeri, ["Oratio in funere cardinalis Prosperi Columnensis"], BAV cod. Vat. lat. 5815, fol. 121ᵛ: " . . . heu, pro dolor, hic morbus communis est et fere naturale vitium Romanae curiae—. . . ."

devotion comes as a surprise, especially when we recall that many of the preachers were mendicant friars. This phenomenon can perhaps be partially explained by invoking the fundamental rhetorical principle of adapting one's discourse to the needs and expectations of the audience. The men of the papal court were not interested in the virtues of the cloister. They were men of the city and the world, and they to a great extent perceived themselves as direct heirs to the great traditions of antiquity—classical, apostolic, and patristic. Their heroes, then, were the Ciceros, the Peters and Pauls, the Augustines and Jeromes—all men of action who dedicated their lives to the service of the public good.

The spirituality which the preachers proposed emerges, therefore, with characteristics distinguishing it from other spiritualities with which it was contemporary or almost contemporary. It stands at the opposite pole from the spirituality of eremitical withdrawal, though we know from figures like Pietro Quirini and Paolo Giustiniani that that ideal was not altogether unfamiliar to the court. It contrasts with the crude devotional and juridical piety that Erasmus decried in such scathing terms. It bears little resemblance to the piety of the Rhineland mystics and the Devotio Moderna. By its relative inattention to the problem of grace and by a similar inattention to the Virgin, Original Sin, and the Real Presence in the Eucharist, it distinguishes itself from the pieties of the Reformation and Counter Reformation that would follow upon it.

There is not much evidence to indicate that the preachers self-consciously proposed their pattern of piety as something new and distinctive. There is, however, considerable evidence to indicate they thought it was authentically Christian and the ideal which Christians should embrace if they wished their lives to conform to their profession. But, as the preachers cast their eyes about them, they saw that this was far from being the case. Whereas on the one hand through the great deeds of God they lived in the happiest of times, on the other hand their times were the worst and the most calamitous of all. Religion had collapsed. Ambition, sensuality, and avarice abounded, and the preachers could not in conscience tolerate such a situation. They had to censure it. We thus enter into the other side of the preacher's art, that is, the art of blame and the rhetoric of reproach.

The preachers spared no portion of the long epoch that we have been examining. Sánchez de Arévalo, preaching in honor of Aquinas during the pontificate of Nicholas V, deplored the lax condition of the religious orders of his day.[68] In 1462 Domenichi wrote to Ermolao Barbaro that their age was a tempest, the worst of times.[69] When he exhorted the cardinals to elect a good successor to Pius II, he lamented that iniquity abounded and that charity had grown cold (Matt. 24:12).[70] Some years later Aurelio Brandolini in the peroration of his panegyric on Aquinas deplored the bad lives of the Christians of his day and the catastrophic condition of "the bark of Peter."[71] Bernardino Carvajal used the word "ruins" to describe to the cardinals the times which the successor of Innocent VIII would have to face.[72] Antonius Manilius told that successor, Alexander VI, that his times were stormy and calamitous, filled to the brim with avarice, luxury, and every species of iniquity, and that all life was tainted and adulterated with vice.[73] Cajetan coolly reminded Alexander that the kingdom of God had collapsed and was rushing into ruin.[74] In a kind of parenthesis, Schomberg mentions in his fifth sermon for Julius II that he is living "in a corrupt age."[75] In the oration given in his name opening the Lateran Council, Julius II informed the Fathers gathered there that ecclesiastical discipline had crumbled and that the morals of men in every station of life had suffered a great shipwreck.[76] Raphael Brandolini is no more encouraging in his oration for the same council.[77] Finally the funeral eulogy for Leo X in 1521 recognized the failing condition of "the Christian Republic."[78]

This depressing litany could be considerably amplified, but even as

---

68. "Sermo in die beati Thomae de Aquino," BAV cod. Vat. lat. 4881, fol. 236ᵛ.

69. "Epistola ad Hermolaum Barbarum," BAV cod. Ottob. lat. 1035, fol. 39ᵛ.

70. "Oratio pro electione summi pontificis," *ibid.*, fol. 14ʳ⁻ᵛ.

71. *Oratio pro sancto Thoma Aquinate* [Rome: E. Silber, 1485/90], GKW #5016, fols. [11ʳ–12ᵛ].

72. *Oratio de eligendo summo pontifice* [Rome: E. Silber, c.1493], GKW #6152, fol. [5ᵛ].

73. *Oratio pro Britonoriensibus ad Alexandrum VI* [Rome: E. Silber, c.1493], Hain #*10701, fols. [2ᵛ–3ʳ].

74. "Oratio de vi cultus divini et orationis efficacia," in *Opuscula*, p. 183.

75. "Quinta oratio. Ductus est Iesus in desertum," in *Orationes vel potius divinorum eloquiorum enodationes*, fol. [17ʳ].

76. For the text, see Nelson H. Minnich, "Concepts of Reform Proposed at the Fifth Lateran Council," *Archivum Historiae Pontificiae*, 7 (1969), 237–38.

77. "Oratio ad Lateranense concilium," BAV cod. Ottob. lat. 813, fols. 3ᵛ, 28ʳ, 50ʳ.

78. "Pro electione summi pontificis," Bibl. del Conte Alessandro Marcello del Majno, Venice, cod. Serie A.I., Busta 5, Fasc. b., fols. [1ᵛ–2ʳ]. This oration is attributed by a late hand to Cristoforo Marcello; see Kristeller, *Iter*, II, 578. McManamon, however, judges it better attributed to Julius Pimpinella, "Ideal Renaissance Pope," p. 18, n. 48.

it stands it shows that the words "ruin," "collapse," and their equivalents sprang easily to the lips of the preachers. There does seem to be a crescendo in the last years of the Quattrocento and early years of the Cinquecento, but this crescendo is due in part to more ample documentation. What the preachers decried remained the same throughout the period—the bad morals of the laity and especially of the higher clergy and Roman Curia; the general collapse of respect for law and discipline and for ecclesiastical authority or "liberty"; the wars among Christian princes; and, finally, the advances of the Turks.

It is important to realize, however, that even while the preachers deplored their age they also perceived enough promise in it to speak of it at times as "golden." By that expression they were not necessarily referring simply to the fact that they lived in the Christian era. They were often referring to something much more specifically contemporary, such as the rebirth of eloquence, the voyages of discovery, and various efforts at reform. These and other factors could elicit from them an enthusiastic response.[79]

Certainly one of the most curious applications of the term golden age comes from Cajetan. In his treatise *De indulgentiis*, dated December 8, 1517, and therefore written without any knowledge of Luther's Ninety-Five Theses of the previous week, Cajetan defends the antiquity and utility of indulgences. If the Church employs them correctly, it will witness the return of the "golden age of the penitent Fathers."[80]

Cajetan's golden age enjoys a privileged historical irony, but otherwise it is typical of the term's easy application in Renaissance Rome. In many of the preachers, a curiously comfortable coexistence of both pessimistic and optimistic assessments of their age is also typical. By now, certainly, some suspicion should be aroused about those assessments and about the logic that underlay them. How did the preachers arrive at their judgments? How much credence can be given them?

The investigation will be simpler if it is limited to the preachers' nega-

79. I have several times attempted to illustrate and document this phenomenon: "Fulfillment of the Christian Golden Age under Pope Julius II: Text of a Discourse of Giles of Viterbo, 1507," *Traditio*, 25 (1969), 265–338; "The Discovery of America and Reform Thought at the Papal Court in the Early Cinquecento," in *First Images of America: The Impact of the New World on the Old*, ed. Fredi Chiappelli et al., 2 vols. (Berkeley: University of California Press, 1976), I, 185–200; *Giles of Viterbo on Church and Reform: A Study in Renaissance Thought*, Studies in Medieval and Reformation Thought, No. 5 (Leiden: Brill, 1968), esp. pp. 100–38.

80. Found in *Opuscula omnia* (Lyons: J. Junta, 1562), pp. 90–97, esp. 97: "Redirent siquidem hoc pacto aurea poenitentium patrum saecula."

tive assessments. As we begin to examine them, we might notice how frequently they are supported by an appropriate authority or historical precedent. Sánchez de Arévalo's immensely popular *Speculum vitae humanae* utilizes this device so regularly and in such exaggerated fashion that it is a good case to study. What is writ so large by Arévalo may be writ less obviously by others.

As Arévalo reviews various occupations and states of life, he discloses the abuses and vices endemic to each. Notaries, for instance, are supposed to be "servants of justice." After that concise definition, Arévalo launches into a diatribe against the deceits, deceptions, and crimes against justice the notaries commit. The long indictment closes weakly with a quotation from Isidore to support it.[81] When he takes the linen weavers to task, his method of argumentation is even more obvious. They weave bad cloth, and they defraud by mixing good thread with bad. It was their crimes that Isaiah castigated (30:1; 59:5).[82] Regarding shepherds, no one will be able to escape their deceitful actions. The prophet Jeremiah says rightly of them: "The shepherds have prevaricated" (2:8).[83]

Arévalo obviously assumes these vices are prevalent, for they are "characteristic" of each of the categories he describes. The witnesses who testify to the existence of the vices allow themselves to be transported across the centuries with facile compliance. When Arévalo turns to various ecclesiastical offices, the same method prevails and the same kind of conclusion emerges, as we have already suggested by the correlation between the popes' short lives and the characteristic gluttony of princes.[84]

The same style of argumentation appears in a more sophisticated contemporary of Arévalo, Domenico de' Domenichi, in his treatise for Pius II on the reform of the Church. Time and again he adduces some authority from the past in order to make his point about a present abuse. He shows a special preference for Saint Bernard and particularly for the *De consideratione*. That long admonition of Bernard to Pope Eugene III was very popular at the court. When Luther reminded Leo X of it in 1520, he was certainly not the first to call it to the attention of Renaissance Rome.[85]

---

81. *Speculum*, pp. 116–18.
82. *Ibid.*, pp. 145–46.
83. *Ibid.*, p. 158.
84. *Ibid.*, pp. 291–93.
85. "Epistola Lutheriana ad Leonem Decimum summum pontificem," prefatory letter to the "Tractatus de libertate christiana" of 1520, in *D. Martin Luthers Werke, Kritische Gesamtausgabe*, VII (Weimar: H. Böhlaus, 1897), 45, 48. See note 85 of Chapter II.

Nicholas V, as a matter of fact, had had it copied for his own use and that of others,[86] and it is frequently cited by the preachers when they address the problem of reform.[87]

Often enough, when Domenichi describes the abuses in the Church of his own day, he does so in Bernard's words. For example, when he speaks about the wealth, extravagances, and splendid tables of the prelates of the mid-Quattrocento, he without historical scruple lifts his words from a sermon of Bernard composed three centuries earlier.[88] In discussing a related question, he uses Henry of Ghent (d. 1293) the same way.[89]

The abuses that Sánchez de Arévalo and Domenichi castigated may very well have been raging when they wrote. By phrasing their criticisms in the words of some venerable authority, they gave them more weight, and they adopted a style of argumentation their age knew and respected. On the other hand, the question inevitably arises: how much was their very perception of abuses conditioned by the authoritative texts they had at hand? If there were classic truths, classic heresies, and classic refutations of heresies, were there not also classic sins and classic abuses? Were not these sins and abuses sometimes seen to be present because they aforehand had to be present?[90] At a minimum, whatever difficulties and dislocations

86. See "J. Merlonis Horstii monitum ad lectores," which introduces the *De consideratione*, PL 182, 725–26.

87. See, e.g., Domenichi, "Quaestio super c. Constantinus," BAV cod. Barb. lat. 1201, fol. 57^r; Domenichi, "Expositio psalmi centesimi," *ibid.*, fol. 21^r; Domenichi, "Oratio die qua intrarunt ad electionem," BAV cod. Ottob. lat. 1035, fol. 5^r; Domenichi, "[Epistola] ad ducem et senatum Venetum," *ibid.*, fol. 63^r; Carvajal, *Oratio de eligendo summo pontifice*, fols. [5^v, 6^r]; Lollio, *Oratio circumcisionis dominicae* [Rome: S. Plannck, 1485?], Hain #*10180, fol. [4^r]; Flores, *Oratio de summo pontifice eligendo*, fols. [3^v–4^r]; Vázquez, *De unitate et simplicitate personae Christi in duabus naturis oratio* (Rome: J. Mazochius, 1518), fol. xxii^r, now in the modern edition of Quirino Fernandez, "Fray Dionisio Vázquez de Toledo, orador sagrado del Siglo de Oro," *Archivo Agustiniano*, 60 (1976), 178.

88. *Tractatus*, fol. [12^v]; Bernard, Sermo in Cant. XXXIII (not XXIV, as given in the text), PL 183, 959.

89. *Tractatus*, fol. [13^r]: " . . . quod, ut dicit Henricus de Ganda: Nimium hoc tempore crevit decus ecclesiae in istis exterioribus. Utinam magis crevisset in interioribus! Ideo timeo, inquit, quod hanc causam utendi talibus nimium extendamus." Cf. Henry of Ghent, *Quodlib.* 3, q. 19: "Sed hanc causam utendi timeo quod nimium extendimus. Crevit enim nimium decus ecclesiae in his et honestas exterior. Utinam magis crevisset interior, . . . !"

90. Arévalo's statement about the vices of nobles graphically displays this mentality. *Speculum*, p. 56: "Habent denique nobiles quaedam peculiaria sibique naturalia, forte dixerim indelebilia, vitia, ad quae teste Philosopho in Rhetoricis quam maxime natura ipsa inclinatur, ipsi tamen actualiter operantur."

the preachers observed in the contemporary scene were categorized according to received formulations.

If we examine the explanations the preachers proffer for the calamities of their day, we can easily isolate them by adducing three familiar words —avarice, luxury, and ambition. These are the three vices the preachers discover in operation all around them, especially in churchmen, and these are the vices that have reduced Christendom to a moral shambles. Such is the stance of Arévalo, Domenichi, Pius II, Aurelio Brandolini, Schomberg, Inghirami, Casali, and others.⁹¹ In Giles of Viterbo's famous description of the Rome of Alexander VI as a city in which gold, violence, and lust ruled, he was saying, more eloquently and perhaps more emphatically, what his colleagues at the court had been saying all along.⁹²

These three classic vices are directly related to the three concupiscences of the First Epistle of John (2:16). They were explicitly articulated from the Epistle by Gregory the Great.⁹³ The three concupiscences are important for Augustine.⁹⁴ More immediately for the preachers, the three vices appear in Bernard's *De consideratione* as part of his attack on what he viewed as the corruption of the higher clergy of his day.⁹⁵ These vices, in fact, were central to the medieval moralistic tradition.⁹⁶

91. See, e.g., Arévalo, "Sermo in die ascensionis Domini," BAV cod. Vat. lat. 4881, fol. 237ᵛ; Domenichi, "Oratio pro electione summi pontificis," BAV cod. Ottob. lat. 1035, fols. 16ᵛ, 18ʳ; Pius II, "Oratio III. In Haspach Pataviensis diocesis," in *Orationes*, I, 59–75; A. Brandolini, *De humanae vitae conditione et toleranda corporis aegritudine* (Basel: R. Winter, 1543), p. 21, and *Oratio pro sancto Thoma Aquinate*, fol. [11ᵛ]; Schomberg, "Prima oratio. Ductus Iesus in desertum," in *Orationes vel potius divinorum eloquiorum enodationes*, fol. [3ʳ]; Inghirami, *Panegyricus in memoriam divi Thomae Aquinatis*, fol. [6ᵛ]; Casali, "Oratio in die cinerum," Bibl. Ambr. cod. G.33 inf., I, fol. 305ʳ. See also Poggio Bracciolini's "Oratio ad patres reverendissimos," 1417, composed for the Fathers of the Council of Constance, in *Opera* (Fubini), II, 15–21. On this oration, see Riccardo Fubini, "Un orazione di Poggio Bracciolini sui vizi del clero, scritta al tempo del Concilio di Costanza," *Giornale storico della letteratura italiana*, 142 (1965), 24–33. On the general problem of the three vices, see Donald R. Howard, *The Three Temptations: Medieval Man in Search of the World* (Princeton: Princeton University Press, 1966).

92. "Historia XX saeculorum," Bibl. Ang. cod. lat. 502, fol. 260ᵛ: " . . . nihil ius, nihil fas. Aurum, vis et Venus imperabat."

93. "Homilia VII in Ezechielem," PL 76, 1024–25. See also "Homilia XVI in evangelia," *ibid.*, 1136, and Howard, *Three Temptations*, pp. 44–56.

94. See, e.g., *Confessions*, III.1–3; X.30–40.

95. See PL 182, e.g., 740–41, 760, 783.

96. See Howard, *Three Temptations*, passim, and Morton W. Bloomfield, *The Seven Deadly Sins: An Introduction to the History of a Religious Concept, with Special Reference to Medieval English Literature* (East Lansing, Mich.: Michigan State College Press, 1952).

When we read the indictments the preachers direct against the prelates of their own day, we must see these indictments, therefore, against the background of classic vices handed down from earlier eras. The catalogue of sins and abuses with which Philip the Chancellor reproved the churchmen of France in the thirteenth century is identical with the catalogue we find in the preachers—simony, ambition for promotion, appointment of unworthy candidates to office, and similar misdeeds. Philip affirmed that in his day there were more students in the school of Satan than in the school of Christ.[97] Bernard, in other words, was not alone in his outrage, and there is evidence to indicate that the same vices were assigned to the same classes of men with the same degree of moral indignation from the twelfth century onwards.

If we approach the three classical vices from a different source, we note that avarice and luxury appear in the very preface of Livy's history as his explanation for the decline of Roman virtue. We must assume that preface was well known to many of the preachers, and it is actually quoted by Domenichi in his panegyric of Rome.[98] From Livy the preachers had a confirmation of the three vices deriving from John's Epistle as adequate categories for analyzing the troubles of their day. Even more important is Aurelio Brandolini's relating these vices to the oratory of the *genus demonstrativum* by making them fundamental categories in the art of vituperation. They were standard weapons in the orator's arsenal.[99]

The mention of Livy's name prompts a question about the interpretation the preachers placed on the course of history. Did they see in that course a decline from a happier era, and, if so, was that decline ineluctable because of some principle of corruption inherent in the historical process itself? I have studied this question in considerable detail in Giles of Viterbo, and I believe I have shown that Giles did subscribe to such ideas.[100] His assessment of his own age cannot be appreciated apart from his conviction that the present had to be bad because it was farther from the

97. See Johannes Baptist Schneyer, *Die Sittenkritik in der Predigten Philipps des Kanzlers*, Beiträge zur Gesch. d. Phil. u. Theol. d. Mittelalters, No. 39.4 (Münster: Aschendorff, 1963). See also Ray C. Petry, "Emphasis on the Gospel and Christian Reform in Late Medieval Preaching," *Church History*, 16 (1947), 75–91, esp. p. 76 for the similar reproaches which a certain Raoul Ardent (d. 1101) addressed to churchmen.

98. "Oratio in laudem civitatis et civilitatis Romanae," BAV cod. Ottob. lat. 1035, fol. 83ᵛ.

99. See *De ratione scribendi*, p. 173.

100. See my *Giles of Viterbo*, esp. pp. 103–8.

source, the beginning, than any previous age. This conviction by no means precluded the possibility of a reform that would restore the earlier and happier condition, a reform that would inaugurate a new golden age. In Eliodoro Tolomei's sermon on the fourth Sunday of Lent, 1520, there is even a vaguely Joachimite suggestion of a new "third age" of reform and triumph to be inaugurated by Leo X.[101]

There are indications that some of the other preachers believed in historical decline. Sánchez de Arévalo and Bartholomaeus Sibylla speak in terms of cosmic senescence.[102] Cusa surely believed that men would get progressively worse as time moved onwards.[103] Arévalo and Cusa, moreover, suspected or even believed that they were living in the "last days,"[104] and Cusa went so far as to conjecture when the final triumph of the Church would come—probably sometime between 1700 and 1734.[105] Maroldi and Galatino assume that they are living near the end, and they know that the situation is inevitably evil because of that fact.[106]

Such views of history were so common among religious thinkers of the era that it can almost be assumed other preachers at the court were somehow affected by them. They are almost totally absent, however, from the sermons coram. But when, or if, these views were operative, they would perforce weigh any assessment towards the negative, even before evidence had been examined. The same can be said of the moral pessimism that occasionally appears in the preachers, despite the optimistic view most of them had about human nature and even man's moral potential.

101. "Oratio tertia de misericordia et iustitia Dei," in *Orationes habitae Romae in pontificio sacello* (Venice: Ioannes Antonius et Fratres de Sabio, 1521), fol. [10^{r-v}]. On Eliodoro, see Adrianus Staring, *Der karmelitengeneral Nikolaus Audet und die katholische Reform des XVI. Jahrhunderts*, Textus et Studia Historica Carmelitana, No. 3 (Rome: Institutum Carmelitanum, 1959), esp. pp. 51–59. On Joachim, see now Delno C. West, ed., *Joachim of Flora in Christian Thought: Essays on the Influence of the Calabrian Prophet*, 2 vols. (New York: Burt Franklin, 1975).

102. See Arévalo, "Libellus de remediis afflictae ecclesiae," BAV cod. Barb. lat. 1487, fol. 151^v, and Sibylla, "Sermo de fine mundi," BN Florence cod. Conv. Soppr. J.VII.5, fol. 4^v.

103. See *De Concordantia Catholica*, ed. Gerhardus Kallen, Opera omnia iussu et auctoritate Academiae Litterarum Heidelbergensis ad codicum fidem edita, XIV (Hamburg: F. Meiner, 1964–68), 39 (I.3).

104. See Arévalo, "Libellus de remediis afflictae ecclesiae," BAV cod. Barb. lat. 1487, fol. 138^{r-v}; Cusa, *De Concordantia Catholica*, pp. 71–72 (I.12), 183 (II.17).

105. See "Coniectura de Ultimis Diebus," in *Opuscula I*, ed. Paulus Wilpert, Opera omnia iussu et auctoritate Academiae Litterarum Heidelbergensis ad codicum fidem edita, IV (Hamburg: F. Meiner, 1959), 91–100.

106. See Maroldi, *Sententia veritatis humanae redemptionis* [Rome: S. Plannck, after March 25, 1481], Hain #*10778, fol. [6^r]; Galatino, "Libellus pro reformatione," BAV cod. Vat. lat. 5578, fol. 101^r.

The French invasions of Italy in 1494 and 1499 shocked Italian thinkers and called forth from them negative evaluations of their age.[107] These
events played practically no explicit role, however, in the liturgical sermons at the papal court. The same certainly cannot be said about the
threat of the Turks. The most terrifying evidence the preachers produced
that the times were bad was the series of Turkish victories over the Christians since the fall of Constantinople in 1453. When the preachers discuss
the desperate condition of the Christian religion, they often are directly
referring to the fact that that religion has now been confined to a mere
"corner" of Europe and that there seems to be no hope of saving even that
corner from the Turkish ravage. The loss of the Savior's Sepulchre, the
loss of the ancient apostolic cities of Antioch and Alexandria, and the fall
of Constantinople all provided grounds for an unflattering comparison of
their own age with an age when these lands were Christian. Even when
Christianity was viewed simply in terms of territory, there was "less" of
it now than in the more prosperous times of the past.

The Turkish victories were not seen, however, solely in terms of lost
territory or in terms of the eternal damnation sustained by those in their
territories who no longer practiced the Christian religion. The Turkish
victories had a moral implication even for the Christians who were not
yet under the sway of the infidel. In blunt terms, the sins of Christians
caused the victories of the Turks.[108]

The sin of war and discord among Christian princes obviously aided the
Turks, for it distracted Christian arms from the common enemy. The
preachers often lamented this sin. But the problem was more general. God
punished Christians with the Turkish scourge because of the sins of private men or because of the private sins of public men that would not
seem to relate directly to the advances of the Turks. If Christians reformed
their lives and abandoned their ambition, avarice, and luxury, God would
in turn aid them in defeating the Turks. Hence, another argument for the

---

107. See, e.g., Charles Trinkaus, *Adversity's Noblemen: The Italian Humanists
on Happiness* (New York: Columbia University Press, 1940), esp. pp. 121–40, and
Felix Gilbert, *Machiavelli and Guicciardini: Politics and History in Sixteenth-Century
Florence* (Princeton: Princeton University Press, 1965).
108. See, e.g., Arévalo, "Libellus de remediis afflictae ecclesiae," BAV cod. Barb.
lat. 1487, fol. 110^r-v; Domenichi, *Tractatus*, fol. [4^v]; Domenichi, "Oratio pro electione
summi pontificis," BAV cod. Ottob. lat. 1035, fol. 18^r; Thegliatius, *Oratio in die
omnium sanctorum*, fol. [6^v]; Thegliatius, *Sermo in materia fidei* [Rome: n. publ., after
Dec. 27, 1480], Hain #*15461, fol. [3^v]; Marsi, *Oratio in die sancti Stephani primi
martyris* [Rome: E. Silber, after Dec. 26, 1487?], Hain #*10786, fol. [5^r].

urgency of the reform of men's lives surfaces. Sin caused the Turks' victories, and virtue will assure their defeat. As Arévalo says with irreproachable consistency: if the cause is destroyed, the effect will be destroyed as well.[109] Such ideas were commonplace in the Renaissance, and the preachers utilized them.

The reverse logic that often seems to be lurking beneath the surface must be carefully noted. The logic that states that the Turks are advancing because of the sins of Christians can be turned around to read: the advances of the Turks prove that Christians are in a state of sin. The Turkish advances prove that the lives of Christians are riddled with ambition, luxury, and avarice. This is the logic that seems to be operative when the preachers review the debased moral condition of their times. Since the preachers were present in the Roman Curia, they were especially sensitive to delinquencies that they in fact observed there or that they in theory were supposed to observe there.

The tendency to deplore the low morals of the age was not confined, however, to those who were eyewitnesses to what went on in the Curia. Pietro del Monte relates how as a young man in Venice he frequently participated in conversations with Guarino, Francesco Barbaro, Andrea Giuliani, and Pietro Miani in which earlier ages were praised, while their own was blamed for its vices and malignancies. In these conversations, voices were sometimes raised in defense of the present, affirming that every age has its troubles and that the present age was no worse than many others. But even such a weak defense does not seem to have been consistently pursued by del Monte's distinguished friends.[110] These conversations confirm what other evidence from Renaissance Italy also indicates: it was not bad form to speak ill of the age, whether one were discussing the subject in the early Quattrocento in Venice or in the late Quattrocento in Rome.

The names of the persons participating in those conversations in Venice also suggest that this distribution of praise and blame to various ages was particularly attractive to students of rhetoric. The tradition can be traced back at least to Petrarch. In particular, to ply the art of praise and blame almost inevitably meant, in an age fascinated by the recovery of great monuments from the past, to distribute that praise and blame over the

---

109. "Epistola de expugnatione Euboiae," BAV cod. Vat. lat. 5869, fol. 102[r-v].
110. "De vitiorum inter se differentia et comparatione," BAV cod. Vat. lat. 1048, fol. 5[r-v].

centuries. In such an exercise one's own age had to be prepared to take its share of the bad with the good. It could not always receive congratulation. Though praise was more effective than blame in inciting to virtue, blame was not without its uses.

Praise and blame, in fact, are correlates. Aurelio Brandolini proposes in his treatise on letter writing that the "difficulties and perversities of the times" are an important element in the rhetoric of congratulation. We augment the praise of the person we are eulogizing by showing how marvelous it was to succeed so well amidst such iniquity.[111] Therefore, just as praise was sometimes blame in disguise, reproach was sometimes an integral part of praise.

Brandolini's proposal shows that "the difficulties and perversities of the times" is, literally, a timeless device in the art of praise and blame. That device has application in all ages and situations. The inference seems valid that the sense of religious security which some preachers described as obtaining in Renaissance Rome encouraged them to indulge in blame just as the insecurities of the Counter Reformation would lead them to restrict it.

In Arévalo's *Speculum vitae humanae*, moreover, an exaggerated form of a presupposition which other preachers shared can once again be observed. This presupposition is what R. G. Collingwood long ago designated as "substantialism," and he identified it as the chief defect of Greco-Roman historiography.[112] An unchanging substance, such as Rome for Livy, voyages through history without being affected by it. That is to say, the unchanging substance is clearly distinguished from the oftentimes sordid contingencies affecting that substance's members. This is how Arévalo views the various occupations and states of life in the *Speculum*. In his dedicatory letter to Paul II, he tells the pope that in the "mirror" he holds up to every occupation the reader will see what deserves praise and what deserves blame. As it turns out, for the occupations themselves Arévalo has nothing but praise—for their nobility, their antiquity, their utility. But for the men who serve in these occupations his blame is severe. When other preachers allotted blame in their sermons and other writings, they similarly allotted it to "men and the times," but not to any radical defects in society's institutions.

111. See *De ratione scribendi*, p. 125.
112. *The Idea of History* (New York: Oxford University Press, 1956), pp. 42–45.

The armchair quality and the stylized categories of the preachers' analysis of "men and the times" should by now be clear. This analysis was accompanied by an easy recourse to moral explanations of exceedingly complex problems. The preachers' assessment of what was happening around them has the advantages and all the disadvantages of such an approach. There is, certainly, some justification for assigning blame for many disorders of society to the disordered passions of its leaders. But this particular assignment of blame does no justice to the other factors—economic, ideological, technological, etc.—that are inevitably involved in any major crisis. Nowhere is the weakness of the remedies proposed by the rhetorical tradition more evident than in its tendency to reduce all evils to moral components.

This tendency suggests, in any event, the final quality the preachers propose as distinguishing the life of the true Christian, especially if he is a public man. He should be an example to others. In him the virtues of his state of life should be operative in such a radiant way as to incite others to imitate him. He could do no greater service to his fellow men than by giving them good example, and he could do no greater disservice than by giving bad example.

Scholarship is well aware of the importance of the "mirror-literature" in the Renaissance, especially as applied to princes. Erasmus's treatise *On the Education of the Christian Prince* written for the young Charles of Hapsburg in 1516 is one of the last important instances of it, and Machiavelli's *Prince* struck the first heavy blow against it. The presuppositions of this genre are particularly noticeable in the funeral eulogies of the preachers. The presuppositions in these cases derive directly from the principles of epideictic oratory. In these eulogies the preachers construct for their listeners the mirror of the good pope, of the good cardinal, of the good bishop, and of the good jurist or public servant.

In panegyrics of the saints, the same principles are in force. The preachers consistently commend the saints' *praecepta* and their *exempla*. The *praecepta* in persons like Augustine and Aquinas are sometimes the equivalent of *doctrina*, and they do not necessarily have a directly moral connotation. But even when *praecepta* are taken to comprise the totality of the saint's teaching, the orators do their best to relate it to the art of good and blessed living. Whatever the saints taught is interpreted in relationship to that art. Since holy thoughts and the contemplation of divine things are part of the art of holy living, the correlation was not difficult. Study of Scripture and sacred letters was a duty incumbent upon all literate men.

Often, however, the preachers try to make a correlation which more immediately relates that study to the lives of others, as we have seen in Inghirami's panegyric of Aquinas. Here the distinction between *doctrina* and *exemplum* begins to dissolve, for part of the good example even a public man provides is his devotion to learning and the sacred texts. His action should spring from his contemplation.

Reductively, therefore, example becomes the dominant category. Aurelio Brandolini, in the impassioned peroration of his panegyric on Aquinas, deplores the crimes, seditions, lack of faith, and contempt for God and religion that he sees all about him.[113] He deplores the fact that so much of the world has been lost to the infidel. All of this would not have happened if Christians had imitated the example of Thomas's pursuit of holiness. The near catastrophic state in which the Christian religion and the bark of Peter find themselves is due to the bad lives Christians lead. As Brandolini addresses his distinguished audience of cardinals and other members of the papal court, he creates the distinct impression that he is laying the blame at the doors of the prelates seated in front of him. The scene at the Minerva must have been tense. Christ founded the Church on poverty, sound doctrine, and chastity. But they by their wealth, their ignorance, and their unbridled passions are overturning it. Condign punishment for their unbelief and pride is coming. Finally, Brandolini implores his listeners to rush to the aid of the Church and restore it to its pristine state of faith and innocence.

The example of God's great deeds, the example of Christ's love and humility, and the example of the learning and virtue of the saints supplied the Christian people with an almost inexhaustible resource of incitements to good and holy living. But more was needed—the good example of contemporaries, especially of leaders in society like princes, bishops, cardinals, and popes. This is what the preachers so often found wanting, and this is what they deplored. This is what they wanted to see remedied by a reform of Church and society.

---

113. *Oratio pro sancto Thoma Aquinate*, fols. [11ʳ–12ᵛ].

CHAPTER SIX. THE REFORM OF CHURCH AND SOCIETY: IN APOSTOLICAE SEDIS SPECULA LOCATI

In their sermons *inter missarum solemnia* and in their other orations and treatises, the preachers presented their goals for a reformed Church and a reformed society. They on occasion enumerate the goals almost programatically, as Domenichi does in his "Ad electionem" for the successor to Calixtus III and as Carvajal does on the same occasion after the death of Innocent VIII.[1] Inghirami provides a similar enumeration in the peroration of his sermon for All Saints in 1497, though in vaguer terms.[2] The last part of de Viana's sermon on Ash Wednesday in the previous year contains, in a less concise way than the others, a program for reform that resembles them.[3] From Cajetan's oration to the Fifth Lateran Council, another such program can easily be reconstructed.[4]

At any given time the preachers tend to urge only one or two of these goals, and they also tend in the sermons *coram* to reserve for a brief peroration their ideas about what the desperate situation of Christendom requires. Some caution must be exercised, therefore, in accepting a composite description of these goals as verifiable in all the preachers. Nonetheless, despite the span of years and the number of individuals involved, the convergence in viewpoint is considerable.

The Roman ideal of reform, as propounded by the sacred orators of the court, focused on five major problems. First of all, the orators keenly felt the need for the moral and disciplinary reform of the city of Rome and the Roman Curia. This meant the transformation of institutions ridden by avarice, ambition, and luxury into institutions where virtue prevailed.

---

1. Domenichi, "Oratio die qua intrarunt ad electionem," BAV cod. Ottob. lat. 1035, fols. 8ʳ–9ᵛ; Carvajal, *Oratio de eligendo summo pontifice* [Rome: E. Silber, c.1493], GKW #6152, fol. [5ᵛ].

2. "In laudem omnium sanctorum oratio," Bibl. Guarn. cod. LIII.4.8, fol. 50ʳ.

3. *Oratio in die cinerum* [Rome: S. Plannck, 1496], Cop. #6198, fols. [5ᵛ–6ᵛ].

4. "Oratio de ecclesia et synodorum differentia," in *Opuscula omnia* (Lyons: G. Rovillius, 1588), pp. 191–92. See also the oration given in Julius II's name opening the council, in Nelson H. Minnich's "Concepts of Reform Proposed at the Fifth Lateran Council," *Archivum Historiae Pontificiae*, 7 (1969), pp. 237–38, as well as R. Brandolini's *Dialogus Leo nuncupatus*, ed. Francisco [sic] Fogliazzi (Venice: S. Occhi, 1753), pp. 65–67, 96–97.

While vice was being replaced by virtue, good learning should also be fostered, and sacred buildings should be restored. The preachers wanted Rome and the Curia to recover the respect and authority they had once enjoyed. This respect and authority was needed for the good governance of the Church, and it corresponded to the intrinsic dignity of these institutions.

When the preachers turned their eyes outwards from the city of Rome, they saw that the appointment of good bishops was as necessary as the election of good popes and the appointment of good cardinals and curial officials. This was their second reform goal, though it was not as often discussed as the other four. The bishops should be true pastors, not hirelings seeking their own gain. They should, consequently, defend the rights and prerogatives of the Church against those who encroached upon them. The preachers often expressed this duty in the classic formulation from the era of the Gregorian Reform of defending "the liberty of the Church."

This meant, in the third place, that the princes had to be reformed. They must be made to respect the Church's liberty. An even more persistent theme in the sermons and orations, however, is that the wars that the Christian princes waged against one another must cease. Nothing was more contrary to Christ's message of love and to the bequest of peace he left his disciples on the night before he died. Nothing was more contrary to the peace and concord that should reign in the universe.

Nothing was more subversive to attempts to remedy the most pressing evil of the day—the threat of the Turks. Remedying that evil was the fourth goal of the preachers. The arms of the Christian princes had to be diverted from one another to the common enemy. The Turk had to be stopped. If possible, the holy places should be recovered. Peace among Christians was the precondition for a successful war against the Turks. Virtue and learning were also proposed as effective measures in the face of the mortal threat, but a military campaign was what the preachers almost invariably urged.

A successful war against the Turks would result in securing the final goal the preachers sometimes proposed: the fraternal union of all men in the love of God and under the one universal pastor. Thus would be accomplished the Savior's desire that the world be constituted as "one flock" with its unity and order assured under the "one shepherd."

These goals and the presuppositions about Church and society that underlay them are not necessarily congruous with the ideals of other reform-minded persons in the fifteenth and sixteenth centuries. The preachers were not Spiritual Franciscans or Florentine republicans. They were not attempting through some special gift of clairvoyance to anticipate Luther. They had in fact adopted a rhetorical tradition that saw one of its chief services to be support of received verities and public institutions. Nonetheless, the preachers were concerned with reform. They could hardly have lived in their era as serious Christians and not be concerned with it. Moreover, as virtuosos in the art of praise and blame, reform talk fell to them almost as their proper métier.

Our task, therefore, consists in discerning how the preachers' ideals differ from others current in the era and how they originate from different assumptions about what characterizes a reformed world. In particular, we must understand the values the preachers cherished, the evils they feared, and the vision of reality they presupposed. If we grant that passion underlies every logic, we must try to grasp the passions that underlay the logic of reform the preachers espoused. To a large extent the book has been dealing with these issues all along. It would thus hope to disclose goals, passions, and presuppositions concerning reform in Renaissance Rome, just as scholars have attempted to disclose them for the Rome of the Counter Reformation.[5]

Several general characteristics of the Roman reform ideal during the Renaissance are already clear from a simple listing of its goals. The reform is this-worldly in the sense that it is concerned with the proper constitution of human society. It is not concerned exclusively with what we might term in-house problems of ecclesiastical management and proper doctrine. It is not content with a private life of piety detached from the world's problems and potential achievements.

Thus it impels to engagement, expecting every person to do his duty according to his state in life. In this engagement the Church is leader, whose own goals are coterminous with what should be the best goals of the other societies and political institutions with which it deals. But the Church has a dignity and identity of its own, which derive in part from the clear tasks set for it. This Church is a Church aware of the benefits it has to offer to the world. The tasks incumbent upon it are somehow con-

5. See esp. William J. Bouwsma, *Venice and the Defense of Republican Liberty: Renaissance Values in the Age of the Counter Reformation* (Berkeley: University of California Press, 1968), pp. 293–338, as well as the series of studies by Romeo de Maio, *Riforme e miti nella Chiesa del Cinquecento*, Esperienze No. 17 (Naples: Guida, 1973).

sequent upon the great realities of the Trinity, Creation, and Redemption. The tasks are not, therefore, particularly subject to reappraisal in the light of empirical evidence.

The goals of the Roman reform ideal are, within a given framework of interpretation, all-encompassing. Though they may begin ostensibly modestly with the reform of the Curia and the city of Rome, they soon expand to embrace all mankind. From this universal scope, as a matter of fact, the preachers could perceive the very nobility of the goals in large measure to originate. Who could challenge the nobility, and the desirability, of a world restored to unity and harmony? The ugly distortions of which such a vision was capable do not trouble orators intent upon depicting and praising an ideal.

The vigor with which these goals are propounded perhaps reflects the preachers' excitement over the vigor of the new Renaissance Rome they saw being created before their eyes after the neglect it had suffered for centuries. The active commitment to accomplishment reflects the activism implicit in the rhetorical tradition the preachers adopted. The urgency that genuinely animates some of the preachers reflects the general sense of religious crisis that had been swelling in Europe at least since the Council of Basel. Although the preachers preached in the atmosphere of stately serenity that was striven for in the *cappelle,* many of them were foreigners who would bring with them to Rome a sense of ecclesiastical disquiet that was at variance with that atmosphere.

But the goals that the preachers proposed do not originate with the Renaissance. For the most part, they are constructed from elements of medieval ecclesiastical polity formulated from the middle of the eleventh century onwards. The reform of the Curia was demanded in Bernard's day. The appointment of good bishops and the defense of the liberty of the Church hark back to the Gregorian Reform and its long aftermath. The call for peace among Christian princes and for war against the infidel dates at least from the times of Urban II. What the Renaissance contributed to these goals was not an impulse to reexamine them but a rhetoric with which to expound them. This does not mean the goals were any less sincere for being traditional. The goals accorded with venerable ecclesiastical tradition. They accorded, moreover, with themes congenial to the rhetorical tradition of antiquity—the glories of the city, the necessity for honest men in public service, and the benefits of peace, especially peace among allies in the face of a common danger. Hence, the goals were rendered all the more genuine and perennial for the preachers.

In describing these goals, the preachers usually employ global terms. They sometimes fill out details, as in their descriptions of the cardinals' godly feasts, but this is not generally true. Detailed recommendations for the cardinals' life-style, for instance, would be rhetorically awkward and even inappropriate in an oration. But closer specifications about goals and means to attain them can sometimes be obtained from the preachers' other writings. For that reason it is important to note how many major state-ments on reform composed at the papal court during the Renaissance relate somehow to the sacred orators of the *cappelle*. At this point a chronological listing of these documents might be helpful.

The earliest is Domenichi's *Tractatus de reformationibus Romanae curiae.*[6] It is one of the "advices" requested by Pius II at the beginning of his pontificate. Cusa's reform proposal was composed at about the same time.[7] Besides this document for Pius, there is a much shorter instruction by Cusa which has never been published or studied, found in one of the Vatican codices of his sermons. This undated instruction, "Considera quomodo istud," is a concise summary of the principles upon which Cusa thought true reform must rest.[8] Next there is Rodrigo Sánchez de Arévalo's "Libellus de remediis afflictae ecclesiae," written during the pontificate of Paul II, probably in 1469.[9] It is a long treatise, never published, whose purpose is to remove initiative for reform from councils and locate it in the pope. Then there is the oration by Raphael Brandolini intended for the Fifth Lateran Council. It exists in at least two manuscript versions. It deserves special mention here, apart from other important orations at the council like Cajetan's, Marcello's, Thegliatius's, and Giles of Viterbo's, because it is so much longer. Also, unlike those orations, it has never been

---

6. Brixen: Baptista Farfengus, 1495, GKW #8638.

7. The proposal was edited by Stephan Ehses in "Der Reformentwurf des Kardi-nals Nikolaus Cusanus," *Historisches Jahrbuch*, 32 (1911), 274–97. See also Erwin Iserloh, "Reform der Kirche bei Nikolaus von Kues," in *Das Cusanus-Jubiläum*, ed. Rudolf Haubst, Mitteilungen und Forschungsbeiträge der Cusanus-Gesellschaft, No. 4 (Mainz: Matthias-Grünewald, 1964), pp. 54–73; Donald Sullivan, "Nicholas of Cusa as Reformer: The Papal Legation to the Germanies, 1451–1452," *Mediaeval Studies*, 36 (1974), 382–428; and James E. Biechler, "Nicholas of Cusa and the End of the Conciliar Movement: A Humanist Crisis of Identity," *Church History*, 44 (1975), 1–17.

8. BAV cod. Vat. lat. 1245, fols. 73ᵛ–74ʳ.

9. BAV cod. Barb. lat. 1487, fols. 107ʳ–156ᵛ.

published or studied.[10] Finally, there are several treatises on reform by Pietro Galatino. These, too, are found only in manuscript and have received scant attention from scholars. The earliest of them, "Libellus pro reformatione," was finished shortly before the death of Leo X in 1521.[11]

There are, in addition, three major reform documents of the court not composed by the preachers but directly or indirectly influenced by some of them. The documents in question are the unpromulgated reform bulls of Pius II, "Pastor aeternus,"[12] of Sixtus IV, "Quoniam regnantium,"[13] and of Alexander VI, "In apostolicae sedis specula."[14] The proposals of Domenichi and especially of Cusa influenced Pius's bull, and Pius's document influenced Sixtus's and Alexander's.[15] The important role played by Oliviero Carafa and Francesco Piccolomini in Alexander's reform commission establishes another link with the preachers; these two cardinals, as must be clear by now, manifested a special concern for promoting excellence in the sermons coram, and many of those sermons are prefaced by dedications to them.[16] Last of all, the decrees published by the Fifth Lateran Council, Gianfrancesco Pico della Mirandola's oration intended for the council, and the Libellus on reform submitted to Leo X in 1513 by the two Camaldolese hermits, Paolo Giustiniani and Pietro Quirini, are significant documents that can be employed as instruments for testing the reform goals of the preachers and for discovering how commonly those goals were shared.[17]

10. "Oratio ad Lateranense concilium," BAV cod. Ottob. lat. 813, and also Bibl. Ambr. cod. Z.65 sup.

11. BAV cod. Vat. lat. 5578, fols. 86ʳ–106ᵛ. Later treatises also deal with reform, e.g., "Opus de ecclesia restituta," BAV cod. Vat. lat. 5576, and "De angelico pastore opusculum," BAV cod. Vat. lat. 5578, fols. 1ʳ–84ʳ.

12. The critical edition is contained in Rudolf Haubst's "Der Reformentwurf Pius' des Zweiten," Römische Quartalschrift, 49 (1954), 188–242.

13. The document is contained in BAV cod. Vat. lat. 3884, fols. 118ʳ–132ᵛ and Vat. lat. 3883, fols. 14ʳ–25ᵛ.

14. There are at least three copies of the bull; see Chapter I, note 2.

15. See the articles by Léonce Celier, "Alexandre VI et la réforme de l'Église," Mélanges d'archéologie et d'histoire, 27 (1907), 65–124, and "L'idée de réforme à la cour pontificale du Concile de Bâle au Concile de Latran," Revue des questions historiques, 86 (1909), 418–35.

16. See Celier, "Alexandre VI," esp. pp. 97–103.

17. See Charles B. Schmitt, "Gianfrancesco Pico della Mirandola and the Fifth Lateran Council," Archiv für Reformationsgeschichte, 61 (1970), 161–78, and Libellus ad Leonem X pontificem maximum, in Annales Camaldulenses, ed. G. B. Mittarelli and A. Costadoni, IX (Venice: J. B. Pasquali, 1773), 612–719. On this treatise and its relationship to Roman reform ideals, see my "The Discovery of America and Reform Thought at the Papal Court in the Early Cinquecento," in First Images of America: The Impact of the New World on the Old, ed. Fredi Chiappelli, et al., 2 vols. (Berkeley: University of California Press, 1976), I, 185–200.

An enlightening way to begin a consideration of the Roman reform ideals is to ask what models were implicitly or explicitly operative in the preachers' consciousness as they projected their ideal to which a renovated Church and a renovated society should conform. In accord with what pattern was their ideal Church and world constructed? For Luther this ideal was the Pauline Church where the evangelical doctrine of justification by faith alone was rightly proclaimed. What was it for the preachers?[18]

There is no simple answer to that question because of the large number of people with whom we are dealing. From the outset, however, it is clear that for the preachers "looking up" to the heavenly Church was at least as important as "looking back" to the primitive Church of the apostolic era or back to any other ideal from antiquity.[19] This fact already distinguishes the Roman reform ideal from other reforms like the Spiritual Franciscans' or Luther's. It distinguishes it from the Gregorian Reform of the eleventh century, which, though it did not precisely "look back" to the apostolic age, did look back to an earlier and purer canonical tradition.

In his *De consideratione*, Bernard invokes the verse from Revelation (21:2), "I saw the holy city, the new Jerusalem, descending from heaven" —"Vidi civitatem sanctam, Jerusalem novam, descendentem de caelo, a Deo paratam." Bernard then affirms that the Church has God as its author and owes its origins to heaven.[20] The same verse from Revelation is utilized by Lodovico da Ferrara, by Cajetan, and by others when they discourse on the model to which the Church should conform.[21]

18. For a general frame of reference in which to place this discussion, see Avery Dulles, *Models of the Church* (Garden City, N.Y.: Doubleday, 1974).

19. See, e.g., Glenn Olsen, "The Idea of the *Ecclesia Primitiva* in the Writings of the Twelfth-Century Canonists," *Traditio*, 25 (1969), 61–86. For a study of the force of the "exemplum vitae apostolicae" in the writings of Aquinas, see Emilio Panella, "La 'Lex Nova' tra storia ed ermeneutica: Le occasioni dell'esegesi di s. Tommaso d'Aquino," *Memorie Domenicane*, NS 6 (1975), 11–106, esp. 59–66.

20. PL 182, 769: "Non est parvi pendendum quod et Deum habet auctorem et de caelo ducit originem." For medieval sources for the idea of the Church as a reflection of the heavenly exemplar, see Yves Congar, *L'ecclésiologie du haut Moyen-Age* (Paris: Cerf, 1968), esp. pp. 98–129. See also Dulles, *Models of the Church*, pp. 104–5. On the ecclesiology of the *De consideratione*, see Elizabeth Kennan, "The 'De Consideratione' of St. Bernard of Clairvaux and the Papacy in the Mid-Twelfth Century: A Review of Scholarship," *Traditio*, 23 (1967), 73–115, esp. 114: "Bernard's vision of the New Jerusalem, or the Church in her destined purity, moreover, is not an historical but a mystical one. The Church in her perfection already exists as the heavenly hierarchy. . . . Therefore, if one is to rule the Church, one must obviously study the heavenly pattern to which she is to be molded."

21. Lodovico da Ferrara, "Sermo de conformitate ecclesiae militantis ad ecclesiam triumphantem," in *Orationes quinque* [Rome: n. publ., after 1492], Hain-Cop. #6983,

Cajetan is especially insistent on the heavenly exemplar in his oration for the council. He repeatedly invites the audience to "look up," and he distinguishes the "Pisan Church" from the true Church by an exegesis of the verse from Revelation. In the heavenly Church Cajetan sees concord and community ("civitas"), holiness ("sancta"), peace ("Jerusalem"), the newness of divine sonship that Christ bestowed in his Incarnation ("nova"), and unity under the one vicar of Christ on earth according to the structure of one God in the heavenly city ("descendens"). Cajetan's goals for the reformed Church emerge from a consideration of the heavenly model. The source for these goals is clearly metaphysical, not historical.

Cajetan's short but important letter on reform to the whole Dominican order while he was Master General, dated May 21, 1513, is permeated with suggestions of the "heavenly fatherland" as justification for the reform measures he enjoins.[22] It is noteworthy that, although one of the principal measures he advocates was a more faithful observance of the share-and-share-alike quality of the friars' "common life," he does not adduce the classical text from the Acts of the Apostles (4:32–35), which could establish historical precedent for it.

Palmeri in his sermon on peace paraphrases the text from Revelation to insist on the unity and monarchical structure that should characterize the Church militant, for that Church is constructed in imitation of "the heavenly and supernal Jerusalem, which is our mother."[23] Similar expressions occur in the orations of Domenichi, Thegliatius, Lodovico da Ferrara, and others.[24] Jouffroy specifies earth's conformity with the exemplar in terms of the beauty and splendor of the liturgical ceremonies, which reflect the beauty and splendor of the heavenly court, an idea we have

---

fol. [17^r]; Cajetan, "Oratio de ecclesia et synodorum differentia," in *Opuscula*, pp. 189–92; Palmeri, ["De pacis dignitate"], BAV cod. Vat. lat. 5815, fol. 92^r.

22. The letter is contained in *Monumenta Ordinis Fratrum Praedicatorum Historica*, ed. Benedictus Maria Reichert, IX (Rome: Domus Generalitia O. P., 1901), 93–94.

23. ["De pacis dignitate"], BAV cod. Vat. lat. 5815, fol. 92^r: "Haec civitas de caelo descendit ad instar caelestis, supernae Ierusalem, quae est mater nostra."

24. See, e.g., Domenichi, "Oratio pro electione summi pontificis," BAV cod. Ottob. lat. 1035, fol. 11^{r-v}; Thegliatius, *Oratio pro die pentecostes* [Rome: S. Plannck, after June 3, 1487], Hain #15456, fol. [5^r]; Lodovico da Ferrara, "Sermo de conformitate ecclesiae militantis ad ecclesiam triumphantem," in *Orationes quinque*, fol. [18^r]; Schomberg, "Quarta oratio. Nox praecessit," in *Orationes vel potius divinorum eloquiorum enodationes* [Leipzig: W. Stöckel, 1512], fol. [12^{r-v}]. See also Galatino, "Opus de ecclesia instituta," BAV cod. Vat. lat. 5575, fol. 2^r and passim, esp. "Liber secundus," fols. 88^v–133^v.

seen before.[25] Sometimes the correlation of the earthly Church with the heavenly is identified with the hierarchical structure found in both, but often the correlation is much more general, as we have seen in Cajetan's oration for the council. Giles of Viterbo's formula to express the inclusive nature of the relationship is taken from the Lord's Prayer—"on earth, as it is in heaven."[26]

The preachers are not immune to the circularity implied in argumentation from a heavenly exemplar. What is seen on earth indicates what will be found in heaven, and what is found in heaven is prescriptive for what should prevail on earth. The authors we have been discussing were trained in metaphysical traditions, and they would, presumably, be more sensitive to heavenly exemplars than their humanist colleagues. We know, for instance, that the heavenly, even trinitarian, exemplar was very important in the reform thought of Jean Gerson.[27] It was important for Cusa as well.[28] But, as we have already seen, the humanists at the court also frequently urged that eyes be raised for the contemplation of a heavenly scene. The humanists depict the beauty of the heavenly fatherland that is our goal. Although not quite so pointedly as the scholastics, they thus suggest that a certain correspondence should prevail between the order and style of our destiny and the order and style of our earthly life.

The preachers did sometimes "look back." Gordon Leff has rightly insisted that in the late Middle Ages the historical ideal of the primitive Church was employed as an instrument of criticism for the actually existing Church, and, hence, it was an important factor in the destruction of the so-called "medieval synthesis."[29] Against the background of Leff's

25. "Oratio in funeralibus Nicolai papae quinti," BAV cod. Vat. lat. 3675, fols. 32ᵛ, 34ᵛ.

26. See my *Giles of Viterbo on Church and Reform: A Study in Renaissance Thought*, Studies in Medieval and Reformation Thought, No. 5 (Leiden: Brill, 1968), esp. pp. 95–96.

27. See Louis B. Pascoe, "Jean Gerson: Mysticism, Conciliarism, and Reform," *Annuarium Historiae Conciliorum*, 6 (1974), 135–53.

28. See *De Concordantia Catholica*, ed. Gerhardus Kallen, Opera omnia iussu et auctoritate Academiae Litterarum Heidelbergensis ad codicum fidem edita, XIV (Hamburg: F. Meiner, 1964–68), 37–38 (I.3); 42 (I.4).

29. "The Apostolic Ideal in Later Medieval Ecclesiology," *The Journal of Theological Studies*, NS 18 (1967), 58–82. See also Leff's "The Making of the Myth of a True Church in the Later Middle Ages," *The Journal of Medieval and Renaissance Studies*, 1 (1971), 1–15, as well as Louis B. Pascoe, "Jean Gerson: The 'Ecclesia Primitiva' and Reform," *Traditio*, 30 (1974), 379–409, and Scott H. Hendrix, "In Quest of the *Vera Ecclesia*: The Crises of Late Medieval Ecclesiology," *Viator*, 7 (1976), 347–78.

observations, the uses to which the preachers put the idea of the primitive Church are particularly intriguing. That idea could be used to support the status quo as well as to corrode it, even when the idea was adduced as a criticism of contemporary abuses. Once again, what is crucial for understanding reform are the specific qualities of the "ecclesia primitiva" which are isolated for commendation. Like everybody who looks back, the preachers looked back selectively.

Arévalo's "De remediis" offers the best example of how the supposed virtues of the primitive Church could be employed in favor of existing institutions. Arévalo concludes that God permits the Turkish ravage because of the sins of Christians. The remedy for this evil is for the Church to return to what was observed "in the nativity of its law and in the primitive Church." The Church is to return, that is, to obedience and reverence for the Holy See. By such a return the problem will be solved.[30]

Domenichi and the author of the oration addressed to the cardinals about to elect a successor to Leo X do not focus on reverence for the papacy as the hallmark of the primitive Church. But when they characterize that Church as one of peace and concord, as a Church without the vice of ambition, they opt for an ideal in which disruptive and "disobedient" elements are incompatible with the good Church of the past.[31] Less congenial to the preferences of the Renaissance popes, however, would be the insistence of Giles of Viterbo and Raphael Brandolini in their orations for the Fifth Lateran Council that the health of the early Church was due in large measure to the frequent convocation of councils.[32] Yet Giles and Brandolini are in these instances directing their words to a council already in session, to a council assembled to assert the authority of a papal council over a schismatic rival. From Giles's other writings, it is evident that his attitude towards councils was much more guarded than his words to the Fifth Lateran would suggest.

30. BAV cod. Barb. lat. 1487, fol. 110ᵛ: "Quare ad aërem nativum, ad aërem patriae redeundum est pro salute fidei catholicae et sanctae matris ecclesiae, videlicet ad manutenendam et augendam antiquam illam reverentiam et obedientiam huius sanctae apostolicae sedis in toto populo Christiano, . . . quae . . . in ipsa legis nativitate et in ecclesia primitiva iussa et observata est." See L. D. Ettlinger, *The Sistine Chapel before Michelangelo: Religious Imagery and Papal Primacy* (Oxford: Clarendon, 1965), pp. 104–19.

31. See Domenichi, "Oratio die qua intrarunt ad electionem," BAV cod. Ottob. lat. 1035, fol. 7ʳ⁻ᵛ; Pimpinella (?), "Pro electione summi pontificis oratio," Bibl. del Conte Alessandro Marcello del Majno, Venice, cod. Serie A.I, Busta 5, Fasc. b, fol. [5ʳ].

32. See R. Brandolini, "Oratio ad Lateranense concilium," BAV cod. Ottob. lat. 813, fols. 17ᵛ–18ᵛ, and my *Giles of Viterbo*, esp. p. 121.

Of all the preachers, Massari and Arévalo most frequently direct attention to the "vita apostolica," and they focus on the critical verses from the fourth chapter of Acts. In his Commentary on Augustine's Rule, Massari sees the apostolic life of his friars articulated in the common table and the communal sharing described in those verses.[33] But his Commentary is traditional, posing no threat to the Church at large. Other preachers propose the simplicity and even poverty of the early Church as an ideal.[34] In the later writings of Galatino, however, poverty becomes a normative preoccupation.[35]

The preachers' caution on the question of poverty should not be surprising. Memory of the conflicts of the popes with the Fraticelli lived on, and Paul II's request of Arévalo to write a treatise for him on the poverty of Christ and the apostles indicates that the pope feared the issue was not dead. Arévalo's treatise was reassuring. First of all, poverty is always relative. It is relative to the end proposed, e.g., to call men back from overly zealous pursuit of the goods of this world or to free men from worldly cares in order to have more time for contemplation. Or poverty is relative to the state of life of the individual concerned, e.g., a poor king may have more wealth than a rich farmer. At any rate, destitution is bad, for it leads the destitute person into crime and it distracts him from higher values. Christ's poverty was the most perfect of all not because it was the most abject conceivable but because it was the most appropriate for his status and for the ends he had in view.[36] Neither Christ nor the apostles nor the Fathers of the Church like Basil, Benedict, Jerome, or Augustine practiced poverty the way the "friars preacher and the friars minor" practice it today. If Christ had practiced poverty "exemplariter" according to the principles of these two mendicant orders, how explain that the Church did not discover this example for twelve hundred years?[37] That poverty is "perfect" and sufficient, even for those who profess it by vow, which excludes avarice and which inhibits excessive solicitude for temporal

33. See, e.g., the "Vita" in *Vita praecellentissimi ecclesiae doctoris divi Aurelii Augustini. Commentarii super regula sancti Augustini* (Rome: G. Herolt, 1481), Hain #*5683, fol. [10ᵛ]; the commentary on the "third Rule," *ibid.*, fols. [24ᵛ, 27ᵛ–30ʳ, 62ᵛ–63ʳ]; the commentary on the "second Rule," *ibid.*, fol. [216ᵛ].

34. See, e.g., Domenichi, *Tractatus*, fol. [3ʳ–ᵛ]; Pimpinella (?), "Pro electione summi pontificis oratio," Bibl. del Conte Alessandro Marcello del Majno, Venice, cod. Serie A.I, Busta 5, Fasc. b, fols. [4ʳ–5ʳ].

35. See, e.g., "Pars prima operis de ecclesia destituta," BAV cod. Vat. lat. 5568, fols. 64ᵛ, 79ʳ–ᵛ; "De angelico pastore opusculum," BAV cod. Vat. lat. 5578, fols. 32ʳ–41ʳ.

36. See "Libellus de paupertate Christi," BAV cod. Vat. lat. 969, fols. 11ʳ–26ᵛ.

37. See *ibid.*, fol. 48ʳ. See also *ibid.*, fols. 36ᵛ, 40ʳ.

goods.[38] As conceived by Arévalo, the poverty of the primitive Church is characterized by its moderation and rationality.

Pius II, even before he became pope, rejected out of hand the idea that the Roman Curia should be "poor and medicant." The pope needed good counselors, and such counselors could not be brought to Rome and supported there without money. According to Pius, nowhere in the world was there another curia so glorious for its learned and morally worthy men— for its wisdom, its order, and its good observances. To say the least, Pius saw no inherent contradiction between the primitive Church and the Curia of his own day.[39]

Aside from the more or less traditional "imitation of Christ" in charity, forgiveness, simplicity, and other virtues, there is very little in the preachers about the "ecclesia primitiva." Giles of Viterbo's "Historia XX saeculorum" describes the poverty of that Church at length. He also draws a number of interesting parallels between various events and institutions of the Old Testament and the history of the Church even in his own times;[40] but these ideas are much less fully developed in the writings of other preachers.[41]

Domenichi and Aurelio Brandolini, on the other hand, surely wanted to witness a rebirth of the eloquence and "pristine dignity" of the Church of the Fathers.[42] Other preachers, by their frequent praise of the *exempla* and *doctrina* of the great figures of the patristic era, betray an appreciation for the accomplishments of that age which made it a model against which to measure the Church that they daily experienced.

In a more immediate fashion than others of their era who spoke of the reform of the Church, the preachers at the papal court were conscious of its "Roman" character. Although their sense of discrimination between Christian and pagan precluded their taking ancient Roman institutions as models in the same degree as the heavenly court and the primitive

38. See *ibid.*, fol. 28[r-v].

39. "Apologia ad Martinum Mayer," in *Commentarii rerum memorabilium* (Rome: D. Basae, 1584), pp. 736–40. Angelo of Vallombrosa (Angelo Leonora) regretted the pope did not have more money—with which to keep kings and princes disciplined and to finance a war against the Turks. *Oratio Angeli anachoritae Vallisumbrosae pro concilio Lateranensi* [n.p.: n. publ., 1511], fol. [3[r-v]].

40. See my *Giles of Viterbo*, esp. pp. 100–38.

41. The first book of Galatino's "Opus de ecclesia instituta," BAV cod. Vat. lat. 5575, fols. 8[r]–88[r], examines the Church according to "figures" from the Old Testament.

42. See Domenichi, *Liber de dignitate episcopali* (Rome: G. Salomoni, 1757), pp. 1–2; Brandolini, "Epitoma in sacram Iudaeorum historiam," BAV cod. Ottob. lat. 438, fol. 8[r].

Church, they looked back at those Roman institutions with genuine admiration.

The Church was the "Res publica Christiana." It was the "Imperium Romanum." Such terminology considerably antedates the Renaissance.[43] The preachers adopted this and similar terminology and used it with some frequency. Though they were perfectly aware of the distinction between the Church and the Empire of their own day, their vocabulary often blurs that distinction. It is noteworthy that in 1517 an Italian Dominican, Isidoro Isolani, published a book *De imperio militantis ecclesiae libri quattuor* in which he explicitly dealt with the question of whether the term "imperium" could appropriately be applied to the Church.[44] He answered affirmatively.

It would take us far beyond the scope of this book to examine what impact this easy exchange of vocabulary had on the thinking of the preachers, especially since this examination would require a detailed study for each individual. The problem, needless to say, is not now being raised for the first time. Even though it cannot here be resolved, we must nonetheless advert to it while we ask what models were explicitly or implicitly operative in the preachers' consciousness as they elaborated their ideal of reform. It can at least be asserted that the loss of territory to the Turks evoked a nostalgic recall of the universality of the ancient empire after Constantine when all the known world was Christian. At the court the voyages of discovery and the overseas conquests of the Spaniards and Portuguese were sometimes viewed as compensation for that loss and as earnests of its imminent recovery.[45]

For the preachers "Rome" meant something even more immediate and important than the great universal institution of antiquity. Rome was the *city*—the city in which they lived and, in most cases, the city they had adopted. On April 20, 1483, Pomponio Leto initiated the celebration in Rome of the legendary anniversary of the founding of the city—Rome's "birthday." The tradition has continued through the centuries down to the present day. During the Renaissance the choir and some officials of the papal court lent the support of their presence and their talents to the

43. On this question, see, e.g., Robert Folz, *L'idée d'Empire en Occident du Vᵉ au XIVᵉ siècle* (Paris: Aubier, 1953); J. B. Sägmüller, "Die Idee von der Kirche als Imperium Romanum im kanonischen Recht," *Theologische Quartalschrift*, 80 (1898), 50–80.
44. Milan: G. Ponticus, 1517.
45. See my "Discovery of America."

festivity.[46] The inauguration of the celebration during the Renaissance was symptomatic of the Romans' new appreciation for their city.

The preachers at the court appropriated and promoted the mystique of Rome that Leto's celebration suggested. Erasmus affirmed that ancient Rome was dead and that the present city, apart from the Curia and its hangers-on, was nothing but ruins. It possessed nothing but the scars and scabs of its mortal wounds.[47] The preachers were aware of the ruins and the wounds. They nevertheless found in the city a meaning that allowed them to transcend its problems and find in its supernatural destiny a basis for hope for all the world. Not infrequently they asserted that the Rome of the Renaissance popes surpassed, or gave promise of surpassing, the excellence of the Rome of Cicero and Caesar. Certainly, Christian Rome was better than pagan Rome.[48] The reproaches the preachers sometimes addressed to the city emanated from their sense of discrepancy between the city's true dignity and the often unworthy lives of the men who now lived in it. As in the case of the Church itself, it was not the institution that was to be faulted but the "men and the times" in which that institution was immersed.

The appreciation that the preachers had for the city of Rome rested in part on their own experience as foreigners who had been received into it as into the "patria communis." The term was traditional, classical in inspiration, but it found frequent use in the Renaissance.[49] When the

46. See Burchard, *Liber Notarum*, II, 278–80; Jacopo Gherardi, *Il diario romano*, ed. Enrico Carusi, RIS, 23.3 (Città di Castello: S. Lapi, 1904), 117. For a description of the images of Rome in the minds of its citizens during an earlier era, see Robert Brentano, *Rome before Avignon: A Social History of Thirteenth-Century Rome* (New York: Basic Books, 1974), pp. 73–90. See also Arturo Graf, *Roma nella memoria e nelle immaginazioni del medio evo* (Turin: E. Loescher, 1915), and David Thompson, ed., *The Idea of Rome: From Antiquity to the Renaissance* (Albuquerque: University of New Mexico Press, 1971).

47. *Ciceronianus*, ASD, I.2, 693–94.

48. See, e.g., Marcello, *Oratio in die omnium sanctorum* [Rome: M. Silber?, after Nov. 1, 1511], fol. [2ʳ]; Domenichi, "Oratio in laudem civitatis et civilitatis Romanae," BAV cod. Ottob. lat. 1035, fols. 86ʳ–87ʳ; Zenobius Acciaiuoli, *Oratio in laudem urbis Romae* [Rome: J. Mazochius, 1518]; my "Man's Dignity, God's Love, and the Destiny of Rome: A Text of Giles of Viterbo," *Viator*, 3 (1972), 389–416. See also Chapter Four, "Roma, Caput Mundi," in Egmont Lee, *Sixtus IV and Men of Letters*, Temi e Testi, No. 26 (Rome: Storia e Letteratura, 1978), pp. 123–50.

49. The phrase was an ancient *topos*, which in fact can be traced back to Isocrates; see James H. Oliver, "The Ruling Power: A Study of the Roman Empire in the Second Century After Christ through the Roman Oration of Aelius Aristides," *Transactions of the American Philosophical Society*, NS 43 (1953), 928. See also Igino Cecchetti, *Roma nobilis: L'idea, la missione, le memorie, il destino di Roma* (Rome: Edizioni arte e scienza, 1953), p. 86, where he lists Cicero [cf. 1 Cat. 7.17], Seneca, the Digest, (Cassiodorus), and Bartolo di Sassoferrato as sources. Bruni applies the term to

Romans conferred citizenship upon Domenichi, he celebrated in his oration the city's character as the "common fatherland," and reviewed the history of great men from antiquity down to his own day who had found in Rome their true home, "communis patria amicorum et sociorum."[50] This sentiment of Domenichi, the Venetian, was shared by other preachers like Carvajal, the Spaniard,[51] like Ioannes Sambocius, the Pole,[52] like Aurelio and Raphael Brandolini, the Florentines.[53] Though Aurelio saw in the open arms Rome extended to foreigners one of the sources of its moral problems,[54] he nonetheless celebrated it as "patria communis" for Sixtus IV, the Ligurian.

Erasmus distinguished *res* from *verba*. He asserted that today, if one looked at reality and refused to be dazzled by words, being a citizen of Rome meant less than being a citizen of Basel. Praise of Rome? Enough of these "epideictics"! How much better it would be to compose orations which lead the soul to the worship of Christ and inflame it with the love of piety![55] Erasmus was a citizen of the world and allowed no city to put a claim on him. The preachers did not wish to embrace such neutrality. Rome was a city like no other. The preachers did not perceive a discrepancy between praise of it and Christian piety.

In his writings, Giles of Viterbo gave elaborate expression to a mystique of the city. In other preachers are found only suggestions of such a mystique, but there is no doubt about their conviction that Rome had a special dignity and responsibility. Domenichi, immediately after his long celebration of Rome as "patria communis," turns in his oration to Rome's more specifically Christian glory. He paraphrases and adapts words from the first Epistle of Peter (2:9) to apply them to Rome and its citizens. Rome

Florence in his *Laudatio*; see the edition by Hans Baron in his *From Petrarch to Leonardo Bruni: Studies in Humanistic and Political Literature* (Chicago: University of Chicago Press, 1968), p. 251.

50. "Oratio in laudem civitatis et civilitatis Romanae," BAV cod. Ottob. lat. 1035, fols. 84^v–86^r.

51. *Oratio super praestanda solemni obedientia sanctissimo domino nostro Alexandro papae VI* [Rome: S. Plannck, after June 19, 1493], GKW #6145, fols. [2^v–3^r].

52. *Oratio in festo solemni divinae Trinitatis* [Rome: S. Guiletus and E. Nani, 1514], fol. [1^v].

53. A. Brandolini, "De laudibus beatissimi patris Sixti IV pontificis maximi libri," BAV cod. Urb. lat. 739, fol. 59^r; R. Brandolini, "Oratio ad Lateranense concilium," BAV cod. Ottob. lat. 813, fols. 50^v–51^r, and *Oratio de obitu Dominici Ruvere* [Rome: E. Silber, 1501], fol. [6^v].

54. "Oratio praeclarissimo viro Antonio Lauredano," BAV cod. Reg. lat. 1368, fol. 66^{r-v}.

55. *Ciceronianus*, ASD, I.2, 694–96.

is "a holy nation, an elect people, a priestly city."[56] This paraphrase is lifted verbatim from Leo the Great's sermon on the feast of Peter and Paul.[57]

Leo's point is that, because Rome is now the "see of blessed Peter," it has become the "caput orbis." The preachers followed Leo's example in conjoining the idea of Rome as the see of Peter and Rome as head of the world. Like Leo, they found universalistic implications in this conjunction. Arévalo, therefore, called upon "Roma felix" to rejoice in its dignity.[58] Domenichi saw Rome as decorated with the "doctrina" and the "vitae exempla" of both Peter and Paul.[59] Rome ought to be, says Raphael Brandolini, "the perpetual domicile of wisdom and virtue." It is "the parent of the whole Christian Republic."[60] This vision of the meaning of Rome is not significant for any originality but for the frequency with which it recurs.

If "public men" and leaders in society have a special obligation to be an example to others and to be a "mirror" of the virtues, the obligation of the "Roman Church" was similar. It was, as Celadoni said in his "Ad elegendum" for the successor to Alexander VI, not only the "caput orbis," but also a "norma" and a "speculum."[61] The most effective causality it could exercise was exemplary.

The application of terms like "norma," "speculum," and "exemplar" to Rome, to the Apostolic See, to the papal household, and to the Roman Curia was common in the documents at the papal court.[62] The applica-

56. "Oratio in laudem civitatis et civilitatis Romanae," BAV cod. Ottob. lat. 1035, fols. 86ʳ–87ʳ.

57. "Sermo LXXXII. In natali apostolorum Petri et Pauli," PL 54, 422–23. See also Cecchetti, Roma nobilis, pp. 85–86.

58. "Sermo in die apostolorum Petri et Pauli," BAV cod. Vat. lat. 4881, fols. 248ᵛ–249ʳ.

59. "Oratio pro electione summi pontificis," BAV cod. Ottob. lat. 1035, fol. 11ʳ.

60. R. Brandolini, "Oratio de obitu Mariani Genazanensis," BAV cod. Vat. lat. 10806, fol. 58ᵛ. See also his "Oratio ad Lateranense concilium," BAV cod. Ottob. lat. 813, fols. 4ᵛ, 8ʳ. Similar ideas occur, e.g., in Schomberg, "Tertia oratio. Ductus est Iesus in desertum," in Orationes vel potius divinorum eloquiorum enodationes, fol. [8ʳ⁻ᵛ]; Casali, "Oratio in die omnium sanctorum," Bibl. Ambr. cod. G.33 inf., II, fol. 9ʳ⁻ᵛ; Galatino, "De angelico pastore opusculum," BAV cod. Vat. lat. 5578, fols. 39ʳ–40ʳ; Andrea Piperari, Oratio de passione Iesu Christi redemptoris nostri ([Rome: E. Silber], 1508), fol. [10ʳ].

61. Oratio ad sacrum cardinalium senatum ingressurum ad novum pontificem eligendum [Rome: J. Besicken, 1503], fol. [5ᵛ], in the modern edition by John M. McManamon, "The Ideal Renaissance Pope: Funeral Oratory from the Papal Court," Archivum Historiae Pontificiae, 14 (1976), p. 68.

62. See, e.g., the "Prima congeries rudior" of Alexander's reform bull, BAV cod.

tion to courts and monarchs was common in the general political literature of the era, but for the institutions we are considering it was
particularly evocative of ecclesiastical traditions that would be familiar to
many of the preachers.[63] As the frequency with which these terms were
employed by the preachers indicates, Rome's obligation to act as exemplary center was certainly among its chief duties. Rome's failure to provide that example elicited from them their severest words of reproach.

Reform your Church, and reform your Curia! This is the message the
preachers delivered in blunt terms. Domenichi's *Tractatus* informed Pius
II that it was futile to try to stave off the rebellion of princes with the
words, "The Temple of the Lord! The Temple of the Lord! That is—The
Roman Church! The Roman Church!" Because of the bad lives of prelates and members of the Curia, the princes called that Church "Babylon,
the mother of all fornications and abominations of the earth!"[64]

With Sixtus IV seated in his presence, Niccolò Capranica in his funeral
eulogy for Bessarion told his audience how the cardinal esteemed and
favored learned and virtuous men and how he hated men who were lazy
and pursued a life of piggish sensuality, the likes of which "the Roman
Curia is full."[65] Jacopo Gherardi reports how vehemently Paolo Tos-
canella, one of the judges of the Rota, reproached Sixtus and his court
in his sermon for Ascension Thursday, 1482, and Gherardi describes

---

Vat. lat. 3883, fol. 142ʳ; Pius II, "Apologia ad Martinum Mayer," in *Commentarii*, p.
744, and "Pastor aeternus," in Haubst's "Der Reformentwurf," p. 210; Arévalo,
Speculum vitae humanae (Paris: M. Soly, 1656), fol. a.vᵛ. See also Flavio Biondo's
"Prooemium" to his *De Roma triumphante* (Basel: Froben, 1531), p. 2.

63. On the force of the idea of moral exemplarity, esp. of the "exemplum cari-
tatis," in the Fathers, its relationship to the question of papal authority and order in
the Church, and its articulation in the canonical tradition of the Middle Ages, see
Ludwig Buisson, *Potestas und Caritas: Die päpstliche Gewalt im Spätmittelalter*,
Forschungen zur kirchlichen Rechtsgeschichte und zum Kirchenrecht, No. 2 (Cologne:
Böhlau, 1958), esp. pp. 17–73.

64. Fol. [4ʳ]: "Et non prodest nobis dicere, Templum Domini, Templum Domini,
Iere. vii, sive Romana Ecclesia, Romana Ecclesia, quia potius appellant Babylonem
iuxta dictum 2 Petri ultimo et Apoc. xvi, matrem fornicationum et abominationum
terrae."

65. "Nicolai episcopi Firmani oratio in funere Bessarionis," in *Kardinal Bessarion
als Theologe, Humanist und Staatsmann*, ed. Ludwig Mohler, III (Paderborn: F.
Schöningh, 1967), 411: "Ingenuos namque et doctos amabat Nicaenus, nec in peni-
tiorem ad familiaritatem admittebat nisi ingenio, doctrina et moribus egregios atque
praestantes. Hebetes, tardos et ventri ac somno deditos tamquam ignavum pecus et
Epicuri de grege porcos a praesepibus, ut sic loquar, arcebat nec quoque pacto eiusmodi ventris animalia, quibus—pro nefas—plena est Romana curia, videre et pati
poterat. Nec minus abhorrebat delatores, susurrores, rumigerulos, adulatores, quos
venenum et pestem curiae appellabat."

the sense of guilt some of the listeners manifested and the satisfaction of others with the oration.[66]

Guillaume Pérès's words to the cardinals about to elect a successor to Sixtus are extraordinarily straightforward about the corruption in the Curia which the new pope must extirpate.[67] Though Pérès and other preachers tried to strengthen their case by insisting that the Curia had once enjoyed a good name, Domenico Capranica was trying to combat its ill fame as early as the pontificate of Nicholas V.[68] As we know from many other sources, slurs against the Roman Curia reach much farther back into history than even that pontificate.[69]

66. *Diario*, p. 100: "Omeliam autem huius diei solemnis peroravit venerandus pater Paulus Tuscanella, ex ordine iudicum Rotae palatinae, vir integerrimae famae et summae auctoritatis apud omnes curiales. Oratio eius vehemens habita nimium. Invectus in pontificem est vehementer, licet absentem, et in suos omnes. A senatoribus etiam non abstinuit, adeo ut chorus universus tali oratione commotus sit; plerique pudore quodam, quod nimis aperte obloquebatur, vultum dimittebant, non ausi illum intueri, plerique fixos oculos in eum tenebant, vim orationis et oratoris intrepidum animum admirantes. Fuere nonnulli qui non tam orationem quam vigorem orationis commendarunt, laetantes inveniri virum fortem et lingua liberum, qui absque formidine loqueretur. Audio relatam fuisse pontifici hominis huius libertatem in dicendo ac subrisisse."

67. *Sermo super electione futuri pontificis* [Rome: S. Plannck, 1484?], Hain #*12588, fol. [4ʳ]: "Romanam curiam facto non inanibus verbis reformare curabit, ut ex ea tantus vanitatis, corruptionis et carnalis immunditiae fetor procul abigatur. Nam ab his letale venenum conficitur quod fidelibus visu vel fama propinatum omnem in eis devotionem religionis extinguit et ecclesiae Romanae perimit auctoritatem. Paulatim haec vitia primo, per quamdam alluvionem multorum animos occuparunt et interdum etiam vindicata fuerunt. At nunc illorum contagio velut generalis pestilentia totam curiam invasit, et corrupti mores quos haec pessima ac diversa inter se mala luxuria atque avaritia gignunt curiam ipsam ab omni honestate dispoliarunt. Quodque deterius est et magis pernitiosum exemplo [sic] inveniuntur multi quibus non satis est haec mala impune perpetrare nisi etiam velut de pudicitia ceterisque virtutibus subversis triumphantes in malefactis publice glorientur. Olim, dum boni mores in Romana curia colebantur, gradus ad dignitates et honores non nisi per virtutes et litteras aperiebatur. At nunc, postquam inter bonos et malos nullum discrimen est et omnia virtutis praemia ambitio possidet ac avaritia cunctas bonas artes subvertit, . . . Eligatur ergo pontifex qui talia abhorreat et pastorali sarculo radicem illorum extirpet."

68. See his "Quaedam avisamenta super reformatione papae et Romanae curiae," BAV cod. Vat. lat. 4039, fol. 17ᵛ. On fol. 17ʳ, he says: "Taceo de moribus curiae, quae polluit terram in fornicationibus suis, nam rei magnitudine et pudore ipso dicendi vincitur omnis sermo." See also Lapo da Castiglionchio's defense of the Curia in his "Dialogus de Curiae Commodis," 1438, in *Prosatori latini del Quattrocento*, ed. Eugenio Garin, La letteratura italiana, Storia e Testi, No. 13 (Milano: Ricciardi, n.d.), pp. 167–211.

69. See, e.g., John A. Yunck, "Economic Conservatism, Papal Finance, and the Medieval Satires on Rome," in *Change in Medieval Society: Europe North of the Alps, 1050–1500*, ed. Sylvia Thrupp (New York: Appleton-Century-Crofts, 1964), 72–85, and Josef Benzinger, *Invectiva in Romam: Romkritik im Mittelalter von 9. bis zum 12. Jahrhundert*, Historische Studien, No. 404 (Lübeck: Mattheisen Verlag, 1968).

Baptista Mantuanus, in the peroration of his sermon for All Saints, 1488, in the presence of Innocent VIII excoriated the luxury and display of high churchmen. These prelates, dressed in purple, own more gold and silver vessels in their private collections than do the basilicas of God and his saints. Christ ate bread, which he often had to beg, but they have set before them at one meal fish and fowl and game—with no thought of God's law, no thought of scandal, no thought of the needs of the poor. Mantuanus's criticisms are the standard ones directed against the lifestyle of the cardinals of the Curia, and he must have had them especially in mind.[70]

On the feast of Saint Stephen, 1496, the Dominican Raynaldus Mons Aureus, in an apostrophe to Alexander VI, told him that it did no good to have recourse to God in prayer unless he provided that the city of Rome be purged of its blasphemies, of its incitements to lust, and of the burdens and vexations of the Curia. By the example of such a purgation, the whole Church would be cleansed.[71] Upon the death of Alexander,

---

70. "Oratio in omnium sanctorum celebritate," Bibl. Com. Ariostea, Ferrara, cod. II.162, fols. 141^v–142^r: "Certe neque Christus neque Christi familia fuit huius tanti luxus exemplar quantus hac nostra tempestate quorumdam virorum ecclesiasticorum mores invasit, et eorum praecipue qui, modum atque modestiam praetergressi, purpurati trabeatique, unguentis delibuti et calamistrati, ferocibus et phaleratis equis quasi de Mithridate triumphantes invehuntur. . . . Christus per omnem vitam una, et ea quidem humili, veste contentus in alienis semper aedibus pane, ut plurimum mendicato, vescebatur. Nos autem, dum quidquid errat in terris, quidquid natat in undis, quidquid volat in aëre una mensa consumimus, nulla de Dei lege, nulla de scandalo, nulla vel certe postrema est cura de miseris. Praetereo vasa aurea, Attalica ornamenta, quorum copia maior est in privatis aedibus quam in sanctorum Deique basilicis. Taceo domos caelo erectas, tot praeambulorum et sequentium pompas, tot servorum greges, tantum lascivae iuventutis pelagus."

71. *Oratio de visione Dei* [n.p.: n. publ., after Dec. 26, 1496], Hain #*11548, fol. [6^r–^{v}]: "Nos enim, pro dolor, neque sanctorum martyrum testimoniis commovemur, neque divinis flagellis emendamur, bellis concutimur, aquarum inundationibus agitamur, pestem et famem instare videmus, et tamen iratum Deum placare non curamus. In qua re, pater beatissime, etsi religiose factum est a Sanctitate tua, cum post formidandum Tiberis excursum ad Deum recurri iussisti, tamen (cum gratia et venia ipsius dixerim) si a tot summi Dei blasphemiis, a tot libidinum incitamentis ac tendiculis, a tot curiae oneribus vexationibusque urbem Romam et eius exemplo universam ecclesiam non purgaveris, frustra recurretur ad Deum, frustra divina poscentur auxilia. Haec enim eiusmodi sunt ut non solum in auctores, verum etiam in permissores indignatio divina descendat. Scriptum est enim, Illi quidem in suo peccato morientur, sanguinem autem eorum de manu speculatoris requiram. Age, igitur, beatissime pater, et sicut moenia urbis erexisti, templa exornasti, arcem sancti Angeli mirabilis artificii et impensae surgere praecepisti, ita ad componendos mores diligentius animum tuae Sanctitatis adiungas, impiissimos blasphemos compescas, obscoenitatis laqueos dissolvas et conteras, avaritiam et cetera quae furorem divinum provocant super grege tibi commisso regnare non sinas. Quae si, ut spero, feceris, placatus Deus aperiet nobis caelos, ut cum beato Stephano videamus Dominum nostrum Iesum Christum sedentem

Celadoni informed the cardinals that there was no health in the body of the Church, for from the head corruption had flowed to the whole organism.[72]

When Pedro Flores addressed the cardinals entering conclave to elect a successor to Julius II in 1513, he begged them to elect a man who would "correct even the offices of this Curia of yours."[73] Flores then shared with the cardinals some of his personal experience. He had spent time in Spain, France, and Germany. In those countries the people were accustomed to reverence the name of the city where the see of Peter and the authority of Christ were located. But Flores had had to contend with them in defense of the present condition of Rome, for they said it had fallen into the hands of pillagers and robbers. Virtue and discipline, Flores warned the cardinals, must replace the pursuit of wealth and worldly gain—good men must replace bad![74]

Raphael Brandolini's oration for the Lateran Council maintains that the corruption of Rome is the cause for the corruption of the Church. "Begin your reform with the reform of this city."[75] A long section of the oration deplores the bad example that Rome, the popes, and the cardinals have given to the world.[76] Brandolini implores the cardinals to lead lives above reproach. He dares not tell them what he hears people whispering behind their backs about their conduct or what horrible fates people wish for them.[77]

---

a dextris Dei patris omnipotentis. Dixi." Cardinal Oliviero Carafa, who was not present for this sermon, requested a copy in writing from Mons Aureus. This request encouraged the friar to have the sermon printed; see fol. [1ᵛ].

72. *Oratio ad sacrum cardinalium senatum ingressurum ad novum pontificem eligendum*, fol. [5ᵛ]; in McManamon's edition, "Ideal Renaissance Pope," p. 68.

73. *Oratio de summo pontifice eligendo* (Rome: n. publ., 1513), fols. [9ᵛ–10ʳ].

74. *Ibid.*, fol. [10ʳ]: "Fui ego apud Hispanos, gentem meam, Gallos, Germanos. Solent ad nomen urbis, ubi sedes Petri, ubi potestas Christi sit, trepidare. Magna tamen mihi saepe cum illis pro dignitate ipsius urbis pugna fuit. Eam enim aiebant expilatoribus esse expositam. Desciscat iam studium a lucro ad virtutem, a divitiis ad disciplinam liberaliorem. Redeat multitudo illa clarissimorum virorum qui ad hanc vestram urbem tamquam ad spem vitae honestissimae undique gentium solebant concurrere! Id facile fiet, si merita hominum non pecuniae censebuntur, si viderimus honoris tantum cuique non esse quantum in censu sit."

75. "Oratio ad Lateranense concilium," BAV cod. Ottob. lat. 813, fols. 56ᵛ–57ʳ: "Hanc [urbem] primum, ut par est, reformate! Huius mores, instituta, ritus disciplinasque ad veterem integritatem, ad pristinam sanctitatem, ad pietatem, ad innocentiam revocate! Amplissimis hanc, ut coepistis, aedificiis decorate, ut ab hac una universi terrarum orbis gentes et nationes veteri instituto privatae ac publicae vitae normam, honorum et dignitatum insignia, calamitatum perfugia et postulent et expectent."

76. *Ibid.*, fol. 23ᵛ–28ʳ.

77. *Ibid.*, fol. 26ʳ: "Supprimam ego honoris ac observantiae causa qui de vestris

Martinus de Viana in his Ash Wednesday sermon of 1496 calls the prelates sitting before him to conversion and to reform of life. He says he fears offending them, but he fears all the more that those who contemn the precepts of God and the Church will persevere in their obstinacy. After a series of indicting rhetorical questions, he exclaims, "The soul is too repelled by the degeneracy of our times to continue!"[78]

One of the longest and most effective reproaches addressed to the cardinals was by Bernardino Carvajal in his oration for the election of a successor to Innocent VIII. The Roman Church was once "the teacher of discipline, the school of virtue, and rich in holy and learned men." Now it is replete with crime and every concupiscence. Who would deny that the city of Rome is "the sinful woman"? She is filled with pride, luxury, avarice—and worse![79] Do not tell me, he continues, that it has ever been

---

actionibus in templis, in compitis, in domesticis penetralibus sermones interim habeantur, qui risus subsannationesque excitentur, quae passim texantur fabellae, quam acuta vestris capitibus atque praecordiis spicula defigantur, quae vestrae ad extremum calamitates atque iacturae prophanis ingratae ac molestae numquam accidant. Quod sane periculum atque discrimen utinam, patres, utinam vestro incommodo ac detrimento non aliquando fecissetis, maior vestrae dignitatis et famae ab universo mortalium coetu ratio haberetur." Brandolini's oration for the council is broader in outlook than Gianfrancesco Pico's, but the moralistic emphasis is similar; see Schmitt, "Gianfrancesco Pico."

78. *Oratio in die cinerum*, fol. [6ʳ]: "Rem profecto terribilem dico. Ex utroque conturbor: timeo auditores offendere, sed plus timeo Dei praeceptorum ac ecclesiasticae honestatis contemptores in sua obstinatione remanere. Consideremus, quaeso, si viri ecclesiastici bonique apostolorum successores simus. Quid in nobis postquam sacros ordines pastoraleque officium suscepimus virtutis accesserit? Quid humilitatis in prosperis? Quid . . . ? . . . . Alii de virtute cotidie transeunt ad virtutem, nos de infirmitate ad infirmitatem. Alii meliores per flagella fiunt, nos deteriores saepe efficimur. Horret animus nostrorum temporum ruinas prosequi!"

79. *Oratio de eligendo summo pontifice*, fol. [4ʳ⁻ᵛ]: "Egressus est a filia Sion omnis decor eius, et quae vere olim magistra fuit disciplinae, virtutum schola, locuplex sanctis et doctis, pro dolor, his omnibus in maiori parte vacua, universorum criminum amaritudine repleta est, et quod Ioannes partit omne mundanum crimen triplici capite, concupiscentia carnis, concupiscentia oculorum, superbia vitae, nonne id omne nos quatit, patres? Utinam quateret modo! Utinam pulsaret tantum et non iam irruisset, quin immo rupisset et violasset claustra pudoris et integritatis Romanae ecclesiae. Famosam peccatricem quis ambigit urbem Romam? De qua et utinam Deus sicut ab illa evangelica septem eiiciat daemonia, quorum servit multitudini. Bone Deus, quanta istic criminum alluvio! Horret tamen animus dicere quando meminit fidem Petri. Sed numquid nos blandiendo silebimus quod in plateis et tectis malefactis nostris publicavimus? Quid enim apud nos non sibi vindicat luxus? Quem locum superbia non implet? Cui parcit avaritia? Quem non subigit auri sacra fames [Verg. A. 3.57]? Quid si ulterius descendam? Iubeat tamen hic Plato quiescere. Fumabunt nempe vitiorum stercora, et sola ipsa narratio templum hoc sacratissimum polluet. Consulto praeteream urbis et curiae nostrae excessus ac deformia membratim distinguere, ne parentis videar pudenda revelare."

thus and that even the just man falls seven times a day. The crimes have never been so monstrous, never so frequent, never so public, never so unpunished—indeed, never so well rewarded as today. If we ask why the whole body of the Church is sick or if we ask whence come these ills, we have to reply that it is from "the head." It is from "the exemplar." Though Carvajal's recriminations are meant at least by implication to include the cardinals as well as the Curia and the whole city of Rome, he clearly has the pope himself in mind when he here speaks of the head and exemplar.

Aurelio Brandolini criticized preachers and orators at the court who did not know how to praise the present pope without reproaching his predecessors.[80] We are thus justified in assuming that such a practice was tolerated and was perhaps even more frequently employed than the documents that survive indicate. As McManamon's study of papal funeral oratory shows, we have what seems to be a uniquely bold and important instance of reproach of a recently deceased pontiff in Celadoni's oration for the election of a successor to Alexander VI.[81]

Raphael Brandolini's correspondence during that pontificate reveals that even while Alexander was alive, Raphael was not hesitant to pass strongly negative judgments on what was happening in the papal palace.[82] When he criticized Alexander by name years later in his dialogue *Leo*, he was not thereby merely indulging in a style of vituperation that was expected or tolerated but that had no basis in the orator's genuine assessment.[83] He was not merely adapting himself "to the subject, the occasion, and the audience."

At least three sermons *inter missarum solemnia* during Alexander's pontificate are notable for calling upon him to undertake the reform of the Church over which he presided. I refer to the orations of de Viana for Ash Wednesday, of Inghirami for All Saints, and of Mons Aureus for the feast of Saint Stephen.[84] The sermons of de Viana and Mons

---

80. *De ratione scribendi libri tres* (Cologne: A. Birckmannus, 1573), p. 65.

81. "Ideal Renaissance Pope," esp. pp. 54–70.

82. See, e.g., the letters to Manfredus de Manfredis, Sept. 13 and Nov. 7, 1500, Rome, in "Einige Briefe von Raphael Brandolinus. Migetheilt von Dr. Gisbert Brom," *Römische Quartalschrift*, 2 (1888), pp. 190–95.

83. *Leo*, p. 78: " . . . qui locupletandae ac supra modum attollendae domesticae posteritatis cupiditate incensus, . . ." See also his "Oratio ad Lateranense concilium," BAV cod. Ottob. lat. 813, fol. 31^{r-v}, for what can be construed as a criticism of both Sixtus IV and Alexander VI.

84. De Viana, *Oratio in die cinerum*, fols. [5^v–6^v]; Inghirami, "In laudem omnium

Aureus are also notable for being delivered in the same year, 1496, the year before Alexander's famous "conversion" after the murder of the Duke of Gandia. It was in June of 1497 that Alexander constituted the reform commission that eventually produced the bull "In apostolicae sedis specula." There is no evidence to suggest that these two sermons had a direct influence on the pope's decision to undertake the reform of the Church, a reform for which pressure came to bear upon him from so many quarters. But we should at least notice that the sermons anticipated the pope's decision and were not composed in order to please him by confirming a decision already taken.

Alexander's bull is dependent upon its predecessors. Pius II begins "Pastor aeternus" with the proposition that the pope, in imitation of Jesus himself, must show the "way of life" to his flock by his deeds as well as by his words. Therefore, he will undertake the reform of the Roman Curia so that others can imitate him.[85] This idea is found in the reform memorials prepared for Pius by Cusa and Domenichi. The bull prepared for Alexander is even stronger. Jesus taught by his deeds *before* he taught by his words. The pope must first reform himself and his household, for the imitation of others.[86] The idea that the pope was a mirror of the virtues and should reform others by his example is often found in the documents circulating at the court.[87]

Domenichi's brief "Expositio psalmi centesimi," almost certainly written to accompany his *Tractatus* on reform, enumerates ten provisions to be observed by "the ideal pope." These ten can be reduced to two: (1) the pope must himself so live that he be "exemplar et regula aliorum"; (2) he must remove vicious men from his household and Curia, and he must replace them with good.[88] That is, he must remove detractors who stir up dissension, cardinals and prelates who pant after dignities, and he must replace them with men who want to serve others. In particular, as Bernard advised Eugene, he must choose cardinals from among men "of every land" and not merely from his own. Domenichi is characteristically con-

---

sanctorum oratio," Bibl. Guarn. cod. LIII.4.8, fols. 48^v–49^v; Mons Aureus, *Oratio de visione Dei*, fol. [6^{r-v}].

85. See "Pastor aeternus" in Haubst, "Der Reformentwurf," p. 205.

86. Alexander VI, "In apostolicae sedis specula," Arch. Seg. Vat., Misc. Arm. XI.88, fol. 1^v.

87. See, e.g., Massimo Miglio, *Storiografia pontificia del Quattrocento* (Bologna: Patròn, 1975), pp. 1–30, 61–118.

88. BAV cod. Barb. lat. 1201, fols. 20^r–21^v.

cerned about the quality of the men who will function within a given structure, not with a change of the structure itself. As he says in the *Tractatus*: "And true reform of the Church consists in this: . . . that virtuous and learned men be promoted to offices."[89]

Both of Domenichi's documents contain clearly implied cautions about nepotism, an abuse to which other preachers also referred. Of particular importance on this question of nepotism is Pérès's "Super electione" for the successor to Sixtus IV. In insisting that relatives not be favored at the expense of the Church, Pérès was undoubtedly criticizing the notorious nepotism of the late pope, whose powerful nephew Giuliano was in his audience.[90]

As Iserloh has pointed out, Cusa's reform memorial contained an important provision that Pius's bull, like those of Sixtus and Alexander, omitted. To assure that the reform of the Roman Church and Curia be carried out effectively, Cusa proposed that these institutions be "visited" by the same three-man commission intended for the visitation of the Church at large.[91] Pius took the much less specific course of calling for "fraternal admonitions from all" as the method for dealing with the reform of Roman Church and Curia. This significant deviation from Cusa's document directs attention to the sensitive issue of the authority of the ideal pope. Jedin has studied in considerable detail the theological and juridical problems concerning the pope's relationship to councils and to the college of cardinals as they were debated in the late Quattrocento.[92]

---

89. *Tractatus*, fol. [14ᵛ]: "Et in hoc consistit vera [text=verae] ecclesiae reformatio potius quam in frenis equorum vel in biretis et habitu, ut scilicet virtuosi et scientifici promoveantur, quia haec graviora sunt legis, quae oportet facere et illa omnia priora [text=prona] non omittere."

90. *Sermo super electione futuri pontificis*, fols. [3ᵛ–4ʳ]: "Non aedificabit Sion, i.e., ecclesiam, in sanguinibus, quoniam Petrus non per carnem et sanguinem sed per patrem caelestem Filium Dei cognovit. . . . Non desunt autem plurimi qui ex hoc sedis apostolicae dignitatem impugnant, dicentes quod ecclesia aedificatur in sanguine quodque prelati ex sanguine nascuntur et ex voluntate carnis generantur. . . . His detractionibus obstruendis opus nobis esset tali pontifice qui ut rex Salem [Heb. 7.3] nec patrem, nec matrem, nec genealogiam haberet aut inordinatam carnis affectionem. . . . Si bonus erit pontifex, ad collegium vestrum quando necessitas exegerit modo canonico et determinatis temporibus viros probos et graves assumet." See also Arévalo's long and outspoken criticism of papal nepotism, *Speculum*, pp. 271–74.

91. Iserloh, "Reform der Kirche," p. 63. See Cusa's proposal in Ehses, "Reformentwurf," p. 292.

92. For example, "Sánchez de Arévalo und die Konzilsfrage unter Paul II," *Historisches Jahrbuch*, 73 (1953), 95–119, and *A History of the Council of Trent*, trans. Ernest Graf, I (London: T. Nelson, 1957), 5–116.

These studies serve as indispensable background for the positions advocated by the preachers at the court, but there is no need to repeat their conclusions here. What is pertinent at present is the more generic depiction of papal authority as it surfaces in the preachers and relates to reform.

Sánchez de Arévalo takes the most extreme position on papal plenitude of power. The pope is not bound by anything that would limit his authority—not by election capitulations or even by decrees of a general council. He has exactly the same power as Peter, and therefore he can change any precepts or laws which Peter and the apostles devised.[93]

Only two points in Arévalo's position require some elaboration. First of all, his argumentation repeatedly has recourse to the verse from Isaiah (5:4): "What more could I have done for my vineyard that I have not done?"[94] Since God, in his liberality and generosity, wanted to endow the Church with all that was most marvelous and useful, he surely would endow it with as unrestricted authority as possible. Argument from God's liberality and generosity is here employed in a way we have not as yet encountered. This use of the argument is unique to Arévalo among the preachers.

Secondly, Arévalo argues to the unlimited nature of papal authority from the fact that the pope is vicar of Christ. Whatever Christ was able to do in governing the Church, his vicar is able to do. Christ, in fact, had universal dominion over all created reality because of his union with the Word in the Incarnation.[95] Thus the pope has dominion over all created reality and especially over princes. Here argument from the mystery of the Incarnation is put to a use we have not as yet encountered. This use, too, is peculiar to Arévalo. Like all his contemporaries, Arévalo of course insisted that, whatever the extent of papal authority, it had to be used for "the public utility of the Christian people."[96] But for him there was no abuse in the Church, except heresy in the pope or Curia, more serious

93. See his "De auctoritate Romani pontificis," edited by Antonio García García, "Un opúsculo inédito de Rodrigo Sánchez de Arévalo: De libera et irrefragabili auctoritate Romani pontificis," Salmanticensis, 4 (1957), 474–502, esp. 486, 488–89.

94. See, e.g., Speculum, pp. 256–57, 299–300; "De auctoritate Romani pontificis," edited by García García, "Un opúsculo," p. 488.

95. See his "De paupertate Christi," edited in part by Teodoro Toni, "La realeza de Jesucristo en un tratado inédito del siglo XV," Estudios eclesiásticos, 13 (1934), 369–98, esp. 377–78, 383.

96. See the "De auctoritate Romani pontificis," edited by García García, "Un opúsculo," p. 489.

than diminishing or injuring the authority of the Holy See.[97] This was the radical abuse that called for reform.

Domenichi opposed some of the more extreme views about papal authority, but he also sustained the hierocratic position that the pope could dispense himself from oaths if it were for the good of the Church.[98] Neither Arévalo nor Domenichi, however, discuss the technical questions about the extent and source of papal authority in their sermons at the court. It is important to realize that even though at least some of the preachers were deeply concerned about these questions and actually entered into controversy over them, yet in their sermons during the liturgy they bypassed them.

The only ecclesiological theme that appears in any notable degree in the sermons and other orations is the monarchical character of the Church. Very frequently this monarchical constitution is intimately linked with the idea of order. Brenta in his sermon for Pentecost, 1483, maintains that just as there is one God in heaven so must there be monarchical government on earth. Otherwise discord and disorder will result.[99] Cajetan argues in the same fashion in his oration for the council,[100] and Carvajal makes an almost stronger connection between order and monarchy in his oration "De eligendo." He adduces in confirmation the line from Aristotle's *Metaphysics* (XII.10, 1076a), quoting Homer, which some of the other preachers also favored: "Non est bona pluralitas principatuum; unus ergo princeps."[101] Palmeri in his oration on peace saw monarchy indicated by

97. "Libellus de remediis afflictae ecclesiae," BAV cod. Barb. lat. 1487, fol. 127[r]: "Non tantum possunt obesse ecclesiae deformatio morum quin immo neque malitia quaecumque illa sit in Romano pontifice aut abusus in curia Romana extra casum haeresis quantum obesse et nocere possunt ecclesiae minuere et laedere auctoritatem illius sanctae sedis aut illi resistere, a qua cuncti ecclesiae status vivificantur et vegetantur, quae quidem laesio a modernis congregationibus satis timetur."

98. See, e.g., his "Consilium in materia creationis cardinalium," BAV cod. Barb. lat. 1201, fols. 32[v]–55[r], esp. fols. 32[v], 43[v]–45[r], and "De potestate papae et termino eius," BAV cod. Vat. lat. 4123, esp. fol. 1[r].

99. *In pentecosten oratio* [Rome: E. Silber, after May 18, 1483], GKW #5100, fol. [7[r]]: "Nam huius beatae Trinitatis et numinis immutabilis una est substantia . . . . Quoniam unus Deus est, eoque uno omnia gubernentur necesse est. Ut enim exercitus et ceterae quaecumque hominum sint congregationes cito dissolvuntur et pereunt plurium administrantium imperium nactae. Quotiens enim plures imperatores aut reges constituuntur totiens plures discordiae, plura odia atque dissidia nascuntur. . . . Sic illa caelestia numquam tanto ordine tamque constanti et unanimi rerum lege atque vicissitudine regerentur nisi essent unum, summum omnipotentemque rectorem Deum sortita." See also Arévalo, *Speculum*, p. 3.

100. "Oratio de ecclesiae et synodorum differentia," in *Opuscula*, p. 191.

101. *Oratio de eligendo summo pontifice*, fol. [3[r]]: "Et ordinatissime quidem Dominus ecclesiae suae unicum primum et universalem pastorem praefecit, ad quem rerum

the order found in nature.[102] The concern for order and the fear of chaos that we noted earlier in a broader context here receives specific application.

If the monarchical constitution of the Church was the guarantee of order, what was the function of the monarch himself? He was to be a pastor. The Petrine text most utilized by the preachers was not the "Thou art Peter" of Matthew's Gospel (16:18) but the "Feed my sheep" of John's (21:16). The pastoral nature of the papal office included the teaching of correct doctrine. Pius's "Pastor aeternus" emphasizes this aspect of pastoral responsibility by quoting verbatim the creed formulated by the Fourth Lateran Council, 1215. None of the preachers adverts to the fact that the new liturgies of the Renaissance *cappelle* had removed the pope from the directly pastoral exercise of preaching correct doctrine to his flock.

The pastor was to be an "oculus" and a "speculator."[103] "Speculator," a term found in the prophet Ezechiel (33:2, 7), is taken as a Latin equivalent for the Greek "episcopos," one who oversees and inspects. The pastor, therefore, was an inspector of good doctrine and of good morals. This highlights the significance of the word "specula" in the opening words of Alexander's bull. The pope, as the preachers often indicated, was on a peak—"specula" or "fastigium."[104] He could easily be viewed there as exemplar. From there he could oversee his whole flock, extended throughout the world.

The application of the term "specula" to the Holy See, along with its implied duty of overseeing the flock, dates back at least to Bernard's *De consideratione*. In using the term, Bernard meant to inculcate that the

---

omnium summa deferretur, ne destituetur ecclesia gubernatione unius quam regnum aut monarchiam vocant quamque omnis humana et divina sapientia ceteris praelationibus anteponit. Tollit enim confusionem, auget reverentiam, exsequitur deliberationem, queunt potiora optimi principatus. Hinc sapientissimus Aristoteles: Entia nolunt male disponi, nec est bona pluralitas principantium; unus ergo princeps. . . . et caelestis Hierusalem, quam nostra quoque in terris militans praefigurat, unico rectore gaudet." For other instances of the quotation from Aristotle, see, e.g., Massari, ["Cum in Bethania"], Bibl. Estense cod. Alpha Q.6.13, fol. 254^r; Domenichi, "Oratio ad Fredericum tertium," BAV cod. Ottob. lat. 1035, fol. 72^v. See also Aquinas, *Summa Theologiae*, I.103.3.

102. ["De pacis dignitate"], BAV cod. Vat. lat. 5815, fol. 93^v.

103. See, e.g., Carvajal, *Oratio de eligendo summo pontifice*, fol. [1^r]; Domenico Capranica, "Quaedam avisamenta super reformatione papae et Romanae curiae [for Nicholas V]," BAV cod. Vat. lat. 4039, fol. 17^r. See also Haubst, "Der Reformentwurf," p. 237, n. 1c.

104. See, e.g., Domenichi, "Oratio in laudem beatissimae Catherinae de Senis," BAV cod. Ottob. lat. 1035, fol. 27^v; Arévalo, *Speculum*, p. 267; Casali, "Oratio in die omnium sanctorum," Bibl. Ambr. cod. G.33 inf., II, fol. 10^v.

papal office was one of service and ministry, not one of domination.[105] At least in some cases, the Renaissance use of the term was seemingly meant to recall Bernard's message. At any rate, it was service and ministry, not domination, which Raphael Brandolini published as the world's expectations for the pontificate of Leo X.[106]

In the preachers, the monarchical and pastoral character of the papal office merge for the accomplishment of what seems to be the principal reason for its establishment. That reason is to symbolize and to effect the unity of mankind in peace and concord, in imitation of the heavenly monarchy and in imitation of the peace and concord that reigns there. That reason is to fulfill Christ's promise of a world united as "one flock" under "one shepherd."

The papal function is seen, in other words, in a larger context than that of chief officer of the Church. When the role of the papacy is described or celebrated, much more than the constitution of the Church is involved. The papal office is related to the destiny of all mankind and to the structure of the universe. In it the many are to become one. It is the guarantor of order; it is the focal point and the efficient cause of that tranquillity of order that is peace. Though the preachers do not make an explicit correlation between Rome's exemplary role and its character as "patria communis," the city in this idealized form would nonetheless serve as a good model for the reformed condition of all the world.

If the preachers were relatively clear about the nature and function of the papal office, they were less so about the cardinals'. In the history of that dignity, the preachers surely enjoy no monopoly on vagueness as to just how the cardinals fit into the scheme of things. The preachers resort to the familiar and erroneous etymology that the cardinals are the hinges on which the Church turns. Their office, consequently, must be important. First of all, the cardinals have the duty of electing the right man as pope, and their obligations in this regard are detailed for them in every oration before a conclave which survives.[107] The only other specific duty that is expounded is their obligation to give honest and religiously inspired advice in the consistories. They were the chief counselors of the monarch, and, as in other Renaissance monarchies, this obligation was considered a

---

105. PL 182, 747: "Blanditur cathedra? Specula est. Inde denique superintendis, sonans tibi episcopi nomine non dominium sed officium."

106. See Leo, p. 115.

107. See McManamon, "Ideal Renaissance Pope," esp. pp. 53–54.

serious one. They were not to be flatterers, and they were not to seek their own advantage.

The pope, in turn, had the obligation to consult them. Both Domenichi and Pérès insist on this obligation to consult, and Domenichi quotes Saint Bernard's *De consideratione*, typically enough, to the effect that there is no greater pride than for one man to prefer his own judgment to that of the congregation, as if he alone were the Holy Spirit.[108] The monarchical character of the papacy was thus tempered by the prudence that insisted upon consultation with the wise. This was what was at issue in the papal consistories.

Besides the good behavior of the pope and cardinals, the reform of "the head" also comprised the reform of certain institutions in Rome through which the head regularly functioned.[109] Primacy of honor was given to the reform of the *cappelle,* as we saw in Chapter One. It is possible to detect an implied criticism of Julius II when Petrus Flores insists with the cardinals about to elect his successor that the new pope must be a man "for whom sacred ceremonies, both public and private, are of the highest importance." The man who does not celebrate the sacred mysteries and observe the holy days in effect declares war on God.[110]

The papal household must be freed of frivolous persons and entertainments.[111] Only the reform bull of the Franciscan Sixtus IV provides that a new office be instituted in the papal palace that will see to it that alms be distributed to the poor and that no person who begs there be sent away hungry. "The name of no office will be a greater ornament to the Apostolic Palace" than that one.[112] The creation of such an office corresponds with a recommendation of Domenichi's *Tractatus* that the pope should see to it that alms were distributed to the poor on a regular basis. The title of "father of the poor" should be one of his greatest glories.[113]

---

108. Domenichi, "Oratio pro electione summi pontificis," BAV cod. Ottob. lat. 1035, fol. 16ʳ⁻ᵛ; Pérès, *Sermo super electione futuri pontificis,* fol. [3ʳ].

109. For details on the many reforms proposed for the offices of the Curia, see Celier, "Alexandre VI," as well as the bulls of Pius, Sixtus, and Alexander.

110. *Oratio de summo pontifice eligendo,* fols. [4ᵛ–5ʳ].

111. See Domenichi, *Tractatus,* fols. [8ᵛ–9ʳ], and the recommendations of Francesco Piccolomini for Alexander VI, in Celier, "Alexandre VI," p. 102: "Ioculatores, histriones, tubicines, ceteri musici, venatores, canes, aves a palatio eiciantur." See also "In apostolicae sedis specula," Arch. Segr. Vat., Misc. Arm. XI.88, fol. 8ʳ⁻ᵛ, where reference is made to Bernard's warning in the *De consideratione* about adolescents.

112. See "Quoniam regnantium," BAV cod. Vat. lat. 3884, fols. 118ᵛ–119ʳ.

113. *Tractatus,* fol. [7ʳ⁻ᵛ].

In all the reform bulls, besides the regulation of the cardinals' tables, there are also regulations about other aspects of their dress, deportment, and households, in an effort to enforce an appropriate measure of simplicity. Abuses in these areas are also addressed by the preachers.[114]

Simony in curial transactions is frequently decried, as well as the promotion to office of the young and unworthy.[115] Thus, reform of the offices of the Curia in terms of adherence to canonical procedures and the elimination of unjust and exorbitant exactions for services is seen as a critical need. Domenichi's *Tractatus*, the reform memorials of Oliviero Carafa and Francesco Piccolomini, and the unpublished reform bulls are in large measure directed against these abuses. More specifically, they try to eliminate unwarranted dispensations, the easy granting of indulgences, and plurality of benefices. They want to control the practice of reservations, expectancies, and the number of curial officials. The system of the Curia was under attack in many quarters of Christendom, and the criticism was not unappreciated by some members of the court. This aspect of Roman reform goals and the ineffectuality of the steps taken to implement them are, however, well enough known to allow here merely a mention of them, which at the same time places them within the larger ideological scheme being depicted.

The insistence of Giles of Viterbo and Raphael Brandolini on the continuation of the construction of the new Saint Peter's and their seeing this project as closely related to reform specifies for the "head" the general commendation of Church construction and restoration that has already been noted as a mark of the good public man.[116] Many years earlier, in a sermon for Calixtus III, Arévalo saw one of the purposes of the Incarna-

---

114. For a long listing of such abuses which, though not restricted to the cardinals, were certainly meant to apply to them, see R. Brandolini's "Oratio ad Lateranense concilium," BAV cod. Ottob. lat. 813, fols. 20ʳ–28ʳ, 53ᵛ–54ᵛ. See also Sixtus IV's "Quoniam regnantium," BAV cod. Vat. lat. 3884, fols. 121ᵛ–127ʳ; Domenichi, *Tractatus*, fols. [10ʳ–14ʳ]; Thegliatius, *Sermo in materia fidei* [Rome: n. publ., after Dec. 27, 1480], Hain #*15461, fol. [4ʳ⁻ᵛ], as well as Hubert Jedin, "Analecten zur Reformtätigkeit der Päpste Julius III. und Pauls IV. 3. Vorschläge und Entwürfe zur Kardinalsreform," *Römische Quartalschrift*, 43 (1935), 87–128.

115. See, e.g., Arévalo, *Speculum*, pp. 329–32; Domenichi, *Tractatus*, fol. [14ʳ⁻ᵛ]; Domenichi, "Oratio pro electione summi pontificis," BAV cod. Ottob. lat. 1035, fol. 16ᵛ; R. Brandolini, *Leo*, pp. 101–4; Flores, *Oratio de summo pontifice eligendo*, fol. [6ᵛ]; de Bagnariis, *In funere domini Petri Ferrici oratio* [Rome: n. publ., 1478?], Hain #9160, fol. [3ʳ].

116. See R. Brandolini, "Oratio ad Lateranense concilium," BAV cod. Ottob. lat. 813, fols. 54ᵛ–56ᵛ, and my *Giles of Viterbo*, pp. 113–14, 136–37. See also Alexander's "In apostolicae sedis specula," Arch. Segr. Vat., Misc. Arm. XI.88, fol. 12ᵛ, on the "Fabrica basilicae principis apostolorum."

tion as the bringing of all fine arts from heaven, as it were, for man's use and convenience.[117] This seems to be simply another way of saying that Christ restored all the goods of creation, including the products of man's genius, to a good and holy status. The Incarnation was thus viewed as the most radical of all possible reforms of man and his world, to whose purposes every other reform must conform. Arévalo's interpretation of that reform in this instance made easy a correlation of patronage of fine building and painting with a reform of the city of Rome.

In summary, the reform of the head so that it would be an example and spur to virtue for the rest of the Church follows the general pattern for the ideal of the Christian life which the preachers proposed. Each person, including the pope, should perform the duties of his office, and those duties are often indicated by law and by the title of the office. Simony was the specific form of avarice that was endemic to the Curia, and it was to be uprooted. The seeking of advancement was the species of ambition that infected the Roman prelates and that had to be extirpated. Sumptuous dress, meals, and households were the forms of luxury that were openly discussed and deplored and that might even be subject to regulation. The bad men must be replaced by the good. Appropriate sentiments of respect and admiration would be evoked by this example of virtue. From respect and admiration would follow imitation. The first step would thus be taken for the reform of the Church as a whole and, accordingly, the Roman Church would thereby recover the authority it had lost in the eyes of so many.

Reform of the head was the first goal of the Roman reform ideal, and it was also the first means for the moral reform of the rest of the Church. The second means for that end was for the pope to guarantee the appointment of worthy bishops. Mariano da Genazzano points out this duty to Innocent VIII and to Alexander VI in his sermons for them.[118] Martinus de Viana does the same for Alexander in 1494 on Ascension Thursday

117. "Sermo in die ascensionis," BAV cod. Vat. lat. 4881, fol. 238ʳ: "Descendit ut et turpissimam servitutem qua misere serviebamus e nostris cervicibus depelleret. Descendit rursus ut iustitiam et fidem, modestiam et frugalitatem ac omnium bonarum artium disciplinas e caelo ipso secum, ut ita dixerim, ad nostras duceret commoditates. Descendit denique ut pristinae dignitatis nostrae statum, ut sanctam civitatem, ut rem publicam, ut patriam qua nihil potest esse iocundius, ut salutem, vitam, spiritum, animam denique ipsam paene ex faucibus truculentissimi hostis ereptam caritate sua nobis restitueret."

118. *Oratio habita dominica tertia adventus* [Rome: E. Silber, after Dec. 16, 1487], Hain-Cop. #7554, fols. [5ᵛ–6ʳ], and esp. *Oratio de passione Iesu Christi* [Rome: E. Silber, after April 13, 1498], Hain-Cop. #7555, fol. [15ʳ].

and on Trinity Sunday.[119] In the second sermon he insists in particular that the bishops be theologically learned, so that they might preach sound doctrine and be able to refute those who contradict it.

Arévalo describes the qualities of a reforming bishop in detail in his "Libellus de remediis afflictae ecclesiae." In this treatise, as elsewhere, he puts great emphasis on preaching and on the study of Scripture as means to reform the Church.[120] He severely castigates the mendicants in his sermon before Nicholas V on Passion Sunday, 1449, because they abuse their preaching office in various ways, including the hawking of indulgences.[121] Marsi in his sermon on Saint Stephen for Innocent VIII criticizes bishops who were absent from their flock.[122]

Worthy bishops would be effective agents in implementing the reform the Church needed. Canonical visitors for various countries and dioceses were also frequently mentioned as effective agents of reform.[123] Cusa, who himself visited Germany for Nicholas V and was Pius II's legate for Rome, constructs a theology to support this office, basing himself on the viewpoint that Christ was sent as a "visitor" to earth by the Father. By instituting such legateships, the earthly Church conforms itself to the heavenly. The office of the visitor or legate, according to Cusa, is to teach the true faith and to see to it that the flock obeys God's laws, the ordinances of the sacred canons, and the duties of each one's state in life.[124]

119. *Oratio de Christi ad caelos ascensione* [Rome: n. publ., 1494], Cop. #6197, fol. [5ʳ], and *Oratio in die sanctissimi Trinitatis* (Rome: [S. Plannck], 1494), Cop. #6196, fols. [4ᵛ–5ʳ]. See also Inghirami, "Pro Iulio II funebris oratio," in *Thomae Phaedri Inghirami Volaterrani orationes duae*, ed. Pietro Luigi Galletti (Rome: G. Salomoni, 1777), pp. 91–92.

120. BAV cod. Barb. lat. 1487, fols. 115ᵛ, 134ʳ–138ᵛ. See also his "Sermo in dominica passionis Domini in quadragesima," BAV cod. Vat. lat. 4881, fols. 233ʳ–234ʳ.

121. "Sermo in dominica passionis Domini in quadragesima," BAV cod. Vat. lat. 4881, fol. 234ʳ: "Equidem, beatissime pater, plenus est mundus non dixerim praedicatoribus sed rapacissimis quaestoribus. Monachorum claustra vacua, mendicantium monasteria deserta paene reperiuntur. Vagantur enim per orbem religiosi, a claustris oberrantes, a vera obedientia lucri gratia apostatantes, diversas ubique indulgentias publicantes. Hi bursas replent, animas decipiunt, nullum apostolicae sedi casum reservant. De omnibus absolvunt, in omnibus dispensant, et, ut paucis dixerim, qui dati erant populo Christiano verbi Dei seminatores iam, pro dolor, facti sunt salutis humanae nundinatores. Horum abusus, horum errores atque scandala non facile dicere posses. Magis quidem remedio quam expressione egent."

122. *Oratio in die sancti Stephani primi martyris* [Rome: E. Silber, after Dec. 26, 1487?], Hain #10786, fol. [8ᵛ].

123. See, e.g., Arévalo, "Libellus de remediis afflictae ecclesiae," BAV cod. Barb. lat. 1487, fols. 144ʳ–145ʳ; Arévalo, "Sermo in die annuntiationis," BAV cod. Vat. lat. 4881, fol. 242ʳ; Sixtus IV, "Quoniam regnantium," BAV cod. Vat. lat. 3884, fol. 124ᵛ.

124. See, e.g., "Intrantes domum invenerunt," BAV cod. Vat. lat. 1244, fols. 7ᵛ–8ʳ;

Restoration of the ancient "liberty of the Church" is sometimes mentioned as a reform goal. Carvajal gives it first place in his program outlined in the "De eligendo" of 1492, and it was important for Pérès in the corresponding oration of 1484.[125] Aeneas Silvius Piccolomini deplored that bishops of his own day allowed the authority of the Church to slip into the hands of princes. This lament occurs, interestingly enough, in his panegyric of Saint Ambrose during the Council of Basel, 1437. Ambrose's resistance to Emperor Theodosius was a commonplace for praise of the saint, and it is that incident in Ambrose's life that prompts Aeneas's lament.[126] It is by no means clear whether the future pope is here referring to anything in particular. Cristoforo Marcello briefly commends Julius II's vindication of the liberty of the Church during his sermon for All Saints, 1511.[127] In a lapse into matters improper for a liturgical oration, moreover, he praises the pope's military campaigns on behalf of the Church and Italy, and he hails him as a "second Julius Caesar."

The relationship between the hierarchy and the princes preoccupied Domenichi. The distinction between the two orders was extremely important for him, and at one point in his *Tractatus*, seemingly quoting Jerome, he affirms: "This is what destroys the Church—the laity is better than the clergy."[128] But Domenichi's more characteristic concern was that the princes usurp the Church's prerogatives, and he returns to this grievance several times. In the "Pro electione" for the successor to Pius, he locates the blame for the princes' insolence on the weakness and fawning ambition of the members of the hierarchy, who strive to please men

---

"Dies diei," BAV cod. Vat. lat. 1245, fol. 30ᵛ; "Dominus Iesus misit me," *ibid.*, fol. 36ᵛ; "Respice Domine," *ibid.*, fols. 107ᵛ–110ᵛ; "Haec est voluntas Dei," *ibid.*, fol. 144ᵛ; "Domine adiuva me," *ibid.*, fol. 229ᵛ; "Loquimini ad petram," *ibid.*, fol. 237ᵛ; "Sic currite ut comprehendatis," *ibid.*, fol. 282ᵛ. See also his memorial on reform for Pius II in Ehses, "Reformentwurf," pp. 281–92.

125. Carvajal, *Oratio de eligendo summo pontifice*, fol. [5ᵛ], and Pérès, *Sermo super electione futuri pontificis*, fol. [1ᵛ].

126. "Oratio II. Habita Basileae in divi Ambrosii celebritate," in *Pii II P.M., olim Aeneae Sylvii Piccolominei Senensis, orationes politicae et ecclesiasticae*, ed. Giovanni Domenico Mansi, 2 vols. (Lucca: P. M. Benedinus, 1755–57), I, 50.

127. *Oratio in die omnium sanctorum*, fol. [6ʳ]. On the "libertas ecclesiae," see also, e.g., Francis of Assisi, "Oratio de iustitia servanda," BAV cod. Vat. lat. 14063, fol. 26ʳ; R. Brandolini, "[Epistola] Raphael Brandolinus Iunior Lippus Nicolao Flisco," Bibl. Ang. cod. lat. 252, fols. 8ᵛ–9ʳ; the reform memorial, 1497, of the Cardinal of Portugal, Jorge da Costa, BAV cod. Vat. lat. 3883, fol. 169ʳ.

128. *Tractatus*, fol. [12ʳ].

rather than God.[129] The good bishop, as well as the good pope, is one who will resist the princes' blandishments and usurpations.

Even more frequently deplored by the preachers are the wars the Christian princes wage against one another. In no other aspect of their lives are they more in need of reform than in this one. Peace and concord must replace the constant warfare, which is the bane of the age.

This assignment of peace and concord to the princes as their characteristic need is surely due in part to observed abuses. It also happens to conform to an ancient liturgical tradition that implores for them from God precisely those blessings.[130] Still, the preachers' emphasis is noteworthy, and it anticipates Erasmus's insistence on "pax et concordia" as the hallmark and goal of Christian life. This emphasis was a specific articulation of the general tendency to see the Christian ideal in terms of man's relationship to his fellow men. Domenichi asks, "With what else do the Gospels and Christ's doctrine resound from beginning to end except charity and peace?" There is no need to belabor how closely Domenichi's question approximates the famous statement of Erasmus many years later, "The sum and substance of our religion is peace and unanimity."[131]

It is impossible to exaggerate how often the "pax-et-concordia" formula recurs in the sermons and orations at the court. Both Campano and Platina, when they commend the oratory of Pius II, commend it for treating peace and concord.[132] It is clear that these two humanists considered

129. "Oratio pro electione summi pontificis," BAV cod. Ottob. lat. 1035, fol. 15ʳ. See also his "Oratio pro parte episcoporum," *ibid.*, fols. 28ᵛ–29ʳ, and "[Epistola] ad ducem et senatum Venetum," *ibid.*, fol. 64ᵛ.

130. Cf. "Litaniae sanctorum," in *Missale Romanum*, "Sabbato sancto": "Ut regibus et principibus christianis pacem et veram concordiam donare digneris, te rogamus, audi nos."

131. "Oratio pro pace Italiae," BAV cod. Ottob. lat. 1035, fol. 50ʳ: "Quid enim [MS=etiam] aliud sonant evangelia et doctrina ipsius a principio ad finem usque nisi caritatem et pacem?" See also Benedictus Maffeus, *Pacis encomion ad amplissimum cardinalem Oliverium Carafam* (Bologna: n. publ. 1557), fol. [5ᵛ]: " . . . si Christianae religionis dogmata inspicimus, quoniam omnis Christi actio est nostra institutio, bella tamquam pestem, luem labemque humani generis omnino fugere et vitare debemus. Christus enim nullam rem pace maiorem apostolis suis dedit aut reliquit. . . ." For Erasmus, see his letter to John Carondelet, Jan. 5, 1522/3, in *Opus Epistolarum*, ed. P. S. Allen and H. M. Allen, V (Oxford: Clarendon, 1924), 177: "Summa nostrae religionis pax est et unanimitas." See also the letter to Jodocus Jonas, May 10, 1521, *ibid.*, IV (1922), 486: "Quid enim est aliud nostra religio quam pax in Spiritu sancto?" See my article, "Erasmus and Luther: Continuity and Discontinuity as Key to Their Conflict," *Sixteenth Century Journal*, 5, No. 2 (October, 1974), 47–65.

132. See their statements printed as prefatory material to Mansi's edition of Pius's *Orationes*, I, xxix, xxx, and see as well Campano's "In exequiis divi Pii II pontificis maximi oratio," in *Opera a Michaele Ferno edita* (Rome: E. Silber, 1495), GKW #5939, fol. [103ʳ⁻ᵛ]. See also Platina's "Tractatus de laudibus pacis," in *Cre-*

peace and concord among the most important topics with which oratory should deal, perhaps even its most characteristic topic.

The preachers insist that peace is a particularly Christian ideal. Massari relates Christian peace to the ancient "pax Romana" by a *quanto-magis* argument.[133] It was easy to relate it to the theological doctrine of the Mystical Body of Christ, the Church, and preachers like Cajetan and others did so.[134] This doctrine was often propounded in the sermons, and it provided an organic model for the harmonious and ordered conditions which should prevail in the Church. When Carvajal comments on the Beatitudes in his sermon for All Saints, 1482, he reserves special praise for the last, "Blessed are the peacemakers." He argues that this is the greatest Beatitude because to it is attached the greatest reward—divine sonship.[135]

But the scriptural text that without question is most frequently adduced in praise of peace is the text from the discourse of Jesus at the Last Supper as reported in John's Gospel: "Peace I leave you. My peace I give you." Repeatedly the preachers insist that this statement indicates Christ's most precious and most characteristic bequest to his disciples. Repeatedly they refer to it as his "last will and testament."[136] Domenichi firmly believes: "No one can be at peace with Christ and receive Christ's bequest of peace, which was his last will and testament, who is not at peace with his fellow Christian."[137]

The duty of effecting peace among Christians fell largely to the pope; it was even an essential part of his office. On occasion the preachers are

---

monensium monumenta Romae extantia, ed. Thomas Augustinus Vairani, 2 vols. in one (Rome: G. Salomoni, 1778), I, 67–106.

133. "Oratio de pace," Bibl. Estense cod. Alpha Q.6.13, fol. 79^{r-v}.

134. "Oratio de ecclesiae et synodorum differentia," in *Opuscula*, pp. 189–90. See also, e.g., Marcus Antonius Ticinensis, *In adventu oratio* [Rome: S. Plannck, after Dec. 6, 1500], fol. [6^v]; Arévalo, *Speculum*, pp. 257–60.

135. *Sermo in die omnium sanctorum* [Rome: G. Herolt, after Nov. 1, 1482], GKW #6154, fol. [7^r].

136. See, e.g., Arévalo, "Sermo in die pentecostes," BAV cod. Vat. lat. 4881, fol. 253^v; Domenichi, "Oratio pro pace Italiae," BAV cod. Ottob. lat. 1035, fol. 46^r; Palmeri, ["De pacis dignitate"], BAV cod. Vat. lat. 5815, fol. 93^r; Massari, "Oratio de pace," Bibl. Estense cod. Alpha Q.6.13, fol. 78^v; Cajetan, "Oratio de ecclesiae et synodorum differentia," in *Opuscula*, p. 190; Flores, *Oratio de summo pontifice eligendo*, fol. [6^v]; Maffeus, *Pacis encomion ad amplissimum cardinalem Oliverum Carafam*, fol. [8^r]. On Guarino's interest in the verse from John, see Remigio Sabbadini, *La scuola e gli studi di Guarino Guarini Veronese* (Catania: N. Giannotta, 1896), p. 139.

137. "Oratio pro pace Italiae," BAV cod. Vat. lat. 4881, fol. 51^v: "Nec poterit ad haereditatem Domini pervenire qui testamentum pacis noluerit observare, nec concors esse cum Christo qui discors fuerit cum Christiano."

specific as was Celadoni before the conclave in 1503. The successor to Alexander VI must be able to establish peace between the kings of France and Spain, who were then at war in Italy.[138] Celadoni presumably would have been gratified by the election of Francesco Piccolomini as Pius III in the election which ensued.

Pius's successor after his extremely brief pontificate was Julius II. This was the man whom Erasmus conceived as the greatest offender against peace because he himself drew the sword against Christians. Inghirami's funeral oration for Julius makes an attempt at justifying his wars, but Flores's "De eligendo" for his successor just a few days later recalls that Christ instructed Peter to put his sword in the scabbard. It is improper, he tells the cardinals, for the pastor of souls to carry a sword and wage wars.[139] On Good Friday, 1510, Battista Casali criticized kings and princes who wage war against one another and draw Christian blood.[140] Though Casali possibly meant to exclude Julius from this category of "kings and princes," his words do not necessarily demand that interpretation, and he in fact exhorts Julius to trust in the power of the cross. With Julius seated in his audience, Giles of Viterbo in his oration opening the Fifth Lateran Council rejected the reliance of the Church on arms, and he adduced the recent defeat of the troops of the Holy League at Ravenna as a sign of divine displeasure at such reliance.[141]

Nonetheless, the sacred orators of the court do not directly and unequivocally confront Julius on this major issue of his pontificate. They perhaps could not be expected to be any bolder under the circumstances, and they deserve some credit for being as outspoken as they were. Less happy, of course, would be commendation of Julius's arms like that of Cristoforo Marcello.

Only rarely do the orators suggest how peace among the princes is to be effected and maintained. The supposition often seems to be that their appropriation of Christ's message and the resulting life of virtue where justice and temperance prevail would be sufficient. Domenichi's oration on

138. *Oratio ad sacrum cardinalium senatum ingressurum ad novum pontificem eligendum*, fol. [5^r]; in McManamon's edition, "Ideal Renaissance Pope," pp. 67–68.

139. Inghirami, "Pro Iulio II funebris oratio," in *Orationes duae*, pp. 98–102; Flores, *Oratio de summo pontifice eligendo*, fol. [7^{r-v}].

140. "Oratio in die veneris sancti," Bibl. Ambr. cod. G.33 inf., II, fols. 6^v–7^r.

141. See Mansi, 32, 674, and now the critical edition by Clare O'Reilly, " 'Without Councils We Cannot Be Saved': Giles of Viterbo Addresses the Fifth Lateran Council," *Augustiniana*, 27 (1977), esp. 173, 199–201. See also my *Giles of Viterbo*, pp. 127–29.

peace, 1468, however, descends to some particulars. First of all, men must love and esteem peace as a gift of God. Secondly, they must avoid sin, for true peace is possible only for good men. Thirdly, they must try to please God by doing his will. The fourth and last recommendation is to repress lust for domination. Let each prince be content with his boundaries and never seek to avenge injuries.[142] This last is the solution that Erasmus would later propose, and it is a solution which coincides with the preachers' general presuppositions about the stability that should characterize institutions.[143] As Palmeri said in his oration on peace: "If you wish to have peace in the commonwealth, observe order."[144] Massari generalizes: "Innovation is dangerous in all commonwealths."[145]

Aurelio Brandolini affirms that peace and concord is the unique end for which government ("civitas") is established.[146] Cajetan, Arévalo, and Domenichi invoke Aquinas's name to support the view that the purpose of government is peace.[147] Cajetan ties this purpose inseparably to order and to monarchical form. The preachers adduce Sallust as their authority to instruct their listeners in the fact that concord is the condition for growth and development, whereas discord inevitably destroys even the greatest institutions.[148]

142. "Oratio pro pace Italiae," BAV cod. Ottob. lat. 1035, fol. 52^r: "Quarto, si pacem retinere vultis, discordiarum materies et quasi seminarium auferenda est cupiditas libidoque dominandi suisque terminis quisque contentus cupiditati modum imponat. . . . Addo ut iniurias spernat nec se vindicare cupiat."

143. See, e.g., "Querela pacis," LB, IV, 637.

144. ["De pacis dignitate"], BAV cod. Vat. lat. 5815, fol. 89^r: "Si pacem in re publica habere quaeris, ordinem serva. Nam si in ceteris rebus, sicut in homine est, pax et ordo deficeret, non solum rem publicam verum etiam universum mundum penitus ruere contingeret."

145. Commentary on the "third Rule," in Vita Augustini, fol. [48^r]: "Namque omnis innovatio in quacumque re publica periculosa est. . . . In omni monasterio, in omni religione, in omni denique re publica illud est praecipue servandum ut non facile quidquam aut leviter varietur. . . ."

146. "De comparatione rei publicae et regni ad Laurentium Medicem Florentinae rei publicae principem libri tres," in Irodalomtörténeti emlékek. II: Olaszországi XV századbeli íróknak Mátyás királyt dicsöitö müvei, ed. Ábel Jenö (Budapest: 1890), p. 172.

147. Cajetan, De Comparatione Auctoritatis Papae et Concilii cum Apologia eiusdem Tractatus, ed. Vincentius M. Iacobus Pollet, Scripta Theologica, No. 1 (Rome: Angelicum, 1936), p. 17; Arévalo, "Libellus de remediis afflictae ecclesiae," BAV cod. Barb. lat. 1487, fol. 128^r; Domenichi, Liber de dignitate episcopali, p. 64. See Summa Theologiae, I.103.3. The relationship between monarchy, unity, order, and peace is succinctly stated by Thomas in this article.

148. See, e.g., Massari, "Oratio de creando novo generali," Bibl. Estense cod. Alpha Q.6.13, fol. 55^v; Carvajal, Sermo in die omnium sanctorum, fol. [8^v]; Domenichi, "Oratio die qua intrarunt ad electionem," BAV cod. Ottob. lat. 1035, fol. 7^{r-v}; Domenichi, "Oratio pro pace Italiae," ibid., fols. 50^v–51^r; Domenichi, "Sermo de

The preachers occasionally insist on the observance of laws and canons as one of the means to insure internal concord.[149] In Francis of Assisi this conjoining of obedience with law, the moral code, and the Church's discipline is especially prominent.[150] The duty of the laity to obey the clergy in ecclesiastical matters is, of course, implied in the stance the preachers take on the "libertas ecclesiae," but that duty enjoys no particular emphasis in the sermons at the court.

Here, again, we find a contrast with Cusa's sermons. Some of the difference can be explained by the different audiences being addressed. Nonetheless, Cusa enjoins upon the members of the laity obedience to their prelates with extraordinary rigor. He says, in fact, during a visitation of a parish in his diocese of Brixen: "Irrational obedience, therefore, is consummate and most perfect obedience, namely, when obedience is given without any reasons being asked, just as a beast of burden obeys its master."[151] As the quotation suggests, this sermon of Cusa betrays one of his implicit models for the reform of the Church, the life of the three vows of poverty, chastity, and obedience. The model is in this instance linked with the model of the heavenly kingdom. Cusa, in general, finds obedience to the law and observance of the duties of one's state in life, indicated by the etymology of one's title, as the indispensable means for true reform and true peace.[152]

Peace among Christians was conceived, therefore, as a good in itself, as a good especially appropriate to princes and as one of the goals of reform. But that peace was often mentioned in the same breath with another major preoccupation of the preachers—the threat of the Turk. That threat

---

sancto Marco," BAV cod. Ross. 1037, fol. 11ᵛ. Sallust, Jug., X.6: "Nam concordia parvae res crescunt, discordia maximae dilabuntur."

149. See, e.g., Domenichi, *Tractatus*, fols. [17ʳ–18ʳ]; Arévalo, "Libellus de remediis afflictae ecclesiae," BAV cod. Barb. lat. 1487, fols. 127ʳ⁻ᵛ, 144ʳ.

150. See, e.g., "Oratio de observantia divinae legis," BAV cod. Vat. lat. 14063, fols. 7ʳ⁻ᵛ, 9ᵛ, 10ᵛ.

151. "Respice Domine de caelo et vide," BAV cod. Vat. lat. 1245, fol. 109ᵛ: "Obedientia igitur irrationalis est consummata obedientia et perfectissima, scilicet quando obeditur sine inquisitione rationis, sicut iumentum obedit domino suo." On the place of obedience in Cusa's thought, see James E. Biechler, *The Religious Language of Nicholas of Cusa*, American Academy of Religion, Dissertation Ser., No. 8 (Missoula, Montana: Scholars Press, 1975), pp. 151–53.

152. See, e.g., *De Concordantia Catholica*, pp. 254–55 (II.27); 261 (II.28); 286 (II.33); 432–33 (III.28–29); 456–59 (III.40); "Deus in loco sancto suo," BAV cod. Vat. lat. 1245, fol. 22ʳ; "Ostendite mihi numisma," *ibid.*, fol. 186ʳ⁻ᵛ; "Domine adiuva me," *ibid.*, fol. 229ʳ⁻ᵛ; "Pater vester caelestis dabit vobis," *ibid.*, fols. 269ᵛ–270ʳ; "Sic currite ut comprehendatis," *ibid.*, fol. 282ᵛ.

could be met only if the Christian princes ceased making war on one another and turned their arms against the infidel. There is hardly a preacher at the court from whom we have more than two or three orations who does not at some time or other direct his attention to the danger in which Christendom finds itself and suggest some remedies. The advances of the Turk were cause and symptom of Christianity's "collapse." The most obvious remedy for this evil and the one most frequently proposed was war.

The preachers often juxtaposed their appeals for peace and their call for war, generally doing this without indicating they saw any inconsistency in it. To untangle the logic behind this juxtaposition is difficult even in individual cases, as I have elsewhere tried to show.[153] The difficulty is geometrically compounded when a number of individuals are involved. However, some generalizations are possible.

First of all, though diatribes against the bloody and cruel Turk sometimes seem to be simply a conveniently dramatic way to end an oration that otherwise lacks obvious immediacy, fear of the Turk in Rome was real. When Giles of Viterbo wrote to the papal nuncio to King Charles of Spain on January 26, 1518, he said, "We are terrified. . . . We fear that Italy and Rome are about to be destroyed." In this case there is no reason to dismiss Giles's words as produced simply for an appropriate occasion.[154] From other sources we know or can assume that Giles was not alone among the preachers in his fears.[155] The decree of the Fifth Lateran Council, "Postquam ad universalis ecclesiae curam," testifies to the concern. The situation, therefore, was considered serious. Though Cusa might

153. See my *Giles of Viterbo*, pp. 127–30.
154. "[Epistola] sanctissimi domini nostri nuntio ad Catholicum regem," BAV cod. Vat. lat. 3146, fol. 37ᵛ: "Romae terror est ingens. . . . Quae res ita metu praesenti omnes occupat ut actum de Italia et urbe Roma esse videatur." Professor Francis X. Martin called this letter to my attention.
155. See, e.g., the letter of R. Brandolini to Antonius de Monte, Sept. 10, 1501, Rome, in "Einige Briefe," pp. 202–3. See also Kenneth M. Setton, "Pope Leo X and the Turkish Peril," *Proceedings of the American Philosophical Society*, 113 (1969), 367–424; E. Guglia, "Die Türkenfrage auf dem 5. Laterankonzil," *Mitteilungen des Instituts für österreichische Geschichtsforschung*, 21 (1900), 679–91. For more general studies, see C. A. Patrides, " 'The Bloody and Cruell Turke': The Background of a Renaissance Commonplace," *Studies in the Renaissance*, 10 (1963), 126–35, and the studies by Robert H. Schwoebel, "Coexistence, Conversion and the Crusade against the Turks," *Studies in the Renaissance*, 12 (1965), 164–87, and *The Shadow of the Crescent: The Renaissance Image of the Turk (1453–1517)* (New York: St. Martin's Press, 1967). Indispensable are the two published volumes of Kenneth M. Setton's projected three volumes, *The Papacy and the Levant (1204–1571)*, Memoirs of the American Philosophical Society, Nos. 114, 127 (Philadelphia: The American Philosophical Society, 1976–78).

in 1453 propose a dialogue with the Turks in his *De Pace Fidei*, in 1456 he invited his flock to rejoice at Christian military victories over them.[156] In 1455 he described Mohammed as one of the beasts of the Apocalypse.[157] Domenichi stated that our battle is not with man, but with a most horrible beast, the enemy of all nature and humanity.[158]

Secondly, some of the preachers indicate that they would not advocate war unless all else had failed. We do find, as a matter of fact, certain alternatives proposed. Casali, for example, suggests that learning is a better weapon than arms. What makes Casali's suggestion intriguing is that it occurs in his sermon for January 1, 1508, where he lauds in his peroration the papal library founded by Sixtus IV as a kind of transfer to Rome of Plato's Academy and Aristotle's Lyceum. In 1508 Raphael began to paint for Julius II the Stanza della Segnatura which contains his "School of Athens," and we possibly have here an instance of a papal sermon influencing a major work of art. Casali's implicit identification of Rome as a "new Athens" also supplies us with another model for the restoration of the city of Rome as a center of good learning.[159] The preachers proposed virtue more frequently and more convincingly than learning, however, as an efficacious measure to overcome the Turks.

Thirdly, the preachers did not disdain the arguments which advocate war as a means to peace. To this effect Domenichi quotes Aristotle, Cicero, and Augustine for Paul II in 1468.[160] Flores and others use the same kind of argument,[161] and Gorgonius maintains that a war of offense against the Turks is the best defense of Italy.[162] Even less easily reconciled with the

---

156. "Laudans invocabo Dominum," BAV cod. Vat. lat. 1245, fols. 164v–165r. For his opposition to a campaign against the Turks, see the letter to John of Segovia, Dec. 28, 1453, in *De Pace Fidei*, ed. Raymundus Klibansky and Hildebrandus Bascour, Opera omnia iussu et auctoritate Academiae Litterarum Heidelbergensis ad codicum fidem edita, VII (Hamburg: F. Meiner, 1959), pp. 97–100.

157. "Iterum venturus est iudicare," BAV cod. Vat. lat. 1245, fol. 125v.

158. "Oratio pro electione summi pontificis," BAV cod. Ottob. lat. 1035, fol. 14v.

159. "Oratio in circumcisione," Bibl. Ambr. cod. G.33 inf., II, fols. 12r–17v. See my article, "The Vatican Library and the Schools of Athens: A Text of Battista Casali, 1508," *The Journal of Medieval and Renaissance Studies*, 7 (1977), 271–87. Heinrich Pfeiffer proposes Giles of Viterbo's commentary on Peter Lombard and his oration on the golden age as the inspiration for the Stanza della Segnatura. *Zur Ikonographie von Raffaels Disputa: Egidio da Viterbo und die christliche-platonische Konzeption der Stanza della Segnatura*, Miscellanea Historiae Pontificiae, No. 37 (Rome: Pontificia Universitas Gregoriana, 1975).

160. "Oratio pro pace Italiae," BAV cod. Ottob. lat. 1035, fol. 50v.

161. See, e.g., Flores, *Oratio de summo pontifice eligendo*, fols. [6v–7r]; Maffeus, *Pacis encomion ad amplissimum cardinalem Oliverum Carafam*, fols. [5r–6v].

162. *Oratio de animae immortalitate* [n.p.: n. publ., after Dec. 20, 1517], fol. [1v].

preachers' general insistence on the blessings of peace that Jesus bequeathed his disciples is Inghirami's depicting Jesus as the person who waged war with the infidels in Africa and brought them to their knees with the capture of Bejaïa (Bougie).[163]

Lastly, the war against the Turks was often ordered towards the most inclusive of all the Roman reform goals, the establishment or restoration of the religious unity of mankind. This war meant that the Christians living under the rule of the infidel would be reunited with their brothers in the West and that the holy places would be returned to their rightful owners. With the defeat of the Turk, the conditions for true and lasting peace would be secured and the world would be ready for its destiny as one flock under one shepherd.[164]

The religious unity of the world was the fifth goal for Roman reform. It was an ideal that easily correlated with the preachers' presuppositions about the harmonious constitution of the universe. Harmony and concord were impossible without unity.[165] The unity the preachers desired correlated also with their presuppositions about the nature and purpose of government, about the papacy's role in the world, and about the "reconciliation of all things" that was the effect of the Incarnation.[166] Moreover,

163. *In laudem Ferdinandi Hispaniarum regis catholici ob Bugiae regnum in Africa captum oratio dicta Iulio II pontifici maximo*, ed. Pietro Luigi Galletti (Rome: A. Fulgonius, 1773), p. 24: "Non Hispana robora pugnabant, non instructa tantum acies Ibera certabat. Ipse ille Iesus Deus omnipotens, cui bellum contra impias nefariasque nationes geritur, ipse inquam Iesus pugnabat, ipse impellebat, ipse fugabat."

164. See, e.g., Flores, *Oratio de summo pontifice eligendo*, fol. [2ᵛ]; de Viana, *Oratio in die Trinitatis*, fol. [5ʳ⁻ᵛ]; Galatino, "In apocalypsim commentaria," BAV cod. Vat. lat. 5567, fol. 1ᵛ, 169ʳ; Piperari, *Oratio de passione Iesu Christi redemptoris nostri*, fol. [10ʳ]; Eliodoro Tolomei, "Oratio tertia de misericordia et iustitia Dei," in *Orationes habitae Romae in pontificio sacello* (Venice: Ioannes Antonius et Fratres de Sabio, 1521), fol. [10ʳ]. See esp. Carvajal's *Homelia doctissima coram maximo Maximiliano caesare semper augusto* [Rome: J. Besicken, 1508] preached on Sept. 14, 1508, when he was apostolic delegate to Emperor Maximilian. This long, thematic discourse, which does not hesitate to adduce the name of Abbot Joachim, marshals arguments from Scripture and from recent political events to show that the time is ripe for the defeat of the infidel. See also my "Discovery of America," and John Shearman, *Raphael's Cartoons in the Collection of Her Majesty the Queen and the Tapestries for the Sistine Chapel* (London: Phaidon, 1972), pp. 78–83.

165. See, e.g., Arévalo, *Speculum*, pp. 257–60; Domenichi, "Oratio pro pace Italiae," BAV cod. Ottob. lat. 1035, fol. 50ʳ⁻ᵛ; Palmeri, ["De pacis dignitate"], BAV cod. Vat. lat. 5815, fols. 85ʳ–86ʳ; Galatino, *Oratio de circumcisione dominica* [Rome: M. Silber, after Jan. 1, 1515], fols. [6ᵛ–8ʳ].

166. See, e.g., Arévalo, "Libellus de remediis afflictae ecclesiae," BAV cod. Barb. lat. 1487, fol. 121ʳ, and his "Sermo in die annuntiationis," BAV cod. Vat. lat. 4881, fol. 242ʳ. Bernard's *De consideratione* emphasizes the relationship between unity and perfection, and it further relates this to the papal office, PL 182, 751–52, 758–60. See also Michele Maccarrone, *Vicarius Christi: Storia del titolo papale*, Lateranum NS

this goal was made explicit in Christ's prayer for unity at the Last Supper and his "promise" of it on that same occasion.

The preachers' persuasion that God's grace was abundantly present and that he willed "all men to be saved" (1 Tim. 2:4) supported their hopes for the religious unity of the world. Filippi admonished Leo X in 1520 that he must remember that Christ was born not "for him alone, or just for us, but for all nations under heaven."[167] Therefore, Leo must try to have the Gospel preached to the unbelievers. Only if that failed should he resort to war. The *Libellus* of Giustiniani and Quirini, as well as some other documents in circulation at the court, show a sense of responsibility for the evangelization of the Turks and of the territories recently discovered by the Spaniards and the Portuguese.[168] Even Alexander VI's famous bull of 1493 on the New World, *Inter caetera*, reflects the canonical tradition that tried to balance the rights of the infidels with papal responsibility for preaching the Gospel, while at the same time not being blind to the political realities of aggressive expansionism.[169]

Among the preachers, Cajetan is unequivocally firm in his conviction that holy words and holy lives, not armies, are the instruments of conversion, and he pronounces the wars of subjugation which the Europeans were waging against the new peoples to be unjust and immoral.[170] Cajetan's courageous practicality was contemporaneous with the universalistic hopes that animated many of the orators at the court and that received their most elaborate expression in the writings of Galatino and Giles of Viterbo.

We might note, finally, that the documents of the Fifth Lateran Council manifest many of the same concerns and reform goals as do the writings of the preachers. The preachers thus mirror, and even seem indirectly to have helped create, the most authoritative formulation of Roman reform

---

18, 1–4 (Rome: Lateranum, 1952), esp. pp. 267–73 on Domenichi, Arévalo, and Pietro del Monte. Maccarrone shows how at Rome the hierocratic theory of papal direct authority over temporalities dominated in the interpretation of the term "vicarius Christi."

167. *Oratio in die epiphaniae MDXX* [Rome: S. Guileretus, 1520], fols. [5ᵛ–6ʳ].

168. See my "Discovery of America."

169. See James Muldoon, "Papal Responsibility for the Infidel: Another Look at Alexander VI's *Inter Caetera*," *The Catholic Historical Review*, 64 (1978), 168–84.

170. See his commentary on Aquinas's *Summa Theologiae*, II–II.66.8 ad 1ᵃᵐ, written in 1517 and published in Aquinas's *Opera omnia iussu impensaque Leonis XIII P.M.*, IX (Rome: S. C. de Propaganda Fide, 1897), p. 94. See also Vincentius M. Iacobus Pollet, "De Caietani scripto: 'Ad septemdecim quaesita responsiones,'" *Angelicum*, 14 (1937), 538–59, esp. 549–53: "Ad sex quaesita a fratribus praedicatoribus in novo continente."

ideals before the outbreak of the Reformation. How effectively that formulation met the needs of the Church and society it addressed is quite another question. The judgment of historians and theologians on the quality of the council has been almost unexceptionally negative from the sixteenth century until today, although recent studies indicate this judgment has been too sweeping and not always well informed.[171]

In any case, these were the five goals that the preachers held up for praise, and their contraries were what they singled out for blame. The blame was sometimes mixed with threat. The destruction of Italy and Rome was not a fear of Giles of Viterbo alone. Thegliatius presents it as a decided possibility in his sermon for the feast of Saint John, 1481.[172] Other preachers were much vaguer about what might be the ultimate result of failure to reform. A favorite theme was that "the kingdom will be taken away" (Matt. 21:43) unless reform were instituted. The phrase, applied to the cardinals and other prelates, appears as early as Domenichi's *Tractatus*,[173] and other preachers quote or paraphrase it, without defining its meaning.[174]

Generally, however, the sermons and orations end with a word of hope and promise. The sacred orators of the court could paint a desperate picture of the problems facing mankind. But God's grace is abundant, and he is not far from any man. He certainly will aid those whose goals correspond to the purposes of his Creation and Redemption. If reform is but undertaken and properly implemented, all will be well.

171. See Nelson H. Minnich, "The Participants at the Fifth Lateran Council," *Archivum Historiae Pontificiae*, 12 (1974), 157–206, and esp. his "Episcopal Reform at the Fifth Lateran Council (1512–1517)," Diss. Harvard Univ., 1977. See also John Headley, "Luther and the Fifth Lateran Council," *Archive for Reformation History*, 64 (1973), 55–78. The most recent comprehensive study of the council is Olivier de la Brosse et al., *Latran V et Trente*, Histoire des conciles oecuménique, No. 10 (Paris: Editions de l'Orante, 1975). This book adds little to our knowledge about the council and repeats the conventionally negative judgments about it.

172. *Sermo in materia fidei*, fols. [3ᵛ–4ʳ].

173. *Tractatus*, fol. [12ʳ].

174. See, e.g., A. Brandolini, *Oratio pro sancto Thoma Aquinate* [Rome: E. Silber, 1485/90], GKW #5016, fol. [11ᵛ]; R. Brandolini, "Oratio ad Lateranense concilium," BAV cod. Ottob. lat. 813, fol. 61ʳ. See also Cusa, "Audistis, fratres, Pium secundum," BAV cod. Vat. lat. 1245, fols. 283ᵛ–284ʳ, and Petrus de Vicentia, *Oratio pro capessenda expeditione contra infideles* [Rome: J. Besicken, after March 25, 1490], Hain #12860, fol. [10ʳ].

CONCLUSION

Historians of the Renaissance, convinced that something new happened in Italy in the fourteenth and fifteenth centuries, yet challenged by the medieval character of so many facets of Italian life and culture, have been especially preoccupied with the problem of the continuities and discontinuities of their era with the Middle Ages. A study of Rome during the Renaissance inevitably evinces that same preoccupation. What was new, and what was old in the culture of the Renaissance? This general question subsumes the more specialized ones posed in the Introduction to this book —questions about the nature of Renaissance preaching, the quality of the religious world view at the papal court, and the character of Renaissance Humanism. Through a study of these three "old problems," the book has addressed a single, altogether more fundamental one: what was Renaissance culture, and what happened during the period that allows or requires distinguishing it from the Middle Ages?

Although most historians willingly concede that the revival of the *studia humanitatis* determined to a great extent the character of the literary and intellectual culture of the Renaissance, they find the precise nature of the change that revival effected elusive and difficult to chart. The focus of this book has been specialized, limited to high churchmen and persons of refined sensibilities in formal settings. Such a focus qualifies any generalizations that might derive from it. But compensatory for the narrowness of focus is the precision which the controlled situation of the papal *cappelle* allows it to achieve. Within the limits of the examination the book undertakes, certain features of Renaissance culture emerge well substantiated.

What was new in that culture? From the perspective of the three "old questions" which were employed to address that question, the same answer recurs consistently. What was new was a new rhetoric. The answer is banal apart from detailed demonstration of how that rhetoric functioned. With such a demonstration, the answer explains how rhetoric changed a literary genre from its medieval and thematic form to something quite different and explains how it helped create a distinctive religious vision. It also explains how rhetoric was integral to the more general revival of the *studia humanitatis* which we identify with Renaissance Humanism.

The rhetoric that Renaissance Rome revived was principally the rhetoric of praise and blame. The cultivation of this rhetoric was part of a more general enthusiasm for antiquity that antedates the revival of the *genus demonstrativum*. Once that *genus* was revived, however, it had a notable impact on culture, promoting and producing certain phenomena which we commonly associate with the Renaissance. Symptomatic of these phenomena, for instance, is the emergence of the theme of the dignity of man.

The *genus demonstrativum* was a literary form. Any prolonged discussion of it in an historical context inevitably raises another fundamental question, one which is in fact addressed throughout the book: the relationship of form to content. The relationship between form and content was first examined in the new liturgical form of the Renaissance *cappelle* and then examined in more specialized fashion through an examination of the new rhetorical form of the epideictic genre. The last three chapters of the book could be said to deal with content, but the conceptually neat distinction between *verba* and *res* cannot be sustained in practice for a relationship which the oratory of the court shows to be so complex.

Nowhere does this complexity more patently manifest itself than in the relationship of the new rhetoric to characteristically medieval ideals, practices, and thought-forms. Some of these *medievalia* are adopted by the orators of the court almost unchanged, some are transformed, some are repudiated, and some are simply bypassed without mention. The oratory of the court reveals with special detail the complexity of the relationship of the new rhetoric to medieval Scholasticism simply because so many of the orators who employed the new rhetoric were men whose mature training had been "in the schools." Even the schoolmen, however, wanted their oratory based on the genuinity of antiquity—classical, biblical, and patristic. Ancient sources, ancient doctrine, and ancient patterns of saintly living were the burdens of their eloquence.

The relationship between form and content, as specified in the relationship between the *genus demonstrativum* and the Christian religion, prompts the generalization that the new oratory highlighted those aspects of Christianity that were conformable to certain values of this world and that stressed the quality of men's dealings with their fellow men. In this sense, the revival of the *studia humanitatis* rendered Christianity more "human." This generalization does not mean to resurrect the old definition of Renaissance Humanism as an affirmation of human values after their negation in the Middle Ages. Nonetheless, these *studia* did have a humanizing influence on traditional religion. The revival of classical form was very much responsible for this influence. But with the revival of form came the concomitant revival of classical content, as is illustrated by the use to which the oratory put classical heroes whose virtues were those of public service.

The most arresting aspect of the influence of the new form on traditional religion was the extraordinarily affirmative interpretation of man and the world that it elicited and made resound. As the orators applied their rhetoric of praise to God's deeds and mysteries, they extolled them as magnificent *beneficia* for the human race. There is evidence that, as the orators indulged in their panegyrics of God, they persuaded their listeners that they were saying something fresh and exciting, no matter how traditional the truths they propounded may have been. They presumably evoked from at least some of those listeners the joy, wonder, and sense of their own dignity that they wanted to evoke, and thus moved them to the practice of good and holy living. Further precision about how effectively the orators touched the lives of their listeners seems almost impossible to ascertain; but, at a minimum, there is no evidence that requires dismissal of their efforts as utterly vain and fruitless.

The emphasis of the new oratory on *res gestae* and the preachers' effective employment of ekphrasis infused an historical, emotional, narrative, and visual quality into Renaissance perceptions that contrasts with the more cerebral and transcendent character of much scholastic speculation. But the substantialism in the scholastic tradition enjoyed some affinity with the willingness of the new rhetoric to transcend the facts in favor of an ideal. In both instances the result was models constructed more immediately from preconceived and inherited elements than from empirical reality. The orators' depiction of the Church exemplifies the tendencies that were operative. The heavenly and idealized character of the Church, as they often presented it, resembles a reality of fully achieved perfection rather than a human and historical institution beset with limitations. The ambivalences of the models, moreover, were not seen or exposed. Even when the preachers engaged in the art of vituperation, they did not mean to deny the idealized models they had constructed. They meant only to face the injuries these ideals suffered from certain regrettable contingencies.

The criticisms that the sacred orators directed against those contingencies could be bold and scathing; and, despite their generally preconceived character, they must in many instances have struck their mark. Insofar as these criticisms were directed against churchmen, they fitted the pattern of an age when criticisms of the Church and the call for its reform were swelling and becoming increasingly strident. However, even as the sacred orators of the court deplored their times, they were in fact affirming received ideals. Theirs was a dogmatic oratory, and they were spokesmen for a system even as they criticized it.

Since peace and order were integral parts of the Roman religious vision, these values confirmed a sense of satisfaction with other traditional values, truths, and goals. Lodovico da Ferrara's confidence in the secure condition of Christian teaching suggests a similar confidence in other, presumably perennial realities—realities affirmed alike by the Greek Fathers, the Latin Fathers, the scholastics, and the classicizing orators of his own day. The preachers of the papal court, in spite of their warnings and in spite of their oscillation between extremes of praise and blame, do not seem to have stirred much deep anxiety in themselves or others about the ultimate viability of the realities they celebrated or criticized. Lodovico's confidence betrays a mentality that could interpret the demands of the Protestant Reformation only as irresponsible defiance of the order of the universe and as dangerous threats to the continuity and coherence of inspired traditions.

Such a mentality even insulated the orators from fully appreciating the novelty inherent in their own enterprise. They proposed medieval and traditional goals for the reform of the Renaissance Church, and they had no intention of inciting a revolution. Nonetheless, their peculiar application of rhetoric to sacred discourse resulted in a "reform" that was impressive, even though they seem to have been only vaguely aware of how great a change they had wrought. They saw its operation in rather modest terms of putting the old truths into new and more attractive dress, not always perceiving that such a change in form was a change in method that was bound to effect some change in message. As new rhetorical methods of addressing religious truths developed, displacing or modifying earlier methods, markedly different emphases in doctrine had to emerge. Whatever the preachers' success or lack of success in winning support for the great reform goals they explicitly espoused, they enjoyed considerable success in effecting this other reform.

The message effected by this reform celebrated, inter alia, the vision of a God who invited man to share his divine powers and prerogatives—God became man, that man might become God. Having created man in his own image and likeness and having invested him with "agendi virtutes," God now endowed him with even more perfect gifts. He lavished these gifts on man not that he might live in seclusion for himself alone, but that he might be active in the service of others. He called man, indeed, to build a community of peace and concord which, though including household and city, extended far beyond these modest confines to reach to the very ends of the earth.

This message, at once congratulatory and challenging, amplified and orchestrated by the new rhetoric, differs strikingly from the ones we conventionally ascribe to the late Middle Ages, the Reformation, and the Counter Reformation. The very recognition of its existence in the Renaissance now enjoins upon us some re-evaluation of these other eras or phenomena. It also helps vindicate a new and distinctive character for Renaissance culture and religion in Italy.

Nonetheless, there is no escaping the fact that Renaissance rhetoric was fundamentally conservative in intent. Its conservative nature, plus its sometimes pompous airs, might make it seem more appropriate, therefore, for the courts of kings than for republican cities. However, every political entity in the Renaissance had its celebratory occasions and felt the need to shore up its traditions by praising them. Thus, considered in itself, the revival of the *genus demonstrativum* was not more compellingly fitting at the court of the papal monarch than it would have been elsewhere in Europe. For the reasons which Aurelio Brandolini states, the *genus demonstrativum* was bound to emerge as the most important *genus* as long as Latin was the language in which the revival of classical rhetoric was carried on. If the revival of that *genus* was more striking in Rome than elsewhere, it was so largely because the public oratory of the court was in Latin and because the orations of the *cappelle* were so frequent and so central to the function of the court.

On the other hand, insofar as epideictic oratory must project an ideal (or its opposite), that oratory could serve Rome as it served no other. Rome was not a commercial or industrial city. It was a city whose chief assets were the memories and monuments of its past and the hopes it might inspire for the future. It was these memories, monuments, and hopes that account for the revival of Rome in the Renaissance and that contributed to the mystique that sustained it once revived. Rome was exemplary center, font of ancient culture, special depository of the apostolic message, see of blessed Peter. Its mystique was at the very heart of its reality.

This mystique was symbolically articulated in the papal *cappelle*. There the apostolic liturgies reflected the heavenly liturgies. When the sacred orators of the court adopted the new rhetoric of praise and blame *inter missarum solemnia*, they adopted a rhetoric marvelously appropriate for those liturgies and for painting a vision of man's life and destiny suggested by the dignified ritual itself.

APPENDIX. A SHORT-TITLE FINDING LIST OF SERMONS CORAM PAPA INTER MISSARUM SOLEMNIA, c.1450–1521

This list contains all the strictly liturgical orations at the papal court that I have identified and examined for the period under consideration. Although this category of orations is not the exclusive focus of the book, it is the most important one, and in the interest of brevity and control I judged it best to limit the list to these orations. In case of doubt whether an oration falls into this technical category, I have included it, but I have excluded others like Magnus's "Oratio de Spiritu sancto" which, though originally intended for the liturgy, was in fact delivered after the Mass was over.

The list does not claim to be complete. It is the result of a systematic search undertaken during the writing of the book, but these sermons are scattered in various libraries and appear in unlikely places. However, even as the list stands, I believe it will be useful to Renaissance scholars for reasons the book has tried to show. Besides standard bibliographical information, I try whenever possible to provide the pope, occasion, and year for the sermon when these are not already clear from the title. I also list one library where I know the sermon can be found.

Alessandri, Carlo, da Perugia
> *Sermo in die parasceve* [Rome: U. Han, after March 23, 1475], GKW #1225. For Sixtus IV, 1475. BAV

Almania, Nicolaus de. *See* Schomberg, Nicolaus

Alpharabius, Iacobus Leonissani
> *In die ascensionis Domini oratio* [Rome: n. publ., n.d.]. For Julius II, year unknown. I have not located this oration.

Ambrosius de Cora, Coriolanus. *See* Massari, Ambrogio

Anonymous
> "Oratio coram pontifice in adventu Domini," BN Florence cod. Conv. Soppr. J.VII.5, fols. 1^r–3^v. Second Sunday of Advent, pope and year unknown.

Anonymous
> ["Oratio in die sancti Stephani"], BAV cod. Vat. lat. 4872, fols. 93^r–97^r. Pope and year unknown.

Anonymous
> "Sermo in epiphania Domini," Bibl. Marc. cod. lat. XI.100 (3938), fols.

54^r–58^r. Pope and year unknown, but before 1454; see Kristeller, *Iter*, II, 255.

Augustinus Philippus Florentinus. *See* Filippi, Agostino
de Bagnariis, Ludovicus, Imolensis, O.M.

1. *Oratio in die sancti Stephani* [Rome: S. Plannck, after Dec. 26, 1481], Hain-Cop. #*9162 (another printing, #*9161). For Sixtus IV, 1481. Bibl. Ang.
2. *Oratio in die prothomartyris Stephani* [Rome: G. Theotonicus, 1482?], Hain-Cop. #9163. For Sixtus IV, 1482? BL
3. *Oratio de nomine Iesu* [Rome: E. Silber?, 1486], Hain #9164. For Innocent VIII, Circumcision, 1486. Bibl. Vall.
4. "Oratio de Christi passione," BAV cod. Vat. lat. 11542, fols. 1^r–20^r. Good Friday, pope and year unknown.

Baptista Mantuanus, O.Carm.

"Oratio in omnium sanctorum celebritate," Bibl. Com. Ariostea, Ferrara, cod. II.162, fols. 130^r–142^r. For Innocent VIII, 1488. Part of this sermon was edited, rather carelessly, by Gabriel Wessels, "B. Baptistae Mantuani oratio habita coram Innocentio VIII et Cardinalibus in Basilica Vaticana," *Analecta Ordinis Carmelitarum*, 6 (1927), 129–34.

Bodivit, Guillelmus, O.M.

1. *In die annuntiationis Virginis sermo* [Rome: B. Guldinbeck, after Aug. 12, 1484], GKW #4503. For Sixtus IV, 1484. BL
2. *Sermo habitus in die Trinitatis* [Rome: S. Plannck, after May 29, 1485], GKW #4505 (another printing, #4504). For Innocent VIII, 1485. BAV

Boussard, Geoffrey (Boussardus, Gaufridus)

Oratio habita Bononiae in die circumcisionis (Paris: G. Eustace, 1507). For Julius II, 1507. BL

Brandolini, Aurelio Lippo, O.E.S.A.

Oratio de virtutibus Iesu Christi nobis in eius passione ostensis [Rome: J. Besicken, after April 1, 1496], GKW #5017. For Alexander VI, Good Friday, 1496. BAV

Brenta, Andrea

In pentecosten oratio [Rome: E. Silber, after May 18, 1483], GKW #5100. For Sixtus IV, 1483. BAV

Brito, D. Guillelmus Iocet. *See* Ioseph Guglielmus (de Britannia), O.M.
Cajetan (Thomas de Vio), O.P.

1. "Oratio de vi cultus divini et orationis efficacia," in *Opuscula omnia* (Lyons: G. Rovillius, 1588), pp. 181–83. For Alexander VI, first Sunday of Advent, 1501.
2. "Oratio de unione Verbi cum natura humana," *ibid.*, pp. 183–85. For Alexander VI, first Sunday of Advent, 1502.
3. "Oratio de causa et origine mali," *ibid.*, pp. 185–86. For Alexander VI, first Sunday of Lent, 1502.
4. "Oratio de immortalitate animorum," *ibid.*, pp. 186–88. For Julius II, first Sunday of Advent, 1503. For an English translation, with introduction, see

James K. Sheridan, "On the Immortality of Minds," in *Renaissance Philosophy*, ed. Leonard A. Kennedy (The Hague: Mouton, 1973), pp. 41–54.

5. "Oratio de modo quo animae patiuntur ab igne corporeo et de corporum cruciatu," *Opuscula omnia*, pp. 188–89. For Julius II, first Sunday of Advent, 1504.

Campano, Giovanni Antonio

1. "Oratio ascensus Domini," in *Opera a Michaele Ferno edita* (Rome: E. Silber, 1495), GKW #5939, fols. [65ᵛ–66ʳ]. Pope and year unknown, incomplete as it stands. BAV

2. "Oratio cineritia," *ibid.*, fols. [76ᵛ–82ʳ]. For Pius II, year unknown.

3. "De Spiritu sancto oratio," *ibid.*, fols. [82ʳ–85ᵛ]. Pentecost, year and pope unknown.

4. "De circumcisione oratio," *ibid.*, fols. [85ᵛ–87ᵛ]. Pope and year unknown.

5. "In festo sancti Stephani oratio," *ibid.*, fols. [87ᵛ–90ʳ]. Pope and year unknown.

de Canali, Mathias

1. *De passione Domini oratio* [Rome: S. Plannck, after April 17, 1489], GKW #5957. For Innocent VIII, Good Friday, 1489. BAV

2. *Oratio cinerum* [Rome: J. Besicken, 1503 (given as 1504 by BM Catalogue, vol. 33, col. 179, but see fol. 1ʳ where date printed is 1503)]. For Alexander VI (or Julius II). BL

Capitaneus, Thomas, O.P.

Oratio in die omnium sanctorum [Rome: S. Plannck, after Nov. 1, 1483], GKW #6023 (other printings, #6021, #6022). For Sixtus IV, 1483. BAV

Cardulus, Franciscus Narniensis

1. "De Ioannis evangelistae laudibus oratio," Bibl. Capitolare, Lucca, cod. 544, II, fols. 81ᵛ–86ʳ. For Alexander VI, 1492.

2. "Oratio de circumcisione," *ibid.*, II, fols. 86ᵛ–90ᵛ. For Alexander VI, year unknown.

Carvajal, Bernardino

1. *Oratio in die circumcisionis* [Rome: S. Plannck, c.1488/90], GKW #6147 (another printing, #6146). For Sixtus IV, 1484. BAV

2. *Sermo in die omnium sanctorum* [Rome: G. Herolt, after Nov. 1, 1482], GKW #6154. For Sixtus IV, 1482. Bibl. Vall.

Casali, (Giovanni) Battista

1. "Oratio in die cinerum," Bibl. Ambr. cod. G.33 inf., I, fols. 303ᵛ–308ᵛ. For Alexander VI, 1502.

2. "Oratio in die veneris sancti [MS, sancto]," *ibid.*, II, fols. 2ʳ–7ʳ. For Julius II, 1510.

3. "Oratio in die omnium sanctorum," *ibid.*, II, fols. 7ᵛ–12ʳ. For Julius II, 1509.

4. "Oratio in circumcisione," *ibid.*, II, fols. 12ʳ–17ᵛ. For Julius II, 1508. For a modern edition, see my "The Vatican Library and the Schools of Athens: A Text of Battista Casali, 1508," *The Journal of Medieval and Renaissance Studies*, 7 (1977), 271–87, esp. 279–87.

5. "In die ascensionis," *ibid.*, II, fols. 18ʳ–22ᵛ. Pope and year unknown.

Columna, Pietro. *See* Galatinus, Petrus

Cortesius, Alexander

    Oratio in epiphania [Rome: S. Plannck, after Jan. 25, 1483], GKW #7796
    (another printing, #7795). For Sixtus IV, 1483. BAV

Dati, Nicoletto

    1. *Oratio die Trinitatis habita* [Rome: J. Besicken and S. Mayr, after June 11,
       1503]; see GKW, VII, 327. For Julius II, 1503/5? BL

    2. *Oratio die circumcisionis habita* [Rome: J. Besicken, after Jan. 1, 1509];
       see GKW, VII, 327. For Julius II, 1509/11? BAV

de' Domenichi, Domenico

    1. "Oratio in laudem beatissimae Catherinae de Senis," BAV cod. Ottob. lat.
       1035, fols. 18^v–28^r. For Pius II, May 2, 1462/63, "in die solemnitatis
       ipsius."

    2. "Oratio pro pace Italiae," *ibid.*, fols. 46^r–52^v. For Paul II, Ascension Thurs-
       day, 1468.

    3. "Oratio pro victoriis Christianorum," *ibid.*, fols. 77^v–83^r. For Paul II, Aug.
       30, 1469, to celebrate the anniversary of the pope's election.

Eliodoro da Siena. *See* Tolomei, Eliodoro

Fernandez de S. Ella, Rodericus. *See* Rodericus de S. Ella

Ferno, Michele

    In Ioannis evangelistae festum oratio [Rome: E. Silber, 1495], Hain #6979.
    For Alexander VI, 1494. BN Milan.

Fichet, Guillaume

    "De divi prothomartyris Stephani laudibus oratio," BAV cod. Chigi J.VI.235,
    now in a modern edition by Paul Oskar Kristeller, "An Unknown Hu-
    manist Sermon on St. Stephen by Guillaume Fichet," in *Mélanges Eugène
    Tisserant*, VI, Studi e Testi, No. 236 (Vatican City: BAV, 1964), 459–97.
    For Sixtus IV, 1476.

Filippi, Agostino, O.S.M.

    1. "Oratio in epiphania," in *Orationes novem coram Iulio II et Leone X*
       (Rome: J. Mazochius, 1518), fols. [2^r–4^r]. For Julius II, 1513. BAV

    2. "Oratio dominica de Trinitate," *ibid.*, fols. [4^r–6^v]. For Leo X, 1513.

    3. "Oratio de sacramentis," *ibid.*, fols.[6^v–8^v]. For Leo X, Epiphany, 1514.

    4. "Oratio de veritate," *ibid.*, fols. [8^v–11^r]. For Leo X, Passion Sunday, 1514.

    5. "Oratio de multiplici adoratione," *ibid.*, fols. [11^r–13^r]. For Leo X, Epiphany,
       1515.

    6. "Oratio in die epiphaniae," *ibid.*, fols. [13^r–14^v]. For Leo X, 1516.

    7. "Oratio de peccato," *ibid.*, fols. [14^v–16^r]. For Leo X, Passion Sunday, 1516.

    8. "Oratio in epiphania Domini," *ibid.*, fols. [16^r–18^r]. For Leo X, 1518.

    9. "Oratio in dominica de passione," *ibid.*, fols. [18^r–20^r]. For Leo X, 1518.

    10. *Oratio die epiphaniae MDXX* [Rome: S. Guileretus, 1520]. For Leo X. BAV

Franciscus de Assisio, O.M.

    1. "Oratio de observantia divinae legis," BAV cod. Vat. lat. 14063, fols. 1^r–12^r.
    For Paul II, second Sunday of Advent, year unknown.

2. "Oratio de immortalitate animorum," *ibid.*, fols. 12ᵛ–17ᵛ. For Paul II, second Sunday of Advent, year unknown.

3. "Oratio de communi resurrectione," *ibid.*, fols. 17ᵛ–21ᵛ. For Paul II, second Sunday of Lent, year unknown.

4. "Oratio de iustitia servanda," *ibid.*, fols. 21ᵛ–28ʳ. For Paul II, second Sunday of Advent, year unknown.

5. "Oratio de transfiguratione Salvatoris," *ibid.*, fols. 28ᵛ–36ʳ. For Paul II, second Sunday of Lent, year unknown.

6. "Oratio de dulcedine vitae aeternae," *ibid.*, fols. 36ʳ–42ᵛ. For Paul II, second Sunday of Lent, year unknown.

7. *Oratio pro defensione fidei Christianae* [Rome: n. publ., after Dec. 10, 1480], Hain-Cop. #7322. For Sixtus IV, second Sunday of Advent, 1480. Bibl. Mazarine, Paris.

Galatinus, Petrus, O.M.
Oratio de circumcisione dominica [Rome: M. Silber, after Jan. 1, 1515]. For Leo X, 1515. BN Rome.

Georgio, Ioannes Antonius de S. *See* Sangiorgio, Giovanni Antonio

Gorgonius, Stephanus Basignanas, O.Carm.
Oratio de animae immortalitate [n.p.: n. publ., after Dec. 20, 1517]. For Leo X, fourth Sunday of Advent, 1517. Bibl. Vall., where it is not listed in the catalogue; shelf number, Inc. Q.V.172(24).

Gravina, Pietro (Panhormitanus)
Oratio de Christi ad caelos ascensu [Rome: S. Plannck, 1493], Hain-Cop. #7925. For Alexander VI, 1493. Bibl. Ang.

Guglielmo, Giuseppe di Brittania. *See* Ioseph, Guglielmus Brito

Guillelmo Raimondo de Moncata. *See* Mithridates, Flavius

Guillermus de Dumo-Quercu
Sermo de Spiritu sancto [Rome?: n. publ., after June 10, 1481], Hain-Cop. #8325. For Sixtus IV, Pentecost, 1481. Bibl. Mazarine, Paris.

Imolensis, Ludovicus. *See* de Bagnariis, Ludovicus

Inghirami, Tommaso "Fedra"
1. "In laudem omnium sanctorum oratio," Bibl. Guarn. cod. LIII.4.8 (formerly 5885), fols. 38ʳ–50ʳ. For Alexander VI, 1497.

2. "De morte Iesu Christi deque eius tormentis oratio," BN Paris cod. lat. 7352B, fols. 221ʳ–236ʳ. For Julius II, Good Friday, 1504.

Ioannes Antonius de S. Georgio. *See* Sangiorgio, Giovanni Antonio

Ioannes de Trevio, O.M.
1. *Oratio de veri Messiae adventu* (Rome: J. P. de Lignamine, 1472), Hain #*15609. For Sixtus IV, second Sunday of Advent, 1472. BAV

2. *Oratio de animarum immortalitate* (Rome: J. P. de Lignamine, 1473), Hain #*15610. For Sixtus IV, second Sunday of Advent, 1473. Bibl. Ang.

3. *De humana felicitate oratio*, *ibid.* For Sixtus IV, second Sunday of Lent, 1472.

Ioseph, Guglielmus (de Britannia), O.M.

In Christi ascensione adhortatio [Rome: E. Silber, after May 24, 1487], Hain-Reichling #9448. For Innocent VIII, 1487. Bibl. Casan.

Lodovico da Ferrara (Ludovicus Ferrariensis), O.P.

1. "Sermo de adventu Christi," in *Orationes quinque in cappella pontificia* [Rome: n. publ., after 1492], Hain-Cop. #6983, fols. [2ʳ–5ᵛ]. For Innocent VIII, first Sunday of Advent, year unknown. BAV

2. "Sermo de pugna Christi cum daemone," *ibid.*, fols. [6ʳ–10ʳ]. For Innocent VIII, first Sunday of Lent, 1492?

3. "Sermo de suprema die," *ibid.*, fols. [10ᵛ–13ᵛ]. For Alexander VI, first Sunday of Advent, 1492.

4. "Sermo de divina gratia," *ibid.*, fols. [14ʳ–16ᵛ]. For Alexander VI, first Sunday of Lent, year unknown.

5. "Sermo de conformitate ecclesiae militantis ad ecclesiam triumphantem," *ibid.*, fols. [16ᵛ–20ʳ]. For Alexander VI, first Sunday of Lent, year unknown.

Lollio, Antonio, da San Gimignano

1. *Oratio circumcisionis dominicae* [Rome: S. Plannck, 1485?], Hain #*10180 (other printings, #*10179, Cop. #3633). For Innocent VIII, 1485. Bibl. Ang.

2. *Oratio passionis dominicae* [Rome: S. Plannck, 1486?], Hain #*10181 (other printings, #10182, Cop. #3634). For Innocent VIII, Good Friday, 1486. Bibl. Vall.

de Maraschis, Bartholomaeus

Oratio in parasceve ([Rome: J. P. de Lignamine], 1473), Hain #10744. For Paul II, 1468. BN Naples.

Marcello, Cristoforo

Oratio in die omnium sanctorum [Rome: M. Silber?, after Nov. 1, 1511]. For Julius II, 1511. BAV

Marcus Antonius Ticinensis, O.M.

In adventu oratio [Rome: S. Plannck, after Dec. 6, 1500, despite Reichling #345]. For Alexander VI, second Sunday of Advent, 1500. BAV

Mariano da Genazzano, O.E.S.A.

1. *Oratio habita dominica tertia adventus* [Rome: E. Silber, after Dec. 16, 1487], Hain-Cop. #7554 (another printing, #*7553). For Innocent VIII, 1487. Bibl. Ang.

2. *Oratio de passione Iesu Christi* [Rome: E. Silber, after April 13, 1498], Hain-Cop. #7555. For Alexander VI, Good Friday, 1498. Bibl. Ang.

Maroldi, Marco, O.P.

1. *Sententia veritatis humanae redemptionis* [Rome: S. Plannck, after March 25, 1481], Hain #*10778 (another printing, #*10777). For Sixtus IV, Annunciation, 1481. Bibl. Ang.

2. *Oratio in epiphania* [Rome: J. Gensberg, after Jan. 6, 1475], Hain #*10779. For Sixtus IV, 1475. Bibl. Ang.

Marsi, Pietro

1. *Oratio in die sancti Stephani* [Rome: S. Plannck, n.d.], Hain #*10785 (an-

other printing, #*10784). Pope and year unknown. Bibl. Ang.

2. *Oratio in die sancti Stephani primi martyris* [Rome: E. Silber, after Dec. 26, 1487?], Hain #10786. For Innocent VIII, 1487? Bibl. Vall.

3. *Panegyricus in memoriam sancti Ioannis evangelistae* [Rome: S. Plannck, after Dec. 27, 1485?], Hain #*10789 (another printing, #10788). For Innocent VIII, 1485? Bibl. Ang.

4. *Oratio in die ascensionis de immortalitate animae* [Rome: E. Silber, n.d.], Hain-Cop. #*10790 (another printing, #10791). For Innocent VIII, year unknown (not 1480 as in Hain-Cop.). BAV

Martinus de Azpetia

De passione Domini oratio [Rome: G. Lauer or E. Silber, after 1492], Hain #2238. For Alexander VI, Good Friday, year unknown. Bibl. Ang.

Massari, Ambrogio, O.E.S.A.

1. "Oratio de laudibus sancti [Augustini]," in *Vita praecellentissimi ecclesiae doctoris divi Aurelii Augustini* (Rome: G. Herolt, 1481), Hain #*5683, fols. [233ʳ–237ᵛ]. For Pius II, 1463. BAV

2. "Oratio de laudibus sancti [Augustini]," *ibid.*, fols. [241ᵛ–247ᵛ]. For Paul II, year unknown.

3. "De incarnatione Verbi [oratio]," Bibl. Estense cod. Alpha Q.6.13 (formerly 894), fols. 28ᵛ–32ᵛ. For Paul II, occasion and year unknown.

4. "De sapientia Christi [oratio]," *ibid.*, fols. 32ᵛ–47ʳ. For Paul II, occasion and year unknown.

5. "Oratio de pace," *ibid.*, fols. 73ᵛ–79ᵛ. For Paul II, occasion and year unknown.

6. "Omelia super capitulo XI° Lucae evangelistae," *ibid.*, fols. 79ᵛ–91ᵛ. For Paul II, occasion and year unknown.

7. "Oratio pulcherrima de ascensione Christi," *ibid.*, fols. 218ᵛ–229ʳ. Pope and year unknown.

8. ["Cum in Bethania"], *ibid.*, fols. 252ʳ–263ᵛ. Pope, occasion, and year unknown.

9. *Oratio de conceptione Virginis* [Rome: S. Plannck, c.1480], Hain #*5686? (other printings, #*5685, #5687, Cop. #1767). For Sixtus IV, Dec. 8, 1472. Bibl. Vall.

10. *Oratio de Ioannis apostoli et evangelistae laudibus* [Rome: B. Guldinbeck, n.d.], Hain #*5688. For Paul II, year unknown. BAV

Miranda, Sancius de

Oratio de divino amore (Rome: n. publ. [1496]), Hain #11239. For Alexander VI, Pentecost, 1496. BAV

Mithridates, Flavius

Sermo de passione Domini, ed. Chaim Wirszubski (Jerusalem: The Israel Academy of Sciences and Humanities, 1963). For Sixtus IV, Good Friday, 1481. BAV

Mons Aureus, Raynaldus, O.P.

Oratio de visione Dei [n.p.: n. publ., after Dec. 26, 1496], Hain #*11548. For Alexander VI, St. Stephen, 1496. BAV

del Monte, Pietro
1. "Oratio in prima dominica quadragesimae," BAV cod. Vat. lat. 4872, fols. 1ʳ–13ʳ. Pope and year unknown (Nicholas V?).
2. "Oratio in die sancto parasceves," *ibid.*, fols. 15ʳ–27ʳ. Pope and year unknown (Nicholas V?).
3. "Oratio in dominica quadragesimae quae dicitur de passione," BAV cod. Vat. lat. 2694, fols. 301ʳ–308ᵛ. For Nicholas V, 1450/51.

Mora, Alphonsus
Oratio de Trinitate [Rome: E. Silber, after May 21, 1486], Hain #*11610. For Innocent VIII, 1486. BAV

Mucagata, Philippus, O.S.M.
Oratio in die epiphaniae [Rome: E. Silber, after Jan. 6, 1488], Hain #11625. For Innocent VIII, 1488. BN Naples.

Nicolaus de Almania. *See* Schomberg, Nicolaus

Nimireus, Martinus
Sermo de passione Domini [Rome: E. Silber, after April 3, 1494], Hain-Cop. #11889. For Alexander VI, Good Friday, 1494. BAV

Nogarola, Leonardo
"Oratio in die nativitatis Domini," BAV cod. Ross. 1124, fols. 1ʳ–14ʳ. For Sixtus IV, year unknown.

Palmeri, Nicolò, O.E.S.A.
1. ["De sacerdotio"], BAV cod. Vat. lat. 5815, fols. 33ʳ–43ᵛ. Passion Sunday?, pope and year unknown.
2. ["De sacrificio"], *ibid.*, fols. 44ʳ–56ᵛ. Passion Sunday?, pope and year un-unknown.
3. ["De veteri et novo testamento"], *ibid.*, fols. 57ʳ–70ʳ. Passion Sunday?, pope and year unknown.
4. ["De divinitate Christi in passione"], *ibid.*, fols. 70ʳ–84ʳ. Passion Sunday, pope and year unknown.
5. ["De pacis dignitate"], *ibid.*, fols. 84ᵛ–101ᵛ. Pope, year, and occasion unknown.
6. ["Oratio de incarnatione"], *ibid.*, fols. 111ᵛ–118ᵛ. For Pius II, Annunciation, 1461?

Passarineus, Petrus Paulus
"Oratio de sacrae circumcisionis mysterio," a manuscript fascicule of twelve folios bound at the end of printed materials bearing the shelf mark Inc. 246 of the Bibl. Ang.; see Kristeller, *Iter*, II, 93. For Sixtus IV, 1481.

Paulus de Roma, O.E.S.A.
["De origine, natura et potestate daemonum"], BAV cod. Ross. 685, fols. 134ʳ–137ᵛ. Pope, year, and occasion unknown.

Petrus, (Frater), O.M. (Petrus Rodolfi Viglevanus?)
Sermo ([Rome]: E. Silber, [c.1482]), Reichling #284. Second Sunday of Advent, pope (Sixtus IV?) and year (1481?) unknown. BN Paris.

Piperari (Piperario), Andrea

    1. *Oratio de passione Iesu Christi redemptoris nostri* ([Rome: E. Silber], 1508). For Julius II, Good Friday, 1508. BN Rome

    2. *Oratio in festo omnium sanctorum* (Rome: [J. Mazochius], 1513). For Leo X, 1513. Bibl. Corsiniana, Rome.

    3. *Oratio de fragilitate humana* [Florence: P. Pacini, 1516]. For Leo X, Ash Wednesday, 1516. BAV

Ptolomaeus, Heliodorus. *See* Tolomei, Eliodoro

Radini Tedeschini, Tommaso, O.P.

    "In die sanctorum omnium oratio," Bibl. Ricc. cod. 904, (fasc. 8), fols. 87ᵛ–92ʳ. For Leo X. 1520.

Rodericus de S. Ella

    Oratio in die parasceve [Rome: S. Plannck, 1480?], Hain #*13933=*13931 (other printings, #*13932, Cop. #2456). For Sixtus IV, 1477. Bibl. Ang.

Sambocius (Sambucus, Samboky), Ioannes

    Oratio in festo solemni divinae Trinitatis [Rome: S. Guileretus and E. Nani, 1514]. For Leo X, 1514. Bibl. Casan.

Sánchez de Arévalo, Rodrigo

    1. "Sermo in dominica passionis Domini in quadragesima," BAV cod. Vat. lat. 4881, fols. 231ᵛ–234ʳ. For Nicholas V, 1449.

    2. "Sermo in die ascensionis Domini," *ibid.*, fols. 237ʳ–239ᵛ. For Calixtus III, 1456?

    3. "Sermo in die annuntiationis," *ibid.*, fols. 239ᵛ–242ʳ. For Calixtus III, 1456?

    4. "Sermo in die sanctae Trinitatis," *ibid.*, fols. 242ᵛ–245ʳ. For Pius II, 1462.

    5. "Sermo in die apostolorum Petri et Pauli," *ibid.*, fols. 247ᵛ–250ᵛ. For Nicholas V, 1448 or 1450.

    6. "Sermo in die pentecostes," *ibid.*, fols. 250ᵛ–254ʳ. For Pius II, 1462.

Sangiorgio, Giovanni Antonio

    Sermo in dominica quinta quadragesimae [Rome: n. publ., c.1480], Hain #7599. For Sixtus IV?, year unknown. Bibl. Ang.

Schomberg, Nicolaus, O.P.

    1. "Prima oratio. Ductus est Iesus in desertum," in *Orationes vel potius divinorum eloquiorum enodationes* (Leipzig: W. Stöckel, 1512), fols. [2ᵛ–4ᵛ]. For Julius II, first Sunday of Lent, year unknown. Bibl. Ang.

    2. "Secunda oratio. Nox praecessit," *ibid.*, fols. [4ᵛ–6ᵛ]. For Julius II, first Sunday of Advent, year unknown.

    3. "Tertia oratio. Ductus est Iesus in desertum," *ibid.*, fols. [6ᵛ–8ᵛ]. For Julius II, first Sunday of Lent, year unknown.

    4. "Quarta oratio. Nox praecessit," *ibid.*, fols. [9ʳ–12ᵛ]. For Julius II, first Sunday of Advent, year unknown.

    5. "Quinta oratio. Ductus est Iesus in desertum," *ibid.*, fols. [13ʳ–17ᵛ]. For Julius II, first Sunday of Lent, year unknown.

Scoptius, Hieronymus

    1. *Oratio de Trinitate* [Rome: S. Plannck, after June 14, 1489], Hain #14540. For Innocent VIII, 1489. BN Paris.

2. *Oratio in die festo omnium sanctorum* [Rome: E. Silber or S. Plannck, after Nov. 1, 1489], Hain-Cop. #14541; Reichling, III, 179, where the date is incorrect. For Innocent VIII, 1489. BN Naples.

Sibylla, Bartholomaeus, O.P.

"Sermo de fine mundi," BN Florence cod. Conv. Soppr. J.VII.5, fols. 4ʳ–7ᵛ. For Innocent VIII, first Sunday of Advent, 1484/85.

Siculus, Guilelmus. *See* Mithridates, Flavius

Signori, Giovan Battista, O.E.S.A.

Oratio de summo Deo [n.p.: n. publ., after Dec. 11, 1485], Hain #14732. For Innocent VIII, third Sunday of Advent, 1485. Bibl. Ang.

Spagnoli. *See* Baptista Mantuanus

Terasse, Petrus, O.Carm.

Oratio de divina providentia [Rome: S. Plannck, after March 9, 1483], Hain-Cop. #*15369 (other printings, #15368, Cop. #5728). For Sixtus IV, fourth Sunday of Lent, 1483. Bibl. Ang.

Thegliatius, Stephanus

1. *Oratio pro die pentecostes* [Rome: S. Plannck, after June 3, 1487], Hain #15456. For Innocent VIII, 1487. BAV

2. *Oratio de passione Domini* [Rome: S. Plannck, 1496], Hain-Cop. #15457. For Innocent VIII, Good Friday, 1492. BAV

3. *Oratio in die omnium sanctorum* [Rome: S. Plannck, 1496], Hain-Cop. #15459 (another printing, #15458). For Alexander VI, 1492. Bibl. Ang.

4. *Sermo in materia fidei* [Rome: n. publ., after Dec. 27, 1480], Hain #*15461 (another printing, #15460). For Sixtus IV, feast of St. John, 1480.

Tolomei, Eliodoro (da Siena), O.Carm.

1. "Oratio prima de temporali Christi nativitate," in *Orationes habitae Romae in pontificio sacello* (Venice: Ioannes Antonius et Fratres de Sabio, 1521), fols. [4ʳ–6ʳ]. For Leo X, first Sunday of Advent, 1520. Bibl. Carmelitana (Via Sforza Pallavicini, 10), Rome.

2. "Oratio secunda de sapientia et caritate Christi," *ibid.*, fols. [6ʳ–8ᵛ]. For Leo X, fourth Sunday of Lent, 1520.

3. "Oratio tertia de misericordia et iustitia Dei," *ibid.*, fols. [8ᵛ–11ʳ]. For Leo X, fourth Sunday of Lent, 1521.

4. "Oratio quarta de paenitentia," *ibid.*, fols. [11ʳ–13ᵛ]. For Leo X, fourth Sunday of Advent, 1519.

Totis, Timotheus de, da Modena, O.P.

1. *Sermo quod omnino datur ultimus finis creaturae rationalis* [Rome: E. Silber, 1496], Cop. #5843, fols. [5ᵛ–8ᵛ] (another printing, Cop. #5844). For Alexander VI, Ascension Thursday, year (c.1493?) unknown. Bibl. Ang.

2. *Sermo qualiter possimus Iesum Christum induere, ibid.*, fols. [8ᵛ–11ᵛ] (another printing, Cop. #5844). For Alexander VI, first Sunday of Advent, year (c.1493?) unknown.

Valla, Nicolaus, O.M.

    Oratio de unione hypostatica Christi [Rome: J. Besicken, after Dec. 4, 1502]. For Alexander VI, second Sunday of Advent, 1502. BL

Vázquez, Dionisio, O.E.S.A.

    1. *Oratio in die cinerum* (Rome: J. Mazochius, 1513), now critically edited by John O'Malley, "An Ash Wednesday Sermon on the Dignity of Man for Pope Julius II, 1513," in *Essays Presented to Myron P. Gilmore*, ed. Sergio Bertelli and Gloria Ramakus, 2 vols. (Florence: Nuova Italia, 1978), I, 193–209.

    2. *De unitate et simplicitate personae Christi in duabus naturis oratio* (Rome: J. Mazochius, 1518), now edited by Quirino Fernandez, "Fray Dionisio Vázquez de Toledo, orador sagrado del Siglo de Oro," *Archivo Agustiniano*, 60 (1976), 105–204 (158–78). For Leo X, third Sunday of Advent, 1517.

de Viana, Martinus

    1. *Oratio in die sanctissimae Trinitatis* (Rome: [S. Plannck], 1494), Cop. #6196. For Alexander VI, 1494. BAV

    2. *Oratio de Christi ad caelos ascensione* [Rome: n. publ., 1494], Cop. #6197. For Alexander VI, 1494. BAV

    3. *Oratio in die cinerum* [Rome: S. Plannck, 1496], Cop. #6198. For Alexander VI, 1496. BAV

Zanni (Zane), Bernardo

    1. *Oratio in festo omnium sanctorum* [Rome: n. publ., after Nov. 3, 1500], Hain #16272. For Alexander VI, 1500. Bibl. Com., Cagli (Pesaro).

    2. *Oratio passionis dominicae* [n.p.: n. publ., after March 25, 1502], Hain #16273. For Alexander VI, Good Friday, 1502. BAV

INDEX OF MANUSCRIPT SOURCES

(All references are to footnotes or Appendix.)

GENERAL INDEX